CONFUCIANISM FOR THE MODERN WORLD

While Confucian ideals continue to inspire thinkers and political actors, discussions of concrete Confucian practices and institutions appropriate for the modern era have been conspicuously absent from the literature. This volume represents the most cutting-edge effort to spell out in meticulous detail the relevance of Confucianism for the contemporary world. The contributors to this book – internationally renowned philosophers, lawyers, historians, and social scientists – argue for feasible and desirable Confucian policies and institutions as they attempt to draw out the political, economic, and legal implications of Confucianism for the modern world. The book is divided into three parts that correspond to the basic hallmarks of modernity as a social and political system – democracy, capitalism, and the rule of law. This is a thought-provoking defense of distinctively Confucian practices and institutions that will stimulate interest and debate among students of politics, law, philosophy, and East Asian studies. Moreover, this book helps to bridge the gap between theory and practice and may be relevant for policy makers as well.

Daniel A. Bell is currently Visiting Fellow at the Center for Advanced Study in the Behavioral Sciences at Stanford University and Associate Professor at the City University of Hong Kong. He has also taught at the National University of Singapore and the University of Hong Kong. He is the author of *East Meets West: Human Rights and Democracy in East Asia* (2000) and *Communitarianism and Its Critics* (1993), and coeditor of *The East Asian Challenge for Human Rights* (Cambridge University Press, 1999).

Hahm Chaibong is Professor in the Department of Political Science at Yonsei University, Seoul, Korea. He is the author of numerous books and articles in both Korean and English, including *Confucianism, Capitalism, and Democracy* (2000) and *Postmodernity and Confucianism* (1998 [in Korean]). He has been a visiting professor at Duke, Georgetown, and Princeton Universities and in fall 2003 will assume the post of Director of Social Science Research and Policies at UNESCO, Paris, France (on leave from Yonsei).

CONFUCIANISM FOR THE MODERN WORLD

Edited by

DANIEL A. BELL

City University of Hong Kong

HAHM CHAIBONG

Yonsei University, Seoul, Korea

CAMBRIDGE
UNIVERSITY PRESS

CAMBRIDGE UNIVERSITY PRESS
Cambridge, New York, Melbourne, Madrid, Cape Town, Singapore,
São Paulo, Delhi, Dubai, Tokyo, Mexico City

Cambridge University Press
The Edinburgh Building, Cambridge CB2 8RU, UK

Published in the United States of America by Cambridge University Press, New York

www.cambridge.org
Information on this title: www.cambridge.org/9780521527880

First published 2003
Reprinted 2005, 2007

A catalogue record for this publication is available from the British Library

Library of Congress Cataloguing in Publication Data
Confucianism for the modern world / David A, Bell, Ham Chaibong
p. cm.
Includes bibliographical references and index.
ISBN 0-521-82100-2 - ISBN 0-521-53788-0 (pbk.)
1. Confucianism - 20th century. 2. Confucianism and world politics.
3. Confucianism and law. I. Bell, Daniel (Daniel A.) II. Hans, Chae-bong.
BL.1852.C65 2003
181'.112 - dc21

2002072899

ISBN 978-0-521-82100-1 Hardback
ISBN 978-0-521-52788-0 Paperback

In memory of

DAVID L. HALL

ABOUT THE COVER ILLUSTRATION

T'ongchon Munam (Rock Gate), by Chong Son (1676–1759), assumed name Kyomjae. A scene of Mount Kumgang off the East seacoast of Korea. In contrast to earlier painters of the Chosŏn dynasty who painted idealized landscapes of China, a country they considered to be the center of civilization ("Middle Kingdom"), Kyomjae started painting real Korean landscapes. At this time, Confucianism came to be fully "indigenized" in Korea and Korean Confucians began to look upon their own civilization with pride. This represented an important case of Confucianism adapting to, and being adopted by, a non-Chinese culture.

CONTENTS

CONTRIBUTING AUTHORS

ROGER T. AMES is Professor of Chinese Philosophy at the University of Hawaii. His recent publications include *Democracy of the Dead* (1999) (with David L. Hall).

DANIEL A. BELL is Visiting Fellow, Center for Advanced Study in the Behavioral Sciences, Stanford University, and Associate Professor, Department of Public and Social Administration, City University of Hong Kong. His recent publications include *East Meets West: Human Rights and Democracy in East Asia* (2000).

JOSEPH CHAN is Head of the Department of Politics and Public Administration, University of Hong Kong. His recent publications include the coedited volume *Political Theory in China* (2001) (in Chinese).

CHAN SIN YEE is Associate Professor, Department of Philosophy, University of Vermont. She has published essays on ancient Confucianism, feminism, and emotions.

CHANG MI-HYE is Lecturer in Sociology at Yonsei University.

CHANG YUN-SHIK is Professor Emeritus of Sociology, University of British Columbia. He is currently engaged in a research project on democracy in South Korea.

ALBERT H. Y. CHEN is Professor, Faculty of Law, University of Hong Kong. His recent publications include *The Rule of Law, Enlightenment, and the Spirit of Modern Law* (1998) (in Chinese).

WILLIAM THEODORE DE BARY is John Mitchell Mason Professor of the University and Provost Emeritus of Columbia University. His recent publications include *Asian Values and Human Rights* (1998).

HAHM CHAIBONG is Professor, Department of Political Science, Yonsei University, and in fall 2003 will assume the post of Director of Social Science Research and Policies at UNESCO (on leave from Yonsei). He has published essays on political theory and Confucianism. His recent publications include *Confucianism, Capitalism, and Democracy* (2000).

HAHM CHAIHARK is Assistant Professor, Graduate School of International Studies, Yonsei University. He is currently working on a study of the political and cultural significance of the Constitutional Court of South Korea.

DAVID L. HALL was Professor, Department of Philosophy, University of Texas at El Paso. His publications include *Richard Rorty: Prophet and Poet of the New Pragmatism* (1994).

GEIR HELGESEN is Senior Researcher, Nordic Institute of Asian Studies, Copenhagen. His recent publications include *Democracy and Authority in Korea: The Cultural Dimension in Korean Politics* (1998).

LUSINA HO is Associate Professor, Faculty of Law, University of Hong Kong. Her current research focus is on the theoretical and practical implications of the new People's Republic of China Law of Trusts.

KIM TAE-EUN is a graduate student at Yonsei University.

LEW SEOK-CHOON is Professor, Department of Sociology, Yonsei University. He is currently working on a comparative study of affective networks in East Asia.

JONGRYN MO is Director, Center for International Studies, Graduate School of International Studies, Yonsei University. He is currently preparing a study on the evolution of governance in newly democratic Asian countries.

GILBERT ROZMAN is Musgrave Professor of Sociology at Princeton University. His recent publications include the edited book *Japan and Russia: The Tortuous Path to Normalization, 1949–1999* (2000).

WANG JUNTAO is a Ph.D. candidate in the Department of Political Science, Columbia University.

ACKNOWLEDGMENTS

People and institutions who have supported our endeavor are legion.

For the conferences we were extremely fortunate to have the use of the ancestral compound of the Kwangsan Kim clan in Kunja-ree, Andong, North Kyongsang Province. The sheer beauty of the natural surroundings and the ancient architecture provided a magnificent venue for our discussions. That the name of the village was "Kunja," meaning "princely man" or "Confucian gentleman," only added to the appropriateness of the occasion. We are grateful to the Kwangsan Kim clan for allowing us to trespass on their hallowed ancestral grounds and for their gracious hospitality throughout our visit. Tongyang University of Andong also hosted a session for a day and provided their state-of-the-art conference hall as well as guesthouse for our use. The two venues provided a clear sense of the contrast between the Confucian tradition and modernity as well as the reality of their coexistence, thus adding a sense of urgency as well as concreteness to our endeavor.

The editors would like to thank the contributors to this volume. They were, one and all, true "friends from afar" with whom we could engage in the kind of sophisticated and animated discussions, as well as camaraderie and friendship, that Confucius himself dreamed of and idealized in the opening lines of the *Analects*. Like true Confucians, they were gracious and extremely patient as the editors made innumerable and, at times, what must have been insufferable demands during the editing stage.

In addition to the paper presenters and contributors, whose work is presented in this volume, numerous scholars enriched our discussions by participating in the conference as discussants. In particular, we would like to thank Chang Hyun-geun, Choi Jongko, Jang Dong-jin, Jon Byung-jae, Kim Bong-jin, Kim Hong-woo, Kim Hyung-chull, Kim Seog-gun, Joe Lau, Lee Dong-hee, Marc Plattner, and Claus-Georg Riegel for their active participation and fellowship.

Han Yong-tak, Lee Soon-kwon, and Park Sang-hyon provided research assistance and logistical support throughout the conference. As Hahm Chaibong's graduate assistants, they were burdened with responsibilities far beyond the call of duty and we are grateful. Hong Seog-geun of *Jontong gua hyundae Quarterly* also provided invaluable assistance during the conference.

Financial support for the conference was provided by Asia Research Fund (ARF), Daewoo Motor Company, and the Ford Foundation. The Andong branch of the Munhwa Broadcasting Corporation Television (MBC-TV) also provided financial support as well as coverage of the proceedings. In particular, we would like to thank Professor Jeong Kap-young, Executive Director of ARF, and Lee Dong-ho, President of Daewoo Motor Sales Corporation, for their continued interest in and support of our project. We would also like to thank Phyllis Chang (formerly) of the Ford Foundation.

We would also like to acknowledge the Institute of East and West Studies at Yonsei University and the (then) director, Dr. Shin Myung-soon, for their support. Thanks are also owed to the Department of Public and Social Administration at the City University of Hong Kong. The Head of Department, Professor Ian Holliday, provided valuable support at crucial times and Paik Wooyeal helped with fact checking and translations. Ng Kwun Kwan helped with innumerable small tasks at the final stage.

We owe a special thanks to our (then) editor at Cambridge University Press, Mary Child, who showed great interest in the project and provided helpful editorial advice, and to Alia Winters, who has guided the publication process since Mary's departure. We are also grateful for the detailed and insightful reports of the three anonymous referees for Cambridge University Press.

We owe the greatest thanks to our family members (Mikyeong, Jeenho, and Seoho for Chaibong and Bing and Julien for Daniel), who understandably could not always sympathize with the argument that we needed to spend so much time away from them in order to construct a theoretical defense of Confucian family values. Alas, a perfect fit between theory and practice continues to elude us.

Lastly, we remember David Hall. From the start, David was the most enthusiastic supporter of and participant in the "Confucian Democracy" project out of which this volume grew. His scholarship, integrity, wisdom, and wit always enriched and enlivened our discussions. We are much the poorer for his untimely death. It is to the memory of this great Confucian democrat and pragmatist that we dedicate this volume.

EDITORS' NOTE

In this volume all Chinese, Japanese, and Korean names appear with family name preceding given name, except for a few Chinese and Korean authors who use the Western style of family name last. The conventional transliterations for Japanese and Korean are used. Chinese characters are used for relevant Chinese concepts, accompanied by the Pinyin system of romanization.

INTRODUCTION

THE CONTEMPORARY RELEVANCE OF CONFUCIANISM

DANIEL A. BELL AND HAHM CHAIBONG

Confucians have long been preoccupied with social and political change. According to the standard account, Master Kong (Latinized name: Confucius; c. 551–479 B.C.) left his native state of Lu, hoping to find a ruler more receptive to his ideas about good government. Unfortunately, Confucius did not have any luck, and he was forced to settle for a life of teaching. Several generations later, a student in the academic lineage of Confucius's grandson named Master Meng (Latinized name: Mencius: c. 390–305 B.C.) committed himself to spreading Confucius's social and political ideas. Like the old master, Mencius moved from state to state, looking for opportunities to put his political ideals into practice. Mencius had slightly more success – he served briefly as Minister of the State of Qi – but he became disenchanted with political life and reluctantly settled for a teaching career.

Several hundred years later, however, the social and political ideas of Confucius and Mencius – as recorded in *The Analects of Confucius* and *The Works of Mencius* – proved to be literally world transforming. Following a short-lived experience with Legalism, the newly founded Chinese state of Han adopted Confucianism as its official ideology. For the next two thousand years, the country's best minds sought to interpret and modify Confucianism to make it more relevant in particular situations with novel features. By the late nineteenth century, the whole East Asian region was thoroughly "Confucianized." That is, Confucian values and practices informed the daily lives of people in China, Korea, Japan, and Vietnam, and whole systems of government were justified with reference to Confucian ideals.

Since the advent of modernity in the latter half of the nineteenth century, however, Confucianism has fared less well. Max Weber, one of the earliest scholars to devote serious attention to the relationship between Confucianism and modernity, singled out Confucianism among the major "world religions" as the least conducive to capitalist development. East Asians, for their part, began to condemn this venerable tradition as they deepened their

I

encounter with the West. Nationalists and militarists held Confucianism responsible for their country's inability to withstand the onslaught of Western imperialism. From the other side of the political spectrum, the communists did their best to extirpate every root and branch of Confucianism that they regarded as a feudal and reactionary world view hindering progress. Indeed, for the vast majority of East Asians, modernity had come to mean overcoming Confucianism.

As such, in the postcolonial era, few, if any, East Asians openly declared allegiance to Confucian ideals. For most of the cold war period, East Asians had to choose between two alternative roads to modernity – Marxism and capitalism – and the Confucian tradition had almost completely disappeared from public discourse. That modernity itself was the ultimate goal was rarely in doubt. In fact, one of the most remarkable aspects of Confucianism's encounter with modernity is that unlike in the case of Islam, Hinduism, and Buddhism, there has never been an organized Confucian resistance to modernization. Confucianism seems to be one "religion" where one would be hard put to find any "fundamentalist" adherents at all.

Perhaps this lack of fundamentalist resistance to modernity underpins the remarkable ability of many of the countries that belong to the "Confucian sphere of influence" to industrialize and, in some cases, democratize. While the contradictions inherent in the communist bloc were becoming more apparent, while other Third World countries were trapped in seemingly inextricable patterns of underdevelopment, and while even the advanced industrialized countries were mired in the vicious cycle of stagflation, the countries of East Asia continued to flourish through the 1960s, 1970s, and 1980s. In fact, the success of the countries in this region became so conspicuous as to require some explanation. The need for a new theoretical framework became all the more acute primarily because the social scientists, both liberal and Marxist, failed to predict or explain the economic success of these "Confucian" states while the Weberian thesis regarding the alleged incompatibility between Confucianism and capitalism rapidly lost credibility.

Since the early 1980s, there has been much discussion regarding the role of Confucianism in the modernization of East Asia, particularly in the economic sphere. Initially, those who found Confucianism to hold the secret to the region's economic success were mostly Western scholars. It was "outside observers" who began attributing the success of East Asia to Confucianism (MacFarquhar, Hofheinz and Calder, Vogel, among others). The irony was that few living in the Confucian world thought that their political and economic success was due to Confucianism. What success they enjoyed, they typically attributed to their success in having overcome Confucianism.

The first among the East Asians to openly and enthusiastically espouse the idea that Confucianism had much to do with the rapid industrialization of the region were politicians. Most notoriously, Singapore's senior statesman Lee Kuan Yew has invoked Confucian values – under the guise of "Asian values" – with the apparent aim of justifying constraints on the democratic process. Authoritarian governments in the region have similarly appealed to Confucian values meant to contrast with Western-style democracy. Even the Chinese Communist Party "rectified" its previous anti-Confucian stance – party leaders have been trying to tap Confucian teachings to help curb rampant corruption and to counter the widespread social malaise that threatens to undermine the Communist Party.[1] These political leaders affirmed the linkage between Confucianism and modernity not only to explain their economic success but also to argue that the political and economic system that they had erected was in many ways superior to that of the West.

Against this trend, anti-Confucian liberal intellectuals and social critics argued that Confucianism is a dead tradition that has been (justifiably) relegated to the dustbin of history. Others recognized that Confucian values continue to exert moral and political influence in East Asia, with the proviso that these values are not desirable in the modern world and thus Confucianism should be opposed whenever it rears its ugly head. Confucianism, it was argued, is incompatible with the social and political manifestations of modernity – democracy, capitalism, and the rule of law. The Confucian emphasis on differentiated and hierarchical relationships as manifested in the Five Cardinal Virtues (*wulun* 五倫) leads inevitably to elitism and authoritarianism. The Confucian dictum that one should pursue justice, not profit, conflicts with the commercial ethos that undergirds capitalism and the ethics of self-interest that drives it. The Confucian emphasis on moral cultivation and reliance on a morally cultivated elite to bring just order to society exposes it to the danger of subjective and hence arbitrary rule and clashes with the modern reliance on institutions and procedures that secure the rule of law.

The debate soon came to be mired in polemics. The argument over the alleged superiority of one set of values over another might have revealed some interesting psychology at work among the participants, but it did little to

---

1 See Tony Lau, "Jiang's Appeal to Virtue Harks Back to Confucius," *South China Morning Post*, February 20, 2001. Some mainland Chinese intellectuals have also "returned" to Confucianism for inspiration: see, e.g., Guoji Ruxue Lianhehui, ed., *Ruxue Xiandai Tansuo* [Search for Contemporary Confucianism] (Beijing: Beijing Tushuguan Chubanshe, 2002), and Tang Kailin and Cao Gang, *Chongshi Chuantong: Rujia Sixiang de Xiandai Jiazhi Pinggu* [Reinterpreting Tradition: Contemporary Evaluation of Confucian Thought] (Shanghai: East China Normal University Publishing House, 2000).

shed light on the linkages between Confucianism and modernity. In fact, given the state of the debate surrounding Confucianism and modernity, it is not surprising that once East Asia was hit by a financial crisis in 1997, those who had been arguing against the Asian values thesis simply began to dismiss the whole issue. Just as the advocates of Asian values tried to reverse Weber's thesis on Confucianism, so now the critics of Asian values tried to treat the whole argument concerning Confucianism as having been completely misbegotten. When they did acknowledge Confucianism's influence on economic development, they now did so only in order to "prove" that it has produced "crony capitalism" characterized by corruption and inefficiency.

In the meantime, another group of East Asian intellectuals and their Western sympathizers has sought to articulate a vision of Confucianism that avoids either of these extremes by highlighting the humanistic and liberal elements in the Confucian world view while recognizing its flaws. Here the assumption has been that Confucianism has indeed underpinned economic and political development in modernizing East Asian societies and the aim has been to understand how Confucianism actually works in economic organization, political ideology, and social behavior.[2] While this enterprise has primarily been descriptive and explanatory, it has also been animated by a normative vision. This group of "Confucian humanists," as Tu Wei-ming puts it, defends Confucianism on the grounds that it expresses values of universal significance for those concerned with leading moral lives. In the contemporary world, this tradition has the added advantage of buttressing valued forms of communal life against the disintegrating and atomizing forces of economic globalization. As shown by "actually existing" East Asian societies, the Confucian cultural heritage can also underpin relatively egalitarian forms of economic development.

This appealing vision, however, often seems to lack specific proposals for social and political change. That is, the debate over Confucianism continues to be based on values and norms as contained in classical texts and historical past. Little work has been done to investigate linkages between Confucian ideals and concrete practices/institutions, be they political, economic, social, or legal, in the existing "Confucian" societies. It is time for the debate to move beyond the theoretical and speculative stage to more practical and institutional considerations. If Confucianism is to remain viable, it will not be sufficient to "apologize" for the supposedly authoritarian tendencies of its theories and tenets. Rather, proponents of Confucianism need to engage in more affirmative and constructive thinking where the institutional manifestations of Confucianism for modern democratic societies are actively sought and

---

2 See, e.g., Tu Wei-ming, ed., *Confucian Traditions in East Asian Modernity* (Cambridge, Mass.: Harvard University Press, 1996).

articulated. This means sorting out and clearly articulating those aspects of Confucianism that are feasible and defensible in the modern world. Thus, those trying to negotiate the relationship between Confucianism and modernity need to tackle the following questions: Which particular Confucian values should be promoted in contemporary East Asian societies? How should they be promoted? What are the political and institutional implications of "Confucian humanism"? How do the practical implications of modern Confucianism differ from the values and workings of liberal capitalist societies? Can these differences be justified from a moral point of view?

This book emerged from a multiyear project on "Confucian democracy." Our contributors have all made a commitment to take Confucianism seriously, to engage in constructive criticisms, and to identify those parts of Confucianism (if any) still worth defending in a contemporary world. They were asked to work out (and defend) in concrete detail the implications of Confucianism in modern societies and to argue for distinctive Confucian policies and institutions that are still feasible and desirable in East Asian states and beyond.

Internationally renowned lawyers, sociologists, historians, philosophers, and political scientists from East Asia and elsewhere participated in a series of conferences.[3] Each scholar was encouraged to go beyond traditional disciplinary boundaries. Theorists and historians were asked to think in practical terms while scholars engaged in more empirically oriented research were encouraged to reflect on the normative and cultural underpinnings of their work and to imagine alternative institutions and practices which could become the vehicle for the norms and values they have observed.

The conferences were held in various Korean sites, ranging from ultramodern Seoul to ancient Confucian academies. The choice of the conference sites, on the part of the organizers, was quite deliberate. The sites were chosen not only to enable the participants to enjoy the beautiful surroundings afforded by centuries old Confucian academies but also to impart a sense of Confucianism as a living reality and an essential part of the daily lives of ordinary people of Korea. By witnessing the ways in which Confucianism continues to be fully integrated into the lives of otherwise "modern" Koreans,[4] the participants once again felt the urgent need for articulating concrete institutional means by which to maintain or reform Confucianism for the modern

---

3 All the essays in this book were presented at these conferences, with the exception of a specially commissioned essay by Wang Juntao.
4 On the process of historical transmission of Confucian values in Korean society, see Martina Deuchler, *The Confucian Transformation of Korea* (Cambridge, Mass.: Harvard-Yenching Institute Monograph Series, 36, 1992). On the continuing relevance of Confucianism in Korea, see Hahm Pyong Choon, *Korean Jurisprudence, Politics, and Culture* (Seoul: Yonsei University Press, 1986).

world. The interest on the part of the "locals" was just as great. The descendants of the illustrious Confucian scholars in whose names the Confucian academies were dedicated were surprised and delighted to see scholars holding an international conference and using the hallowed halls to debate the implications of Confucianism for the modern world. The interdisciplinary dialogues were filmed and broadcast live on the Internet, and participants were occasionally surprised to see themselves on the evening television newscast.[5]

During the proceedings, the papers were submitted to rigorous scrutiny and critical questioning by the participants.[6] The editors then made certain that the papers were revised for inclusion in this book. The book is divided into three parts that correspond to what we take to be the basic hallmarks of modernity as a social and political system – democracy, capitalism, and the rule of law.[7] Our contributors offer Confucian perspectives on these themes and attempt to draw political/economic/legal implications for the modern world. The book ends with an epilogue by William Theodore de Bary.

CONFUCIAN PERSPECTIVES ON DEMOCRACY

Modern-day governments, it is commonly argued, must be constituted "by the people." Whatever the practical arguments for and against democracy,

5 Korean participants may have been less surprised, since they are living in a context where academics are given uncommon amounts (by Anglo-American standards) of respect and public attention. The relevance of the value of respect for educated persons – traceable, arguably, to the Confucian value of respect for exemplary persons (or *junzi* 君子) – can also be illustrated by the fact that teachers are given 10% discounts on national airlines for intra-Korea travel (it is interesting to note similar policies in "communist" China, where teachers are given 50% discounts on ferry tickets – e.g., between Hong Kong and Shekou – during summer holidays).

6 The critical exchanges were occasionally "formal" by Anglo-American academic standards – for instance, the Korean professors, even the best of friends, referred to each other as "Professor" in both public and private contexts. This did not, however, prevent participants from exchanging critical views. In fact, it can be argued that appropriate decorum may occasionally allow for more productive exchanges than relative informality. If the critic says, "Sam, I object to . . . ," this can be interpreted as a personal attack on Sam and he may be needlessly defensive. But if the critic says, "Professor X, I object to . . . ," this show of respect may allow the recipient to focus on the substance of the criticism without feeling that his or her whole personhood is being targeted for attack.

7 This classification of the "basic hallmarks of modernity" is, of course, contestable (for a similar account, see Randall Peerenboom, *China's Long March Toward Rule of Law* [Cambridge: Cambridge University Press, 2003]). Focusing primarily on the "subjective" components of modernity, Charles Taylor argues that "the affirmation of ordinary life" constitutes part of the modern identity (*Sources of the Self* [Cambridge, Mass.: Harvard University Press, 1989]). From a Confucian perspective, the affirmation of ordinary life has long been a staple of the tradition (see, e.g., *Confucianism and the Family*, eds. Walter H. Slote and George A. DeVos [Albany: State University of New York Press, 1998]).

this form of government has emerged as an ineliminable symbol of equal political recognition in modern societies. Even autocratic leaders such as Lee Kuan Yew recognize that democracy is the best form of government and that all modern countries must eventually adopt this political ideal. The history and culture of the East Asian region, however, may seem to hinder this development. Prior to the twentieth century, not a single political regime in this region was democratic. That is, ordinary people did not have a say in choosing their country's most powerful political decision makers by means of competitive elections, and the majority of "citizens" did not have any other mechanisms for participating in the political process. As the first two contributions show, however, this does not mean that political rulers were "authoritarian" despots who could operate without any checks on their power.

Hahm Chaihark, who teaches Korean studies at Yonsei University, argues that the Confucian concept of ritual propriety (*li* 禮) functioned as a public political norm that effectively restrained and disciplined political rulers in premodern East Asia. The Confucian rulers' political legitimacy depended on correctly regulating their conduct according to *li*, and this meant that rulers had to pay the utmost attention to detailed specification and correct observance of ritual propriety. More importantly, the rulers were surrounded by Confucian scholar-officials who were themselves disciplined by *li* and believed that their mission was to discipline the highest political leader of the country according to ritual propriety.

In modern East Asia, many of the idioms and vocabularies for making sense of politics and rendering value judgments are derived from the Confucian tradition. Given that constitutional norms are more likely to be effective if they are grounded in a society's political culture, Hahm argues that these norms must resonate with the idea of *li* in the East Asian context. Thus, the ruler's power could be effectively checked by modern-day Confucians who are socialized into "the role of disciplinarians of political leaders." Confucian political education can be promoted in families, schools, and other settings with the aim of teaching people the importance of effective and regularized restraints on their government.

It would also be in the ruler's interest to be disciplined by *li*, since this could help to secure legitimacy for the government. Here too, we can learn from past practices. In Korea, Chosŏn dynasty rulers were properly disciplined by various mechanisms and by being educated in the art of governance. For example, the king was obliged to listen to policy lectures by Confucian scholars and he was not allowed to hold audience with his ministers unless he was accompanied by two court historians, one of whom recorded all the verbal transactions while the other recorded all physical movements. Hahm argues that "we should retrieve the notion that a ruler can and should be disciplined by being lectured to all the time, and put under constant surveillance." The need for disciplining political rulers has certainly not diminished in the modern world, and such Confucian disciplinary mechanisms could arguably be adapted to fit modern governmental structures. This may not make the ruler into a paragon of virtue, but it should at least help to prevent obvious corruption – not to mention other indiscretions in presidential offices.

Jongryn Mo, who teaches international political economy in the Graduate School of International Studies at Yonsei University, draws on the example of the Censorate in Korea to argue that there were effective institutional restraints on the ruler's power in Confucian political regimes. In the Chosŏn dynasty, the Censorate consisted of three organs that were designed to prevent abuses in the exercise of political and administrative authority. Mo shows that the censors were not only judicial and auditing agents, "but also voices of dissent and opposition, playing the roles of mass media and opposition parties in modern democracies." Moreover, he argues that the Censorate was well designed for effective horizontal accountability, meaning that Confucian scholar-officials were able to hold agencies of equal power accountable. In effect, the Censorate was a branch of government in a system of checks and balances.

Mo argues for the need to reintroduce elements of the Censorate – such as the practice of appointing censors whose job is to write critical reports on the ruler's conduct – in contemporary East Asian political systems, especially that of Korea. For one thing, this institution is compatible with Confucian political culture and may resonate with the habits and values of East Asian people. With respect to the contemporary Korean context, the Censorate could also help to increase the quality of governance, given that major political actors and some top political organizations have not completely shed their authoritarian ways.

The weakest link in Chosŏn's system of accountability, according to Mo, was the absence of vertical accountability. That is, ordinary people had virtually no way to keep political leaders accountable. More generally, the various Chosŏn checks on abuses of power described by Hahm and Mo are fully compatible with what John Rawls terms a "decent, well-ordered society"[8] – a political regime that satisfies the main requirements of good governance with the exception of democracy. In the East Asian context, this might translate into a constitutional arrangement that provides Confucian junzi (君子) ("gentlemen," or "exemplary persons") with institutional mechanisms to check the ruler's power[9] but without empowering the people with the right to choose their country's political rulers.

8 See John Rawls, *The Law of Peoples* (Cambridge, Mass.: Harvard University Press, 1999).
9 For another institutional suggestion along these lines, see Daniel A. Bell, *East Meets West: Human Rights and Democracy in East Asia* (Princeton: Princeton University Press, 2000), ch. 5.

In short, Hahm and Mo persuasively argue against the conventional view that Confucianism is an ideology that encourages conformity and submissiveness toward authority. But is there anything specifically Confucian that might also justify democracy in the ordinary sense of "power by the people"? The next two papers turn to this topic.

Wang Juntao's essay challenges the perception that political dissidents in China favor uprooting their own tradition in favor of wholesale Westernization.[10] Wang, a doctoral candidate in political science at Columbia University, argues that many of the key figures in the various democracy movements in contemporary Chinese history drew inspiration from Confucian values. From the late nineteenth century onward, leading Chinese intellectuals have struggled to promote "minimal" democracy (i.e., free and fair competitive elections to select political leaders) in their country. It turns out that nearly all the important figures in the history of Chinese democracy movements – Kang Youwei, Zhang Jian, Sun Yatsen, Liang Qichao, Zhang Junmai, Wang Xizhe, and Chen Ziming – tried to revive Confucianism in order to support democratization. Several had received a traditional Confucian education and they argued that democratic institutions such as parliamentary systems, elections, and equal rights are natural extensions of Confucianism. For example, Sun Yatsen, the founding father of the Republic of China, said:

> Our three-*min* (三民) principles [nationalism, citizen rights, and the welfare of human beings] originate from Mencius and are based on Cheng Yichuan [a Song dynasty Confucian]. Mencius is really the ancestor of our democratic ideas. . . . The three-*min* principles are a completion of the development of those three thousand years of Chinese ideas about how to govern and maintain a peaceful world.

Others admitted the existence of some weaknesses in Confucianism that blocked China's march toward democracy but added that Confucianism can be reinterpreted to make it consistent with democracy. This project was successfully carried out in the case of Catholicism – Wang reminds us of Samuel Huntington's argument that Catholicism was transformed from an important obstacle to democratization into one of the major ideological factors underpinning the "third wave" of democratization in the world – and Confucianism may hold similar potential.

The political importance of Wang's argument is that democracy may be easier to implement in the Chinese context if it can be shown that it need

---

10 Wang Juntao's personal history is sufficient to cast doubt on this claim. He is a long-time democratic activist who was labeled (by the Chinese government) one of the two "black hands behind the scenes" of the May/June 1989 Tiananmen democracy movement. Arrested after the June 4, 1989, massacre, Wang spent five years in jail before being released to the United States on medical parole.

not conflict with traditional political culture. As Wang puts it, "If Confucianism is consistent with democracy, the traditional culture may be used as a means of promoting democratization in East Asia. At the very least, the political transition will be smoother and easier, with lower costs, since there will be less cultural resistance."

Chang Yun-Shik's essay shows that Confucian values do not merely have the *potential* to support democracy. In the Korean context, Confucianism *in fact* helped to bring about a transition to a democratic form of government. Chang, Professor Emeritus of Sociology at the University of British Columbia, focuses on the ethic of mutual help. This communal ethic has long been embedded in rural farming communities, but it was reinforced and modified by the importation of Confucian values from China. Koreans incorporated the idea of the community compact articulated by the great twelfth-century Neo-Confucian Zhu Xi. Eventually, the community compact – self-regulating local communities under the leadership of an educated moral elite – became the norm in rural farming communities.

Over the last century, social bonds of mutual obligation and trust spread from rural to urban settings. In contemporary Korea, kinship ties continue to play an important role by linking clan members residing in the city to those remaining in the same surname village (*tongjok maŭl*).[11] Moreover, cities provided people with new opportunities to meet and interact, and the ethic of mutual help came to underpin personal relationships beyond the confines of neighborhood and kinship organizations – in schools, workplaces, training centers, churches, and prisons.

Chang argues that this ethic initially proved to be inimical to democracy. Democratic constitutional forms imposed by Western occupying forces were molded by traditional person-oriented norms, with each president fortifying his position by staffing governmental offices from the personal circles of close kin members, friends, and acquaintances who pledged personal loyalty to him. This led to "administrative despotism," corruption, the decline of party politics, and other ills associated with authoritarian government.

However, this same ethic of mutual help also informed the workings of opposition social forces in Korea. Pro-democracy students and dissident church leaders led the struggle for democracy, and the student-church nexus was molded by the ethic of mutual help. For example, groups of students from the same high school or hometown or church formed "study circles"

---

11 Project participants benefited from this cultural phenomenon. Lew Seok-Choon, one of the project organizers, has extensive networks in his ancestral home of Andong, Korea. Due to these networks, local help could be mobilized to organize enjoyable and affordable social and academic events for visitors in Andong. This region is also renowned for its commitment to Confucianism.

that served as the basic organizational unit for demonstrations. These close ties ensured unity of purpose and mutual support in difficult times. Other groups joined forces to launch their own democratic campaigns, and the increasing number of civic groups committed to the public interest eventually helped to consolidate democracy in Korea.

Democracy, however, is neither stable nor necessarily desirable if it is limited to the minimal idea of free and fair competitive elections. Chang suggests that "personalist democrats" can also help to support more participatory forms of democratic politics. In contrast to "individualist democrats,"

> personalist democrats are not likely to ignore each other or make their political decisions on their own. They will encourage consultation with or advice seeking from others in making decisions on political matters, and they will share information and lend moral support. Does the individual know his interest best? The personalist democrat is likely to think that the group decision is better, wiser, and safer than individual decision making. . . . With emphasis on mutuality, not on individual autonomy per se, personalist democracy might be able to avoid the widespread tendency among many citizens in individualist democracies to exclude themselves from political processes.

The next contribution develops this vision of a "Confucian democracy" that avoids the excesses of liberal individualism. David Hall and Roger Ames argue that democratic practices should not threaten the preservation and appropriate exercise of Confucian sensibilities when they are imported into East Asian countries. In the contemporary world, it is difficult to detach democratic models from elements of "Westernization" – such as legal formalism that mitigates the role of rituals in the socializing process and an insistence upon individual rights to the detriment of social responsibilities – that worry "communitarian Confucians." To meet this challenge, Hall, formerly of the University of Texas,[12] and Ames, who teaches at the University of Hawaii, appeal to John Dewey's understanding of democracy as a "communicating community." This concept was designed precisely to address these concerns and thus holds the greatest promise for achieving a Confucian democracy in which central Confucian values are still largely intact.

In an ideal Confucian society, human relationships are largely noninstrumental and communication appeals to a shared repository of discourse. As Hall and Ames point out, this ideal still informs conversations among educated Chinese: "Such conversations tend to be highly allusive, involving citations of classical texts and the employments of apothegms and proverbs

---

12 We are saddened to report that David Hall has passed away.

common to the tradition."[13] This form of communication has the effect of promoting affective bonding and reinforcing attachment to commonly acknowledged cultural models. Moreover, local groups in rural China have been "slowly and quietly enchanting the routine habits of the day" during the course of their struggles for social and political change. But how can affective bonds of this sort be maintained against the seemingly inevitable trend toward the "disenchantment of the modern world"? More ambitiously, how can these bonds be generalized to the national level, particularly now that an extreme form of "winner take-all" capitalism seems to be taking shape in China? The coauthors suggest that John Dewey's educational theory may have something to offer. Dewey particularly emphasized the educative processes meant to realize and sustain "communicating democracy." The aim of education, according to Dewey, is the creation of a community of affect where everyday communication helps to maintain and promote noninstrumental relationships of the sort Confucians value. If Dewey's theory of education is institutionalized in mainland China, this may help to promote an "enchanted world" where desirable traditional values are exhibited on a day-to-day level. In this context, the importation of democracy need not threaten Confucian sensibilities.

Geir Helgesen, Senior Researcher at the Nordic Institute of Asian Studies (Copenhagen), develops a similar argument for the Korean context. He points to the negative social and political effects of globalization and argues for moral education that strengthens affective ties and resonates with Confucian values. According to Helgesen, survey research reveals that globalization contributes to "existential insecurity" among people that can have grave political consequences. If individuals feel helpless and alienated from the political process, they will retreat to the passive realm of consumption. The "centers of meaning production" will shift from the local community and national culture to the standards set by profit-seeking multinationals, resulting in what Helgesen terms "individualistic uniformity." Individual "citizens" will lose their sense of attachment to the political community, participation in national affairs will decline, and "democracy" can only be realized on a formal, institutional level. Without strong affective bonds underpinning relatively participatory forms of democracy, individual "citizens" will lack the motivation to sacrifice for the common good and they will fail to show solidarity with needy members of the political community. This will increase the likelihood of social breakdown and exacerbate economic inequality.

---

13 Project participants witnessed a contemporary manifestation of this ideal. One alcohol-fortified evening, members of the Korean contingent composed free-flowing poetry using classical Chinese characters.

In Korea, the Kim Dae Jung administration promoted restructuring the economy according to the requirements of the International Monetary Fund (IMF). Helgesen argues, however, that it may not have been doing enough to strengthen the affective bonds that underpin "communalistic, solidarity-oriented" democracy. These bonds have been influenced by Confucian social morality for more than half a millennium, and authorities should draw on Confucian resources to combat existential insecurity and strengthen cultural rootedness. More concretely, this means promoting particular Confucian values in Korean schools. Empirical research shows that there is widespread support for such values as ancestor worship, and Helgesen describes his call for a moral education policy as "less of a 'social engineering' project and more of an effort to build on the strengths of continuity and self-confidence." However, this policy should modernize aspects of Confucianism, for example, by challenging gender inequality though without "copying the emancipation struggle of women in the Western world."

The last two essays may contribute to the impression that Confucianism is fundamentally antagonistic to the requirements of global capitalism. The best that Confucianism can do, it seems, is build walls that protect communitarian cultures from the "atomizing" forces of globalization. But is it possible that Confucianism can also help to shape modern market economies in desirable ways? The contributors in the next section examine the Confucian potential for abetting economic development and promoting social justice in market-based economies.

CONFUCIAN PERSPECTIVES ON CAPITALISM

Just as it seems impossible to imagine successful nondemocratic societies in the modern world, so capitalism – an economic system that is dominated by owners of capital who hire wage laborers and produce for profit – seems to be an essential feature of all developed societies. As Karl Marx himself recognized, economic and technological development proceeds more quickly than ever before under capitalism, because capitalists compete with one another to make a profit, and hence they have a special incentive to develop new, ever more efficient means to produce goods. Contrary to Marx's expectations, however, capitalist societies in the West have managed to mitigate some of the negative consequences of capitalist development by redistributing (some) wealth from the capitalist classes to the rest. To what extent does Confucianism provide resources for those thinking about the requirements of modern-day capitalist societies?

Gilbert Rozman, Musgrave Professor of Sociology at Princeton University, argues that Confucianism can provide the ideological underpinning for further dynamism in East Asia. One of the effects of economic globalization is that the state is losing the capacity to control economic activity within its borders. Given the increased tendency toward multiple levels of economic power – both below and above the state – Rozman argues that Confucianism may be particularly appropriate for justifying the transition from state-controlled economies in East Asia.

On the one hand, Confucianism can provide the intellectual and moral resources for promoting an agenda of economic decentralization. By looking back at the history of East Asian countries, Rozman makes the case that Confucian ideals justified limitations on central power and encouraged family and social solidarity to balance controls from above. This translated into reliance on market mechanisms, dynamic local economies, and complex urban networks. Of course, Confucian decentralization has often faced political obstacles, but it has helped to counter the centralizing messages put forward by militarists in Japan and (more recently) by communists in China.

On the other hand, Confucianism can serve as an integrating force for East Asian regionalism. Following the formation of regional trading blocs in Europe and North America, East Asians have been exploring the possibility of their own regional trading bloc that would bring economic payoffs. Rozman suggests that regionalism based on Confucian values and local net-works can be enhanced without artificial state manipulation. He points to the formation of hierarchies of cities across borders such as the Hong Kong-Taiwan-Guangdong-Fujian natural economic territory. As intraregional trade of this sort accelerates, people will form their own economic and cultural ties. Through agreeing on a shared agenda of "open, decentralized, Confucian regionalism," East Asian states "could breathe new life into the way each of them develops and create a vision of how the past brings them together as they expand cooperation for the future."

Rozman does, however, cast some doubt on the Confucian agenda. He warns of continued obstruction from those in East Asia who claim to be defenders of traditional values such as community harmony, state benevolence, and family solidarity while protecting narrow vested interests. He also sees a need to embrace more fully meritocracy and openness to globalization as a prerequisite to reviving Confucian themes as a forward-looking foundation.

The next essay – by Lew Seok-Choon, Professor of Sociology at Yonsei University, and two of his graduate students, Chang Mi-Hye and Kim Tae-Eun – points to the economic benefits of Confucian-style affective networks (social ties bound by what Chang terms the "ethic of mutual help") in an overall capitalist context. Focusing on the case of Korea, the coauthors show that individuals are actively involved in the "social investment" of building up affective networks. These networks – rooted in school ties, marriage, work, hometown, and region – have been blamed for corruption, nepotism, tax evasion, and other economically harmful phenomena denounced by critics of "crony capitalism." That, however, is not the whole story.

For one thing, it is a mistake to regard these networks as "premodern" practices that will disappear as the economy develops. Contrary to the predictions of "modernization theorists," the coauthors show that these networks are alive and well in Korea and cannot easily be removed by legal or institutional reform. Moreover, affective networks can be functional for further economic development. The social trust embedded in these networks lowers the costs of supervision and provides for economic efficiency: "When a person is recruited by a company through recommendation or connection, he/she tends to work harder not to disappoint those who recommended him/her and to secure his/her position within the network of personal relations provided by that connection." These networks can also reduce transaction costs, as the strong trust eliminates the need for detailed contracts and modes of enforcement. What makes the Korean affective networks particularly functional is that they are not exclusive or closed to outsiders.[14] An individual can belong to several affective networks simultaneously and boundaries between groups are flexible and extendable depending on circumstances.[15] In this globalizing world of fast-paced, relatively unpredictable change, such open networks can facilitate rapid adjustment and economic restructuring in times of crisis.

Of course, economic development per se may not be desirable if it leads to radical inequalities and social upheavals. As noted above, however, the "East Asian model of economic development" managed to combine rapid economic development with relatively egalitarian distributions of income (relative to many Western countries). In East Asia, the most developed economies are also the most egalitarian.[16] The next two chapters discuss Confucian

---

14 The Korean hosts for this multiyear project organized several communal events that may have led some foreign participants to conclude that they had been inducted into a new "network." What is clear is that many participants felt the need to reciprocate in some way or other, and this helped to ensure compliance with the demands of an edited book (e.g., revisions, meeting deadlines) without the need to rely on financial inducements.

15 In the Philippines, by comparison, the social network rooted in ties to college fraternities is the most important network in legal, government, and business circles. These networks have been blamed for promoting graft and corruption outside the university, and loyalty to fraternity "brothers" usually overrides other ties in cases of conflict (Mark Mitchell, "Frat Brats," *Far Eastern Economic Review*, February 15, 2001, pp. 62–63). In Korea, the various cross-cutting, relatively open networks help to ensure that no single network can operate unchecked.

16 See Peter Passell, "Asia's Path to More Equality and More Money for All," *New York Times*, August 25, 1996, E5.

perspectives on wealth distribution and social justice that may help to explain this phenomenon.

Throughout Chinese history, Confucians opposed heavy-handed government control and warned of the negative effects of state intervention in the economy. This did not translate, however, into endorsement of an unfettered private property rights regime. As Daniel Bell – a political theorist at the City University of Hong Kong – argues, Confucius and Mencius defended constraints on the free market in the name of more fundamental values. These constraints have influenced the workings of East Asian economies and continue to play a role today.

Firstly, the state has an obligation to secure the conditions for people's basic material welfare, an obligation that has priority over competing political goods. The government realizes this aim, according to Mencius, by means of the "well-field system" that allows farmers to make productive use of land while ensuring that enough food is supplied to the nonfarming classes. Chinese rulers adapted the principles of this system to their own circumstances, and Bell suggests that even Deng Xiaoping's rural land reform program may have been influenced by Mencius's ideas.

Secondly, Confucians argued that ownership rights should be vested in the family, not the individual, so as to facilitate the realization of "family values" such as filial piety, the care of elderly parents. Family joint ownership was institutionalized in traditional legal systems – for example, junior members of families could not be accused of stealing, but only of appropriating (for their own use) family property. While modern East Asian countries have incorporated "individualistic" conceptions of property rights to a certain extent, Bell argues that they still tend to emphasize, in both law and public morality, the duty to regard property as an asset of the whole family, including elderly parents.

Joseph Chan, a political theorist at the University of Hong Kong, delineates the basic Confucian principles of social welfare and draws implications for contemporary societies. Taking Mencius's influential view on social welfare as the basis for discussion, Chan argues that Confucians endorse the idea of a multilayered system of welfare assistance in which the family, social networks, and government all have a specific role to play. Welfare responsibility lies first with the family – Confucians are quite explicit that obligations to the family are the most basic. The principle of family caring should then be extended outward. The local community serves as the second tier of help, mutual care being provided through the well-field system and other networks of communal relationships. The government plays the role of last resort, providing direct help to people who cannot help themselves and lack adult family members to turn to.

Chan shows that these principles were put into practice in premodern China. Confucian principles may also help to explain the fact that contemporary East Asian states rely mainly on nonstate agencies – community, firm, and family – to finance and provide welfare services, with significantly less direct state financing of services than other developed states.[17] To further close the gap between the ideal and reality, Chan proposes a voluntary donation scheme that would allow individuals to choose between various charity groups and aid packages. This scheme would be similar to the United Way, except that the central agency would be a government-run institution that expresses, in a symbolic way, public support for voluntary help and mutual caring. Though this proposal might further reduce the need for direct state financing of welfare, it is not meant to completely eliminate the state's welfare responsibilities.

In short, the ongoing, living Confucian tradition helps to explain the distinctive characteristics of East Asian economic systems and welfare states. This tradition may also help those thinking about an economic reform that strikes the right balance between productive economic activity and meeting the needs of the "worst-off" in an overall capitalist framework. All this, however, would seem to assume the presence of a reliable and transparent legal system to enforce Confucian-style contracts, property rights, and welfare entitlements. Not even the most idealistic Confucian argues that the ethic of mutual help could suffice to regulate conflicts in the modern world. Does this mean the Confucian perspective on law – including its notorious aversion to litigation – is completely out-of-date? Put positively, can Confucianism offer any insights for those thinking about legal reform in modern-day societies? The next section turns to this topic.

CONFUCIAN PERSPECTIVES ON LAW

The third main social plank of modern-day societies is the rule of law. Individuals in contemporary societies must be able to rely on a relatively stable, predictable, and transparent legal system that upholds the ideal of equality before the law and promises restitution in cases of injustice. Of course there is often a gap between the ideal and the practice, but any successful contemporary society must at least aspire to this ideal and devote resources to its practical implementation. On the face of it, it may appear that

---

17 See Gordon White and Roger Goodman, "Welfare Orientalism and the Search for an East Asian Welfare Model," in Roger Goodman, Gordon White, and Huck-ju Kwon, eds., *The East Asian Welfare Model: Welfare Orientalism and the State* (London: Routledge, 1998), pp. 13–14. But see White and Goodman's account of the more immediate social and political explanations for the "East Asian welfare model" (ibid., pp. 14–20).

Confucianism is fundamentally incompatible with contemporary notions of the rule of law.[18]

In traditional China, mediation rather than litigation was the preferred means of dispute resolution. According to Albert Chen, professor of law at the University of Hong Kong, the theory and practice of mediation have largely been shaped by Confucian philosophy. Confucians value social harmony, and litigation was considered to be a negative social phenomenon because it exacerbates ruptures and poisons social relationships beyond the point of repair. Litigation was also viewed with disdain because the pursuit of material self-interest that underlies civil litigation was perceived to be inconsistent with the Confucian valuation of moral self-cultivation over selfish interests. Thus:

> in case of potential conflicts with others, the correct attitude would be that of self-scrutiny (to examine oneself to see what wrong one has done and what moral failings one should be responsible for), self-criticism, politely yielding (*rang* 讓) or giving concessions to others, complaisance and compromise, rather than to assert one's interests, claim one's "rights," and press one's case by taking the other party to court.

In practice, the dominant Confucian philosophy translated into reliance on officials to mediate disputes and search for solutions agreeable to and voluntarily accepted by the disputants. By relying on persuasion and education (as opposed to binding judgments on the parties), the ultimate aim was "the reconciliation of the disputants to each other and hence the restoration of the personal harmony and social solidarity that have been temporarily breached by the conflict."

From a modern liberal standpoint, however, the Confucian theory and practice of mediation is deeply flawed. Due to differences in power, wealth, knowledge, and influence, mediated "compromises" often produce unjust outcomes that disadvantage the weaker parties. In contrast to modern litigation, there are no procedural or institutional safeguards to ensure that the mediator is not biased against the socially inferior or weaker party. What looks like social harmony is often obtained at the expense of justice, and the party who has been genuinely wronged gets less than his or her due. Thus, liberals argue that litigation followed by adjudication by the court according to the law is a better vehicle for the realization of justice.

18 This topic relates to the question of the compatibility between Confucianism and modern ideas of human rights. Recent works have explored this question in detail – see especially Joseph Chan, "A Confucian Perspective on Human Rights for Contemporary China," in Joanne R. Bauer and Daniel A. Bell, eds., *The East Asian Challenge for Human Rights* (New York: Cambridge University Press, 1999), and the articles collected in William Theodore de Bary and Tu Wei-ming, eds., *Confucianism and Human Rights* (New York: Columbia University Press, 1998) – so this book does not focus directly on human rights.

Despite these criticisms, Chen argues that suitably transformed mediation can still have a useful role to play in modern societies. This is recognized in the Anglo-American world, where a movement to introduce means of "alternative dispute settlement" is gaining influence. Various arrangements (e.g., appointing mediators from diverse class backgrounds) can help to minimize the problem of power imbalance, and it may be possible to reach truly consensual settlements that facilitate reconciliation and accommodation. In China, traditional thinking and practice regarding mediation can be revised in light of the modern liberal understanding of the rule of law. For example, it should be ensured that mediation is noncoercive and does not diminish the parties' rights to litigate the matter in court. Mediation may be particularly suitable in cases involving human associations that depend on spontaneous and informal collaboration and where parties have an incentive to maintain collaboration in the future. In such cases, it may not be unreasonable to require mandatory mediation before litigation can be entertained. Chen notes that mediation continues to play an important role in dispute settlement in China (compared to Western countries), and these normative concerns can help to provide guidelines for reform.

Lusina Ho, who teaches law at the University of Hong Kong, considers how Confucian values have been or could be given effect through concrete legal institutions comparable to those in established Western legal systems. Focusing on legislative debates over the law of succession in predominantly Chinese communities, Ho shows that these laws resulted from the influence of Confucian values on the minds of legislators. This is particularly obvious in the case of intestate succession, which involves applying rules devised by the state to distribute a deceased's properties when he or she fails to leave a will. In such cases, the state cannot be neutral – it must appeal to some value system to decide how to distribute the deceased's assets. In mainland China, the state explicitly invokes "traditional Chinese values" to justify maintenance of the elderly, the young, and the needy, with the parents of the deceased being heirs of the first priority. Ho notes, however, that exactly the same rule can be found in the Russian Civil Code, which shows that this rule is not *uniquely* Confucian. But this should not be viewed as a problem; rather, it shows that such laws can also be justified on non-Confucian grounds and thus could potentially be "exported" to non-Chinese communities that do not necessarily subscribe to Confucianism.

In the last part of her paper, Ho draws on the laws and practices surveyed to develop a model of a law of succession with a Confucian foundation that can be accommodated in a Western legal framework. In accordance with the Confucian principle that citizens should be encouraged to practice benevolence, which involves a graduated love depending on the nature of the relationship, the order of the rights of inheritance should correspond to the

Confucian hierarchy of relationships. These substantive Confucian norms can be embedded within the technical framework of the laws of common law jurisdictions that balance the conflict between clarity and flexibility. Ho argues that this model can help remedy the defects of poorly thought out succession laws in predominantly Chinese communities such as Hong Kong, where haphazard mixtures of Confucian values and common law frameworks can (unintentionally) lead to anti-Confucian consequences.

Note, however, that Ho does not defend the traditional patriarchal succession laws – prior to the 1931 Civil Code of China, women were not given equal rights of inheritance. In the same vein, Chen takes it for granted that "creatively transformed" mediation will not be biased against women – more than that, he suggests that there is a special affinity between Confucian values and "feminist values," such as compromise, empathy, and sensitivity to context. More generally, none of the contributors discussed above seek to defend traditional patriarchal social and political arrangements in East Asia; it is simply assumed, it seems, that Confucianism for the modern world need not take on "patriarchal characteristics." But is this assumption warranted? The domination of men over women seems to be one of the defining characteristics of Confucian theory and practice – one might even say that patriarchy is the "Achilles heel" of Confucianism. Does it make sense to discuss "nonpatriarchal" Confucianism? Can Confucianism take on board feminist insights without altering its major values? To what extent can legal systems shaped by Confucian values accommodate the interests of women?

Chan Sin Yee, who teaches philosophy at the University of Vermont, discusses the Confucian conception of gender and draws implications for contemporary legal systems. Focusing specifically on the yin-yang (陰陽) distinction, Chan argues that *complementariness*, rather than subordination, should be emphasized in women's gender roles. The yin-yang distinction is an integral part of Neo-Confucianism, and it was taken to imply a hierarchical relationship between the "female" yin (陰) (associated with dark, cold, night, passivity, softness, weakness, and the moon) and the "male" yang (陽) (associated with light, warmth, day, activity, hardness, strength, and the sun). However, Chan argues that yin and yang were not correlated with the genders of male and female when these ideas first emerged in early Confucian texts. Moreover, the yin and yang were said to be complementary forces in early Confucianism, and yin was not meant to be denigrated in comparison to yang: "For example: 'Music comes from yang, rituals come from yin, when yin and yang harmonize, myriad things are fulfilled' (Li Ji 禮記 11:5). Since rituals (li) are of utmost importance in Confucianism, to conceive of yin as their source is indeed to accord yin a very respectable status." It was only in Han dynasty Confucianism – not coincidentally, perhaps, the first dynasty to lift

Confucianism into official state ideology – that the alignment between *yin-yang* and male-female became codified. Their hierarchical relationship was stressed at the expense of complementariness, and the oppression of women became much more severe than under early Confucianism.

According to Chan, there are no clear philosophical grounds for treating the *yin-yang* distinction as a hierarchical polarity, and whatever practical advantages men enjoyed in Confucian China cannot be justified with reference to this distinction. Still, she recognizes that the *yin-yang* distinction can imply gender essentialism and this may have some implications for gender issues in contemporary society. At most, however, *yin-yang* gender essentialism might justify "ritual" respect accorded to males. This "ritual" respect is similar to the "ritual" honor accorded to the elderly, and it need not affect the distribution of important opportunities and resources. There may also be positive Confucian grounds for the inclusion of women in powerful positions: "the [Confucian] sage-ruler is supposed to act like the parents and assume the roles of both the father and mother to the people. Consequently, in Confucianism, women cannot be excluded from politics on the ground that they lack full human potential as they were in the West." In fact, the practical implications of the *yin-yang* distinction (properly understood) significantly overlap with those of contemporary liberal feminism – "both support the idea of shared parenting, the elimination of many kinds of traditional sexual segregation in the workplace, and equal opportunity of political leadership and political participation." Chan shows, however, that both "schools" will reach these conclusions via different values and justifications. Moreover, there may still be particular areas where the *yin-yang* based conception of gender can lead to legal and political conclusions that worry liberal feminists – for example, *yin-yang* Confucians may be less tolerant of single-parent families that fail to allow interactions and complementariness of the two genders in the family setting and may support divorce laws that discourage the breakup of families and tax laws that reward married couples. One way to address the problem of Confucian intolerance of deviations from gender norms, Chan suggests, is to detach the *yin-yang* based conception of gender from core Confucian ideas, as in pre-Han Confucianism.

Hahm Chaibong, a political theorist at Yonsei University, turns to the more specific issue of Confucian-inspired marriage laws in Korea. On July 16, 1997, the Constitutional Court of Korea struck down the law that maintained the centuries old prohibition of marriages between men and women who have the same surnames and ancestral seats. Confucians were in an uproar whereas liberals celebrated the court's decision, and Hahm argues that these divergent reactions are rooted in deeper philosophical differences.

For the liberal, the family is not valuable in and of itself. It is the means to greater goods that are realized outside the family, such as creativity in work and success in politics. Thus, relegating "women or anyone to the family is seen as a mode of repression, as taking away that person's right to individual freedom and self-expression." Any law that reinforces ties to the family at the expense of opportunities in the public realm should therefore be struck down.

Confucianism, on the other hand, values the family as an end in itself, as an essential part of the good life. It fosters the sense of intimacy and caring that most "civil societies" tend to lack. It is the site where people learn the ties of affection that are subsequently spread to other segments of society. Thus, Confucians argue that the state should do what it can to support the institution of the family.

In Korea, the prohibition on marriages between men and women who have the same surnames is widely regarded as a crucial bulwark of Confucian familism. This prohibition owes its origins to Song dynasty Confucianism. The Song Neo-Confucians sought a means of guaranteeing their social status even in the event of a failure to pass the examination, and they resolved this dilemma by reconstructing the family system along the ancient *zong* (宗) system, that is, the principle of descent through male heirs. The reconstruction of the family was also justified on the philosophical grounds that the family was the main realm in which the Confucian ideals of *li* could be taught and practiced.

These Neo-Confucian ideas were rigorously implemented in Chosŏn Korea, a fascinating example of the way in which philosophies developed in one place actually find their fullest and most "orthodox" expression in another. Through a massive state-led effort in translating, interpreting, and disseminating Neo-Confucian philosophy and institutions, Korea was transformed into an exemplary Confucian society. The prohibition of marriage between men and women who have the same surname and ancestral seat was one of the means of enforcement of the Neo-Confucian family system, because pre-Chosŏn marriage customs often confounded the hierarchy of a family organized along patrilineal descent. The different clans have kept strict genealogical records of all their descendants, and today these records, some going back over five hundred years, still top the best-seller lists in Korea.

However, Hahm suggests that the marriage prohibition may be less defensible today, given the population explosion that coincided with rapid modernization: "Today there are 3,760,000 Kimhae Kims, 2,740,000 Milyang Parks, and 2,370,000 Chŏnju Lees, the three largest clans in Korea. The chance of meeting and falling in love with someone from one's own clan is much greater in modern-day South Korea, highly urbanized and with a population of forty-five million." In this context, the marriage prohibition becomes counterproductive since many young people, denied the chance to marry the person they love, are turning away from the institutions of marriage and family. Thus, Hahm suggests that Confucians should endorse the Constitutional Court's decision while searching for new institutional means for preserving the family. This would also pave the way for further nonpatriarchal interpretations of Confucianism.[19]

DOES CONFUCIANISM REALLY MATTER?

This book ends with an epilogue by William Theodore de Bary, Provost Emeritus of Columbia University. Professor de Bary – one of the pedagogical pioneers of core curricula in the humanities – stresses that Confucianism is relevant not only in East Asian societies. A multicultural education in the twenty-first century will have to combine an understanding of local and world cultures. He argues that Confucianism should be given a definite (though not uniquely privileged) place within multicultural educational curricula. At minimum, this would include study of the *Analects* – generations of readers have been attracted by the person of Confucius revealed in its pages. The appeal of Confucius as a person – how he triumphed over political failure and achieved a measure of self-fulfillment (and humility) in difficult circumstances – might help one achieve a sense of personal ease and contentment, whatever the social and political relevance of Confucianism.

Still, the skeptic may be left with a sense of lingering unease. The contributors to this volume may seem to bend over backward to identify those parts of the Confucian tradition consistent with democracy, capitalism, and the rule of law while deliberately ignoring or downplaying those inimical to modernity. Put more bluntly, it may appear that the contributors to this volume are Westernized liberals who scan the Confucian tradition for values and practices that seem to fit their preexisting political agenda, without any deep or real interest in the Confucian tradition per se. These values and practices are stripped of any social and political context and chosen just because of their compatibility with modern liberal capitalist democracy.

But this would not be a fair characterization of what motivates this project.[20] For one thing, most of our contributors are from and/or live in East

---

19 One of the editors of this book had an interesting experience with Korean-style feminism. He asked a Korean graduate student at Yonsei University who expressed feminist ideals to explain what exactly she would want to challenge in the social and political practices in Korea. The student replied that she was particularly irked that she did not have the "right" to perform rituals of ancestor worship (typically, only males have the "right") and that as an eldest daughter she did not have the "right" to continue the family lineage. In other words, she wanted an equal opportunity to participate in Confucian rituals.

20 For de Bary's own reflections on the negative and unresolved problems of the Confucian tradition, see his *The Trouble with Confucianism* (Cambridge, Mass.: Harvard University Press, 1991).

Asian societies with a Confucian heritage, and they identify with and take pride in that heritage; they do not begin with a liberal-democratic framework that is used as the normative template for picking and choosing desirable values. More concretely, some contributors (e.g., Chang Yun-Shik, Gilbert Rozman, and Hahm Chaibong) make detailed use of historical material to show how Confucian values emerged and trace their development to the present day. Others (e.g., Chan Sin Yee) try to show why it makes philosophical sense to distinguish between defensible Confucian values relevant for the present day and problematic "contingent" features tied to their original context. Yet others (e.g., Hahm Chaihark, David Hall, Roger Ames, Lusina Ho, Lew Seok-Choon, Jongryn Mo, and Daniel Bell) select defensible Confucian values not part of (if not inconsistent with) Western liberalism partly to avoid the criticism that the project is driven by the purely strategic consideration of picking and choosing elements from the Confucian tradition that fit with Western liberal-democratic norms. This latter group is concerned to show that modernity in East Asia may have distinctive "Confucian" characteristics.

Put differently, the contributors to this volume are somewhat disenchanted with Western-style liberal modernity. Most important of all is its inability to articulate and institutionalize the kind of communal life that can ensure human flourishing. Confucianism can help to remedy this flaw, thus altering the character of the modern world as currently defined. At the same time, we do not argue for the wholesale restoration of premodern Confucianism. Obviously the main social and political features of modernity – democracy, capitalism, and the rule of law – are here to stay. The effort to secure human freedom had a historical inevitability and normative force that is hard to deny. Moreover, democracy, capitalism, and the rule of law are still values that need to be defended above and beyond all others in many parts of the world, including parts of East Asia. There is a sense in which the development of democratic rights and the affirmation of the positive role of the market are not only the requirements of globalization, but quite necessary for securing the good life. The rule of law continues to be the minimum standard necessary for any human flourishing.

What then is the sense in which we are questioning these essential features of modernity? Is it not the case that Confucian East Asia needs more of these rather than less? Indeed, East Asians have been actively working to overthrow Confucianism for the better part of the past century. Clearly, many in East Asia continue to argue for more "modernity," not less. Those who still do not enjoy the luxury of democracy cry out for even the most basic human rights and procedural justice. For countries mired in corruption and inefficiency, the introduction of free market principles and private property laws are urgent matters that go beyond considerations of tradition and culture. In countries where women are still relegated to second class citizen status, if not subjected to outright abuse and blatant discrimination, the call for the restoration of "family values" and talk of Confucianism can seem to be nothing less than reactionary.

However, the contributors to this volume have decided to look beyond, to look to the next stage with a willingness to err on the side of Confucianism, so to speak. Our view is that there is little danger that any argument in favor of Confucianism would bring about a reaction to turn the clock back to the Confucian past, however defined. This perhaps arises from the fact that most of the contributors, with important exceptions, hail from countries where basic human rights are secure and the rule of law and democracy have begun to take root. This, coupled with the fact that East Asia continues to exhibit a remarkable ability to generate economic growth and political stability, has provided the authors with the luxury of speculating about improving modernity with Confucian norms and institutions, an idea that might be viewed with skepticism, if not outright suspicion, under different circumstances. Of course, the burden is on us to define what that good life is, in what ways modernity does not measure up, and how Confucianism can contribute to the rearticulation and reformulation of modernity in ways that would measure up to our standards of the "good life."

From the Confucian perspective, what we are doing is rearticulating Confucianism for our modern world in the same way Confucians of the past rearticulated it for theirs. Throughout its long and illustrious history, Confucianism was able to survive as a coherent system of thought, a world view, because it was able to engage its philosophical opponents in creative debates through which it was constantly reformulated and reinvented. Confucius and Mencius were themselves able to articulate the visions and ideals of what we have come to call Confucianism by actively engaging in debate the Legalists, Mohists, and innumerable others who made up the "Hundred Schools of Thought" (*zhuzibaijia* 諸子百家) during the Spring and Autumn and Warring States periods.

When "all under heaven" were united into a single empire by Qin Shihuang, who adopted Legalism as his ruling ideology, Confucianism with its essentially "feudal" (*fengjian* 封建) characteristics seemed to have no future. However, Confucianism was able to survive by quickly reinventing itself during the Han dynasty as a bureaucratic ideology prepared to serve the interest of the empire. Philosophically, Dong Zhongshu of the Han dynasty was also to redefine Confucianism within the context of a universal empire by creatively combining it with the theories of *yin-yang* and Five Elements (*yin-yang-wu-hang-shuo* 陰陽五行説), which were then popular.

That Confucianism constantly reinvented itself by coming to terms with the dominant philosophical and political orientations of the time is nowhere more clearly illustrated than in the case of Song Neo-Confucianism. Neo-Confucians of the Song were able to reinvent the tradition that eventually became the "orthodoxy" for most parts of East Asia by constructively engaging the Buddhist and Daoist philosophies that were then sweeping China. In fact, it was only because they had a deep appreciation of Buddhist and Daoist thought that Neo-Confucians could adopt what they thought were undeniably universal elements within these philosophies all the while criticizing them for their shortcomings within their particular historical context. The new schools of Confucianism clearly, sometimes blatantly, incorporated into their doctrines everything from Buddhist epistemology and Daoist cosmology to philosophical diagrams and methods of contemplation. Of course, their rhetoric tended to be anti-Buddhist and anti-Daoist, sometimes vehemently so. Given their ultimate agenda of philosophically and politically reviving Confucianism this was understandable. However, their criticism was based on a deep understanding and appreciation of the theoretical insights and institutional manifestations of Buddhism and Daoism, while remaining fully cognizant of the mass, universal appeal that these world views had among the people.

What we are doing, then, is reviving Confucianism for the modern world by bringing about a creative synthesis between the two, an endeavor that would have been entirely familiar to Confucian intellectuals of the past. Which part of the multifaceted, centuries old Confucian tradition is most relevant for this project? We left it up to individual contributors to decide this. Our view is that it would have been too constraining to attempt to provide an "index" of Confucian values that all our contributors must adhere to.[21] For our purposes, Confucianism was defined broadly as the school of thought developed by Confucius and his interpreters (up to the present), along with the practices and institutions that these ideas (at least partly) gave rise to. This broad definition allowed our contributors to draw inspiration from the ideas of Confucius and Mencius, Song and Ming dynasty Neo-Confucians, as well as modern Confucian thinkers, and to creatively articulate particular Confucian values and practices they would like to defend as appropriate for the modern era.

21 For an interesting effort to put forward a "measurable" index of Confucian convictions and practices, see Koh Byong-ik, "Confucianism in Modern Korea," in Tu Wei-ming, ed., *Confucian Traditions in East Asian Modernity* (Cambridge, Mass.: Harvard University Press, 1996), pp. 197–198. This index, however, takes sides in the debate over the nature of Confucianism and eliminates from consideration parts of the Confucian tradition that may be relevant for the modern world (e.g., the item "Belief in the inherent goodness of human nature" would not allow defenders of Confucianism to look to Xunzi for inspiration). It would be difficult if not impossible to formulate an index that avoids this flaw.

Given that our contributors also share the view that Confucianism is a living heritage in East Asia, the more serious challenge was perhaps to detect contemporary manifestations of Confucianism and explain why they should be labeled "Confucian." To be sure, during those periods in East Asian history when a particular version of Confucian philosophy was accepted as the orthodoxy and efforts were made to have practices and institutions cohere with it, it was easy enough to discover and define Confucianism. However, in the modern era, when few publicly espouse Confucianism as their world view or philosophy, it is much more difficult to detect manifestations of Confucianism.[22] Rather than point to vague principles said to influence the "habits of the heart" of East Asians, our contributors tended to focus on particular practices and institutions still relevant and defensible today. In other words, they focus on concrete phenomena in East Asia, ideally tracing their historical evolution from their Confucian origins to the present day. It is certainly possible that contemporary East Asians have lost sight of that history, in which case it may not be implausible to argue that Confucianism can operate "behind the backs" of the people involved. For our purposes, it was (only) necessary to show in concrete detail how the particular practice or institution relates to the Confucian tradition[23] – and to further think normatively about which practices and institutions are still defensible in the modern world.

In sum, what emerges from our project is something more than the strategic use of Confucian values and practices for the purpose of promoting Western-style modernity in East Asia but less than an alternative theory of modernity appropriate (only) for the East Asian context. Confucian values may have universal appeal and they may be feasible and desirable even in societies without a Confucian heritage (though defenders of Confucianism may face more of an uphill struggle in such contexts). Our aim is not to

---

22 For some empirical evidence that points to the resilience of Confucian cultural traits in Japan, China, and Hong Kong, see Ka Lin, *Confucian Welfare Cluster: A Cultural Interpretation of Social Welfare* (Tampere: Tampere University Press, 1999).

23 We drew the line, however, at the argument that anti-Confucian thinkers (such as Mao Zedong) and associated practices should still be seen as extensions of the Confucian tradition. This kind of argument is not unusual. For example, Simon Leys argues that "Mao Zedong est imprégné de mentalité confucéenne, et de façon d'autant plus profonde qu'il en est moins conscient" (Mao Zedong is impregnated with a Confucian mentality, and in a way so deep that he is less conscious of it) (Leys, *Essais sur la Chine* [Paris: Robert Laffont, 1998], p. 132), and Donald Munro argues that long-entrenched Confucian values and habits continued to provide the background assumptions and values even during the darkest "anti-Confucian" days of the Cultural Revolution (Munro, *The Concept of Man in Early China* [Stanford: Stanford University Press, 1969], pp. 165–167). These arguments are not necessarily wrong, but they are difficult to substantiate and thus we have asked contributors to refrain from such arguments.

replace Western (liberal) modernity with an East Asian version but rather to articulate some Confucian values and practices that could shape modern political, economic, and legal institutions in desirable ways, mitigating some of their more obvious excesses. This book is a starting point for debate, as there may well be relevant and defensible Confucian values and practices not discussed here. Still, what makes our book original is that concrete discussions of Confucian values and practices for the contemporary era have been conspicuously absent from the literature. The essays presented in this volume thus represent the most cutting-edge and potentially relevant efforts to modernize Confucianism and Confucianize modernity at the same time.

PART I

CONFUCIAN PERSPECTIVES ON DEMOCRACY

CHAPTER 1

CONSTITUTIONALISM, CONFUCIAN CIVIC VIRTUE, AND RITUAL PROPRIETY

HAHM CHAIHARK

I CONSTITUTIONALISM AND THE IMPORTANCE OF CIVIC VIRTUE

These days, we are apt to combine the two terms "democracy" and "constitutionalism" and talk about "constitutional democracy," without giving much thought to the nature of the relationship or connection between the two. If we do think about it, however, we will find that there is something of a tension between the two. For democracy usually refers to a form of politics in which the people are the source of power and legitimacy, and it is thus associated with the idea of majority rule. Of course, this is not the whole story, and there may certainly be other, more sophisticated conceptions of democracy. Yet, by and large, it is intimately associated with the ideas of self-rule and self-determination through various forms of participation in the political process.

Constitutionalism, on the other hand, refers to the notion of regulating and restraining the political process and government power according to some higher norm that cannot be changed even if the majority wants to change it. It is grounded in the idea that there are some things that are so important that they should be protected against the majority will, which is bound to be always changing and may even be fickle. Of course, in a democratic polity, constitutions can always be amended or revised by the people. Yet, most constitutions provide for a special procedure for amendment or revision that makes it harder for a simple majority to make changes. Even in countries where in theory the constitution can be changed by a simple majority, the weight of tradition and usage makes change practically impossible.[1] Thus, it is safe to say that the point of having a constitution is to set apart some things

---

1 The British constitution is nominally one which can be changed by a simple majority of the Parliament. Yet, even in Great Britain, the doctrine of parliamentary supremacy is in practice significantly circumscribed by certain implicit, shared understandings regarding the sanctity of the constitutional system.

from the normal political process. The idea of constitutionalism can also be implemented through institutions designed to protect the rights of the minority. Viewed in this light, constitutional democracy is a form of politics that tries to combine two distinct values which are somewhat at odds with each other. One is based on an implicit trust in the people's capacity for governance, while the other is related to an attitude of distrust toward governments, be they democratic or not.

This is not to say that constitutional democracy is ultimately an incoherent idea or that it is riddled with some "fundamental contradictions." Among legal scholars who have grappled with the issue, Frank Michelman has argued that the two elements can be mediated through what he calls a republican "jurisgenerative" politics, in which the people can see themselves as the author of laws that they agree to live by.[2] The idea is that the requirements of both democracy and constitutionalism can be satisfied when people participate in the process of establishing the rules that will govern their lives, including their political life. Similarly, Ronald Dworkin argues that democracy cannot be equated with mere majoritarianism. For him, democracy is a moral value according to which each citizen should be treated with equal respect and concern. This in turn gives rise to the moral rights of the individual which demand protection against infringement by the majority. From this perspective, the fact that these basic rights of citizens can "trump" the laws of a democratically elected legislature is not antidemocratic at all – democracy is actually promoted by it.[3]

Without attempting to settle the debate regarding how to harmonize these two values, both of which I believe are important for any political ordering in the modern world, I wish to concentrate in the following pages on just one of the two, namely, constitutionalism, and to explore the possible resources within Confucianism for the proper practice and understanding of this ideal. I shall define constitutionalism in functional terms as the ideal of establishing some form of effective and regularized restraint on the government.[4] In other words, "constitutionalism," as I am using the term here, is shorthand for the project of preventing abuse of government power. By this I am not denying that modern constitutions often have many functions other

---

2 Frank Michelman, "Law's Republic," *Yale Law Journal* vol. 97, no. 8 (1988), pp. 1499–1503. Michelman's idea of "jurisgenerative" politics is taken from Robert Cover. See Robert M. Cover, "The Supreme Court 1982 Term – Forward: *Nomos* and Narrative," *Harvard Law Review* vol. 97, no. 1 (1983), pp. 4–68.

3 Ronald Dworkin, Introduction, in *Freedom's Law* (Cambridge, Mass.: Harvard University Press, 1996), pp. 15–19. Dworkin uses the term "constitutional conception of democracy" to describe his understanding of democracy. On his theory of rights, see, generally, Ronald Dworkin, *Taking Rights Seriously* (Cambridge, Mass.: Harvard University Press, 1977).

4 This definition is taken from Carl J. Friedrich, *Constitutional Government and Democracy*, 4th ed. (Waltham, Mass.: Blaisdell Publishing Co., 1968).

than limiting government power.[5] I also agree with Stephen Holmes that constitutionalism is as much about enabling and constituting power as it is about disabling power.[6] Here, I am merely employing the term "constitutionalism" as it is commonly understood in Western political and legal discourse. While a constitution may have a number of functions, the term "constitutionalism" is usually used to refer to the project of restraining the government from abusing its power.

There are many ways of preventing abuse of government power, of course. One way is to design institutional devices to check the power of each government agency. The separation of powers into several branches (e.g., legislative, executive, and judicial) or the division of government functions into multiple levels (e.g., federal, state, and local) are examples of this. Another way is to entrench certain basic rights of the individual, which will be protected by independent courts against encroachments by either the government or other citizens.[7]

Yet, ultimately, I believe the success of a constitutionalist government depends on the disposition of its citizens. One might call this the "political culture"; it might also be described as the civic virtue of citizens. Whatever the label, it points to the importance of the citizens' willingness and ability

5 For example, Ulrich Preuss identifies at least four different functions of a constitution in a modern state: i) limitation of power, ii) authorization of power, iii) legitimization of political authority, and iv) integration of society (Ulrich Preuss, "Patterns of Constitutional Evolution and Change in Eastern Europe," in Joachim J. Hesse and Nevil Johnson, eds., *Constitutional Policy and Change in Europe* [New York: Oxford University Press, 1995], pp. 98–101). According to this, my understanding of constitutionalism might appear to encompass only the first of the four functions enumerated by Preuss. I would argue, however, that my use of the phrase "effective and regularized restraint on the government" is broader than the mere application of limits on power. In a sense, these four functions are the consequences of restraining the government through constitutionalism.

6 Stephen Holmes, "Precommitment and the Paradox of Democracy," in Jon Elster and Rune Slagstad, eds., *Constitutionalism and Democracy* (Cambridge: Cambridge University Press, 1988), pp. 195–240. My discussion below on the constitutional aspect of ritual propriety (*li* 禮) is essentially consistent with Holmes's thesis that putting restraint on government power is not necessarily a negative affair; that power can also be "limited" through "constitutive rules" which "make a practice possible for the first time" (ibid., p. 227).

7 In the United States, courts of law have assumed such an important role in enforcing constitutional restraints on government that the phrase "rule of law" has become all but synonymous with constitutionalism. To be sure, there are significant overlaps, but I believe it is good to maintain an analytical distinction between the two terms. For one thing, the rule of law encompasses nonpolitical areas of law such as enforcement of contracts among private individuals. More importantly, while law and the courts form a vital component of constitutionalism, constitutional politics requires other norms and customs of nonlegal nature which are not amenable to judicial enforcement. As a result, it is possible for a form of rule of law regime to coexist with a quite authoritarian government that acknowledges little constitutional restraint. It is also possible to have a constitutional regime that relies far less on law and the courts as is the case in the United States, and more on tradition, conventions, and other mediums of political regulation.

to put some form of restraint on the government. In other words, constitutionalism requires a certain type of citizens in order to function properly. Now, it is often said that people are not born democratic citizens, but they are made. The same is true of constitutionalist citizens. It takes certain conscious efforts to make a citizenry of a certain disposition that will enable and empower them to demand and maintain restraint on the government. If this is the case, then it would be logical to be mindful of the processes through which this disposition is shaped. We need to think carefully about political education or political socialization. To have a constitutionalist form of government, we need to think about the kinds of civic virtue that should be instilled in the people.

Of course, I am aware that this is not an uncontroversial position. According to some proponents of liberalism, government can be so organized that one need not worry about the character of the people. Indeed, the argument that the point of having a constitution is to form a government that would work regardless of the people's virtue has a long pedigree. Immanuel Kant famously suggested that a proper institutional arrangement could make it possible even for a "nation of devils" to govern themselves peaceably.[8] Similarly, James Madison can be read as having argued that the U.S. Constitution is an instrument designed to achieve precisely that goal.[9]

This faith in the capacity of institutions to filter out bad opinions and to refine the political sentiments of the people is also revealed in the principle of state neutrality. According to this principle, which many liberals believe is at the core of liberalism, the state must remain neutral with regard to the various conceptions of the good life. Thus, the state has no business in trying to promote certain beliefs or attitudes on the basis of some estimation by the state that such beliefs and attitudes will be conducive to the state's political health. Part of the rationale for this seems to be that since the citizens' character has no effect on the political process anyway, the liberal state has no reason to get involved in the business of trying to foster civic virtue.

Recently, however, civic virtue has become a hotly debated issue among Western political theorists and moral philosophers. This is related to the so-

---

8 Immanuel Kant, "Perpetual Peace," in Hans Reiss, ed., and H. B. Nisbet, trans., *Kant: Political Writings* (Cambridge: Cambridge University Press, 1970), pp. 112–113. Kant also wrote that men need not be angels to be able to form this kind of government (ibid.).

9 Madison, echoing Kant's supernatural metaphor, wrote that if humans were angels, we would need no government in the first place. James Madison, "Federalist No. 51," in Alexander Hamilton, James Madison, and John Jay, *The Federalist Papers*, Clinton Rossiter, ed. (New York: Mentor Books, 1961), p. 322. More importantly, Madison argued that the U.S. Constitution would neutralize the selfish ambitions of men and the pernicious effects of factions, so that government will function even though "enlightened statesmen will not always be at the helm" ("Federalist No. 10" [James Madison]).

called revival of the "civic republican" tradition, but discussion of civic virtue is by no means limited to the writers of that camp. Many liberals nowadays acknowledge the need to promote civic virtue and to educate people with the habits, beliefs, and attitudes necessary for citizenship.[10] These writers argue that even a liberal government is dependent on the habits and dispositions of its citizens and that the liberal state need not – indeed, should not – be neutral as to the process of character formation.[11] I believe this recent interest in civic virtue reflects a renewed appreciation for the importance of the human dimension in political ordering. Actually, even in the United States, a country regarded by some as a state embodying the liberal principle, this human dimension has always been recognized by the political leadership. Ever since its founding, America has had a deep commitment to fostering the necessary civic virtues,[12] so that despite the rhetoric of state neutrality, its educative debates and practices reveal a continuing concern over what kind of people should be created and molded through schools and other institutions. To be sure, the U.S. Constitution is famous for attempting to establish a system of government institutions that will work to prevent the abuse of power, regardless of the amount of civic virtue, and it is also true that not one word on education is mentioned in that document. Nevertheless, it would be a mistake to infer from this that constitutionalism in America is unconcerned about the character of citizens.[13] People may have disagreed about the

10 For an interpretation of the major founding figures of the liberal tradition, including Kant, which stresses the vital place occupied by virtue within liberalism, see Peter Berkowitz, *Virtue and the Making of Modern Liberalism* (Princeton, N.J.: Princeton University Press, 1999).
11 For example, Stephen Macedo has consistently drawn our attention to the fact that liberal governments can ill afford to be indifferent about the citizens' beliefs, habits, and attitudes, and the process of their formation. See Stephen Macedo, *Liberal Virtues: Citizenship, Virtue, and Community in Liberal Constitutionalism* (Oxford: Clarendon Press, 1990); Stephen Macedo, "Transformative Constitutionalism and the Case of Religion: Defending the Moderate Hegemony of Liberalism," *Political Theory* vol. 26, no. 1 (February 1998), pp. 56–89; Stephen Macedo, *Diversity and Distrust: Civic Education in a Multicultural Democracy* (Cambridge, Mass.: Harvard University Press, 1999). For a similar argument that the liberal state need not maintain neutrality, see William Galston, *Liberal Purposes: Goods, Virtues, and Diversity in the Liberal State* (New York: Cambridge University Press, 1991). For a more philosophical statement of liberal theory that rejects the neutrality principle, see Joseph Raz, *The Morality of Freedom* (Oxford: Oxford University Press, 1986).
12 On the educational ideas of the founding generation, see Lorraine Smith Pangle and Thomas L. Pangle, *The Learning of Liberty: The Educational Ideas of the American Founders* (Lawrence: University Press of Kansas, 1993).
13 Michael Sandel thinks that with the triumph of the liberal "proceduralist republic" in America, state neutrality became a political orthodoxy and the government was effectively removed from the task of attending to its citizens' character. He also argues that liberalism is incompatible with what he calls the "formative project" of caring for the character of the people, and that by mid-twentieth century, Americans essentially gave up their

particular contents of civic virtue to be promoted; yet they never for a moment doubted the need for educating for citizenship.

Particularly, during the American founding period, the overriding political issue was whether Americans possessed enough virtue to make their political experiment work, that is, whether the citizens would be able to exercise effective and regularized restraint on the government so as to prevent tyranny.[14] Thus, the same generation that produced the Constitution also started busily working on a system of public schools which would inculcate what were called "republican virtues." This public school system was perfected within the next generation and has been one of the main agencies of assimilating newly arrived immigrants and propagating "Americanism." Obviously, the Americanism of the nineteenth and early twentieth centuries included many cultural, racial, and religious prejudices which are frankly quite offensive to many of us living on the threshold of the twenty-first century. Nevertheless, this system's remarkable success in establishing a set of mainstream American civic virtues is evidenced by the fact that people who did not wish to be so assimilated (most notably the Roman Catholics) were forced to set up their own independent school systems.[15]

Of course, the current state of American public schools is far from ideal. Many deplore the dismal conditions of inner city schools and the less than stellar performance of students in basic subjects such as math and the sciences. However, I am not discussing the efficacy of these schools' instruction in factual knowledge or technical skills. I am pointing to the fact that schools have been instrumental throughout American history in producing citizens who believed, for example, that their government is, or at least should be, "of the people, for the people and by the people." To be sure, this may be just rhetoric, but it is nevertheless a powerful cultural idiom which provides people with a criterion for evaluating and criticizing their government. For some, it may even motivate them to certain political actions to make this belief a reality. Being inculcated in this belief, then, is a form of political education that gives people a vocabulary with which to talk about the legitimacy of their government.

When discussing political education, people are apt to think only of classes with names like "Civics" or "Government." Yet, it should be pointed out that

formative project. Michael J. Sandel, *Democracy and Its Discontent* (Cambridge, Mass.: Harvard University Press, 1996). Yet, I submit that a liberal polity depends no less than other kinds of polity on its citizens' being equipped with certain virtues appropriate for its maintenance and reproduction.

14 See Gordon Wood, *The Creation of the American Republic, 1776–1787* (New York: W.W. Norton and Company, Inc., 1969).

15 For a review of the fortunes of the American common school system, and the response of Catholic schools, see Macedo, *Diversity and Distrust*, pp. 41–147.

education for citizenship can be, and often is, carried out in a number of other settings. If, for example, a society's ideal of a virtuous citizen is one who possesses great pride in his or her country's historical achievements, instruction in the history and the arts and literature of that society will be as important as the "Civics" class. In American public schools, it is not hard to imagine that the idea (and ideology) of Manifest Destiny in the presentation of national history would have operated to instill in generations of students a sense of national pride and purpose. Of course, when a particular subgroup in the polity feels left out or underrepresented in the telling of the national history, or in the selection of literary works to be read in the national language class, it will no doubt demand to be included in the citizenship ideal of the society. We witnessed this in recent years in America with the debate about multiculturalism and "cultural canons." In a sense, the history of American public education is the story of how different ideals of citizenship strove to gain the upper hand through endless political debates.[16] Moreover, schools are not the only setting for engaging in political education. Political education is also crucially dependent on civil society, the nonpolitical spheres of life, including family, church, and other civic organizations.[17] In fact, according to the conventional liberal position, another reason why the state should not be involved in political education is because that role belongs to civil society. Yet, arguing for a more conscious and perhaps more active role by the state in promoting civic virtue does not mean civil society should relinquish that role.

I have used the example of American education to highlight a more general point about constitutionalism. It is not my claim that all debates about education have constitutional implications. My point here is merely that, since constitutionalism depends on the disposition of the citizens to put effective restraint on the government, anyone concerned about practicing constitutionalism can ill afford to ignore educational debates relating to the business of preparing the next generation of citizens.

II CONSTITUTIONALISM AND CULTURE

Before turning to the relevance of Confucianism for constitutionalism or political education, I believe a few words about cultural traditions and

16 "Many groups have contested with one another to define and create model citizens through schooling, and this political debate has shaped the course of public education" (David Tyack and Larry Cuban, *Tinkering Toward Utopia: A Century of Public School Reform* [Cambridge, Mass.: Harvard University Press, 1995], p. 2).

17 As is well known, this was recognized early on by Tocqueville. Alexis de Tocqueville, *Democracy in America*, J. P. Mayer, ed., and George Lawrence, trans. (Garden City, N.Y.: Anchor Books, 1988).

constitutionalism are in order. I think it should be fairly uncontroversial to
say that political institutions and legal rules should be supported by the local
culture. This should be quite elementary for anyone who has thought seriously about transplanting legal institutions from one context to another.[18]
One need not be an adherent of Savigny's historical school of jurisprudence
or a Burkean conservative to appreciate the importance of any law's historical and cultural context. It was Montesquieu, the great admirer of the English
constitution, who cautioned: "Laws should be so appropriate to the people
for whom they are made that it is very unlikely that the laws of one nation
can suit another."[19] Another famous Frenchman who admired the democracy
in another English-speaking country (this time, the United States) similarly
warned that the democratic institutions of America should not be regarded
as the universal model for all to follow. For Tocqueville, despite his percep-
tive and enthusiastic praise for American democratic institutions, those institutions were worthy of praise because they reflected the uniquely American
democratic mores. He therefore urged his fellow Europeans to seek their
own paths to democracy.[20] Whether one calls it culture, mores, tradition, or
Volksgeist, one cannot afford to be inattentive to the constellation of contextual elements that can impede or enable the proper operation of legal ideas
and institutions.

18 The phenomenon of "legal transplants" or "legal borrowing" is a fascinating subject which
has been studied by many scholars from diverse backgrounds. In legal history, Alan Watson
has advanced the famous thesis that legal transplants are often the most significant cause
of legal change in any regime. See, e.g., Alan Watson, "Legal Change: Sources of Law and
Legal Culture," *University of Pennsylvania Law Review* vol. 131 (1983), pp. 1121–1157; Alan
Watson, *Legal Transplants: An Approach to Comparative Law*, 2d ed. (Athens, Ga.: University of Georgia Press, 1993). In cultural studies and legal anthropology, the phenomenon,
sometimes referred to as "legal pluralism," is often analyzed in relation to the experience
of colonialism. See, e.g., M. B. Hooker, *Legal Pluralism: An Introduction to Colonial and Neo-
colonial Laws* (Oxford: Clarendon Press, 1975); Clifford Geertz, "Local Knowledge: Fact and
Law in Comparative Perspective," *Local Knowledge: Further Essays in Interpretive Anthropology*
(New York: Basic Books, 1983), pp. 167–234. With the increase of international legal
transactions and a growing concern for uniformity among legal regimes, scholars special-
izing in the more "conventional" fields of law (e.g., corporations, civil procedure, or
constitutional law) are also showing a greater interest in the idea of legal transplants
or borrowing. See, e.g., Symposium, "Contextuality and Universality: Constitutional
Borrowings on the Global Stage," *University of Pennsylvania Journal of Constitutional Law*
vol. 1 (1999); Oscar G. Chase, "Legal Processes and National Culture," *Cardozo Journal of
International and Comparative Law* vol. 5, no. 1 (1997), pp. 1–24 (examining the feasibility
and desirability of importing the German system of civil litigation into the United States).
19 Montesquieu, *The Spirit of the Laws*, Anne Cohler, Basia Miller, and Harold Stone, eds. and
trans. (New York: Cambridge University Press, 1989 [1748]), p. 8. For his admiration
and novel interpretation of the English constitution, see ibid., pp. 154–166. In invoking
the "authority" of Montesquieu, I am not thereby endorsing his description of Chinese
laws and Confucian political morality.
20 Tocqueville, *Democracy in America*, pp. 18 and 309–315.

In the words of Robert Cover: "No set of legal institutions or prescriptions exists apart from the narratives that locate it and give it meaning."[21] For Cover, such narratives, which provide meaning to legal institutions, are what he calls *nomos*, a normative universe that all of us inhabit. It is by reference to this nomos that we give meaning to law and attribute legal meaning to our actions. Therefore, depending on the nomos that we inhabit, the same physical acts and the same legal texts can have very different meanings. Thus Cover writes: "If there existed two legal orders with identical legal precepts and identical, predictable patterns of public force, they would nonetheless differ essentially in meaning if, in one of the orders, the precepts were universally venerated while in the other they were regarded by many as fundamentally unjust."[22]

With regard to constitutions, Frederick Schauer makes a similar argument concerning constitutional rules on free speech. After observing that "the prelegal instantiations of terms like 'political' and 'free speech' will vary dramatically from culture to culture," Schauer writes that it would then be logical to conclude that "differences in the scope of constitutional protection [will] vary far more than might be expected merely by inspecting the relevant constitutional language."[23]

The normative power of law, especially a constitution, therefore derives from its being embedded in a nomos, the normative cultural vocabulary of a people through which they understand and evaluate political action. In any society, law is a part of its normative culture and as such operates by interacting with other parts of that culture. To use Clifford Geertz's famous expression, law is a "system of meaning," a way of "imagining the real," a distinctive grammar of the society according to which people make sense of the world and interact with one another.[24] Then, to be effective and relevant to the society, constitutional norms must partake of that society's "system of meaning" whose grammar is its culture.

The concept of "culture" is undoubtedly a very porous one, and it can mean many things to many people.[25] This is not the place – nor am I competent

---

21 Cover, "*Nomos* and Narrative," p. 4.

22 Cover, "*Nomos* and Narrative," p. 7. Again, *nomos* is what allows us to understand the "difference between sleeping late on Sunday and refusing the sacraments, between having a snack and desecrating the fast of Yom Kippur, between banking a check and refusing to pay your income tax" (ibid., p. 8).

23 Frederick Schauer, "Free Speech and the Cultural Contingency of Constitutional Categories," in Michel Rosenfeld, ed., *Constitutionalism, Identity, Difference, and Legitimacy* (Durham, N.C.: Duke University Press, 1994), p. 367.

24 Geertz, "Local Knowledge," pp. 173 and 184.

25 As historian E. P. Thompson observes, "we should not forget that 'culture' is a clumpish term, which by gathering up so many activities and attributes into one common bundle may actually confuse or disguise discriminations that should be made between them" (*Cus-*

– to elaborate a comprehensive theory of culture. I will just mention that I am using the term here in an admittedly imprecise and eclectic manner to mean the relatively stable system of shared signs, symbols, beliefs, assumptions, habits, and norms which allows us to make sense of the world, make value judgments, and communicate with one another. It is a system of meaning, but it is also a normative enterprise. Culture is in one sense more fundamental than the individual because culture precedes the individual and it is culture that defines what an individual is. As Geertz says, we are all "cultural artifacts."[26] Nevertheless, it would be inaccurate to regard culture as some relentless, inexorable force that determines one's entire existence. Culture is a human construct, and as such it is always undergoing change and adjustments brought about through the agency of individuals in that culture. Culture constantly reproduces itself by cultivating the next generation who grow up internalizing the same beliefs and norms, and so it may seem at times irresistible and oppressive. Yet, culture is never a fully integrated, coherent, static, totalizing, seamless whole.[27] There are always gaps, fissures, ambiguities, inconsistencies, and contradictions within any given culture, and this allows for transformation and reconfiguration of the signs, symbols, habits, beliefs, and norms that make up the culture. Culture always has room for subcultures and countercultures, and it is always possible that these may eventually become the dominant culture.

According to this understanding of culture, law itself is a cultural system, for law trades on the meanings and value judgments made possible by the culture that produced it. This is what Geertz means when he says that law is a system of meaning. When a constitution is borrowed from another country, it has to resonate with the ways that the people of the borrower country attribute meaning and make normative value judgments, that is, with its culture. One legal scholar has stated that the constitution of a state must be connected with its own particular "religion," by which he means "the most important, most binding ideas at the heart of that culture."[28] This

toms in Common [New York: The New Press, 1991], p. 13). For a more recent attack on the usefulness of the concept for anthropological studies, see Adam Kuper, *Culture: The Anthropologists' Account* (Cambridge, Mass.: Harvard University Press, 2000).

26 Clifford Geertz, "The Impact of the Concept of Culture on the Concept of Man," in *The Interpretation of Cultures* (New York: Basic Books, 1973), p. 51.

27 Sally E. Merry, "Law, Culture, and Cultural Appropriation," *Yale Journal of Law and Humanities* vol. 10, no. 2 (1998), pp. 582–584 (describing recent theories of culture which criticize the overly consensual and homogeneous conception of culture presupposed in conventional anthropological studies).

28 Lawrence W. Beer, "Introduction" to Lawrence W. Beer, ed., *Constitutional Systems in Late Twentieth Century Asia* (Seattle: University of Washington Press, 1992), p. 16. As such, Beer adds, "[h]uman rights standards must deal effectively with such 'constitutional religion'; they must be linked with what is already seen as most important in a community, or fail" (ibid., p. 17).

is so because a constitution, probably more so than any other law, is expressive of that country's legal and political culture. In many instances, constitutional issues force the decision makers to "reflect upon the legal culture in which the dispute is embedded," such that the resulting decisions can be interpreted as "expressions of the decision makers' constitutional identities."[29]

In arguing that constitutional issues are intimately related to culture and that constitutional norms should be articulated in terms of the normative vocabulary provided by the surrounding culture, I am not implying that cross-cultural interaction between different constitutional systems, or legal transplantation in general, is impossible or useless. I believe that cross-fertilization is an important way in which different countries can develop and enrich their own practice and theory of constitutionalism. I am, however, arguing that recognition of the cultural dimension in law and constitutionalism should lead us to question the meaningfulness and the effectiveness of a constitutional discourse that is conducted solely, or mostly, in terms of concepts and categories imported from another culture. Further, I am suggesting that we should at least query whether the current constitutional discourse in East Asian countries is not a case of such discourse carried on in terms of borrowed idioms.

For at least a century now, we have often heard the complaint lodged by various observers of East Asian politics and law to the effect that the formal political and legal institutions imported from the West are not functioning properly due to "cultural elements." For example, one frequently hears of the "failure" of political parties in East Asia. It is a fact that no East Asian country has established the stable two-party system that is regarded as the norm in the West. Similarly, people have noted that the electoral system does not function as a means for focusing on the issues, but rather becomes an occasion for reinforcing and exacerbating favoritism, nepotism, regionalism, and so forth. The conclusion that many drew from this state of affairs was that East Asians must change, or "modernize," their culture. In a way, that is still true; a means must be found to root out corruption in politics and government.[30] On the other hand, it is not self-evident that the problem is with the culture alone.

29 George P. Fletcher, "Constitutional Identity," in Michel Rosenfeld, ed., *Constitutionalism, Identity, Difference, and Legitimacy* (Durham, N.C.: Duke University Press, 1994), p. 223. Of course, the constitutional culture of America, or anywhere else, is not monolithic. There are always multiple strands within it, whose mutual interaction and even conflict are normal ingredients in the development of any constitutional culture. See, e.g., J. David Greenstone, "Against Simplicity: The Cultural Dimensions of the Constitution," *University of Chicago Law Review* vol. 55 (1988), pp. 428–449.
30 Here, I do not intend to go into the by now familiar criticisms laid on the so-called modernization theory. Suffice it to say that in light of the ongoing scholarly reexamination and problematization of the concept of modernity itself, it has become less than obvious what it means to pursue modernization.

It is worth asking whether the imported political institutions and idioms might not be the source of the problem. What is needed instead may be a new and imaginative way of talking about and conducting politics that is more sensitive to the culture. What is needed may be a political idiom and institutional arrangements grounded more firmly in the cultural traditions of East Asia. If that is the case, I believe the only way to come by such a new idiom or institutions will be through a serious meditation on the culture itself.[31]

III RITUAL PROPRIETY AS CONSTITUTIONAL NORM

Turning now to the prospects of constitutionalism in East Asia, I believe that many of the idioms and vocabularies used by East Asians for making sense of the world and rendering normative judgments are derived from the Confucian tradition. The way an East Asian interprets another person's actions and makes normative judgments is still powerfully informed by Confucian teachings.[32] This is true even in the political sphere. To be sure, no one these days talks in terms of emulating the ancient sage-kings, and no one quotes the Confucian classics in support of a policy argument, except as occasional rhetorical flourish. On the other hand, the qualities of a political leader esteemed by the people are by and large virtues extolled by Confucian teaching. For example, in Korea, people still demand such qualities as uprightness (or righteousness) and humility (or knowing one's station), and they still have the expectation, however unrealistic it may be, that their political leaders should be "honorably poor" (chŏngbin in Korean, qingpin 清貧 in Chinese), that is, unsullied by material greed.

31 Of course, I am not arguing that East Asians should scrap all the political and legal terms and institutions that they learned from the West. Indeed, they were fast learners, and commentators have noted the speed with which they picked up Western political idioms like democracy, freedom, equality, separation of powers, party system, and rule of law. In a sense, East Asians have already adopted these and made them their own, such that the current East Asian political and legal culture is a hybrid. As such any search for political idioms and institutions more sensitive to the East Asian culture will have to take this into consideration. In other words, it cannot be an exercise in reactionary restorationism.

32 I am aware of the peril in using another lumpish term "East Asia." By using that term, I am certainly not implying that East Asia is a homogeneous region. Similarly, I am not suggesting that we can generalize about Confucianism, for claiming that such and such is *the* Confucian position always risks ignoring the remarkable diversity of views within the tradition. It is sometimes difficult to know whether or not certain common "East Asian" traits can be attributable to the shared Confucian background, and whether or not such attribution adds anything to our understanding of East Asia. While I am skeptical about "explaining" general values or ideals (e.g., priority of community over individual, preference for harmony etc.) by reference to Confucianism, I do think it is plausible to attribute certain shared symbols, vocabulary, and rhetorical strategies (e.g., Five Cardinal Relations) to Confucianism.

Given this situation, I believe that in East Asia the constitutionalist goal of putting effective restraint on the government and the educative goal of creating citizens who will demand such restraint should be pursued by taking into account this cultural idiom and vocabulary of Confucianism. Among the Confucian terms and concepts, I would like to suggest that "ritual propriety" (*ye* in Korean, *li* 禮 in Chinese) can provide a fruitful means of appropriating the Confucian cultural idiom for the project of establishing constitutionalism. Given the richness and fertile ambiguity of the term, I believe that it is a field that will reward our cultivation and exploration. Variously translated as ritual, rites, ceremony, propriety, manners, or etiquette, et cetera, this concept of *li* may at first seem an unlikely candidate for the job of restraining political power or of creating such a disposition in the citizenry. Once we properly understand its significance, however, we will see that it is particularly well suited for the job. This is because the Confucian notion of *li* lies at the intersection of politics and education. It is a marvelous combination of education, self-cultivation, training, discipline, restraint, authority, and legitimacy.

On the educative side, *li* is a behavioral norm that operates by being internalized by the person, so that in effect it becomes part of his or her entire being. Proficiency in acting according to ritual propriety is something that is learned and acquired through practice and repetition. I believe this aspect is captured well by the notion of "discipline." It is well known that Confucius once defined the supreme virtue *ren* (仁) (or *in* in Korean; variously translated humanity, human-heartedness, benevolence, charity, etc.) as "disciplining oneself and returning to ritual propriety" (*keji fuli* 克己復禮 in Chinese, *kŭkgi bongnye* in Korean).[33] This shows, at the least, that discipline and ritual propriety are closely related.[34] In fact, the idea of discipline is very helpful for understanding both the educative and constitutional aspects of *li*. Particularly, I believe that the idea of discipline as developed by the French philosopher Michel Foucault captures many aspects of *li* that

---

33 *Analects* 12:1.

34 Thomas Stephens has employed the term "discipline" to describe the Chinese approach to dispute resolution. He contrasts it to the Western approach which he labels "adjudication." According to his usage, discipline presupposes a world ordered in hierarchical terms and seeks to maintain that hierarchical order through enforcement of duties without rights (Thomas B. Stephens, *Order and Discipline in China* [Seattle: University of Washington Press, 1992]). The implication is that politically powerful persons were not subject to any discipline at all. As will be seen below, my claim is that ritual propriety was a powerful means of disciplining political leaders as well. One misses an essential feature of Confucian political theory if one starts with the assumption that premodern Chinese or Korean politicians were subject to no discipline. Even though Stephens states that his categories are not intended to describe types of political authority or government structure, he nevertheless appears to be working under such assumption (ibid., pp. 7 and 16–39).

are vital for understanding its significance as political education for
constitutionalism.[35]

According to Foucault, discipline is a highly individualized mode of
regulatory norm which operates through minute training of the human body,
under continuous observation and surveillance, so that the person ultimately
internalizes what Foucault calls the "normalizing gaze" and arrives at self-
surveillance. Discipline is thus essentially an educative process that can be
contrasted with a different form of regulation which operates through spo-
radic applications of coercion and terror.[36] Like Foucault's idea of discipline,
li operates by ceaseless and constant application, so that it penetrates into
the body's movements and becomes a part of its reflex system. As with
disciplinary power, training in *li* ultimately results in self-surveillance
through the person's internalization of the prescribed value and behavior.[37]
As with discipline, *li* is concerned with a person's reform and transformation,
rather than with mere external conformity or coercive submission.[38] It works
through a subtle process of habituation and "ritualization."

Yet, *li* is corrupted or violated once its performance becomes routine or
automatic. As Herbert Fingarette noted, one has to be "present" in it and
one's action must be "spontaneous."[39] For the Confucian, learning to discipline oneself according to *li*, so that one spontaneously knows how to act in
a ritually proper manner, is actually the process of learning to become human.
Humanization requires discipline. We might even say that for the Confucian,
human beings are "rites-bearers," whose humanity is secured by "grasping"
the prescriptions of *li*.[40] This is what Tu Wei-ming means when he says that

35 I should note that Foucault did not argue that "discipline" had a constitutionalist dimen-
     sion of restraining political power. Rather, he saw it as a form of power directed at the
     common people for increased control and efficiency. My argument is that *li* (禮) was a
     similar form of power, or restraint, which was directed not only at the common people,
     but also at the political elite, including the monarch. For Foucault's exposition of the rise
     of disciplinary power in Western history, see Michel Foucault, *Discipline and Punish: The
     Birth of the Prison*, Alan Sheridan, trans. (New York: Vintage Books, 1979).
36 "Juridical power" is the label used by Foucault to describe this latter type of regulation.
37 Foucault's notion of constant visibility as an element of the disciplinary technique, i.e.,
     the idea of having to behave as if one is always under surveillance, has a parallel in the
     Confucian idea of "watchfulness over oneself when one is alone" (*shendu* 慎獨 in Chinese,
     shindok in Korean), mentioned in the *Great Learning* and *The Doctrine of the Mean*.
38 The analogy between Foucault's opposites, i.e., discipline and juridical power, and the oppo-
     sition in Chinese tradition between *li* and *xing* (刑) (punishment) (or between Confucian-
     ism and Legalism) should be obvious to anyone familiar with Chinese intellectual history.
39 Herbert Fingarette, *Confucius: The Secular As Sacred* (New York: Harper and Row, 1971).
40 According to a common representation of liberalism, liberals view human beings as
     "rights-bearers" who come together to form a society in order to safeguard their pre-social,
     pre-political rights. By suggesting that for Confucians, human beings are "rites-bearers,"
     I do not mean to imply that people are similarly endowed with rites even before they enter
     society. Indeed, it would be difficult for Confucians to conceive of human beings in a pre-
     social state.

"[i]n the Confucian context it is inconceivable that one can become truly human without going through the process of 'ritualization.' "[41] To paraphrase Clifford Geertz, human beings are "ritual artifacts."

On the political, or constitutional, side, *li* is vitally concerned with the notion of restraining the government and of a regime's legitimacy.[42] This is apparent if we survey the role of *li* throughout premodern history. In these limited pages, I cannot review the entire political and intellectual history of imperial China or premodern Korea; suffice it to say that *li* was part of the Confucian conception of law, and that it was actually codified and continually revised by the successive dynasties as the norm directly applicable to the throne and the ruling house.[43] Observance of the prescriptions of *li* was of the utmost importance for each ruler because that was what secured the legitimacy of a Confucian ruler. Because their political legitimacy depended on correctly regulating their conduct according to *li*, rulers had to pay the utmost attention to the detailed specifications and correct observance of *li*, and this meant that they had to surround themselves with experts on matters of ritual propriety.

More importantly, as experts on *li*, the Confucian scholars who staffed the central bureaucracy naturally had a vested interest in making sure that the ruler and the entire government operated according to ritual propriety. Their scholarly discussions on *li* unavoidably had a political dimension. Indeed, discourse on *li* often became a constitutional discourse on the legitimacy of the ruler, or the lack thereof. Confucian scholar-officials made sure that the ruler knew that he had to be disciplined by *li* before he could claim the authority to rule over others.[44]

41 Tu Wei-ming, "*Li* as Process of Humanization," *Philosophy East and West* vol. 22, no. 2 (1972), p. 187.
42 Recall that, according to Ulrich Preuss, conferral of legitimacy to political authority was one of the key functions of a constitution. See note 5 above.
43 In my opinion, our understanding of law in a Confucian society is still in a state of infancy. Here, I only register my view that in order to find out what "the law" was during premodern times in China or Korea, we need to be mindful of at least three categories. The first is the various penal codes promulgated and continually revised by the court, the second is the body of administrative codes that set out the responsibilities of the bureaucracy, and the third is the numerous ritual codes compiled to regulate the "ritual" duties of the state and the throne. I submit that since at least the Tang dynasty, each so-called Confucian dynasty had this tripartite structure of law.
44 For more on the role of *li* as a constitutional norm which regulated and even "constituted" the throne during imperial China, see, e.g., Howard J. Wechsler, *Offerings of Jade and Silk: Ritual and Symbol in the Legitimation of the T'ang Dynasty* (New Haven, Conn.: Yale University Press, 1985); Ron Guey Chu, "Rites and Rights in Ming China," in Wm. Theodore de Bary and Tu Wei-ming, eds., *Confucianism and Human Rights* (New York: Columbia University Press, 1998), pp. 169–178; Carney T. Fisher, *The Chosen One: Succession and Adoption in the Court of Ming Shizong* (Sydney: Allen and Unwin, 1990); Angela Zito, *Of Body and Brush: Grand Sacrifice as Text/Performance in Eighteenth-Century China* (Chicago: University of Chicago Press, 1997); Joseph P. McDermott, ed., *State and Court Ritual in China*

Further, believing themselves to be the true custodians of the Confucian tradition, they were convinced that they had the right to "discipline" the ruler with *li* because they themselves were so disciplined. In other words, when applied to the ruler, *li* functioned as a constitutionalist norm. When applied to the Confucian scholars, it functioned as a form of political education that created people who believed that their mission was to discipline the highest political leader of the country. This is captured in the well-known maxim *sugi ch'iin* in Korean (*xiuji zhiren* 修己治人 in Chinese), which means "cultivate oneself and govern others" (or "governance of people through self-cultivation"). For *li* was the very link that connected the two parts of the maxim. *Li* was at once a medium of cultivating the self and a mode of governing the state. In the case of the Confucian scholar-officials who participated in the governance of the state, their self-cultivation through *li* was a process that prepared them for the constitutionalist task of disciplining the ruler.

In such a context, the phrase *keji fuli* ("disciplining oneself and returning to ritual propriety") was not only a "private" moral precept but also a "public" principle of political education for Confucian citizenship. It is in this sense that I am claiming that *li* combined the educative and the political. It educated people to become "constitutionalist citizens" who were able to demand that the ruler be restrained and disciplined in his actions. Being disciplined with ritual propriety was thus a form of Confucian "civic virtue." Put differently, Confucian political education consisted in disciplining citizens with *li* so that they would in turn be able to discipline their ruler with *li*.

IV CONTEMPORARY RELEVANCE OF RITUAL PROPRIETY: CONFUCIAN CIVIC VIRTUE

If what I said earlier about the need for constitutional norms to be grounded in a society's nomos is true, then in the case of contemporary East Asia, it would be reasonable to claim that constitutional norms must resonate with the idea of *li*. Indeed, one might even argue that they should be articulated in terms of *li*. To be sure, discussions of ritual propriety do not predominate the political arena; the concept is not even mentioned in the current constitutions of East Asian countries. I would nevertheless contend that matters of

(Cambridge: Cambridge University Press, 1999). For similar works on premodern Korea, see JaHyun Kim Haboush, "Constructing the Center: The Ritual Controversy and the Search for a New Identity in Seventeenth-Century Korea," in JaHyun K. Haboush and Martina Deuchler, eds., *Culture and the State in Late Chosŏn Korea* (Cambridge, Mass.: Harvard East Asian Monographs, 1999), pp. 46–90; JaHyun Kim Haboush, *A Heritage of Kings: One Man's Monarchy in the Confucian World* (New York: Columbia University Press, 1988).

li still remain a very "public" concern. People learn to relate to one another and define one's place in family and society in terms of *li*. As such, *li* constitutes for East Asians what Cover called nomos, a normative universe, or a structure of meaning, what Geertz calls "the fabric of meaning in terms of which human beings interpret their experience and guide their action."[45] It provides "the narratives that locate . . . and give meaning"[46] to one's actions and speech, and it acts as the normative criteria by which to evaluate them. It is very close to what Tocqueville called the mores of a society.[47] Therefore, any political institutions and legal rules, including constitutional norms, will derive effectiveness and legitimacy to the extent that they are connected to and supported by the prevailing notions of ritual propriety.

In light of this, it is highly regrettable that most contemporary discussions about *li* tend to miss its constitutionalist aspect. On those few occasions when *li* is discussed for its political significance, it is usually understood as a means for taming and controlling the populace. Combined with the conventional view that Confucianism is an ideology that encourages submissiveness toward political authority, this leads to a distorted understanding of *li*. I believe we need to recall that *li* is not only a method of education but also a tool for disciplining the political leader. The educative dimension of *li* should be combined with its constitutionalist dimension.

Political theorist Michael Oakeshott once said that political education consists in "the pursuit of intimations." And he believed that those intimations should be sought in the tradition and history of one's culture.[48] In the East Asian context, I think such pursuit of intimations should begin with an appreciation for the "ritualist" constitutionalist discourse in the tradition. One fruitful way of exploring the intimations of this ritualist discourse, I submit, would be to reappropriate the constitutionalist moment in traditional Confucian discourse and to incorporate it into a "ritualist" approach toward education for citizenship. In this regard, I believe current East Asians have a valuable traditional resource for creating citizens whose role it is to ensure that there is effective regularized restraint on their government.

Ritualist political education is ritualist not only in terms of method but also in relation to the goal of education. And it applies equally to everybody,

---

45 Clifford Geertz, "Ritual and Social Change," in *The Interpretation of Cultures*, p. 145.

46 Cover, "*Nomos* and Narrative," p. 4.

47 At one point, Fingarette actually uses the word *mores* in his interpretation of *li*: "Characteristic of Confucius's teaching is the use of the language and imagery of *li* (禮) as a medium within which to talk about the entire body of the *mores*, or more precisely, of the authentic tradition and reasonable conventions of society" (Fingarette, *Confucius: The Secular As Sacred*, p. 6).

48 Michael Oakeshott, "Political Education," *Rationalism in Politics and Other Essays* (Indianapolis, Ind.: Liberty Press, 1991), pp. 43–69.

including the occupant of the highest political office. Through "ritualization"
it seeks to instill in everyone those habits, attitudes, and beliefs according to
which one's constitutional role is to discipline – to discipline through ritual
propriety not only one's self but also one's political leaders. If political
education becomes ritualist only in its method, it can even be a threat to
constitutionalism, for it is likely to be abused by those in power to "mold"
people's habits and attitudes into submissive obedience to authority.[49] That
is why the constitutionalist dimension of the Confucian ritualist tradition
must be combined with the educative dimension. Without the constitutionalist dimension, any reappropriation of the Confucian ritualist tradition
would merely be a pretext for authoritarian politics.

Thus, for East Asians, political education should start with a deeper appreciation of both the constitutionalist and educative dimensions of the Confucian tradition. If political education is, as Oakeshott says, "not merely a matter
of coming to understand a tradition," but rather "learning how to participate
in a conversation" and being "initiat[ed] into an inheritance in which we have
life interest,"[50] it would then appear reasonable to start engaging in a conversation with the Confucian tradition. At a minimum, this requires getting
beyond crude generalizations about whether Confucianism does or does not
promote authoritarianism. It requires starting to ask such questions as: How
did the ritualist constitutionalist order actually operate? What were the terms
of Confucian political and constitutional discourse? What resources (symbolic,
rhetorical, philosophical) were available for socializing people into the role of
disciplinarians of political leaders? It requires problematizing our conceptions
of the Confucian tradition. At the same time, I believe we should free ourselves from the habit of trying to find *the* correct meaning of Confucianism.
To obsess about arriving at "the essence" of Confucianism is to ignore the fact
that, as a living tradition, Confucianism has always undergone revisions and
transformations. In a way, it is peculiarly "un-Confucian" to ignore changed

---

49 Examples would be the efforts of the governments of South Korea, Singapore, and China
   to reinvigorate selected parts of the Confucian tradition in their education programs. Utilizing strong nationalist sentiments of the people, the governments of these states are promoting Confucianism as an important cultural heritage, while emphasizing such elements
   as filial piety and loyalty to the state, which tend to habituate the mind into conformity
   and obedience. For an account of the development of "moral education" in Korean schools,
   see Geir Helgesen, *Democracy and Authority in Korea* (New York: St. Martin's Press, 1998),
   pp. 143–189. The most extreme example would be the education policy of Japan during
   its militarist/imperial era when Confucian rhetoric was employed to cultivate blind devo-
   tion and loyalty to the emperor. The famous Imperial Rescript on Education issued by the
   Meiji government is widely regarded as having served as the ideological focal point of such
   education. See, e.g., Yamazumi Masami, "Educational Democracy Versus State Control,"
   in Gavan McCormack and Yoshio Sugimoto, eds., *Democracy in Contemporary Japan*
   (Armonk, N.Y.: M.E. Sharpe, Inc., 1986), pp. 90–113.
50 Oakeshott, "Political Education," p. 62.

historical circumstances and to insist on identifying an eternal and immutable core of Confucianism. Premodern Confucians themselves were constantly reinterpreting and re-presenting the tradition to meet the exigencies of their days. As is the case with other traditions, Confucianism began to function as an agent of oppression and repression when people lost that ability to reinterpret and re-present the inherited tradition. As participants in a living tradition, modern-day East Asians should not be afraid to so reinterpret and re-present their Confucian heritage to meet the challenges of our day.

This task of conversing with Confucian tradition should be carried out not only in the classroom but also at other sites. As mentioned before, the schools are obviously a vital setting for political education. Such reinterpretations and re-telling of the Confucian tradition should occur not only in "Civics" class but also in national history or national language classes. Yet, given that the process of ritualization through *li* is the process of learning to become human, the conversation with tradition will inevitably start at an earlier stage. Indeed, for the Confucian, ritualization is a process that starts in the family and continues throughout one's life.[51] This suggests that political education too starts from within the family and continues throughout one's life. In other words, the nongovernmental sector of society has an important role to play in the task of disciplining people to become constitutionalist citizens.[52]

Aside from the immediate goal of preventing the abuse of government power, a ritualist political education that instills in people the value of discipline through *li* can also lead to securing legitimacy for the government. This is so because, as seen above, discipline according to *li* is an important route to self-cultivation,[53] and self-cultivation within the Confucian tradition is what gives authority to the person. Or, as some scholars put it, it is what makes a person authoritative.[54] And in light of the fact that political legitimacy according to Confucianism requires that an authoritative person be in

---

51 Confucius's statement in the *Analects* 2:4 that by the age of seventy he was able to follow his heart's desires without overstepping the line should be a warning to anyone who thinks that disciplining oneself with *li* is a process that one goes through once during childhood.

52 The article by Geir Helgesen in this volume raises some important questions regarding the feasibility, in this age of globalization, of such political education rooted in one's cultural tradition. While I too worry about "MacDonaldization" and the numbing effects of global pop culture, I am inclined to believe with Clifford Geertz that at least for the proximate future, the trend is not toward a uniform legal or political culture but rather toward further particularization, and that "multinational corporations and computer technology will [not be shaping] the minds of Tongans and Yemenis to a common pattern" any time soon (Geertz, "Local Knowledge," p. 216).

53 For an interpretation of *li* as a way to self-cultivation and ultimately to sagehood, see Robert Eno, *The Confucian Creation of Heaven: Philosophy and the Defenses of Ritual Mastery* (Albany: State University of New York Press, 1990).

54 For a rendering of the highest Confucian ideal *ren* (仁) as "becoming an authoritative person," see David Hall and Roger Ames, *Thinking Through Confucius* (Albany: State University of New York Press, 1987), pp. 110–125.

the position of leadership, discipline through *li* would be the ultimate way to secure the legitimacy of one's rule.

In this connection, we would do well to recall Fingarette's interpretation of *li* as an idiom for understanding the human community in general. In a revealing passage, he writes: "Furthermore, to act by ceremony [*li*] is to be completely open to the other; for ceremony is public, shared, transparent; to act otherwise is to be secret, obscure, and devious, or merely tyrannically coercive. It is in this beautiful and dignified, shared and open participation with others who are ultimately like oneself (12:2) that man realizes himself."[55] Now, Fingarette did not write this passage with his mind on the political dimension of human interaction. Indeed, it appears in the context of discussing the religious character of *li*. Yet, I think its implications for politics and constitutionalism should be obvious. A political leader who is disciplined by *li* is completely open to others; his actions are transparent; and he works through noncoercive measures based on public, shared understandings. The virtue of transparency in politics, especially democratic politics, needs no explanation. It is intimately bound up with the notion of accountability and thus with legitimacy. Thus, a government disciplined through *li* would be regarded as legitimate by East Asians.

From the perspective of the citizens, this means that in order to have a legitimate government, a regime that is accountable to the people, they must make sure that their chosen rulers are properly disciplined with *li*. Ideally, a democratic citizenry that has been properly educated through *li* will be one that has acquired the habits and beliefs – civic virtues – that enable it to "work[] through spontaneous coordination"[56] toward ensuring that elected officials will be so disciplined. Of course, this ideal may seldom be realized. Thus, in the event that citizens cannot elect a person who is already so disciplined, they must at least institute measures which will ensure that occupants of the higher offices will be appropriately disciplined.

In other words, in a Confucian constitutionalist polity, the government apparatus must include institutional mechanisms for carrying out and ensuring this discipline of the ruler. If we look to history once more to pursue our intimations, we learn that premodern governments indeed had such mechanisms. For example, during the Chosŏn (朝鮮) dynasty in Korea (1392–1910), the central bureaucracy included many offices whose explicit duties were to educate, correct, and criticize the behavior of the ruler. These included the famous Royal Lectures (*kyŏngyŏn* in Korean, *jingyan* 經筵 in Chinese), the Censorate, and Court Historians. And the subject of their

---

55 Fingarette, *Confucius: The Secular As Sacred*, p. 16.   56 Ibid., p. 8.

criticism was not limited to "ceremonial" or "liturgical" ritual matters but included the entire range of policy issues. Here we must bear in mind that the term *li* encompasses not only the performance of ritual ceremony but also matters of the state in general. For example, the term "rituals of a country" (*pangnye* in Korean, *bangli* 邦禮 in Chinese) referred to the entire government institutional framework of a country, including the six ministries and all the auxiliary agencies.[57] Therefore, it is by no means an overstatement to say that these institutional mechanisms were charged with ensuring that the ruler was properly disciplined according to *li*. In other words, in the case of a ruler, discipline according to ritual propriety also meant being educated in the art of governance and policy science. It meant something far beyond mere decorous behavior or correct performance of state ceremony; it meant acquiring proficiency in statecraft. The ruler of a country was thus subject to a discipline much more rigorous than his subjects.

I suspect that most East Asians today still harbor similar attitudes, even if subconsciously, toward their highest political leaders. They are likely to think that their head of state should be someone who is more disciplined, if not more knowledgeable, than the average person on the street.[58] This means that the occupant of such an office will be regarded as legitimate only to the extent that he or she can successfully discipline himself or herself with ritual propriety, which in this case includes submitting him/herself to rigorous training and instruction in the art of statecraft (i.e., competency in domestic and foreign affairs, including economic, military, and social policy making). This also means that government offices must be instituted which can carry out this function of formal instruction of political leaders. Modern-day analogues of the Royal Lectures or the Censorate should become regular parts of the government and be staffed with those who have shown themselves to be similarly disciplined at least in their own fields of expertise. This should not

---

57 Similarly, in the Confucian vocabulary, the compound word "rituals-music-punishments-regulations" (*ye-ak-hyŏng-jŏng* in Korean, *li-yue-xing-zheng* 禮樂刑政 in Chinese) stood for the totality of the sociopolitical institutional framework necessary for decent human existence. See, e.g., *Li Chi*, James Legge, trans., and Ch'ü Chai and Winberg Chai, eds. (New Hyde Park, N.Y.: University Books, 1967) vol. 2, p. 93 ("The end to which ceremonies, music, punishments, and laws conduct is one: they are the instruments by which the minds of the people are assimilated, and good order in government is made to appear").

58 It might be objected that having a higher expectation of political leaders is contrary to democracy. On certain conceptions of democracy, democracy is a superior form of politics precisely because it enables the peaceful, orderly coexistence among equally fallible human beings. To that extent, my reappropriation of the Confucian constitutionalist moment may entail preserving an undemocratic aspect of East Asian culture. Yet, I believe it is unrealistic to ignore the discrepancies found in people's skills, aptitudes, and talents, and utopian to hope for a polity that can govern itself without attending to the special requirements of political leadership.

be mistaken as a call to make the president a moral exemplar, a paragon of Confucian virtue (i.e., *the* filial son), to be emulated by all the citizens. The heightened discipline demanded of the president is not primarily about the moral quality of the person's private life but more about competency and proficiency in the art of governance. It means ensuring that the president is constantly educated about the requirements of statecraft.

In my view, in the age of democracy, the position of head of state is paradoxically even more elevated than during the period of hereditary monarchy, so that nowadays it is deemed highly "improper" (i.e., contrary to *li*) if anyone dares to "lecture to" the president. In the past, the system of "lecturing to" the king was institutionalized and thus a part of the regular government structure. Today, constant, institutionalized criticism directed at the president would not sit very well with many of our current political leaders. Yet, that is precisely what was practiced during the Chosŏn period through the office of the Censorate.[59] I believe we should revive the notion that the ruler can and should be disciplined by being lectured to all the time and by being under constant surveillance. This will be a small step toward securing transparency in the government. As a way of reinstituting constant surveillance, we might also revive and modernize the office of the Court Historian. As is well known, the king of Chosŏn was not allowed to hold audience with his ministers unless he was accompanied by two historians. One recorded all the verbal transactions, while the other recorded all physical movements. For Korean Confucians, this practice was mandated by the Classics.[60] Beyond simple descriptions of facts, the historians also recorded their critical judgments on whatever issues were being discussed at the court. Empowered with the mandate to closely watch and quietly criticize the monarch on a daily

59 The Censorate during Chosŏn was in actuality made up of two separate bodies: Office of Remonstrance (*Saganwŏn* 司諫院) and Office of Inspection (Sahŏnbu 司憲府). The latter was originally designed as an office in charge of surveillance and impeachment of the officials, but it evolved into an organ whose primary function was understood to be remonstrating with the king on affairs of the state. In effect, Chosŏn government had not one, but two institutions whose constitutional function was to criticize the king according to the ideals of Confucian governance. It may be thought that I am romanticizing the role of the Censorate during the Chosŏn dynasty. Yet, many historians have noted the active role played by the censors in Korean history. For example, JaHyun Kim Haboush has written: "In Korea, regarded as the conscience of the nation, the censorial voice was as relentlessly sharp in its admonition of the throne as in its censure of high-ranking ministers. The Censorate, in effect, emerged as a full-fledged member along with the executive branch and the throne in a tripartite power structure" (JaHyun K. Haboush, "The Confucianization of Korean Society," in Gilbert Rozman, ed., *The East Asian Region: Confucian Heritage and Its Modern Adaptation* [Princeton, N.J.: Princeton University Press, 1991], p. 96).

60 Korean Confucians were being quite literalist with regard to a practice that was described in Chapter 13 ("Yuzao") of the *Liji* (禮記) [Record of Rituals], a book which often presents highly idealized pictures of the ancient Zhou dynasty.

basis, historians thus could exercise the most "regularized restraint" upon the ruler.[61] I believe a system of record keeping on a similar level of detail could be instituted in order to ensure transparency and accountability in the government. Indeed, with the help of modern technology, it would be easier to make a record of all the transactions of the chief executive.[62]

Yet, all this can be realized only if citizens are appropriately disciplined to know that their constitutional role is to demand such discipline from their ruler. Their *li* would consist of understanding that their watchful vigilance is needed in order to prevent abuse of political power. In other words, they need to be disciplined so that their exercise of this role becomes second nature, or in Fingarette's terms, spontaneous to the extent of seeming effortless and even "magical." Once the citizens of modern East Asian countries begin to emulate their Confucian scholar-official ancestors, who first disciplined themselves with ritual propriety and then demanded the ruler's discipline, their countries will become constitutionalist states. It might be objected that this is too demanding. Perhaps it is. Yet, according to political theorist Benjamin Barber, the ideal of democratic education consists in "an aristocracy of everyone," that is, in "raising the common denominator, transforming the individual through education into a deliberative citizen."[63] Nothing less will do for the task of creating constitutionalist citizens.

61 According to Tu Wei-ming, "[t]he historian so conceived is the conscience of the collective memory we all share. . . . To write history is therefore a political act committed in the name of the human community as a whole" (Tu Wei-ming, "The Way, Learning, and Politics in Classical Confucian Humanism," in *Way, Learning, and Politics* [Albany: State University of New York Press, 1993], pp. 7–8).

62 Ideally, the records made would be maintained in the national archives under the strictest security, and kept classified for an appropriate number of years, during which time no one, not even the president, would be given access to them. This in fact was the practice during the Chosŏn period. More importantly, however, a means should be devised to supplement records made by machines with the critical judgment of the historian. During the premodern era, it was the combination of factual record and critical judgment that made the Court Historians a constitutionalist institution that could exert restraint on the ruler.

63 Benjamin Barber, *An Aristocracy of Everyone* (New York: Ballantine Books, 1992), p. 265. Barber goes on to say: "Citizens are aristocrats of the polity and in a democracy everyone is a citizen. . . . Commoners and democrats can claim . . . today that they truly are aristocrats, practitioners of the government of excellence. It is just that their aristocracy, having emerged from democracy's schools, is an aristocracy of everyone" (ibid.).

CHAPTER 2

THE CHALLENGE OF ACCOUNTABILITY

IMPLICATIONS OF THE CENSORATE

JONGRYN MO

I INTRODUCTION

Governance is currently a fashionable topic. Not only does the political establishment debate the issue, unlikely participants such as corporate boards (à
la corporate governance) and development banks (e.g., the World Bank's New
Development Paradigm) have also been drawn into the debate.

Despite the growing interest in the problem of governance, it is not clear
whether we understand how to define, measure, and attain it. Governance
itself can be broadly defined as the traditions and institutions by which
authority in a country is exercised.[1] But the quality of governance is another
matter. So long as the question of whether governance is a means or an end
remains unresolved, it will be difficult to arrive at a consensus measure of
governance quality. If governance is a means to certain policy outcomes, one
good measure should be the ability of a political system to produce sound
policy. Good policies are generally oriented toward desirable social goals (such
as economic growth), are consistent and coherent, and reflect broad national
interests rather than narrow special interests.[2]

The performance of a political system in producing good policy outcomes,
however, turns out to be difficult to measure. Mayhew, for example, evalu-
ates the performance of Congress in terms of how many significant laws it
passes in each session.[3] But a simple count of laws that Congress passes is
misleading because it does not take into account the nature and scope of the
agenda given to Congress. To be objective, one has to measure how effective
or successful Congress is in accomplishing what it set out to do.

---

1 See Daniel Kaufmann, Aart Kraay, and Pablo Zoido-Lobaton, "Governance Matters II:
  Updated Indicators for 2000–2001," *Mimeo* (the World Bank 2002).
2 See Gary Cox and Mathew McCubbins, "The Institutional Determinants of Economic Policy
  Outcomes," in Stephan Haggard and Mathew McCubbins, eds., *Presidents, Parliaments, and
  Policy* (New York: Cambridge University Press, 2001).
3 See David Mayhew, *Divided We Govern* (New Haven, Conn.: Yale University Press, 1991).

Deciding how to attain good governance is an equally challenging problem. Scholars have long searched for institutional arrangements conducive to the formulation and implementation of sound policy. Although democracy has been offered as an ideal institutional solution, it is often more of a principle or value than a practical guide. Most people certainly desire and understand democracy as self-government under the rule of law. But given the current state of knowledge, one cannot be certain about which one among many variants of democracy will work best for a given society. Moreover, there is an influential school of thought in political science that questions the primacy of democracy in the success of national development.[4]

The preoccupation with an institutional solution also makes it easy to overlook the broader social environment in which institutions are embedded. Broad social conditions are important because they affect the choice of institutions as well as their subsequent effectiveness. Take democracy as an example. Democracy will be neither chosen nor sustained unless people are committed to it.[5] The success of democracy also depends on the sharing of certain values and attitudes such as trust, tolerance, and accommodation at all levels of society. While the search for the conditions necessary for successful governance continues on the theoretical front, there seems to be a strong consensus on how to improve governance among the "practitioners" of democracy, that is, those activists and scholars active in promoting democracy. Grounded in the Western philosophy of liberal democracy, this consensus view prescribes a standard set of solutions for countries wanting to improve their governance: making governments accountable and transparent in their functions, increasing broad-based participation in the political process, and strengthening the capacity and transparency of political parties.

In Asia, concerted effort to promote the "Washington consensus" encountered resistance from some political leaders such as Lee Kuan Yew,[6] spawning a vibrant debate on Asian values in the mid-1990s. According to supporters of Asian values, Western liberal democracy, with its emphasis on individual rights, will not work in Asia where collective interests take precedence over individual rights. Unfortunately, the Asian values debate has lost some of its appeal since the Asian economic crisis of 1997 because the apparent failures of Asian governments and corporations to prevent and manage crises cast serious doubt on the performance of institutions based on Asian values.

---

4 See Samuel Huntington, *Political Order in Changing Societies* (New Haven, Conn.: Yale University Press, 1969).
5 See Larry Diamond, *Developing Democracy: Toward Consolidation* (Baltimore, Md.: Johns Hopkins University Press, 1999).
6 See Lee Kuan Yew, "Culture Is Destiny – A Conversation with Lee Kuan Yew," *Foreign Affairs* (March–June 1994), pp. 109–126.

Nevertheless, it is my view that the Asian values debate is still relevant and should continue for no reason other than that it forces scholars and political leaders to grapple with the role of culture and values in democratic governance. One particular issue that I want to address is whether or not Asian values are incompatible with the idea of accountability. This issue is important because the failure of accountability in many Asian governments has been attributed to cultural factors. My argument is that even if some contemporary Asian political leaders may not be committed to the principle and practice of accountability, it is wrong to attribute that to Confucianism, which is rather rich in ideas and practices promoting accountability.

To illustrate the Confucian tradition of government accountability, I show how effective the Confucian system of horizontal accountability could be, using the Censorate of the Chosŏn dynasty (1392–1910) as a case study. Furthermore, the design of the Censorate gives some lessons on how to improve the contemporary system of accountability. First, keeping each individual member of an accounting agency independent is the key to ensuring the independence of the whole agency. Second, more authority should be given to young officials who have a vested interest in strengthening the system of checks and balances in government.

II THE MODERN THEORY OF ACCOUNTABILITY

To show that the Chosŏn's Censorate was an effective institution of accountability, we need a conceptual framework for understanding what makes a system of accountability effective. For a long time, political theorists have thought that the key to good governance is to keep power under control. The government must be able to control the governed and it must also be able to control itself. At the conceptual level, accountability indicates the degree to which power is kept under control, domesticated, or subject to the rule of law. In terms of institutions, accountability describes a relationship between accountable and accounting parties, that is, the degree to which "accountable" parties are accountable to accounting parties. Formally, we can say that "A is accountable to B when A is obliged to inform B about A's (past and future) actions and decisions, to justify them, and to suffer punishment in the case of eventual misconducts."[7] Accounting agents have to possess the capacity to demand public officials to inform them about and explain their activities and the capacity to impose sanctions on office holders who violate

---

7 Andreas Schedler, Larry Diamond, and Marc Plattner, eds., "Conceptualizing Accountability," *The Self-Restraining State: Power and Accountability in New Democracies* (Boulder, Colo.: Lynne Rienner Publishers, 1999), p. 17.

certain rules of conduct. Types of accountability vary according to its standards and sources. Different standards of accountability apply to public officials – political, administrative, professional, financial, moral, legal, and constitutional. In terms of sources, O'Donnell (1999)[8] makes a key distinction between vertical and horizontal accountability, depending on the hierarchical relationship between accounting and accountable agents. If accounting agents hold agencies of equal power or position accountable, they are said to be exercising horizontal accountability. A system of checks and balances among the three branches of government is an example of horizontal accountability. Agents of horizontal accountability also include ombudsmen, auditors, prosecutors, financial accounting offices, and anticorruption commissions within the executive branch. In modern democracies, voters are the main agent of vertical accountability because they have the ultimate authority to install and replace administrations and assemblies.

Establishing agencies of horizontal accountability by itself, of course, does not guarantee the effectiveness of the accountability system. According to O'Donnell, certain conditions must be met for effective horizontal accountability:

1. The existence of vertical accountability.
2. The accounting party must be independent of the accountable party in all decisions that concern its field of competence.
3. The existence of multiple accounting agencies. Effective horizontal accountability is not the product of isolated agencies but of networks of agencies that include at their top courts committed to such accountability.
4. Overlapping jurisdictions of institutions of accountability. By building several strong powers that partially intrude on each other, we can enhance the autonomy of each of them with respect to what would have resulted from a simple separation of such powers.
5. Recursive and reciprocal accountability – accounting agents "check and balance" or are accountable to each.

Condition 1 emphasizes the mutual reinforcing effects of vertical and horizontal accountability in a democratic system. Condition 2 addresses one of the two problems that the designer of an accountability system should solve, *how to create accounting agencies that are sufficiently powerful or autonomous to do their job.* Conditions 3–5 are intended to solve the second, more difficult problem of second-order accountability, *how to hold accounting agencies themselves accountable.*

8 See Guillermo O'Donnell, "Horizontal Accountability in New Democracies," in Andreas Schedler, Larry Diamond, and Marc Plattner, eds., *The Self-Restraining State: Power and Accountability in New Democracies* (Boulder, Colo.: Lynne Rienner Publishers, 1999).

III THE CENSORATE OF THE CHOSŎN GOVERNMENT

If O'Donnell's theory that accounting agencies cannot be effective without satisfying certain conditions is right, it should also explain the performance of the Censorate of the Chosŏn government because the logic of bureaucratic behavior does not change much over time. Indeed, I argue that one of the reasons why the Censorate was effective was that it met O'Donnell's conditions for effective horizontal accountability.

The Censorate consisted of three censoring organs, the Office of the Inspector-General (OIG) (司憲府, sahŏnbu), the Office of the Censor-General (OCG) (司諫院, saganwŏn), and the Office of Special Counselors (OSC) (弘文館, hongmun' gwan). The Samsa, as the three were known, were designed to prevent abuses in the exercise of political and administrative authority. The OSC's main functions were to search out administrative and legal precedents, write major state documents, and advise the king on public affairs.

Among the three, the OIG and the OCG, which came to be known as *taegan* (臺諫) or Censorate, represented the two main agents of accountability within the government. Officially, the OIG was charged with "criticizing public policy, scrutinizing the conduct of the officialdom, rectifying mores, redressing public wrongs, and preventing forgery and fraudulent misuse of public credentials." The authority of the OCG, on the other hand, was to offer remonstrance to the king and to lodge complaints against office holders. The restraint on the conduct of the king himself by the OCG was perhaps the most innovative feature of the Chosŏn's structure of horizontal accountability. On paper, there were clear differences in the authority of the OIG and the OCG. The OIG's main task was censuring (*t'anhaek* 彈劾) while that of the OCG was remonstrance (*kanjaeng* 諫諍), that is, evaluating the king's conduct. But their jurisdictions overlapped in practice, and it is more accurate to say that the OIG and the OCG worked together to monitor and oversee "all aspects of royal, official, popular (principally *yangban*) conduct and mores." The censors' actual activities were much broader than the formal descriptions of their authority indicate. According to Choi (1994),[9] censors' activities consisted of opinion giving (*ŏllon* 言論) (on the king's conduct, censure, policy choice, and official appointments), participation in policy making (*chamjŏng* 參政), attendance to the king (*shishin* 侍臣), review of personnel appointments (*koshinsŏkyŏng* 考臣書經), implementation of laws and ordinances, censuring, and monitoring (*jiucha* 糾察), prosecution (*kukmun* 鞫問), and adjudication of legal disputes (*kyŏlsong* 決訟). Thus, censors were

---

9 See Choi E-Don, *The Structure of Samrimchongchi in the Middle Chosun Period* (Seoul, Korea: Il Cho Kak [in Korean], 1994).

not only judicial and auditing agents (judges, prosecutors, and auditors) but also voices of dissent and opposition (ŏnkwan 言官), playing the roles of mass media and opposition parties in modern democracies. This aspect of the Censorate reflected a strong Confucian belief that the king should encourage open discussion and criticism within the government. At the same time, censors also acted as policy advisors and counselors by offering opinions, recommendations, and guidance to the king and high officials on the basis of their knowledge of history and Confucian philosophy.

Furthermore, the Censorate was an accounting agency in a modern sense because it could subject public officials to the threat of sanctions, oblige them to conduct their duties in transparent ways, and force them to explain or justify their actions; that is, the censors exercised powers of information, justification, and enforcement.

The censors had several sources of information: First, they participated in the formative stage of policy making by attending Royal Lecture sessions. Every OSC counselor was a member of the Office of Royal Lectures. The Censorate was allowed to join the morning and afternoon sessions. The Censorate also insisted on participating in other arenas of policy deliberations such as the king's meetings with high officials (sangcham 常參) (Choi, 1974).[10] Second, important policy and appointment decisions were subject to formal review by the Censorate. Appointment of every official of fifth grade and below was to be approved by the Censorate. "In accordance with a procedure known as sogyong, a document bearing the name, lineage, and career data of each such appointee was submitted to the Censorate for endorsement, and if the Censorate officials failed to give their approval within fifty days, the appointment would be rescinded."[11] In addition, Censorate reviews were required before promulgating new and amended laws.[12] The third source of information was the reporting of acts of official misconduct to the Censorate, typically through memorials to the king, by those who suffered from or witnessed them.[13]

---

10 See Choi Seung-Hee, *A Study on the Censors and Censuring System of the Early Chosun Period* (Seoul, Korea: Seoul National University [in Korean], 1974), pp. 46–49.

11 Edward Willett Wagner, *The Literati Purges: Political Conflict in Early Yi Dynasty* (Cambridge, Mass.: East Asian Research Center, Harvard University, 1974), p. 15.

12 There is some doubt as to whether this review amounted to a formal veto because the Censorate intervened after the king had already approved the new laws that were legislated by the state council. At this stage of the legislative process, the Censorate may have simply screened the language of new laws for legal consistency and enforceability instead of deliberating their substance.

13 Other than these ex ante sources of information, it is not clear whether they had ex post capabilities to gain information through regular and irregular audits. They may have relied mainly on memorials sent to the king even though they may not have had access to them before they reached the king. Neither is it clear whether the Censorate was allowed to review the records of official historians and the diaries of government agencies.

The power of justification was implicit in the way that the censors went about "prosecuting offenders." The first thing that the censors would do was to make accusations. The accused party would then be forced to defend himself to the king against the charges made by the Censorate. This way, the censors were able to demand and receive explanations.

Most importantly, the Censorate was capable of enforcing its authority. The censors had many opportunities to present their views to the king. They could offer remonstrance during Royal Lecture sessions. They were also invited to important meetings convened by the king. The regular channel of communication to the king was direct reporting (*chikŏn* 直言) in writing (*sangso* 上疏) or verbally. The Censorate could report twice a day. In times of emergency, they could do so as many times as necessary.

The main instrument of enforcement was censuring. Censures were recommended to the king against officials who committed misconduct and broke laws. In the recommendations, censors not only explained the nature of the infraction and misconduct but also suggested specific measures of punishment. The king, upon receiving a censure request, decided whether or not to prosecute the accused.

As one would expect, the king did not always follow censure recommendations. Chung reports that the acceptance rate (which is defined as the proportion of censure recommendations that were fully or partially accepted by the king) was 14.1 percent during the reign of Sŏngjong (1469–1494). More often than not, the king, especially Sejo (1455–1468), tried to suppress the censors by employing a variety of tactics including interrogation of censors over the identity of the censor who first conceived and suggested the censure.[14]

However, the low acceptance rate does not necessarily mean that the Censorate was ineffective or not influential. First, it took a number of censures (over one hundred in the case of Han Myŏng-hui, a leading merit subject under Sejo) to "nail" a target. Therefore, we have to ask how often the Censorate eventually succeeded once they set their target. Second, somewhat counterintuitively, the low success rate may indicate that the Censorate was being faithful to their mandate. The censoring bodies as a check on royal conduct were expected to offer recommendations that the king did not like; they were not supposed to be the executors of the king's will. If the censors had simply followed the king's wishes, the acceptance rate would have been much higher.

To understand the effectiveness of the Censorate, it is necessary to examine its design. Remarkably, the Chosŏn's Censorate satisfied all the strict condi-

14 See Chung Doo-hee, *Censoring System of the Chosun Dynasty* (Seoul, Korea: Il Cho Kak [in Korean], 1994).

tions for effective horizontal accountability that we impose on modern pol-yarchies: (1) the autonomy of accounting agencies, (2) the existence of mul-tiple accounting agencies, (3) the presence of overlapping jurisdictions among the accounting agencies, and (4) reciprocal accountability.

Let us begin with the autonomy issue. Since the censors' main targets were high officials and the king, we have to investigate what kinds of mechanisms were in place to protect the censors from political influence. At the ideolog-ical level, the prevailing moral philosophy of Confucianism with its strong emphasis on moral rectitude and historical example provided the raison d'être for the censoring system. As long as Confucianism remained a state ideology, there was always going to be a certain level of support for it. For effective implementation, however, the idea of strong accounting agencies has to be embodied in specific institutions and practices and, more importantly, has to be politically supported by a sufficient number of important stakeholders in the government.

A number of protective devices were used to ensure the autonomy of the Censorate. The two suggested by Lee (1994)[15] are the placement of the Censorate directly under the king, outside the formal line of administration, and the ban on the censors holding a concurrent position to avoid possible conflicts of interests.

It is interesting that the government did not fix and guarantee censors' terms of office, which would have helped enhance their independence. Records show that there was a high degree of turnover in the Censorate. But censors typically received promotion after the end of their tenure and were not assigned to provincial positions immediately after leaving the Censorate (Choi, 1974). Both of these measures were intended to prevent the use of demotions as a way of influencing their decisions. Censors were also exempted from biannual merit reviews, which were required for other officials.[16]

But the most important institutional underpinnings of the Censorate's autonomy were its leverage over the personnel directors who appointed the censors and the independence of the personnel directors themselves from the king and ministers. Since it was four personnel directors (*yijǒnlang* 吏銓郎) with the relatively low ranks of fifth or sixth grade in the Board of Person-nel, not high-ranking officials, who made appointments to key junior-level positions (*chǒngyojik* 清要職) in the Censorate and elsewhere, censors were able to denounce high officials without fearing retaliation in the immediate future.

---

15 See Lee Jae-ho, *A Study on the Political Institutions of Lee's Dynasty* (Seoul, Korea: Il Cho Kak [in Korean], 1994).
16 It is not clear to what extent the censoring organs were financially independent, which would be a plausible indicator of their independence.

Political leaders also gave the Censorate the means for checking the personnel directors, such as censuring and the ex post veto, *sogyŏng*, over their appointment so that personnel directors would not have an excessive amount of influence over the Censorate.

Entrusting censor appointment to personnel directors was predicated on the assumption that personnel dirctors themselves were politically independent of high officials and the king. Indeed, personnel directors with responsibility for assigning all lower-ranked officials of fourth grade and below were the most autonomous agents in the entire officialdom because they alone enjoyed the authority to handpick their successors (*chadaekwŏn* 自代權). The Censorate also satisfied the conditions for solving the problem of second-order accountability. The designers of the Censorate set up multiple accounting agents, made their jurisdictions overlap, and allowed them to monitor one another, thus creating a system of reciprocal accountability within the Censorate. Moreover, individual censors of the three censoring organs enjoyed such a degree of independence that we can say that each one of them was an accounting agency in his own right.

Although the only formal area of overlapping between the jurisdictions of the OIG and the OCG was the power to review personnel and legislative decisions, their jurisdictional boundaries converged in practice much more than the law provided, especially in the areas of remonstrance and censuring. The convergence of jurisdictions, in turn, allowed the censoring organs to hold one another accountable. And the censors did hold each other accountable by denouncing other censuring agencies. More remarkably, the censors of the same agency censured each other without regard to hierarchy; it was not uncommon that censors denounced their own superiors.

Given the amount of authority and autonomy given to the Censorate and the personnel directors, it is easy to see why they comprised one of the three power centers in the Chosŏn government; the other centers were the king and the ministers. Being young and at the junior level, censors and personnel directors were reform oriented and, thus, naturally positioned to check and balance the power of merit subjects and high officials. Thus, the Censorate provided a critical link to the relationships of reciprocal accountability among key governmental actors (see Figure 1). Many believe that this system of checks and balances was one of the key factors contributing to the stability and longevity of the Chosŏn dynasty.

The weakest link in the Chosŏn system of horizontal accountability was, of course, the absence of vertical accountability. Unlike voters in modern democracies, the people of Chosŏn had virtually no institutional means (such as voting) for holding political leaders accountable. The only outside

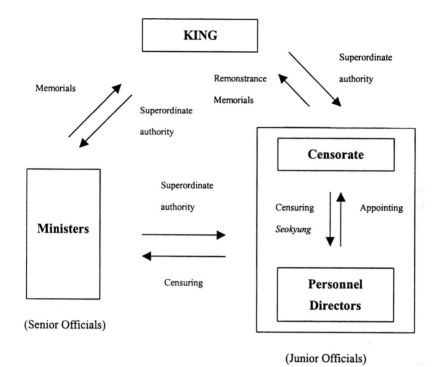

Figure 1. The Chosŏn System of Checks and Balances

restraints on the king came from the threat of revolt and coup. To be fair, however, political leaders were aware or were taught to be aware of the importance of popular support even though they may not have been institutionally constrained by it.

For example, Mencius taught that the king is the son of heaven and heaven bestowed on its son a mandate to provide good government, that is, to provide good for the people. If he did not govern righteously, the people had the right to rise up and overthrow his government in the name of heaven. Mencius even justified regicide, saying that once a king lost the mandate of heaven he was no longer worthy of his subjects' loyalty. The ancient Chinese philosophy of "people-based politics" (*minbon jŏngchi* 民本政治) emphasized that the will of the people was the will of heaven. Therefore, one can say that Confucians believed in a government for the people, if not by or of the people.

Discourse on policy advice is another tradition indicating the extent to which political leaders tried to take into account "public opinion." Giving policy advice to the king was not limited to scholar-bureaucrats. Confucian scholars out of office, who were either preparing to enter the bureaucracy or educating students in local schools, actively participated in policy making as opinion leaders.

Therefore, the historical account of the Censorate shows not only that the idea of accountability was a classic Confucian value but also that Confucian leaders successfully implemented it with an elaborate and surprisingly "modern" construct.

IV THE RISE AND FALL OF THE CENSORATE SYSTEM

Given that the Chosŏn dynasty lasted over five hundred years, it is not surprising that the performance of the Censorate changed over time; the Censorate system at the end of the dynasty was not the same as in the beginning. From historical accounts, we can identify three turning points that significantly transformed the character of the Censorate system: the embracing of the Censorate by Sŏngjong, the breakout of factional politics under Sŏnjo (1567–1608), and the de facto withdrawal of Censorate autonomy by Yŏngjo (1724–1776). These three events then divide the history of the Censorate into four periods: from the foundation to Sŏngjong, the *sarim*'s rise to political dominance between Sŏngjong and Sŏnjo, the era of factional politics, and the rise of powerful clans after Chŏngjo (1776–1800). Many believe that the influence of the Censorate reached its highest point in the second period, especially during the reign of Sŏngjong, the heyday of the Censorate. Therefore, it appears that only in the second period the Censorate system approximated its ideal role.[17]

The early Chosŏn period saw constant struggle over power between the king and the officialdom. Confucian scholar-officials, who played a critical role in overthrowing the Koryŏ dynasty and founding the Chosŏn dynasty, wanted to establish an ideal Confucian government in which they would take

17 This begs the question of how unique the Chosŏn's Censorate was compared to similar institutions in other Korean and Chinese dynasties. Some Korean historians argue that the Censorate was more effective than the preceding Koryŏ dynasty because it was placed apart from other government agencies and was, thus, organizationally independent. See Lee Sung Mu, *How Did the Chosun Combat Corruption? Stories of Censors* (Seoul, Korea: Chunga [in Korean], 2000). But there is a dissenting view that Koryŏ censors were more powerful because their *sogyŏng* authority was extended to all officials, not just the lower ranked, and they did not have to bring hard evidence to denounce. The Censorate, of course, originated from China where it was institutionalized in the Tang dynasty. Although some Korean scholars claim that the Chosŏn's Censorate was more effective than that of any Chinese dynasty, the Tang's version, especially under Taizhong (627–649), appeared to be as effective with a very similar organizational structure. See S.E. Finer, *The History of Government II: The Intermediate Ages* (Oxford: Oxford University Press, 1999 [1997]).

the primary role in realizing Confucian ideals. Some kings like Taejong (1400–1418) and Sejo (1455–1468) did not subscribe to this idea and wanted to extend and assert royal prerogatives. One of the main issues over which the king and the officials clashed was the authority of the Censorate. For example, the officials wanted the Censorate to review the appointments of all officials while the king wanted to limit their veto power to lower-grade officials.

When Sŏngjong ascended to the throne, the conflict between the king and the officials receded. Both sides learned to compromise after having paid heavy political costs in previous conflicts that often led to coups and succession crises. As a result, the system of government, including the Censorate, became more stable and institutionalized. With the rules of the game firmly established, the Censorate was able to perform its duty effectively. Another reason the Censorate blossomed under Sŏngjong was Sŏngjong's personal support. Being a man of letters, he wanted to be faithful to Confucian teachings, so he protected and encouraged the censors as a matter of personal principle.

Since Sŏngjong was an exceptional figure in his commitment to the Censorate, the level of royal support inevitably declined after his reign. But the activities of the Censorate remained vigorous and relatively free of reproach for another hundred years. This was remarkable because a series of literati purges during the second period claimed the lives of many censors.

I argue that the success of the Censorate in the second period had a political foundation, the implicit alliance between the king and rural Neo-Confucian literati, known as *sarim* (*shilin* 士林). As outsiders, the *sarim* fiercely challenged the establishment, represented by merit subjects and royal marriage kin, for political power. The Censorate became the *sarim*'s main platform because it gave authority to young officials of *sarim* background who started entering the government in large numbers through the civil service examination. At the time, the king had incentives to promote *sarim* and, thus, the Censorate because he needed to counterbalance the merit subjects.

When the strength of this alliance changed over time, however, so did the influence of the Censorate. When the king did not feel that the Censorate served his interests, he was willing to punish and even purge the censors as Yŏnsan-gun and Chŏngjong did on four different occasions.

The irony of history is that the Censorate's ultimate loss of effectiveness came when the *sarim* themselves lost interest in horizontal accountability after finally winning power during the reign of Sŏnjo. Without a common opponent like the merit subjects, the unity of the *sarim* broke down, and the *sarim* divided into different factions mostly on the basis of school and regional ties. With the arrival of factional politics, the Censorate became a battleground between competing factions. Each faction relied on its allies in the Censorate to discredit political opponents. Although many criticisms had been leveled at the censors from the early days of the dynasty, such as making accusations on the basis of rumors and conjectures (*poongmon t'anhaek* 風聞彈劾), promoting factional interests had not been one of them before. As factional politics became more fractious over time, the Censorate became increasingly intolerant and partisan. By the eighteenth century, the abuse and decline of the Censorate was so serious that a noted reformer of the time, Chŏng Yak Yong, openly supported its abolition.

Responding to widespread discontent with the Censorate, the two kings in the late eighteenth century, Yŏngjo and Chŏngjo, carried out a series of reforms, resulting in a weak and dependent Censorate. The most fatal of them turned out to be Yŏngjo's decision in 1741 to revoke the authority of personnel directors to appoint key junior officials and nominate their own successors. Although it is true that some factions blatantly used the Censorate for political purposes, it was still the only institutional mechanism of accountability within the system. With the power of the Censorate thus diminished, the Chosŏn system of government proved unable to restrain powerful officials from creating their own family-based political groups. As different ruling families took turns in "capturing" the government throughout the nineteenth century, the Chosŏn dynasty gradually weakened as a result of their misadministration and eventually succumbed to Japanese imperialism in 1905.

V IMPLICATIONS FOR CONTEMPORARY DEMOCRATIC GOVERNANCE

In many ways, participants in the Asian values debate have talked past each other. Proponents of Asian values like Lee Kuan Yew are guilty of denying the democratic traditions of Asia, while their critics like Kim Dae Jung (1994)[18] tend to downplay the limitations of liberal democracy in prevailing Asian culture. The debate now has to move forward in two directions.

First, we have to accept the destiny of democracy and ask which contemporary Asian values and attitudes obstruct the performance of Asian democracies. Asians have to improve their democracies, regardless of whether they have democratic traditions or not. In the case of Korea, I have argued else-

18 See Kim Dae Jung, "Is Culture Destiny? The Myth of Asia's Anti-Democratic Values," *Foreign Affairs* (November/December 1994), pp. 189–194.

where that it is the prevailing (anti) negotiation culture that has proved most damaging to the performance of democracy.[19]

Second, Asians should be willing to borrow ideas from their past as they are looking to improve their democracies. If there are historical institutions and practices that can be adapted to the modern democratic environment, they are more likely to succeed than those simply transplanted from the West. I argue that the Censorate is one of those historical institutions. There are two ways of introducing elements of the Censorate into a contemporary political system, especially the one in Korea. The direct approach is to appoint modern-day censors in the office of the president whose job would be to write critical reports on a whole range of issues related to presidential conduct.[20] Since a high level of distrust exists between political parties and between the government and the media, the president may actually benefit from having an institutionalized source of criticism within his own staff.

Borrowing certain ideas behind the design of the Censorate and applying them to improve the performance of existing institutions is another, and perhaps better, way of learning from the Censorate. The most important idea is to keep each individual "censor" independent; it is not enough for the organization as a whole to be independent. This idea is very relevant for Korea because it is struggling to make the criminal prosecution system politically independent. The lesson from the Chosŏn government is that Korea should pay as much attention to changing the top-down organizational culture of the Office of the Public Prosecutor as to making the office autonomous of outside political pressure.

The second important idea is to empower young officials to become internal agents of change within the bureaucracy. The Chosŏn system of checks and balances shows that it is plain wrong to associate Confucianism with seniority-based organizational hierarchy. Promising young officials in the Censorate and the Ministry of Personnel wielded an amount of real, independent power that is unthinkable in contemporary Korean bureaucracy.

The current movement toward decentralization in government is encouraging as it gives more power to lower-level officials. But Korea may want to become much bolder in institutionalizing the relative power of junior officials. As the Chosŏn government did, the Korean government can send top young officials to "censoring" agencies such as the Board of Audit to work for five to seven years before assigning them to individual ministries. To make

---

19 See Mo Jongryn, "Political Culture and Legislative Gridlock: Politics of Economic Reform in Pre-Crisis Korea," *Comparative Political Studies* (June 2001).
20 See Park Jae Wan, "A Small and Capable Government," *Mimeo* (Department of Public Administration, Sungkyunkwan University [in Korean], 2001).

this effective, the government should allow the Board of Audit to be run by young auditors on temporary assignment, not by permanent staff. A more drastic measure would be to allow junior officials to make, or at least have a say over, some important appointment decisions as lower-level personnel directors did in the Chosŏn dynasty.

CHAPTER 3

CONFUCIAN DEMOCRATS IN CHINESE HISTORY

WANG JUNTAO

I INTRODUCTION: CONFUCIANISM AND DEMOCRATIZATION

Whether or not Confucianism conflicts with democracy is an important question not only for the future democratization of China but also for the future political development of other East Asian countries with a Confucian heritage. If Confucianism is consistent with democracy, the traditional culture may be used as a means of promoting democratization in East Asia. At the very least, the political transition will be smoother and easier, with lower costs, since there will be less cultural resistance. In this essay, it will be argued that Confucianism and democracy are compatible.

The compatibility of Confucianism with democracy may refer to the strong thesis that Confucianism is always supportive of democratization. Here, however, I defend the weaker thesis that Confucianism is not inherently incompatible with democracy. Put positively, it means that Confucianism is capable of embracing the idea of democracy and that it can be developed for this purpose.

There are two ways to validate or invalidate my assumption. One way is through content analysis. Scholars analyze the theoretical tenets of Confucianism and democracy to determine if they are consistent. Those sympathetic to Confucian democracy would define their terms and then try to reveal some elements in Confucianism that can support, or at least be consistent with, some elements of democracy. Although this method seems reasonable, it has provoked endless debates. The most obvious problem is that there is no consensus about the meanings of democracy and Confucianism. Democracy, for example, is notoriously hard to define. Moreover, it is a developing process and meanings change over time – if we evaluate American politics in the early nineteenth century by the current standard, it must be nondemocracy. Confucianism is also an ambiguous and evolving theory that changes with place and time. The original scriptures alone do not represent the entire discourse. They need to be applied and interpreted depending on the specific situation. New situations in different regions or during different periods present new challenges and thus necessitate new interpretations. Such interpretations and reinterpretations also become part of the discourse.

Nor are there straightforward orientations toward certain specific political institutions. In fact, this ability to be adaptable to new situations is (partly) what constitutes a great system of thought. It is thus inappropriate to make a simplistic prediction about a negative relationship between a particular principle and a specific institution.[1] Consider the evolution of Confucianism. It has been used to support political regimes that are radically different from those that existed at the time of Confucius. Without such reinterpretations, Confucianism surely would have been abandoned very early in Chinese political history.

The other approach, which I employ in this article, is historical analysis: looking into Chinese history to determine whether or not political actors embraced both Confucianism and democracy. Ideally, one would collect data on all Confucians in Chinese history in regard to their attitudes toward democracy, or perhaps infer from their other beliefs, if they have not thought explicitly about this question. This exercise would not be feasible in a short essay, however. Thus, I limit myself to an examination of some typical cases – influential political actors – in the period from the late nineteenth century to the present when Chinese intellectuals forcefully engaged with the question of democracy. If it turns out that major Chinese intellectuals recognized the important role of Confucianism in their pro-democracy struggles, this will show that Confucianism can be developed in ways compatible with democracy.

The critic may reply, however, that relying on the views of political actors is also problematic.[2] Those who try to combine democracy and Confucianism in fact betray Confucianism because their ideas are different from the core ideas of the Confucian tradition. Since my purpose here is only

---

1 One famous example of erroneous thinking along these lines is Max Weber's prediction that Catholicism conflicts with modernization and democratization. As Samuel Huntington has argued, Catholicism became transformed from an important obstacle to democratization into one of the major ideological factors underpinning the "third wave" of democratization in the world (Huntington, *The Third Wave: Democratization in the Late-Twentieth Century* [Norman: University of Oklahoma Press, 1991]).

2 The basic compatibility of Confucianism and democracy can perhaps more straightforwardly be established by pointing to democratization in countries with a Confucian heritage such as South Korea and Taiwan. It can always be argued, however, that these countries democratized in spite of (by "overcoming") their Confucian heritage. Moreover, my focus here is China, and it may be more relevant to examine Chinese history in this case.

to determine whether Confucianism can be made consistent with democracy, I do not need to take a stand on what constitutes "real" Confucianism. All schools of Confucianism are fair game for my question. Instead, I will define Confucians as those people who consciously declare themselves to be Confucians and who have some grounding in the tradition. While this definition can seem overly embracing, it has the virtue of limiting the investigation to thinkers who openly identified themselves as defenders of the Confucian tradition and who consciously adhered to Confucianism as they struggled for democracy. I can therefore avoid more contestable arguments about Confucianism operating "behind the backs" of the people involved.

The historical approach raises another potentially problematic question: What is meant by accepting democracy? How can we determine if those people who were influenced by Confucianism also embraced democracy? Did they truly understand the meaning of democracy? This question inevitably involves the definition of democracy. Theoretically, this is a difficult question since there are many conflicting opinions about what democracy is. The least controversial definition, however, is one that involves government "by the people." At minimum, this means some form of competitive procedure, usually elections, for the selection of political leaders. This definition may seem vague, so I will propose an additional condition for identifying a "democrat" – he or she clearly stands on the side of democrats in the actual political struggles between proponents and opponents of democracy. Democratization is an open-ended evolving process, and those involved in the practical step-by-step process may not necessarily completely understand all its theoretical tenets. But we can recognize democrats through their political alignments or partisanship.

In order to show the consistency between Confucianism and democracy in political practice, I will focus on some key political figures in Chinese history. In the case of those who are usually labeled "Confucians," I will show that either they actively pursued democracy or they stood on the side of the democratic bloc in the political struggles. In the case of those who are usually labeled "democrats," I will offer as an example their positive remarks about Confucianism and about what they took to be the positive role of Confucianism in democratization.

The Chinese began to struggle for democracy over one hundred years ago. Since then, there have been three distinct periods. From the late nineteenth century to the 1920s, the Chinese set up and tried to maintain the first republic. From the late 1920s to the late 1970s, the Chinese were under the authoritarian Guomindang regime and the totalitarian communist regime, but there were still some democrats who opposed the dictatorship and appealed for democracy. Since the mid-1970s, there have been new waves of democratization in all parts of China, including the mainland, Taiwan, and Hong Kong. According to the criteria I have presented above, I have chosen Kang Youwei, Zhang Jian, Sun Zhongshan (Sun Yatsen), Liang Qichao, Zhang Junmai, Wang Xizhe, and Chen Ziming as key figures in the democratization of China during their respective periods. I will analyze these figures in chronological order.

II THE ESTABLISHMENT OF THE FIRST REPUBLIC

The Chinese imperial system lasted for well over two millennia and only came under serious political scrutiny following defeats by Western powers in the mid to late nineteenth century. In 1911, the imperial system came to a formal end and China established the first republic in Asia. China underwent four political events in the evolution to republican rule: the Institutional Reform Movement, the Constitutional Reform Movement, the Xinhai Revolution, and the War to Defend the Republic and Uphold the Constitution. Kang Youwei, Zhang Jian, Sun Zhongshan, and Liang Qichao represented these efforts during their respective periods.

1 THE INSTITUTIONAL REFORM MOVEMENT: 1895–1898

The Institutional Reform Movement was the first attempt to reform and set up a modern political system in China. The most prominent leader in this movement was Kang Youwei. He was also one of the most influential Confucians of his day, famous for trying to revise Confucianism to serve as a basis for the setting up of a constitutional monarchy. Kang's case will show that, during China's first attempt at democratization, the leading Confucians embraced democracy and the leading democrats recognized the positive role of Confucianism in the democratization process.

Kang Youwei was born into a Confucian family in Nanhai County of Guangdong Province in 1858. Although his early education was traditional, he began to think about reform when he was thirty years old. In 1888, he had a chance to visit Hong Kong and various parts of China, leading him to realize how backward the Chinese political system was compared to Western modes of governance. Kang wrote to several ministers in Beijing appealing for reform. On his way home to Guangdong, Kang bought a number of translated Western books that further exposed him to new ideas. Beginning in 1891, Kang began to promote ideas of reform among the young people of Guangzhou, one of the most developed and open areas in China at that time. He trained a number of outstanding young people who were supportive of his reformist ideas. Among his best students was Liang Qichao, another leading figure among the Confucians and democrats in the early years of Chinese democratization. After having passed the national Confucian exam and receiving an official title in 1893, Kang wrote several books calling for reform. As a result, he became well known throughout the country. In 1895, the news arrived that China had been defeated by Japan. Kang then led six hundred Confucian candidates for higher examinations from eighteen provinces to deliver a joint petition to the emperor calling for complete reform. In the following years, Kang tried to mobilize more people to participate in further petitions. He also founded an organization and published newspapers to spread his ideas. Although Kang was not the first person to discuss the possibility of establishing a parliamentary system in China, he was the first to call for political reform so as to introduce such a system into China. Finally, in 1898 Kang was successful in his pleas and the young emperor met with him and accepted his ideas for reform. This period later came to be known as the Wuxu Reform, and Kang was appointed as an official to help the emperor. But the reform lasted only 103 days, ending in failure due to a coup by the empress dowager. Kang was sent into exile, but in 1900 he tried to initiate a military attack to save the empire and continue the reform. However, this attempt ended in failure. During his period in exile, Kang continued to research about Chinese reform, to propagate his ideas, to train young reformers, and to set up organizations and publish newspapers.

It has been argued that Kang was not really a democrat because he insisted on the establishment of a constitutional monarchy. In particular, after the Xinhai Revolution, he opposed the republic and tried to restore the Qing dynasty. However, this misinterprets Kang's ideas about a constitutional monarchy. Such critiques of Kang Youwei and other conservative reformers confuse democracy as a goal with the transition strategy. For Kang and the other so-called conservative reformers, a successful democracy required a well-designed strategy to allow for a smooth transition and to reduce the costs. He opposed political revolution on the grounds that this would lead the Chinese to abandon their tradition.

This leads to another dispute about Kang Youwei, that is, whether or not he was a Confucian. It is commonly held that Kang misinterpreted the original meaning of Confucianism and its scriptures, with the implication that Kang was not a "real" Confucian. Recall, however, that for our purposes a Confucian is whoever defines himself or herself as such and who has some grounding in the tradition. From this point of view, Kang was indeed a Confucian. He received a typical traditional Confucian education in his youth. At the age of six, he began to study the Confucian scriptures. By the age of twelve, his knowledge of Confucianism surprised even his neighbors. He maintained a lifelong attachment to the tradition.

Still, let us try to respond more explicitly to the critique that Kang was not a "real" Confucian. His aim was to revise the dominant tradition and his argument was based on an understanding of some selected scriptures. Kang was involved in the debates between two different schools of Confucianism. Previously there had been two branches of Confucianism, the Old Script School (Guwen Xuepai 古文學派) and the New Script School (Jinwen Xuepai 今文學派). The difference between the two schools had emerged during the Han dynasty, two thousand years earlier. Confucianism had once been popular in the Zhou dynasty but it was destroyed and banned by China's first emperor, Qin Shihuang. During Qin's reign, many Confucian masters were killed and Confucian scriptures were burned. During the Han dynasty, Confucianism gained political recognition and Confucian masters became officials who wrote out their interpretations of Confucianism as texts for education and politics. These are called the New Scripts because they were written in the Chinese characters of the Han dynasty. It is commonly argued that these scriptures do not represent "real" Confucianism. Only the scriptures that were preserved by Confucius's family during the Qin dynasty, according to this view, should be considered Confucian classics. Because those scriptures were written in ancient Chinese characters, this school is called the Old Script School. This dispute generated fierce debate that lasted over two millennia.

Another significant difference between the two schools is that the Confucians of the New Script School usually flexibly reinterpreted Confucianism according to the situation and their understanding of current political demands, while the Old Script School insisted on a strict interpretation of the classical literature. Because of the cruel suppression of intellectuals by the Manchu government, the Confucians during the Qing dynasty ended up following the Old Script School, focusing on investigations, examinations, and explanations of the classical literature. This work diverted their attention from politics. In the mid nineteenth century, after a series of military frustrations, some intellectuals began to criticize the Old Script School and they came to believe in the necessity of introducing new knowledge into China that would contribute to its modernization. For example, Gong Zizhen and Wei Yuan followed the New Script School and wrote some books that influenced many Chinese youth.

Following these figures, Kang Youwei tried to introduce democracy through a reexplanation of the Confucian scripts and became the greatest thinker of the New Script School of Confucianism at the time. From *Gongyang Chunqiu* 公羊春秋, a scripture of the New Script School believed to have been written by Confucius,[3] Kang developed the so-called Three Generations

3 The Old Script School believes it is a fake document.

Theory (*San Shi Shuo* 三世説).[4] This theory maintained that human societies had to undergo three periods in succession: Chaos (*Ju Luan Shi* 据亂世), Peace (*Sheng Ping Shi* 升平世), and Paradise (*Tai Ping Shi* 太平世). According to Kang's interpretation of the *Gongyang Chunqiu*, each period was represented by one political regime: chaos for Chaos, dictatorship for Peace, and the republic for Paradise. Confucius lived during the Chaos period and tried to enter the period of Peace. From the Han dynasty onward, the Chinese had lived in Peace for two thousand years. In Kang's opinion, this period was too long and it explains why China was relatively backward compared to the Western powers. He argued that it was time to enter the period of Paradise and he proposed a constitutional monarchy to smooth the transition from dictatorship to republicanism.

Kang also argued that Confucius himself was a perfect model to embody the reform. Kang argued that democratic institutions, for example, parliamentary systems, elections, and equal rights, were not only consistent with but also implied in Confucianism.[5] For example, Kang wrote: "Yao and Shun [Chinese political heads of dominant tribes in mythical ancient times] are the masters of democracy, peace, and humanity";[6] in Paradise, "all is based on public principles. Public principles means every one is equal with no differences between rich and poor, man and woman."[7] Due to misinterpretations by Confucians in later times, Kang argued that democracy was ignored and Chinese political development was delayed. He traced his ideas about reform to the classical Confucian scriptures *Shijing* 詩經 (Poems), *Shangshu* 尚書 (Records), *Liji* 禮記 (Rites), *Yue* 樂 (Music), *Chunqiu* 春秋 (History), and *Yijing* 易經 (Natural Arithmetic). Even though China seemed relatively backward, overall guidance was still to be derived from traditional Chinese ideals. Kang also studied the situation outside: The cases of France, Poland, Japan, and Russia show that the reformed countries survived while the conservative countries were destroyed. But his theory opposed any attempt to skip a stage in the evolutionary chain or firmly break with tradition.

2 THE CONSTITUTIONAL REFORM MOVEMENT: 1900–1911

Although the failure of the Wuxu Reform temporarily ended political reform, the empress dowager herself soon resumed it. Upheavals such as the Boxer Uprising in 1900 and the military victory of the Japanese over Russia in 1905

4 The Three Generations Theory, originally in *Gongyang Chunqiu*, is a story about human development. In Kang's theory, it serves to justify his idea about political reform by returning to Confucius's original thought.
5 Yan Binggang, *Dangdai Xinruxue Yinlun* (Beijing: Beijing Library Press, 1998), p. 8.
6 Kang Youwei, *Kongzi Gai Zhi Kao* (Shanghai: Shanghai Bookstore, 1992).
7 Wang Rongzu, *Kang Youwei Sixiang Yanjiu* (Taipei: Lianjing Chubanshe, 1988), p. 77.

shocked the empress and the Chinese elites. They attributed their failure to the difference between the constitutional monarchy in Japan and the dictatorships in China and Russia. Urged on by the elites throughout the country, the empress decided to reform the Chinese political system in 1906, leading to the Constitutional Reform Movement. During this period the Chinese were almost successful in setting up a constitutional monarchy, but their efforts were interrupted by a revolution two years before it could be completely implemented. By the time of the outbreak of the revolution of 1911, the dynasty had created a constitution that promised to secure a responsible parliamentary system, judicial independence, and local self-government. This movement was led by a brilliant constellation of democratic reformers who were educated in Confucianism and supportive of the political role of Confucianism. Zhang Jian is one such example.

Zhang Jian was renowned for his many-sided talents: He played a significant role in many fields – industrial, commercial, educational, political, and intellectual. Before the Constitutional Reform Movement, he urged some pivotal officials to appeal for reform. When the dynasty declared its support of reform, Zhang was elected chairman of the provincial assembly in Jiangsu and became the leader of public opinion in the most developed area of China. At a crucial point during the provisional constitution period, Zhang initiated and led petitions to shorten the preparations for elections to the National Assembly. When the revolution broke out, Zhang urged Jiangsu Province to declare autonomy. Thereafter, he favored the abolition of the Qing dynasty and he helped the provisional president find the financial support necessary to set up a new government. During the parliamentary period, Zhang established several political parties in order to establish a multiparty system in China.

Zhang was also one of the best-known Confucians of his day. He received the top title honored by official authorities, *zhuangyuan* 狀元, in the national examination that was held every four years. Because Zhang Jian insisted on some traditional values and rules, Cheng Cangbo comments: "He was not only an educator, businessman, and politician, but he was also a master of civilization, a typical traditional Confucian master."[8] Shao Jingren, a legislator in republican China, noted that the great thinker Hu Shi respected Zhang Jian very much, "because he based his achievements on the traditional Confucian Scripts, and, thus, he could be successful and become a great person in China."[9] Other famous members of the Constitutional Reform

8 Cheng Cangbo. "Mr. Zhang Jizhi and Jiangsu Province," in *In Memory of Zhang Jizhi Forty Years After His Death*, ed. by Li Tongfu (Taipei: Wenhai Chubanshe, 1979), p. 17.
9 "Shao Jingren Xiansheng Yanjiang," in ibid., p. 189.

Movement, such as Yang Du (the leader of the Chinese students in Japan) and Tang Hualong (the chairman of the Provincial Assembly in Hubei), had backgrounds and ideas similar to those of Zhang Jian.[10]

3 THE 1911 REPUBLICAN REVOLUTION

In 1908, the empress dowager and Emperor Guangxu both died. Although reform still continued according to the previously announced schedule, the new ruling core of the royal family rejected and suppressed petitions from constitutional reformers calling for a shorter schedule. Such actions led the constitutional reformers to join the Republican Revolution. In 1911, the revolution broke out. Soon thereafter, the first republic in Asian history was established. What is interesting for our purposes is that the founding fathers of the republic recognized the role of Confucianism in democratization. Sun Zhongshan (Sun Yatsen) is the best-known example.

Sun's contribution to the first republic is so significant that following his death in 1925 all political forces proclaimed him the father of the Chinese democratic republic. Although he was primarily educated from Western sources, he received a traditional Confucian education during his teenage years. As early as 1885 when the French defeated the Chinese, Sun began to think about overthrowing the corrupt Qing dynasty and setting up a democracy in China. In 1892, Sun graduated from medical school, but his real interest was in setting up underground organizations and networks to bring about a political revolution that would end the imperial regime of the Qing dynasty. In 1894, Sun proposed the revolutionary goal of driving out foreign invaders and establishing a republican government. In 1896, Qing dynasty officials tried to kidnap him in London. Released under pressure from the United Kingdom, he became the worldwide symbol of the Chinese Republican Revolution. In 1905, he founded the first Chinese political party, the *Tong Meng Hui* 同盟會. He tried to initiate a series of military rebellions in southern China. When revolution finally broke out in 1911, the joint-provisional senate elected him to be the temporary president of the new republic. In exchange for gaining Yuan Shikai's support of the republic and thus avoiding a war between north and south China, Sun soon resigned as president in

---

10 Professor Zhang Pengyuan has systematically analyzed the importance of Confucians in the Constitutional Reform Movement. During this period, 90% of members of the National Assembly and 46% of members of provincial assemblies won officially honored titles for Confucians through examinations in the Confucian scriptures (Zhang Pengyuan, *Lixianpai yu Xinhai Geming* [Taipei: Zhongyang Yanjiuyuan Jindaishi Yanjiusuo, 1983], pp. 247–316). During the republican period, constitutional reformers organized the so-called Progress Party which proposed to make Confucianism into a national religion (Wang Rongzu, *Kang Youwei Sixiang Yanjiu* [Taipei: Lianjing Chubanshe, 1988], p. 118).

favor of Yuan. When Yuan tried to become a dictator in 1913, Sun called for a second revolution. This ended in failure and Sun once again went into exile. Yuan could not sustain the empire and died during another uprising against him shortly thereafter. As a result, China became trapped in the warlord era, but Sun continued his efforts to save the democratic republic. In 1917, he led a movement to defend the constitution against the warlords who tried to abandon it. He established the military government of the Republic of China, of which he was elected the great marshal. In 1924, he reorganized the Guomindang into the party that would eventually reunify China in the 1930s. But Sun died before this historical achievement.

Sun's influence in the struggle for democracy in China is unsurpassed, and he insisted that Confucianism played a crucial role in this struggle.[11] He argued that Confucianism was not only consistent with but also necessary for a democratic republic to take hold in China. In his work *The History of the Chinese Revolution*, Sun wrote that his ideas about revolution originated from traditional Chinese thought, Western experience, and his own innovations. He criticized ideas that maintained that democratization implied a complete transplantation of Western thought and institutions into China. In 1924, he told Japanese journalists: "Our *three-min principles* [nationalism, citizens' rights, welfare of human beings] originate from Mencius and are based on Cheng Yichuan.[12] . . . Mencius is really the ancestor of our democratic ideas. . . . The *three-min principles* are a completion of the development of those three thousand years of Chinese ideas about how to govern and maintain a peaceful world."[13] According to Sun, Confucianism also plays the crucial role of building up an identity for Chinese citizens in a democratic republic.[14] As the main tradition in Chinese history, Confucianism can help to provide a common identity that binds citizens in a democratic republic.[15]

11 Zhang Taiyan, an influential Chinese revolutionary with relatively profound knowledge of Confucianism, similarly drew on Confucianism for the purpose of establishing a democratic republic.
12 Cheng Yichuan, a well-recognized Confucian master during the Song dynasty. Together with Zhu Xi, he developed a New Confucianism that saw the original Confucianism as being in conflict with Buddhism.
13 Jiang Linxiang, *Zhongguo Ruxue Shi* (Guangzhou: Guangdong Education Press, 1998), Vol. 7, p. 215.
14 Ibid., Vol. 6, pp. 211–221.
15 In its founding moments, many members of parliament proposed that Confucianism be the guiding national thought. Although parliament did not ultimately approve this, the draft of the Constitution for the republic endorsed Confucianism as the fundamental principle underlying citizen conduct in national education (Wang Rongzu, *Kang Youwei Sixiang Yanjiu* [Taipei: Lianjing Chubanshe, 1988], p. 118).

4 *DEFENDING THE REPUBLIC*

The republic soon degenerated into instability, and many Chinese began to worry about potential chaos and disintegration. This led to two short periods of restoration of the monarchy: the Hongxian dynasty set up by Yuan Shikai in 1915 and the restoration of the Qing dynasty by General Zhang Xun in 1917. Liang Qichao was a key figure at this time among the Chinese democrats in the defense of the republic. Like Kang Youwei, he was also one of the best Confucians of his day. His story also shows that Confucians can indeed be democrats.

Liang was born in Guangdong Province in 1873. He joined in political activities as Kang's student and assistant. During the Wuxu Reform, Liang spent much time trying to build up a political base in Hunan Province. Like his teacher, he was sent into exile after the failure of the reform. During this time, he set up organizations, published newspapers, and initiated movements in order to resume the reform that had been interrupted in 1898. Under his influence, many Chinese became reformers – joining the Constitutional Reform Movement, the Republican Revolution, and other progressive movements in the 1920s and the 1930s.[16] Liang was the real soul of the Constitutional Reform Movement even though he was not even in China at that time. He wrote influential documents that promoted ideas of constitutional reform among the Qing leaders, and the movement actually developed under his guidance. He also tried to establish a Chinese constitutional party in Japan. Although he opposed the revolution due to concerns about transition problems, he mobilized constitutionalists to support the republic soon after it was set up. During the parliamentary period, he encouraged all the anti-Guomindang forces to organize a so-called Progressive Party, one of the two main parties in the parliament, almost making a two-party system (the Guomindang and the Progressive Party).

His most valuable contribution to democratization in China was to defend the democratic regime when Yuan Shikai tried to dominate the parliament and overthrow the fledgling democracy. In defending the republic, he played a unique role by forging a majority in parliament that enacted a constitution designed to restrict Yuan's activities. Until Liang's participation, there had not been a successful anti-Yuan movement. In 1915, Liang initiated another military movement against Yuan when Yuan tried to restore the empire. First, he rejected Yuan's 200,000-yuan bribe and wrote an article criticizing the

---

16 Even anti-Confucian intellectuals such as Lu Xun, Hu Shi, Guo Moruo, and Mao Zedong admitted Liang's influence over them (Li Ping and Yang Boling, *Liang Qichao Zhuan* [Hefei: Anhui Renmin Press, 1997], pp. 282–285).

restoration of the imperial system. His article was so successful that the newspapers sold out immediately and people had to transcribe the article in restaurants. Then, under his advice, his student, Cai Er, initiated a military rebellion in Yunnan Province. Cai's army then entered Sichuan Province. Although Cai forced Guizhou Province to declare anti-Yuan independence, he was ultimately blocked there. Liang engaged in the risky venture of visiting Guangxi Province in order to elicit the support of this province in the anti-Yuan alliance. After a hard, uncertain, and dangerous time, Liang's rebellion was successful. Yuan resigned from the crown and died during the height of the opposition movement.

In 1917, Liang again played an important role in opposing Zhang Xun's attempt to restore the Qing dynasty. He wrote the official declaration urging the republican army to mobilize the entire republic for the purpose of overthrowing the restored Qing dynasty. He also held several positions in the subsequent government. During the warlord period, he lost an effective means to influence politics when Cai Er died, but he continued to promote democracy through research, propaganda, and education.

As one of the most prominent Confucians of his time, Liang is mentioned in every book about the history of contemporary Confucianism or the intellectual history of China. He adapted Kang's Three Generations Theory and supported an argument that is still influential in contemporary democratic transition theory: that culture matters in democratization. According to Liang's theory, the three generations were multi-majesties, one-majesty, and democracy.[17] Furthermore, they could be divided into six generations: the chiefs of tribes, feudal princes, monarchy, monarchy and republic, presidential republic, and republic without republic.[18] A democratic republic was higher than a constitutional monarchy, but a republic required better citizens. Unlike Kang who focused solely on the regime, Liang paid attention to the requirements for qualified citizens. Because people in China at the time had a low level of education and the Western powers intended to divide China, he argued that it was not appropriate to attempt a radical change in society and politics. The first task of democratization was to develop the minds of the citizens under a democratic monarchy and Confucianism was a prerequisite part of this education.

In his later life, after observing class conflicts and World War I, Liang sharpened his views on the role of Confucianism in a democratic polity. He argued that Western-style democracy (and science) could not solve all the

17 Deng Mingyan, *Liang Qichao de Shengping Jiqi Sixiang* (Taipei: Tianshan Press, 1981), pp. 108–109.
18 Ibid.

problems in industrial societies. Confucianism could complement democracy by appealing for moderation and modesty, thus minimizing competition between individuals and maintaining the unity of the society.

III DEMOCRATIC OPPOSITION TO THE GUOMINDANG (KMT) AND THE CHINESE COMMUNIST PARTY

Following the death of Yuan Shikai, China was trapped in a period of bloody chaos until 1927 when the Guomindang reunified China under the leadership of Jiang Jieshi (Chiang Kai-shek). But Jiang did not restore a democratic regime as the Guomindang had promised in their struggle against Yuan. Instead, he set up an authoritarian regime under his dictatorship. The Guomindang eventually lost the civil war against the Chinese Communist Party (CCP) and fled to Taiwan. In 1949, the CCP established the People's Republic of China (PRC) and set up a totalitarian regime. In both Taiwan and mainland China, however, Chinese liberal intellectuals and democrats continued to struggle to establish a democratic regime.

1 THE THIRD FORCE

During the period of Guomindang authoritarian rule, political freedoms were restricted and opposition movements suppressed. Many well-known democrats and intellectuals fought against such political restrictions and tried to promote an opening of the regime. These people have been referred to as the "third force" that wanted to take the road of liberal democracy, different from both the fascism of the Guomindang and the totalitarianism of the communists. Zhang Junmai is representative of such liberal democrats. He was also one of the leading figures in the so-called third generation of Confucians. His case also shows that Confucians can be democrats.

Zhang Junmai was born in Jiangsu Province in 1887. He became politically conscious during his period of study in Japan from 1906 to 1910 and in Europe from 1913 to 1916 and 1918 to 1922. Zhang joined the overseas Chinese democracy movement in Japan and declared himself a follower of Liang Qichao. As an active member in Liang's Zheng Wen She 政聞社 (Political Information Network), a type of political party, he debated with the republican revolutionaries about how to reform China. After the revolution in 1911, he was elected chairman of Baoshan County on the outskirts of Shanghai. In 1912, he took part in the founding of the Democracy Party, one of the opposition parties at the time. Among the constitutional reformers, he was the earliest to criticize Yuan Shikai. When Yuan tried to set up the Hongxian dynasty, Zhang joined the exile opposition movement. In 1922,

he wrote a constitution for eight political organizations, marking the beginning of a civil society in China. In addition, he wrote articles to spread ideas
of democracy. In 1923, in order to provide education in democracy, he reorganized the National Political University, but the Guomindang soon closed
it down because Zhang refused to obey its instructions that the students recite
the premier's dying words daily. In 1928 Zhang was again frustrated when
the Guomindang banned his publication, the *Xin lu* (新路) (New Way) magazine. Zhang continued his opposition activities and set up an underground
party, the National Socialist Party. Thereafter he became one of the main
opposition leaders and his party was part of the "third force."

In 1938, however, his fate changed. Due to the Japanese invasion, Jiang
Jieshi opened up the regime and Zhang was invited to be a member of the
National People's Political Council. In 1941, along with members of several
other parties, Zhang set up the League of Chinese Democratic Political
Groups to serve as a balance between the Guomindang and the Chinese
Communist Party. He also participated in initiating two constitutional move-
ments. After the anti-Japanese War, he joined the Political Consultative Con-
ference and wrote the new constitution. In 1949, however, the Communist
Party put his name on the most-wanted list as a war criminal and he became
one of several democracy leaders punished after the establishment of the PRC.
In 1951, Zhang set up the Chinese Liberal Democracy Fighters Association
in Hong Kong.

Zhang Junmai was also one of the most important Confucian thinkers of
his time. After Liang Shuming, he was the second master to develop neo-
Confucianism following the critiques of the May Fourth Movement.[19]
Zhang's main aim was to reinterpret Song-Ming Confucianism as favoring
liberal individualism in intellectual and political life. According to
Song-Ming Confucianism, Confucians had to train and develop their minds
in order to achieve a morally perfect self. Zhang thought that such perfect
selves were a necessary basis for democracy. He set up two schools, the Xuehai
Shutang in 1935 and the Institute of National Culture in 1939, both aimed
at training such perfect selves with Confucian minds. In these schools, a
contemporary education system was combined with practices from the
traditional private educational systems. During the 1950s and 1960s,
Zhang ended his political activities and devoted himself to developing
Confucianism. In 1958, Zhang joined the three other great masters of neo-
Confucianism, Tang Junyi, Xu Fuguan, and Mou Zongsan, to publish *A
Declaration to the World for Chinese Culture*. In this historical document, they
established a foundation for neo-Confucianism. Not only did Zhang write

---

19 In fact, Zhang read more books on Confucianism than Liang himself (Zheng Dahua, *Zhang
Junmai Xueshu Sixiang Pingzhuan* [Beijing: Beijing Library Press, 1999], pp. 63, 332).

books, he also traveled widely to spread Confucian ideas on campuses and elsewhere. In his later life he followed the ideal Confucian model: After participation in political activities designed to realize Confucian political and cultural ideas, he wrote books and taught people to spread the influence of Confucianism. Zhang also criticized classical capitalism and insisted on social democracy. He felt that social democratic theory could be a basis for Confucianism.[20] He traced the socialist element to the classical Confucian scriptures, the *Li Ji* 禮記 (The Book of Rites), and he tried to compare socialism in different countries including China to present his political ideas.[21] He also argued that there were seeds of democracy in Confucianism, for example, in its defense of the freedom of speech.[22] In the same vein, many other leaders of the "third force" – Liang Shuming, Huang Yanpei, Shen Junru, and Zeng Qi – identified themselves as Confucians, participated in pro-democracy struggles, and tried to find theoretical linkages between Confucianism and democracy.

2 DISSIDENTS IN THE TOTALITARIAN PERIOD OF THE COMMUNIST REGIME

Although the CCP had promised a democratic regime during their struggle against the Guomindang, they set up a totalitarian regime that was much more invasive of social and political life than the authoritarian rule of the KMT. All independent political activities, media, publications, demonstrations, and organizations were banned, and not only were democrats deprived of the opportunity to speak out but attempts were made to ensure that they did not even hold ideas different from those of the authorities. In 1957, the Chinese Communist Party systematically persecuted all intellectuals and democrats during the Anti-Rightist Movement, and the opposition was further weakened. Many of these former "rightists," however, are now thought of as the old generation of democrats. Several had received a traditional Chinese education, including training in Confucianism.

During the Cultural Revolution (1966–1976), an entire generation of Chinese youth received communist education in which both democratic and Confucian values were denigrated. But the Cultural Revolution also weakened communist control, leading to the appearance of new opposition movements and dissidents in the late Cultural Revolution period. The earliest democrats to have grown up during the communist era were the members of the so-called Li-Yi-Zhe李一哲 group.

---

20 Yan Binggang, *Dangdai Xinruxue Yinlun* (Beijing: Beijing Library Press, 1998), pp. 167–178.
21 Zheng Dahua, *Zhang Junmai Xueshu Sixiang Pingzhuan*, p. 169.
22 Ibid., pp. 256–261.

The name of this group, representing the generation of those educated under the communists, was derived from the surnames of its three leaders. In 1974, they posted a big-character poster in Guangzhou that called for the establishment of a socialist democratic and legal system in China. The leaders were ultimately arrested but not before they had a chance to defend their ideas in officially organized public demonstrations. As a result of these debates, their ideas spread and became popular among Chinese youth. Of the three leaders, Wang Xizhe is the only one known to have continued his democratic activities and he remains an active figure at the present time. In 1980, he tried to set up an independent publications union (*Quanguo minkan xiehui* 全國民刊協會). But Deng Xiaoping decided to crack down on the democracy movement and Wang Xizhe received a fourteen-year prison sentence in 1981. After his release in the mid-1990s, he again became an active democrat in China. He initiated the founding of several opposition parties, the China Democracy Party, the Chinese Justice Party, the Chinese Freedom Labor Party, and the Free China Movement.

Although Wang did not receive a Confucian education, he read several books about Confucianism when he was in prison. He still defends values and knowledge that are typically linked to the anti-Confucianism of the May Fourth Movement and believes that Confucianism, without a focus on individualism, is inconsistent with basic human rights. But he argues that Confucianism can be reformed and developed into a new system that is indeed compatible with democracy and human rights. According to Wang, we must return to the original Confucian ideas in order to develop both Confucianism and democracy. When he was asked about the "Confucian style" of his political activities and writings, he noted that he has been greatly influenced by Confucian works. He said that *ren* (仁), the core idea of Confucianism, "is rooted in my heart and conscience very deeply."[23] In addition, he mentioned that his character and behavior, which are willing to challenge the communist authorities, are partly derived from the Confucian moral model for critical intellectuals.

3 THE THIRD GENERATION OF NEO-CONFUCIANS

In 1958, a group of so-called third generation of Confucians, largely based outside mainland China, reached a consensus about the direction of Chinese political development and Confucianism. Confucian masters Mou Zongsan, Xu Fuguan, Zhang Junmai, and Tang Junyi published *A Declaration to the World for Chinese Culture*. This declaration critically examined Confucianism

---

23 Personal interview with the author.

and the development of mainstream human civilization. It insisted on the basic values of liberal democracy and proposed revising Confucianism to support such values. The document also analyzed the current problems in the Western world and posited that revised Confucianism could mitigate these problems.

The term "third generation of Confucians" was introduced by Mou Zongsan in 1948,[24] and it has since been widely accepted in Chinese intellectual communities. The "first generation of Confucians" refers to those Confucians who lived from the time of Confucius to the Han dynasty. During this period, Confucianism emerged to become the dominant Chinese ideology. The "second generation of Confucians" appeared in the Song and Ming dynasties after Confucianism was reinterpreted in response to the challenge of Buddhism in China. The third generation of Confucians grew in response to the challenge from Western civilization.

A core problem of the third generation of Confucians was to relate Confucianism to democracy. They were perplexed by three questions: Is Confucianism compatible with democracy? What are the obstacles to Confucian China's becoming a democracy? And which parts of Confucianism should be reformed in order to support democracy? They basically agreed that original Confucianism is consistent with democracy. While they pointed to weaknesses in Confucianism that had prevented China from becoming a democracy, they were confident that a reformed Confucianism could support democracy.

According to Mou Zongsan, a necessary precondition for democracy is an independent individual conscience. Confucianism insists that all beings strive for a perfect mind. This idea implies the individual equality of human beings, which can be a starting point for democracy. The difference between Confucianism and mainstream Western thought is that Confucianism pays attention to the morally independent existence of the individual while Western thought focuses on the cognitively and politically independent existence of the individual. Thus, the Chinese tried to develop self-improvement of the free mind through individual reflection, and Western thought made an effort to set up institutions to ensure that individual rights be protected in a democratic polity. But this apparent conflict can be resolved because a morally independent mind can also realize the necessity of a cognitively and politically independent mind. Confucianism could therefore be reformed so as to develop a cognitive and political conscience that will ensure democratization.

Tang Junyi believed that liberalism was the spiritual condition for contemporary democracy and he tried to discover the seeds of liberal ideas in Confucianism. He argued that the conscience of moral improvement means

---

24 Yan Binggang, *Dangdai Xinruxue Yinlun*, pp. 442–445.

equality between individuals and freedom of the individual. But the lack of a political conscience led the Chinese to put too much weight on self-improvement by individual reflection, and thus they did not establish a democratic system with checks and balances and divided power. However, the conscience of individual freedom in a moral sense can be developed into a conscience of the political rights of the individual.

Xu Fuguan discussed the political implication of the assumption that Confucianism is made for the nature of human beings. He argued that the good nature of human beings assumed by Confucianism not only leads to an emphasis on freedom of the individual, but that it also implies limited government. The problem with traditional Confucianism is that it appealed for self-control of behavior and did not search for appropriate institutional arrangements to restrict government. The natural conclusion of Confucianism is the setting up of a democratic regime to guarantee individual freedoms.

In short, the third generation Confucians tried to develop democracy from Confucianism by revealing the seeds of democracy in Confucianism, isolating the problems blocking democracy, and proposing new ideas to reform traditional Confucianism. Although the political situation on the mainland did not allow for substantial political action, they helped to lay the intellectual foundations for Confucian democrats.

4 PRO-DEMOCRACY STRUGGLES IN THE REFORM ERA

When the third wave of democratization swept the world in the 1970s, pro-democracy movements began to grow in both Taiwan and the mainland. In Taiwan, democrats with a strong Confucian intellectual spirit challenged the authorities. This was not surprising because Confucianism remained part of the official education system in Taiwan. Mainland China is a more difficult case for our purposes because when the pro-democracy movement was launched, Confucianism had already been banned for over thirty years and the only works available were negative evaluations written by those who had been strongly influenced by the May Fourth Movement. Despite these adverse conditions, an account of one key figure – Chen Ziming – still reveals a positive relation between Confucianism and democracy.

After Mao Zedong's numerous political campaigns ended in disaster, the younger generation of Chinese began to search for a better society. Democratic ideas were introduced as a possible alternative. From the Li-Yi-Zhe 李一哲 big-character poster in 1974 to the founding of the China Democracy Party in the late 1990s, many political actors have made important contributions to the progress of the democracy movement. Chen Ziming is among the best known.

Chen began his opposition activity in 1974 when he tried to build up a network among independent-minded young Chinese. One of his letters was intercepted, and he was arrested and sent to a labor camp. On the way to the camp, he joined the April fifth demonstration in Beijing in 1976. He was one of six representatives elected to negotiate with the government at that time. In 1978 he became a member of the editorial committee of *Beijing Spring*, the largest independent publication during the Democracy Wall Movement. Because of its influence, its name soon came to be identified with the entire movement. In 1980, Chen initiated the first free elections to be held in Beijing since 1949. He urged people to be the first independent candidates from eight of the fourteen schools where such elections were held, including Beijing University, Qinghua University, People's University, and Beijing Normal University. He himself was elected from the Chinese Academy of Sciences. In the mid-1980s, Chen established a group of independent organizations, including political, social, and economic research institutes, high-tech institutes, a credit union, foundations, a print factory, a newspaper, magazines, a publication group, a survey center, and correspondence schools. In 1989, he supported the student movement and tried to serve as a bridge between the students and the government. Because of his activities in 1989, as well as his continued participation in the democracy movement, he was sentenced to thirteen years in prison in 1991, the longest sentence of all the Beijing intellectuals. Once in prison, he struggled to improve the living conditions of his fellow prisoners. He was released on medical parole in 1994, and he once again began to initiate an open opposition movement. He helped to plan, draft, and organize a series of petitions calling for political reform. Although two of these petitions were accepted, Chen was again imprisoned in 1995 even though he was in poor health due to cancer.

Although the CCP banned all political ideas other than communism, Chen learned Confucianism on his own and came to appreciate the actual and potential role of Confucianism in the democracy movement. Based on his political experience and his understanding, he holds the following ideas about Confucianism.[25] First, he thinks that Confucianism was initiated as an independent school and developed into a semi-civil society. The contributions of Confucius and his three thousand students, as well as the contributions of the Neo-Confucians, all flourished when they were independent. Second, historically Confucianism was a source of morality and justice and provided checks and balances to absolute political power. The Confucians attached higher priority to the people than to the dynasty or the emperor. Confucian thought not only provided a standard and theoretical basis to evaluate political performance in accordance with the people's will and interest, but it was also

25 Letter to the author.

important in encouraging the Confucians to defend the people and to oppose the emperors and officials if they violated the will and interests of the people. Finally, Chen argues that Confucianism is an important source for the development and acceptance of democratic ideas among the Chinese people. Despite the fact that Chen grew up during the worst period for developing an appreciation of Confucianism, he still came to believe in the value of Confucianism for democratization.

IV CONCLUSION: CONFUCIANISM AND DEMOCRACY

The relationship between traditional Confucianism and democracy has long been the subject of heated controversy among Chinese political and intellectual elites. The core of the debate is whether or not the basic elements of Confucianism are consistent with democracy. In this essay, I have approached this issue in a new way, namely, through historical analysis, by determining whether in political history Confucianism has been supportive of democracy. It would have been difficult to conduct this research when the Chinese first began to launch their democratization movement due to lack of evidence; but now, after a century of political struggles, many cases can help us evaluate competing claims. I have tried to point to several influential cases from different periods of recent Chinese history to validate the assumption that, in practice, Confucianism can be supportive of democracy.

One might then ask why, despite such a strongly positive relationship between Confucianism and democratization in contemporary Chinese history, it is widely believed that Confucianism plays a negative role in democratization. We know that the most severe attack on Confucianism occurred during the May Fourth (1919) Movement. After the failure of two attempts to restore the imperial system in China (by Yuan Shikai and Zhang Xun respectively), a group of Chinese intellectuals attacked Confucianism because reactionary attempts had been made to try to establish Confucianism as a national religion to support the imperial system. These supporters of republican ideas believed that Confucianism had been a key factor leading to the failure of the Xinhai Revolution and the revival of the old political order. In order to establish democracy in China, the Chinese therefore had to fight attempts to restore official Confucianism. It is worth noting, however, that they did not typically reject Confucianism as a total package; what they rejected was the role of Confucianism as a national religion that would assist the restoration of the imperial system.

Unfortunately, these subtleties were lost on subsequent radical reformers and revolutionaries. The communists in particular took a very strong stand against Confucianism and came to oppose the entire tradition. After a century replete with disasters due to the totalizing tendencies of radical political forces, the role of Confucianism in pro-democracy struggles can now be recognized.

Let me put these arguments aside for a moment and ask why we should care about this whole intellectual exercise. In fact, there are good practical reasons for democrats to value the role of Confucianism in their struggles.

First, a Confucianism that is consistent with democracy can reduce the resistance and costs during a democratic transition. When Liang Qichao distinguished the *guoti* (國體) (polity) from the *zhengti* (政體) (regime), his real purpose was to emphasize the immutability of the *guoti* (國體). In his argument, reform of the *zhengti* (政體) was sufficient for the renaissance of China because on the one hand the government would be democratic, and on the other hand, changing the *guoti* (國體) would not result in a stable democracy but would likely result in disaster, as the base and identity of the entire nation might be destroyed during the transition. Similarly, Confucianism should not be abandoned but reformed because China is largely based on a Confucian cultural identity and destroying this identity might lead to civil war and reduce the likelihood of a transition to democracy. Sun Zhongshan, in his arguments about the applicability of democracy to China, also emphasized the indigenous conditions in China that were conducive to the newly emerging democratic republic. He argued that democracy cannot work if it is inconsistent with the basic situation in the country (*guoqing* 國情). This is why Sun tried to coordinate Confucianism with his democratic strategy. The tragedy of the failure of the first republic supports the prediction that a boldly radical democratization would lead to chaos and the disintegration of China. After forty years of chaos, the Chinese finally restored political order in 1949, but it was not the democratic experiment Liang and Sun had in mind.

Second, Confucianism can actually improve upon classical democracy; it is not merely a question of using Confucianism as a strategic means to promote democratic ideas and institutions. As early as the late 1910s, leading Chinese intellectuals identified problems with Western civilization and contemplated the possibility of using Confucianism to improve upon it. For example, Liang Qichao, in his famous "Reflective Mind in Europe," reported that Europe was in chaos and needed the Chinese to direct its development at a spiritual level. Zhang Taiyan made a similar argument. Sun Zhongshan advocated five branches of power to balance one another on the grounds that three were not sufficient. After World War II, when the West seemed to have overcome its deep crises, the Confucians developed new arguments for the East Asian region in particular. In an overall democratic political context, Confucianism can help to promote a moral sense and good values that help to elevate members of the community and to combat tendencies to narrow self-interest.

CHAPTER 4

MUTUAL HELP AND DEMOCRACY
IN KOREA

CHANG YUN-SHIK

I INTRODUCTION

The political scientist Juan Linz considers it a fact that "There is no alternative to democracy as a principle of legitimacy."[1] The Nobel Laureate economist Amartya Sen goes one step further in claiming that "this recognition of democracy as a universally relevant system, which moves in the direction of its acceptance as a universal value, is a major revolution in thinking, and one of the main contributions of the twentieth century."[2] He then reminds us that "we do not have to establish afresh, each time, whether such and such a country is 'fit for democracy'" (1999: 5). Such an observation is rather reassuring to those of us whose interest in democracy is more than academic. Democracy in South Korea is likely to stay. It is comforting to hear President Kim Dae Jung say, in response to Lee Kuan Yew's now famous (or infamous) claim "culture is destiny,"[3] that "democracy is destiny."[4]

It is the burden of this essay to demonstrate how Kim's claim is plausible despite a political climate which has not been congenial to democracy. In doing so, I will not, however, search for pointers in Korean traditional values that are compatible with democracy, as Sen insists that we do. Recently it has become fashionable among social scientists to reinterpret Asian values with the intention of looking for certain cultural features that are consonant with those values that underlie democratic political institutions. The trouble

---

1 Juan Linz, "Change and Continuity in the Nature of Contemporary Democracies," *Reexamining Democracy: Essays in Honor of Seymour Martin Lipset* (Newbury Park: Sage Publications, 1992), p. 182.
2 Amartya Sen, "Democracy as a Universal Value," *Journal of Democracy* Vol. 10, No. 3 (July 1999), p. 5.
3 See Fareed Zakaria, "Culture Is Destiny," *Foreign Affairs* Vol. 73, No. 2 (March/April 1994), pp. 109–126.
4 See Kim Dae Jung, "Is Culture Destiny: A Response to Lee Kuan Yew," *Foreign Affairs* Vol. 73, No. 6 (November/December 1994), pp. 189–194.

with this approach is that it fails to pay attention to those features that were, not long ago, blamed for the failure of democracy in Asia. If, indeed, there are elements in Asian values that may or may not promote democracy, we need to find out under what conditions they cease to be antagonistic to this new political ideal and system. Otherwise, we will end up saying that it is Asian values that explain the success of democracy when it succeeds and the failure of democracy when it fails. Instead, my attention will be focused on one specific Confucian ethic, the ethic of mutual help, which at first proved to be inimical to democracy and then slowly revised itself to fit the new form of polity through a dialectic process. I will first discuss how mutual help as a communal ethic was practiced in preindustrial hamlets and later developed into a personalist ethic in the industrial urban community,[5] and then I will analyze how the personalist ethic met the challenge of the new historical project of establishing a democratic political order, the goal that South Korea set out to achieve after three and a half decades of colonization.

II THE *HYANGYAK* (COMMUNITY COMPACT) AND MUTUAL HELP IN RURAL COMMUNITIES

The ethic of mutual help did not derive directly from the Confucian canons. It was Zhu Xi in the twelfth century who sought to incorporate the principle of voluntary cooperation into community structures.[6] He adopted the community compact put forward by Lu Dajun in the eleventh century as an instrument of achieving this goal and revised Lu's compact to incorporate his own principle of community building. The revised Lu-Zhu compact consisted of four main provisions: (1) mutual encouragement in the performance of worthy deeds, (2) mutual admonition in the correction of errors and failings, (3) reciprocal engagement in rites and customs, and (4) mutual aid in times of distress and misfortune (de Bary 1998: 59). De Bary summarizes the key aims of this compact as "the establishment of stable self-regulating local communities through the leadership of an educated moral elite that encouraged self-discipline, mutual respect and assistance, voluntary efforts, and joint ritual to provide for the needs of the community as a whole" (de Bary 1998: 63). "For many later scholars," de Bary further notes, "Zhu's advocacy of

---

5 While conflict, or more specifically class struggle, is firmly established as a useful conceptual apparatus for explaining the historical processes of social change, mutual help has hardly received the scholarly attention it rightly deserves. The notable exception is Prince Petr Kropotkin, *Mutual Aid: A Factor of Evolution* (New York: Alfred A. Knopf, 1925 [1902]). This essay intends to stress the significant role that mutual help played in the social history of the traditional communal order and in the recent history of democracy in Korea.
6 Wm. Theodore de Bary, *Asian Values and Human Rights: A Confucian Communitarian Perspective* (Cambridge, Mass.: Harvard University Press, 1998), p. 59.

the community compact had an importance at least equal to that of his philosophical ideas, and for historians too it has proved of major significance" (de Bary 1998: 58).

During the Chungchong reign (1506–1544), the Chosŏn dynasty (1392–1910) government initiated the community compact (*xiangyue* 鄉約 in Chinese or *hyangyak* in Korean) movement. It was widely felt, after more than a century of trial of politics by moral suasion, that the family alone was not sufficient to produce action according to the Confucian moral precept. The idea was to establish self-governing local communities with moral codes derived from the Lu-Zhu community compact, thereby more effectively teaching the local populace the Confucian ethic and supplementing the family moral codes with communal ethics as conceived by Zhu Xi.

After the launching of the *hyangyak* (鄉約) movement by the imperial government, many noted Korean Confucian scholars further revised the Lu-Zhu community compact to resonate with "the Korean situation." Local *yangban* (兩班) elites directly adopted either the Lu-Zhu version or one of the Korean versions in organizing their own communities into self-governing corporate structures. The central government recognized their leadership in the local community and in the moral education (or indoctrination) of peasants in accordance with Confucian teachings. This movement gradually spread throughout the country, and by the end of the eighteenth century, the idea of self-government under the leadership of local elites became firmly established.[7] Even in those hamlets without a resident *yangban* (兩班) family (or families), peasants organized themselves into corporate units by adopting one of the local codes or formulating one of their own in Korean (many peasants were not able to read and write in Chinese characters).

The mutual help ethic in Korea, however, did not begin with the launching of the *hyangyak* movement in the seventeenth century. We need to identify the two sets of mutual help ethic that had long been embedded in the peasant community and the gentry community. As owners or tenant cultivators, peasants developed the custom of labour exchange among neighbours within the hamlet (often known as the natural community) as was necessary in a small wet-rice farming community. For many centuries, farming remained relatively nonmechanized, based predominantly on animate sources of power such as humans and domesticated animals. The major source of labour for household farming was the human power available within the household. But the seasonal nature of farming was such that it made mutual help among neighbours for farm activities necessary. In fact, such obligatory

---

7 See Shikata Hiroshi, "Yicho Chitai Kyoyaku no Rekishi to Seikaku" (The History and Characteristics of Community Compact in Yi Dynasty Period), *Keijo Teikoku Daikaku Hogaku Nonshu* (Keijo Imperial University Essays on the Study of Law) Vol. 14, No. 4 (1943), pp. 421–496, at p. 438.

neighbourly cooperation and reliance had long been institutionalized in the hamlet in the custom of labour exchange called *pumasi*. Two or three neighbours agreed to help each other for individual household farming needs in a busy season. Person A came to neighbour B's house for, say, weeding and finished the work with B. Then, person B did the same job for A the next day. Neighbours also helped each other with any household work which required more than the human power in the house – be it constructing a house, re-thatching a roof, digging a well, mending a wall, or repairing farm tools. Each peasant also willingly shared what he owned with his neighbours. Borrowing farm tools and other implements was an everyday affair. On ceremonial occasions, which were not infrequent – weddings, funerals, memorial services for the dead, birthdays (especially the first and the sixtieth, among others), and the like – neighbours usually sent gifts or donations, and women came to the house to prepare for the ceremony. This informal ideology of mutual help growing out of the labour exchange practice was extended to other areas, becoming a basis for organizing an informal association known as *kye* (*qi* 契) (rotating interest association) which was designed to meet individual financial needs in a collective manner. The *kye* (*qi*) was a traditional device for ensuring against special or crisis situations that the individual cultivator or household might encounter.

Since the hamlet was of a small size where everyone knew everyone else and interacted with them on a daily basis, labour within the community was often mobilized community-wide. This entailed a form of hamlet-wide labour mobilization *dure*, the practice primarily designed for farming activities within the hamlet. Peasant residents of the hamlet then developed the practice of celebrating and recreating together on festival occasions related to the annual cycle of farm activities and the changing seasons – such as the New Year, May 5, June 7, and August 15 (by the lunar calendar). The hamlet residents were also united in efforts to protect themselves from unusual events, crises, or disasters – including droughts, floods, crop failures, and epidemics. Collectively they turned to the hamlet patron god and regularly offered sacrifices and prayers for the wealth and security of the hamlet as a whole. In the process of community building, peasants developed the skill to mobilize resources (grains or money) within the hamlet through organizing community-wide *kye* (*qi*) in order to finance community events. In short, the custom of mutual help through labour exchange became the basis of the solidarity of the village community and the formation of peasant culture.

Local *yangban* (gentry) elites established their own separate community on the basis of kinship bonds. At the beginning, the Chosŏn dynasty did not recognize the status privileges of the existing gentry class in recruiting for imperial administration, central as well as local. Recruitment was, in theory, based on merit, that is, passing the civil service examination. Any man, regardless

of his status, was able to write the examination. Early Chosŏn dynasty verit-
able records indicate that some commoners wrote and passed the examination,
thereby becoming government officials.[8] Local control was in the hands of the
magistrate, who was sent by the central government, with the help of the
middle status group known as *hyangri* (鄉吏) serving as yamen clerks. Local
gentry, whose elite status was established during the previous dynasty (Koryŏ
918–1392), was quick to respond to this policy. They organized themselves
into an identifiable group by establishing the *hyangan* (鄉案) (local register)
system in order to differentiate themselves from the *hyangri* (the status group
primarily responsible for clerical roles in local administrative offices), as most
of them had been *hyangri* themselves before they were elevated to the current
status of gentry toward the end of the Koryŏ period, and to protect themselves
from the potential tyranny of the local magistrate.

The *hyangan*, established at the *eup* (邑) (township) level (usually the seat
of the local magistrate office), was the local gentry register which listed
members of the gentry status group residing in surrounding areas. A man
would be qualified for inclusion in the *hyangan* if he had been born into a
family or married a woman from a family which had produced a civil servant
within three or four immediate generations. Those listed in the local register formed themselves into an organization known as *hyangso* (the office of
local councillors) with the purpose of assisting the local magistrate and
overseeing the yamen clerks. This organization, voluntarily formed by local
gentry, was later recognized as a semigovernment organ. Thus, local gentry,
as an organized political force, were sanctioned by the government as an elite
group with certain privileges but without pay. Over the years, as the size of
the gentry status group increased, they were dispersed into different areas,
with each group that had the same surname establishing itself as an exclusive community. Since residents of this community shared the same surname
with the descendants of a single ancestor, this community came to be known
as *dongchok maul* (同族마을) or *purak* (部落) (the same surname village). The
dongchok maul as a gentry community was another representative hamlet community, differentiating itself from the peasant commoner community.

As neighbours residing in the same community, members of the gentry
community, like those of the peasant community, exchanged gifts, rejoiced
together on happy occasions, shared suffering, and helped each other in death,
illness, and other personal crises. But unlike most of the peasant communities, they were more than neighbours as they formed a clan originating from

8 See Choe Yong-ho, "Commoners in Early Yi Dynasty Civil Examinations: An Aspect of
  Korean Social Structure, 1392–1910," *Journal of Asian Studies* Vol. 33, No. 4 (August 1974),
  pp. 611–631.

their ancestor who had founded the community. As members of the same clan, they cooperated with each other in revering their ancestors, especially the first ancestor and other eminent ones, by taking care of their graves, building a shrine where they could store ancestor tablets and regularly observe reverence ceremonies in their memory – both on death days and the New Year – and compiling the clan genealogy. All these ritual activities surrounding eminent ancestors were intended as a way of collectively claiming their gentry status.

The relative status ranking of each clan clustered in a same surname village was closely associated with the number of eminent ancestors (who passed the civil service examination and became government officials or noted scholars) that each clan had produced and the official rank in the central administration that they had attained. It therefore became equally important to produce sons to follow the path of their eminent ancestors. The gentry community as a whole considered itself responsible for the education of male children within the clan to prepare them for the national civil servant examination. Although a public school system existed, the gentry community provided education for the children by building their own schools and inviting teachers into the community. It was the collective responsibility of clan elders in the community to see to it that clan members were properly educated in and practiced the gentry (Confucian) way of life. They also cooperated with each other in retaining their gentry status by marrying off their daughters to men of the gentry elsewhere. Any individual family considering marrying down in status did so at the risk of being marginalized or alienated from others or eliminated from the community. Through marriage, a number of gentry clans were confederated into a powerful group. Local gentry houses, through this process of consolidating by the extension of the principle of kinship, developed themselves into a solidified status group, occupied a leadership position in the countryside (outside the hamlet), created a gentry elite culture to differentiate themselves from the peasant folk culture, and assumed the responsibility of establishing a new social order based on the Confucian moral precepts.

Equally important in collective efforts to uphold gentry status and way of life was the need to maintain a certain level of economic well-being of clan members. The community readily came to the aid of those families in financial need or facing a financial crisis. Consequently, there were fewer disparities in material wealth between families in the gentry community than in the peasant community.[9] Most of these collective projects were financed by the incomes from the corporate property in the form of land, forest, or moun-

---

9 Kim Tu-hon, *Hankuk kachok chedosa yonku* (A Study of the History of the Korean Family Institution) (Seoul, Korea: Seoul daehakkyo chulpanbu, 1969), p. 119.

tain or the funds raised through the clan *kye* (*qi*), as was also the case in peasant communities. Prior to the spread of the *hyangyak* system, many gentry communities had their compact modeled after the Lu-Zhu compact as it appeared in *Chuja Daechon* [朱子大全], stipulating membership criteria of the gentry, the code of conduct, et cetera (Kim 1969: 126). At the local level, they represented the great tradition of Confucianism as against the small tradition of the peasant culture.

As shown above, the mutual help ethic was firmly rooted in both the gentry and peasant commoner communities, and the newly imported community pact from Song China did not introduce a new moral code. It merely officially recognized both traditions, articulating, in Confucian terminology and with the moral authority of Zhu Xi, what had long been the rules of interpersonal relationships among peasants and augmenting this small tradition to the level of (or incorporating into it) the great Confucian tradition under the tutelage of the *yangban* elites.

Moreover, the *hyangyak* movement let to establishing a new autonomous community on the basis of the principle of voluntary cooperation that encompassed both *yangban* elites and peasant commoners. In this process, the former did, however, ensure their status superiority. Most Korean versions of the local community compact made a clear distinction between the gentry – the big man (*daein* 大人) – and the nongentry member – the small man (*soin* 小人) – and further stipulated a relationship between the two status groups. Any form of contempt or abuse of the superior by the inferior was not to be tolerated. The compact called for proper respect and decorum from yamen aides and commoners toward the gentry members. While all the residents became members of the *hyangyak* assembly, it was run by gentry members.

This added emphasis on status hierarchy and distinction reflects structural conditions that made full inter-status cooperation difficult. As landowners, *yangban* elites needed the labour of the peasants, many of whom cultivated their land as tenants, but they were only interested in increasing the amount of farm land, not in farming itself – that is, increasing productivity and the income therefrom. Management of the farm land they owned was left largely to a hired worker known as *marum*. Peasants were left on their own and enjoyed a degree of autonomy in managing their own communal affairs.

While subscribing to the egalitarian ideal of mutual help under the *hyangyak* system, in practice, inter–status-group cooperation remained rather limited, if not entirely one-sided. The gentry negotiated with the local administrative office about the amount of tax community members should pay in order to reduce the tax burden that commoners had to bear. The gentry also protected peasant members from the exploitation of the yamen aides. In the early Chosŏn period, before the *hyangyak* system was instituted, the gentry established and managed the *sachang* (社倉) or community granary system – designed by Zhu Xi – to make grain available to poor peasants in the community at a low price in the spring when it was in short supply, on the promise of reimbursement in the fall. Indeed, the local gentry had the power, influence, and material means to help the peasant in time of need and crisis, and some, under the influence of the *hyangyak* ideology, did so.

Peasants did not possess much in the way of resources other than their own labour, and they offered their labour willingly to their gentry neighbours even when they were not obliged to do so. But the gentry did not reciprocate the labour received from commoner neighbours with their own labour. While agriculture was considered the basis for building a prosperous kingdom (and some Confucian scholars authored books on farming), there was an inhibition among the gentry against engaging in labour activities. Only the peasants soiled their hands, so they believed. Being mostly landlords, they exchanged their land with peasant-tenants' labour. When they received labour from peasant neighbours in the labour exchange, they sent their slaves in return for the labour received. When there were weddings, funerals, birthday celebrations, or other big events in the gentry family, the peasant neighbours gave their help in the form of labour. The gentry family did not do the same for the peasant families. Instead, they supported community-wide affairs such as festivals and hamlet patron-god worship ceremonies by making donations in kind or in cash, but they did not directly participate in these activities.[10] Consequently, the principle of mutual help and cooperation became largely the intra–status-group ideal – gentry members helped each other as kin members while peasant members did likewise as neighbours. In the domain of moral and ritual conduct, the gentry taught the peasants Confucian ethics and punished their wrongdoings. The gentry did not allow the peasants to correct their own immoral behavior. The gentry considered themselves guardians of the community mores – based on Confucian teachings. The gentry's perception of commoner peasants was that they were ignorant and needed their teachings. Peasant commoners were constantly referred to as illiterate louts for whom the educated gentry would provide moral enlightenment.

III   MUTUAL HELP AND THE CITY

In the rural setting before industrialization, close personal ties or social bonds were formed largely between neighbours or kin members within the village community, rarely going beyond its boundaries because the physical boundaries of the small community more or less determined the extent of social

---

10 See Kim Taek-Kyu, *Ssichok burak ui kuchoyŏnku* (A Study of a Same Surname Village) (Seoul, Korea: Ilchokak, 1979).

interaction.[11] In the city in industrial Korea, by contrast, where it is impossible to know personally all the people with whom one interacts, Koreans tend to form personal networks through many channels. Kinship ties continue to play an important role in network formation within a city or in linking clan members residing in the city to those remaining in the same surname village. These kinship groups established in the cities may be considered an extended kinship network, the roots of which go back to the rural village where it began. But the urban community also provides people with numerous opportunities to meet, interact, make friends or acquaintances, or establish enduring personal relationships beyond the confines of neighbourhood and kinship organizations – schools, workplaces, training centres, churches, and prisons.

With the disappearance of the traditional status distinction, social bonds of mutual obligation and trust that existed in the rural community among neighbours may be built into both horizontal (between friends, between neighbours, between classmates) and vertical relations (between teachers and students, between employers and employees, and between seniors and juniors in the same school). Thus the ethic of mutual help that developed originally as a neighbourhood or communal ethic becomes the code of conduct among a group of selected persons who are closely tied to each other through blood relationship or a long period of acquaintance. It becomes a network ethic. In the city, the mode of approach to others clearly differentiates strangers from friends and acquaintances. Thus, the traditional communal ethic of mutual help becomes a specific person-oriented ethic or a personalist ethic.

Unlike in the small hamlet community, in the cities, friends and acquaintances do not necessarily live in the same neighbourhood and work at the same place. They therefore make deliberate efforts to maintain their bonds through talking to each other on the phone; exchanging messages; meeting for tea, meals, or drinks; going fishing, hiking, or sight-seeing; gift giving on the occasions of *myongchol* – New Year's day (both lunar and Western calendar), August the Full Moon (August 15 by the lunar calendar), birthdays, marriages, and funerals – or meeting regularly (once a month) on various pretenses.

City residents may withdraw from this circle if they so wish. But the informal personal relationship of bondage, mutual trust, and reciprocal obligation and indebtedness is widely valued in and of itself, and it is expected to be maintained even at the expense of self-interest. An act which places one in debt to others is expected to be reciprocated. Failure to do so, if continued,

11 This section expands the concept of the personalist ethic developed in my "The Personalist Ethic and the Market in Korea," *Comparative Studies in Society and History* Vol. 33, No. 1 (January 1991), pp. 106–129.

may be interpreted as an act of severing ties. But the art of reciprocating a favour is to return it in a spontaneous way rather than in a way calculated to repay what one owes. One does not pay off a personal debt completely, as one does when owing money – a social bond once established is not supposed to be terminated.

Furthermore, in the close relationship of personal bonds, one is encouraged to seek out advice from others. Not to do so is very likely to give offence. In other words, there is a mutual expectation to consult on matters that might, in another cultural context, say in Canada, be considered entirely private. In Canada, minding one's own business is condoned as much as minding other people's business is frowned upon. In Korea, failure to involve one's close friend in making a decision on an important personal matter, whether getting married or divorced, buying a car, or going abroad, may easily offend. Individualism is a concept imported from the West and carries pejorative overtones of selfishness. In interpersonal relations based on the rule of mutual obligation, one acts according to one's own will, but also according to that of others, who will assume responsibility for acts not of their own doing. A person who gave advice to his friend may be blamed should it turn out to be unwise. A prime minister may declare that a political decision he has just made is partly an expression of his own will and partly the will of others. The binding forces of personalism make disengagement from these relationships difficult, for that would violate the ethic of mutual obligation.

In a personalistic relationship, favours exchanged may not be separated from the persons involved – one party cannot be a means to the other for achieving the latter's ends. They always interact with each other as complete persons, not partial persons. A person is, in the words of the anthropologist Robert Redfield, "myself in another form, his qualities and values are inherent in him, and his significance for me is not merely one of utility."[12]

To emphasize human ties is to know *uiri* (義理), the concept more widely known as *giri* in Japanese. To say that a person does not know *uiri* is a negative reflection on his personality. Within the *uiri* network of interpersonal relationships, emphasis on the person is likely to override impersonal concerns of the wider world – formal rules, ideology, the public interest and welfare, or patriotism – should there be a conflict between the two. Shifting loyalty from the person to nonpersonal concerns does not take place easily. Thus the maintenance of interpersonal ties often becomes an end in itself.

The personalist relation is characterized as diffuse, the contractual relation as specific. In the latter, activities, considerations, rights, obligations, or

---

12 Robert Redfield, "The Folk Society," *American Journal of Sociology* Vol. 52, No. 4 (January 1947), p. 301.

performances covered within it tend to be precisely defined and delimited, whereas in the former, they are not. In the personalistic relationship, unlike the contractual one, the element of affectivity looms large. Both parties tend to be sensitive to each other's feelings in their interactions. One risks a great deal in ignoring the other's feelings for impersonal ends. This tendency to be susceptible to human feelings (*inchong e yakhada*) develops into a tendency to share others' feelings or emotions – anger, hate, fear, love, or pity.

This urban personal network continues to flourish not only as a preserve of the traditional norm of mutual help but also in clear appreciation of its economic and status implications. To know someone well implies a mutual personal obligation. The larger the number of persons known personally, the greater is one's personal influence and prestige.[13] In urban life, an influential friend, relative, or acquaintance frequently becomes a means to material benefits, for "getting around" or "getting ahead." Such influence, through a multitude of friendships, facilitates life in the city, making it easier to avoid red tape in dealing with a government office, to get a loan from a bank, and to find a good job or to be promoted ahead of others. Sociologists now recognize the economic implications of personal or affective networks as social capital.[14] When social capital involves luminaries, it also becomes symbolic capital, as Pierre Bourdieu calls it, in that the connection bestows honour and unofficial social ranking which gives advantage in pursuing political or economic ends.

Urban Koreans are increasingly making efforts to organize people on the grounds that they are related through a shared lineage, or have attended the same school or short-term training program, come from the same town or province, or served three years in the army in the same company. Friendship circles formed by members of the same school continue to survive after graduation as alumni associations. In some circles, notably business and politics, connections, ties, and bonds are deliberately established through marriage. Two executive directors of big corporations or banks become more than business partners when they become in-laws with their children tying the knot. Various reasons can be found for creating a new bond. It is said that the major aim of such gatherings is to maintain solidarity, and yet one can always count on others from within the same group or association to promote one's personal interests. In this utilitarian context, an elaborate principle of reciprocity develops within the personal network. Any help rendered by one to another is regarded as a personal favour, to be appreciated and at some future time reciprocated. If one is without personal connections that could

13 Ronald P. Dore, *City Life in Japan* (Berkeley: University of California Press, 1958), p. 259.
14 See James S. Coleman, "Social Capital in the Creation of Human Capital," *American Journal of Sociology* Vol. 94, Supplement, pp. S95–S120.

facilitate one's affairs, one can borrow them through friends or acquaintances, as long as one can pay for the borrowed favour. Thus the personalism that originates from the small rural community continues to prevail in the city, and the urban Korean is neither free from personal ties nor completely alienated from others.

How then did the personalist ethic as it developed in the city from the traditional mutual help ethic practiced in the hamlets cope with the democratization process? More succinctly, how did personalism interact with constitutionalism? We now turn to this question.

IV THE PERSONALIST ETHIC AND DEMOCRACY

In 1948, the newly established Republic of Korea adopted a constitution.[15] Although this first ever democratic constitution has been criticized for conferring excessive powers on the executive office, it was a remarkable (almost revolutionary) document in that it provided not only a framework for democratic political order but also a blueprint for a new society.

The constitution furnished and guaranteed each individual a set of rights, making each former imperial subject a full-fledged citizen of the new republic. These rights included the right to participate in the political process or to exercise political power, the right to express differing political opinions and to organize political opinions through political parties, the right to one's own corporate property, freedom to change residence, freedom of speech, freedom of assembly, freedom of belief, the right to education, the equality of men and women, basic labour rights, and equality before the law. The constitution also provided institutional mechanisms to safeguard the individual rights and liberties of citizens, including a popularly elected legislature, a president elected indirectly by the legislature and independent judiciary, separate central and local administrations, and a competitive party system. Finally, it urged acceptance of a new set of values under the label "constitutionalism," providing a moral basis for conferring those individual rights and freedoms mentioned above to all citizens and establishing new political institutions, centered on individual freedom, equality, legalism (or the rule of law), human rights, social justice, and universalism.

The birth of a democratic government in Korea was not the outcome of a long evolutionary process of political change. It came as a legacy of the Western occupied forces that replaced the imperial colonial authorities. The newly adopted government system represented the liberal tradition of

---

15 This section is partly based on my "Confucius Meets John Locke: Constitutionalism and Personalism and Dialectics of South Korean Democracy," in Sang-Oak Lee and Duck-Soo Park (eds.), *Perspectives on Korea* (Sydney: Wild Peony, 1998), pp. 585–608.

the West, directly challenging the virtues and legitimacy of the dynastic and colonial political order, and demanding a radical break with the past. The kind of political life or political culture that a democratic polity required was not the one to which Koreans were accustomed. The new political institutions provided by the constitution and the values embodied in it stood in sharp contrast to those of the Chosŏn dynasty and colonial Korea under Japanese rule. But traditional norms molded the democratic political process. In the absence of established constitutional norms, democracy first became Koreanized rather than Korea becoming democratized. In describing this process, we will focus on the fact that while constitutional norms tend to emphasize the supremacy of the rule over the person, Korean traditional norms tend to be predominantly person oriented, as indicated above.

The main stumbling block to the democratization of Korea was the executive office, the incumbent of which was elected by the people. It has been occupied by three autocratic personalities who used it to build their personal power bases within the democratic political system for the continuation of authoritarian rule.

Syngman Rhee, the first president elected by the legislature, created a government which was almost completely dominated by the executive office and which he ran for ten years until a student uprising brought it to an abrupt end. Park Chung Hee, who came to power through a coup d'état, revived and expanded Rhee's formula and ruled the country for eighteen years until he was gunned down by Kim Jae-Kyu, his right-hand man, the director of the Korean Central Intelligence Agency. Chun Doo Hwan inherited Park's despotic government after he successfully staged yet another coup d'état, and he stayed in power for seven years. Initially Chun appeared to have every intention of staying beyond the first term (in spite of his promise of not seeking a second term), but he succumbed to the pressure of organized opposition forces and was apparently persuaded by his colleagues within the ruling party to honour his pledge, thereby making a peaceful succession of power possible. Altogether, nine-tenths of the four decades of the republican era have been under three authoritarian regimes, with two brief democratic interludes brought about by the downfall of two of the presidents. For the purpose of analysis, the development of the authoritarian regime within a democratic political framework will be understood as the process of a Caesarian leader coming to dominate parliamentary politics.

Over the years, each president fortified his elected position and authority by staffing his own executive office, cabinet, administrative offices, police, security forces, and the military from personal circles of close kin members, friends, and acquaintances. When he recruited from beyond personal circles, appointees were carefully screened and their loyalty was ensured. Once in office, their activities were monitored and anyone suspected of disloyalty was dismissed under one pretext or another, while those who remained unconditionally loyal were handsomely rewarded with presidential favours in the form of job guarantees within elite circles, career progress, and wealth.

Park also created the Central Intelligence Agency. As the most powerful intelligence and investigation agency, with an enormous extralegal authority and financial resources, the Korean CIA undertook a loyalty check which involved the screening of all major political figures and high-ranking government employees, eliminating anti-Park elements within and without the power circle. The Korean Central Intelligence Agency served as the eyes and ears of Park and became the government organ most feared by the people. After the fall of Park, Chun replaced the KCIA with the Agency of National Safety Planning, which more or less performed the same function as its predecessor.

Each of the three authoritarian presidents formed his own party as he moved into the executive office. The ruling party consisted of those people and organizations who pledged undivided loyalty to the president as a person, not to his political philosophy or ideology (if he had any). High-ranking party members were recruited more or less in the same way the president selected his personal aides in the offices surrounding him. They were not fee-paying members. In Korea, the political party recruitment of fee-paying members has never been institutionalized. The executive office was financially responsible for managing party headquarters offices and the personal welfare of high-ranking officials. The president held the final authority to nominate party members for National Assembly seats and provided a good portion of campaign funds. He then fully utilized his executive authority and influence to help elect the party nominees to the National Assembly. The ruling party virtually became an extension of the executive office. Party members aspiring to be members of the National Assembly needed the approval and assistance of the executive office, and the president needed his party candidates to get reelected in order to control the National Assembly.

With the support of loyalists and control of resources – arms; treasury; information; and judicial, security, and emergency power – the executive office established a firm grip over the legislature through the ruling party. The president fully utilized his executive authority and influence to help elect his party's nominees to the National Assembly in order for the ruling party to control the majority of seats. Should he fail to achieve this goal, the president used his executive power to persuade some opposition party or independent National Assembly members to join his party by offering rewards or threatening to reveal whatever past wrongdoings his security officers could uncover. Once the ruling party members formed a majority force in the

National Assembly, given the control the president had over them, the legislature was under his thumb. If the executive did not concur with the assembly, the ruling party assembly members would have to defer in a demonstration of loyalty to the president. Failure to do so was regarded as an act of defiance of the executive authority and would result in dismissal from the party. Those assembly members seeking reelection at the next election thus risked their nomination and careers should they decline to follow presidential instructions. The ruling party became "built in voting machines."[16] The assembly was reduced to a "marginal" or "minimal" legislature.[17] With the National Assembly dominated by the ruling party members, the legislature's checks on the executive were thus rendered ineffective, and the legislative initiative was usurped by the administrative office.

Park, however, went a little further in strengthening his presidential power. In 1972, he suspended the legislature and ruled through the Emergency Council of State, issuing decrees that had the effect of law. He then revised the constitution to reorganize the structure of the government to solidify his position within it. Under the new constitution, the president was not elected by the people but by a newly introduced National Council for Unification (NCU) which dealt with all issues of unification. The chairman of the NCU, who is the incumbent president, nominates its fifty-member steering committee, which then, under an acting chairman whom it selects itself, conducts the election of the next president. The president so elected appoints one-third of the National Assembly with the approval of the NCU. In sum, the downgrading of the National Assembly in the new constitution reduced party politics to insignificance. Indeed, the president could dissolve political parties. When Park died, Chun Doo Hwan was elected president by the NCU and inherited and ran for seven years the new government system that Park had built.

If the assembly became the maid of the "power" (executive), the judicial branch of the government never had had any constitutional autonomy in its operation. Initially, the president appointed a chief justice with National Assembly approval, and judges' appointments were limited to ten years, with renewals subject to executive review. Subsequent revisions reduced the chief justice's term of office to ten years in 1962, six years in 1972, and five years in 1980, limiting it to one term only. Since the president controlled the legislature through his party, assembly approval of the president's appointment of judges became a mere formality. Executive office control over the appoint-

16 Gregory Henderson, *Korea: The Politics of the Vortex* (Cambridge, Mass.: Harvard University Press, 1968), p. 293.
17 Kim Ho-Chin, *Hankuk chongchi checheron* (A Discourse on the Korean Political System) (Seoul: Pakyongsa, 1990), p. 366.

ment of the top officials of the judicial branch gradually resulted in the ascendancy of the administration over the judicial branch. The former gradually came to have the power to determine the appointment, firing, promotion, transfer, and demotion of judicial officials, which translated into the subjugation of the judiciary by the executive and administrative power. The administration came to dominate the criminal justice system. Rarely were requests of arrest by the police and prosecutor turned down by public judges. Prison terms were usually determined for "political" cases (related to violation of the Anticommunism Law, the National Security Law) by the Blue House (the presidential mansion). Judges were not expected to take an independent stance on trials of political dissidents critical of the government.

In the Fifth Republic under Chun Doo Hwan, a new system was introduced in order to avoid any possible conflict between the judiciary and the administrative branch. This involved sending judges over to the presidential and intelligence offices. The intention was to have the judges understand the mood of the administration, the proper assessment of which would help the judiciary not to offend the administration in handling political cases. The administration also had secret agents stationed in the courthouses, monitoring and reporting on the trial process. Their reports on the performance of individual judges during the trials of important political cases served as a basis for the judges' promotions or demotions.

Once the legislature and judiciary were brought under the control of the executive office, the government came to be largely identified with the administrative bureaucracy, with the executive office at the top. The legislature failed to represent the masses of people, and the judiciary failed to defend those dissidents who fought to regain their constitutional rights. The president and his administration came to loom large in the government process, with the president becoming a virtual despot within the democratic (or quasi-democratic) framework. It was the birth of administrative despotism.[18]

Two of the incumbents of the executive office, Syngman Rhee and Park Chung Hee, built a personal network consisting of their personal followers within the government structure and successfully distributed patronage and personal executive favours for their followers' loyalty in such a way as to perpetuate their own power. They amended the constitution to allow them, first, to serve a third term and then to stay in office without term. The incumbent of the executive office thus successfully personalised the parliamentary process and emerged as a most formidable anticonstitutional force, undermining the democratic process.

18 See Alexis de Tocqueville, *Democracy in America* (The Henry Reeve Text as Revised by Francis Bowen, Now Further Corrected and Edited by Phillips Bradley), Volume II (New York: Alfred A. Knopf, 1948 [1840]), pp. 316–321.

V MUTUAL HELP AND DEMOCRATIZATION

Despotic regime building eliminated the majority of citizens from the political process, blocked all venues through which public opinion could be channeled, and thereby deprived citizens of many of their constitutional rights, thus creating discontent. Discontent ultimately turned into dissension and opposition to the government. Park Chung Hee and Chun Doo Hwan offered the mandate of development combined with "Korean-style democracy" as a rationalization for the authoritarianism of the regime, yet they did not gain popular support. Discontent increased gradually, and dissension and political opposition to the government eventually became widespread and coalesced into a growing antigovernment force.

Antigovernment groups first sprang up separately in reaction to the oppressive government and then consolidated their forces into a people's force strong enough to bring down the government. This happened in 1959 (the April Nineteenth student uprising), 1979 (the Bu-Ma struggle – assassination of Park Chung Hee by Kim Jae-Kyu), and 1987 (the June resistance).

The struggle to regain their lost constitutional rights also helped the people to appreciate and defend the virtues of constitutional democracy of which they had little understanding when it was first bestowed upon them, and to internalize democratic norms and values. As they fought for democracy, they also came to realize the weaknesses of the traditional person-oriented norm which had provided a moral basis for the authoritarian regime. Democracy or constitutionalism as a political ideology began to assume a new moral authority among the antigovernment forces. As the government refused to accommodate the antigovernment forces, tension between the two increased, threatening the legitimacy of the authoritarian system. The dialectic of democracy was underway.

What lay behind these movements were the opposition forces that grew up during the despotic era. Though opposition within the government was supposed to have been institutionalized under the two-party system, the opposition parties had not been able to effectively challenge the authoritarian president. More outright political opposition was of an extra-parliamentary nature, with students and dissident Christian church leaders forming the major opposition forces against the undemocratic regime.

University students have traditionally been a source of political opposition in modern Korea. Frustrated and angered by the antidemocratic behaviour of the president and his administration, especially by the fraudulent rigging of the presidential election in 1960, students took to the street. They led a nationwide demonstration which was later joined by their mentors and ordinary citizens and supported by the army and the United States, eventually leading to the overthrow of Rhee's government and paving the way for a new democratic regime. This revolutionary outcome enabled students to redefine their social task. They identified themselves closely with the new democratic Korea and assumed responsibility for its future, expressing their distrust of the adult generation whom they tended to view as representing traditional past practices of corruption, opportunism, and defeatism. Students thus rapidly established themselves as a powerful opposition force against the government and as informed critics of the society in general, remaining so throughout the despotic era.

In their struggle for democracy under the Park (1961–1979) and Chun (1980–1987) regimes, students engaged in two battles against the government. First they fought for democracy and later they turned against the system of capitalist economy. In the early period, student activists were mainly concerned with such political issues as the guarantee of freedom of the press and of dissent; release of jailed political dissidents; freedom to act according to one's conscience; restoration of the human rights of political prisoners; an end to torture, surveillance, political oppression, and the politics of intelligence; an end to the suppression of political dissidents and student activists under the National Security Law and the Anticommunism Law; and the disbanding of the Central Intelligence Agency (or the Agency of National Safety Planning). After the establishment of the Yushin (維新) regime, they turned to economic issues generated by the capitalist economy. The Park government had earlier adopted its development policy of economic growth through an increase of trade volume and by the importation of foreign capital. To make this plan work, the government had to keep industrial wages and the price of grain low. Ultimately this policy had the effect of helping a small number of the economic elite to amass wealth, while keeping the urban industrial workers and rural farmers in poverty and misery. Students regarded the current system as essentially "antipeople." Furthermore, they thought that, as it was absorbed into the world economy, the national economy was becoming increasingly dependent – reliant on foreign capital – and that the domestic market had been forced to open up to foreign products under the pressure of the trade protectionism of advanced industrialized countries. They thought that South Korea had thus turned into a branch office of the giant firms of Japan and the United States; that South Korea became a puppet regime of the United States, and South Korea was a testing ground for nuclear weapons; that military ties with the allied forces enabled the United States to continue to command the Korean army, while Korea served as a dumping ground for American goods; that South Korea was not a liberated country but an American colony; that the United States still held firm control over South Korea through its military presence; and that "liberation" from the

United States was a step toward unification since the continuing American occupation of South Korea was a barrier to unification. Characterization of the Yushin and Chun regimes as such gave the student movement a clearly defined set of goals. They advocated that the current regime be overthrown and a new society established that was democratic (*minchu*) (*minzhu* 民主), nationalistic (*minchok* 民族), and people (*minchung* 民衆)-oriented. This *sammin* (three *min* 三民) idea became a guiding principle of the student movement in the 1980s. Such articulation of the goals of the student movement with distinctly ideological overtones based on the "scientific understanding" of the structure and dynamics of the current political and economic establishment meant that the student movement was evolving slowly into an organized movement.

Student activists were joined by dissident church leaders who represented the liberal segment of both Protestant and Catholic church communities. Both groups agreed that the revival of democracy meant the liberation of the people. They advanced their conviction that liberal democracy was the best system for the realization of individual freedom and social justice. For two decades – the 1970s and 1980s – the dissident church leaders carried on their struggle for democracy, campaigning against the authoritarian regime. They dealt with numerous political issues: subordination of the Korean economy to Japan and the United States, recovery of a democratic order, respect for human and civic rights, press freedom, freedom on campus, release of arrested students and political prisoners, guarantee of religious freedom, withdrawal of the Yushin constitution and revision of the constitution through a national election, an end to police investigations on campus, guarantee of the minimum wage and the social welfare of industrial workers, withdrawal of emergency decrees, autonomy of the judiciary branches, guarantee of the three labour rights, ending the autocratic regime, abolition of unpopular laws such as the National Security Law, and abolition of torture.[19] They also took initiatives in organizing civilian antigovernment groups in which they played a key role, readily supported other dissident groups or organizations, and joined them in various antigovernment activities such as collecting one million signatures for the petition to demand revision in the constitution, boycotting the referendum for the Yushin constitution, forming a ballot inspection group in the thirteenth National Assembly election (1988), and offering their churches or cathedrals as places to hold meetings, prayers, vigils, fasts, and sit-ins. Their efforts to publicly oppose the regime may not have accomplished their professed objectives, but they were important in that

---

19 See Yi Su-On, "70 nyondae'ui bancheche moksadul" (Anti-Establishment Pastors in the 1970s), *Sindong-A*, September 1984, pp. 168–193.

while severe measures of government oppression silenced almost all opposition forces, the dissident church leaders, together with student activists, continued to express their displeasure at the weakening and attempted extinguishment of democracy.

One should bear in mind that the democratization movement described above was carried out under Emergency Decrees 1 and 2 which prohibited any act which negated, opposed, distorted, or criticized the (Yushin) constitution and any act demanding, proposing, or requesting revision of the constitution. The dissident church leaders' role was doubly important since the press had already been silenced and was colluding with the government. They took it upon themselves to inform the people of government wrongdoings and corruption. They were determined to disclose publicly what the government did not want people to know. More importantly, in the eyes of the public, the church leaders represented an opposition force at the forefront of the struggle for democracy. They came to be accepted as a legitimate force in the political process. As the involvement of the church leaders in the democracy movement continued, their focus gradually came to rest on the human rights issue. In 1973, the National Christian Council of Korea issued the "Human Rights Declaration" in which the concept of human rights was clarified and the aims of the anticipated human rights movement were spelled out. Human rights were construed as individual autonomy. Autonomy is bestowed on man by the Creator; God created men and women according to his image and granted them the right to live on their own with what nature supplies; thus the autonomy of the individual is a God-given right; depriving the basic right of living and autonomy by the authority is considered a betrayal of God's will; therefore, Christ's church must oppose the secular authoritarian power that violates human rights. The dissident church leaders considered it their duty to be on the side of the oppressed and to help them to recover their human rights.

The student-church nexus gradually became a rallying point for opposition forces. Subsequently other citizens expressed their support for the movement by organizing anti-authoritarian-regime groups or joining the many demonstrations organized by the students and church leaders. The opposition forces thus formed continued to struggle for the installment of real democracy in South Korea until the end of Chun's regime. In 1987, Chun's heir apparent, Roh Tae Woo, staged a quiet coup within the ruling party, accepted the opposition New Democratic Party's demands for constitutional revision and direct presidential election, and further promised democratic reforms – a promise which came to be known as the June Twenty-Ninth Announcement.

The rise of administrative despotism described above was attributed to the personalist ethic that permeated those responsible for running the government. How, then, in this personalist society, did the democratic ideal find such a strong following, so much so that in the end the opposition forces prevailed? There is no doubt that the two dissident groups, students and church leaders, and those who joined them, came to value the virtues of the new political philosophy and institutions, committed themselves to them, and were determined to fight for them. This process of the democratization movement as a struggle for an ideology has now been well documented. What is not well known, however, is how this process actually came about. Was it merely ideology that became a driving force behind student activism? Or did the personalist ethic, in some way, play a role? The *International Herald Tribune* of June 21–22, 1986, carried an article which described South Korean university student radical activists. It reads as follows: "Radical thought is passed on in clandestine 'study circles,' groups of students who may come from the same high school or hometown or church. These study circles . . . served as the basic organizational unit for demonstrations and other protests" (quoted in Coleman 1988: S99). Members of a study circle, as the reporter points out, had been friends since high school days or before and formed friendship circles or became friends at the university partly because they shared the same interests. The label "study circle" is given to the group primarily because its members read and discussed together books of their choice in accordance with their ideological orientations and in order to establish a theoretical rationale for their involvement in radical student movements. Commitment to a radical political ideology and action is usually a group decision arrived at by mutual consultation, persuasion, encouragement, and criticism within a circle of close friends. They became more united when they took political action such as engaging in street demonstrations and occupations of targeted buildings (for example, a United States Information Office office or university administration building) and joining factory workers or farm workers in their protest actions. When one of the circle members got into trouble with the law because of his or her political action, others helped the member find a place to hide. A student activist serving a jail term could rely on his circle friends to visit him, to provide what he needed in his cell, and to fulfil his duties outside of the jail which he could not attend to. They felt strongly obliged to help, support, encourage, and protect each other in order to promote their political goal. A sense of obligation to one's friend became an effective driving force within student circles.[20] The same mutual help ethic facilitated and sustained the political actions of those dissident

20 I am indebted to Professor Ronald Dore for this point. See Ronald P. Dore, "Modern Cooperatives in Traditional Communities," in Peter Worsely (ed.), *Two Blades of Grass* (Manchester: Manchester University Press, 1971).

church leaders who carried out "the democracy struggle" under the despotic regime.[21]

VI DEMOCRATIC CONSOLIDATION AND KOREAN DEMOCRACY

Legal political opposition to the government institutionalizes conflict. But when it is restricted and ineffectual, political opposition becomes extra-parliamentary and sometimes illegal. The government uses its legal author-ity to constrain extra-parliamentary opposition, whereas the opposition justifies its activities on the moral and ideological ground that its aim is to restore democracy, which the government undermined despite its official endorsement. Dissidents refuse to accept the legal authority of the govern-ment to counter their "antigovernment" activities on this very moral ground. The government relies heavily on physical force and violence in countering extra-parliamentary opposition, but essentially it is on rather weak ground. This fact not only gives the opposition psychological strength but also helps it to gain growing support.

The extra-parliamentary opposition breeds further political opposition. Dissidents criticize, denounce, and protest against the government for its undemocratic actions; demand a constitutional amendment; or even urge that the president step down, all at the risk of suffering physical harm, arrest, incarceration, or even death. Many dissidents willingly give their lives for the cause of the opposition movement. Under the authoritarian regime, opposi-tion produces victims. Victimization of dissidents, an unavoidable feature of political opposition under an authoritarian regime, becomes an additional cause of opposition. At the same time it enhances the commitment of sur-vivors to the opposition movement.

The authoritarian regime failed to stand on a firm ideological or moral basis and countered the antigovernment elements with sheer force. Conse-quently, the opposition gained moral superiority by opposing an undemoc-ratic government, which, ironically, does not denounce its commitment to a democratic ideal. This moral superiority of the opposition made it a formi-dable force in the continuing struggle for democracy.

But political opposition requires a strong commitment, and the govern-ment constantly tried to co-opt the opposition. Many opposition activists suc-cumbed to this temptation. The government used various means — money, sex, government positions, overseas trips, et cetera. The opposition had to

21 See Hankuk kitokkyo kyohoe hyopǔihoe, 1970 nyondae minchuhwa undong (The Democra-tization Movement in the 1970s) (Seoul: Hankkuk kitokkyo kyohoe hyopǔihoe, 1987), Vols. 1–5.

battle temptation in order to continue its opposition activities. In Korea, personal affinity easily justifies the betrayal of an abstract ideology or principle to which one is committed. Some opposition members succumbed to the temptation but others warded it off. There was little tangible reward for maintaining the struggle.

Student activists and dissident church leaders criticized those who hesitated to join them in opposing the government and urged them to do so. Some did, and others did not. Those who did not join the dissidents stood on the other side of the democracy campaign. The opposition movement put pressure on citizens to decide whether they were for or against democracy. Anti- and pro-government forces were sharply divided, and tension and antagonism between the two sides escalated, forcing the system to respond.

Political opposition within a democratic political framework, whether parliamentary or extra-parliamentary, legal or illegal, has now firmly established a moral basis and developed inner mechanisms of continuity, taking root in a culture that was originally hostile to the idea. It is increasingly accepted as a feature of the South Korean political system.

Political opposition also socializes those who oppose the government into a democratic political culture. By opposing the government's undemocratic actions, the opposition promotes democracy by urging struggles on behalf of constitutional rights arbitrarily denied by the government. Political opposition, therefore, is an exercise in democracy.

Roh's announcement of democratic reform consisted of eight points: granting amnesty to the opposition party leader Kim Dae Jung and reinstating his civil rights; release of political prisoners; a direct presidential election within a year; revision of the presidential election law; replacement of the infamous Basis Laws on the press with a more democratic regulation; establishment of local assemblies and assurance of the autonomy of the university in particular and the educational process in general; guarantee of freedom of political parties; introduction of radical social purification plans. Accepting most of the requests made by the opposition party, Roh adopted this reform as a way of unlocking the political stalemate. Furthermore, it was a way of recognizing the opposition forces and could be viewed as a step toward the institutionalization of democracy.[22]

Democratization, indeed, is steadily taking place in a personalistic political climate. Then, what type of democracy is emerging in South Korea? It is difficult to predict exactly what form the South Korean political system will crystalize into, as it is currently going through waves of reform in response

22 See Victor M. Perez-Diaz, *The Return of Civil Society: The Emergence of Democratic Spain* (Cambridge, Mass.: Harvard University Press, 1993), pp. 54–107.

to changing needs over time and criticisms of the way it is being practiced. But, given the general direction it is going, one can identify some main features of South Korean democracy. At the risk of oversimplification, I will present them in outline fashion.

1. Who will become the government elites?

The democratic government system consists largely of two types of elites, those who are elected by the people through free voting and those who are recruited directly by the administrative offices through examinations. The former represent the will of the people as the president and national assemblymen and make the government a democratic institution. The relationship between the two types of elites determine the form of democratic governance.

(a) The president and the national assemblymen

(a-i)   Elected elites. Political parties are largely responsible for providing elected officials. The central party located in the capital grooms candidates for the executive office and the district party candidates for National Assembly seats.

The central party. The central party is formed of members who seek a political career in the National Assembly and administrative offices and are attracted to leaders of a party with notable characters, not because of the political doctrine or policy lines the party adopts, but because of personal ties – friendship, kinship, school and regional connections, and others. It tends to be divided into factions of personal allegiance, each faction usually identified with the name of its leader. Competition for the leadership often results in a split in the party. Rarely does a political party last more than two national or presidential elections. Personal loyalty to a leader tends to persist through the formation of a party to its breakup.[23] The party leader and the faction leader are responsible for their supporters' career promotions, a portion of campaign expenses, and sometimes living expenses. The leader tends to be possessive of his party and to give it a strong personal stamp. Such a tendency makes the party a highly centralized and hierarchical organization which is unable to develop a wider subscription among lay citizens.

23 Han Y. C., Sejin Kim, and Chang Hyun Cho (eds.), "Political Parties and Elections in South Korea," *Government and Politics of Korea* (Silver Spring, Md.: The Research Institute on Korean Affairs, 1972), p. 133.

(a-ii) District parties. Parties also exist in local areas, but only nominally and organized around a national assemblyman in his own
electoral district. Like the central party, it is based on personal
bonds between a member of or candidate for the National
Assembly as the leader and his (or her) supporters and followers. It is "a personalized instrument"[24] for the leader to utilize
to establish contact with constituents for reelection or election
and offer what favours he or she can render in return. His (or
her) supporters, who become members of his district party,
mediate other constituents of his (or her) electoral district. The
district party is not " 'a policy-responsive linkage' mechanism
but rather a political machine based on patron-client ties" (Park
1988: 1051).

(a-iii) Presidential election. In the largely conservative political
climate, political parties are not divided along ideological
lines, hence the presidential election does not revolve around
ideological cleavages. With democratization, the presidential
candidates no longer represent antidemocratic forces and democratic forces, as they did under the authoritarian regime. Accordingly, for some time to come, regionalism will play a key role in
the presidential election. Voters in three provinces (Kyongsang,
Cholla, and Chungchong) will vote for the candidate of the party
headed by the politician from their own province – usually the
head of the party is the presidential candidate – or the candidate
of another party who is either supported by his followers within
the same party who are from their own province or forms an
alliance with the leader of the party headed by politicians from
their own province. In the remaining provinces (Seoul, Kyonggi,
and Kangwon), those who were not born there will vote for the
candidate of their home province, while native residents will cast
their votes for presidential candidates on the basis of their
regional preferences and their perception of the overall performance of the current regime.

(a-iv) National Assembly election. A National Assembly aspirant has
to jump over two hurdles – party nomination and election. The
party's nomination of National Assembly candidates is largely
made by the party leader, with the advice of a group of high-
ranking officials (mostly faction leaders). Nomination for

---

24 Park Chan Wook, "Legislators and Their Constituents in South Korea," *Asian Survey* Vol.
28, No. 10 (October 1988), p. 1051.

electoral district (*chiyokku* 地域區) is determined by personal loyalty to the party or faction leader and the perceived probability of one's getting elected. Nomination for the national electoral district (*chonkukku* 全國區) is mostly based on one's national reputation (in the case of the ruling party) and financial contribution to the party (in the case of opposition parties).

As for election itself, three factors – the candidate's personal reputation, his or her constituency service, and the popularity of the candidate's party in the electoral district – largely determine eligibility. Of the three factors, constituency service is considered the most important. Ruling party candidates, with the advantage of support from local administrative offices and of better-financed campaigns, tend to focus more on constituency service and establishing informal, personal face-to-face ties with voters in their districts. On the other hand, opposition party candidates tend to make up for the disadvantages they suffer by bringing to the attention of their constituents the failures of the current regime and corruption in the government.[25]

One should also note that there is an increasing tendency for those who do not get party nominations to leave the party and run as independent candidates. They then join the party of their choice once they get elected.

(b) Bureaucrats. Bureaucrats are recruited into administrative offices largely through open competition at various levels – civil service examinations. As society becomes more differentiated and complex through industrialization, urbanization, and globalization, administrative offices require specialized and expert knowledge as a requisite for entry. Furthermore, administrative offices encourage and provide financial support for high-ranking officials (above Grade 5) to receive further professional training provided by universities within the country, and they regularly send selected numbers of officials overseas. Bureaucrats build up their careers within a government office and their performance is constantly evaluated, determining how far they can move up the ladder of success within the government. Although patronage – who you know who could help you get a job and promotion – plays a significant role, patronage alone is not sufficient for one's career promotion.

---

25 Park Chan Wook, "Home Style in a Developing Polity: How Korean Legislators Communicate with Their Constituents," *Korea Journal* Vol. 30, No. 5 (May 1994), p. 9.

2. Who governs?

(a) Separation of power

The executive office continues to dominate the government process but both legislative and judicial branches are trying to assert themselves and slowly gain further autonomy.

(a-i) The National Assembly. The president remains the head of his party and hence the boss to those party members who get elected to the National Assembly, and he demands their loyalty. When the ruling party occupies the majority of seats in the assembly, it comes directly under the president's control. In fact, the president nominates candidates for the speaker and the chairs of various committees in the assembly, and ratification is a mere formality.

Ruling party legislators are not likely to act as a unified entity against the president or the administration. They have little autonomy to decide about the legislative bills and annual budget plan proposals submitted by the administrative branch. Their primary task is to defend the administration against criticism by opposition party members. Not voting for bills submitted by the executive or administrative office may be regarded as an act of disobedience, and one does so at the risk of not being renominated for the next election, or even being dismissed from the party. The president often issues instructions to his party members in the assembly – even if informally – which are usually understood as "orders."

(a-ii) The cabinet and the administrative bureaucracy. The president nominates and dismisses his cabinet members or ministers at will. With the exception of the prime minister, his ministerial nomination is not subject to confirmation by the National Assembly. While an appointment to the cabinet is based on qualification, it is often regarded as a personal favour to, or reward for, the appointee. To distribute favour to those people to whom he owes political debt, the president makes ministerial changes fairly frequently. The average length of the ministerial stay in office has been about one year. The brief stay in a ministerial post does not allow the incumbent to exercise whatever power the post bestows on him or her or to engage in long-term planning.

The cabinet is empowered by the constitution to make decisions on policy matters. But it is up to the president to make it an independent decision-making body. The president may have the prime minister preside over a cabinet meeting or he may do it himself. When he does, few ministers dare to disagree with him. Some presidents are willing to share power with the prime minister by allowing him to be the chair of the cabinet, whereas others regard him as merely another minister.

Presidential control extends to the administrative bureaucracy through exercise of his power to make appointments for what are known as "vital" positions (*yojik* 要職) in the administrative bureaucracy largely for his friends, personal acquaintances, and followers who have remained loyal to their benefactor. When a minister makes appointments for other high-ranking positions within his ministry, he does so with the understanding or approval of the president or his executive assistants.

(b) Policy making

In principle, the primary role of the National Assembly is to legislate, while the president, his cabinet, and administration implement the policy guidelines approved by the former. Indeed, the National Assembly is the final authority to pass or reject legislative bills. But under the previous authoritarian regime, government policies and budget plans were largely formulated and decided by the president and the office of presidential secretaries in consultation with ministers and high-ranking technocrats. They were ratified over the objection of opposition party members, who sometimes tried to block the passage of bills that the executive office proposed.[26] Given the presidential power over the National Assembly noted above, the administrative branch can be expected to continue to dominate the legislative process.

Aside from the power imbalance, however, national assemblymen tend to be more concerned with reelection through cultivating cordial relationships with their constituents than with engaging in legislative activities, since the latter does not appear to contribute to their reelection as much as the former. Elected officials spend inordinate amounts of time in constituency service by visiting their electoral districts, writing letters to their constituents, receiving visitors from their electoral districts, finding jobs, obtaining bank loans, securing relief funds, bringing government public projects to their electoral

---

26 Ahn Byung Young, "Hankuk ŭi ŭihoe chongch'i" (Parliamentary Politics in Korea), in Kim Wun-tae (eds.), *Hankuk chŏngchiron* (On Korean Politics) (Seoul: Pakyongsa, Fourth Edition, 1999), p. 778.

districts, et cetera. Constituency service leaves little time for legislative work. Consequently, assemblymen lack the information they need for devising legislation and rely instead on administrative officials. More importantly, many of them lack professional knowledge to intelligently evaluate the content of the budget plans prepared by the economic planning board and to formulate policies on the environment and financial matters.

Administrative officials, on the other hand, are engaged in the management of issues of public and national interest on which they develop special and expert knowledge and have direct access to relevant information. National assemblymen tend to take care of local or district interests, while the administration addresses matters of national interest.

(c) Increasing constraints on presidential domination

As such, presidential power reaches almost every corner of the government and is not directly accountable to the legislative branch. The incumbent of the executive office is often described as the "imperial" president, but he is not without constraints. With a constitutional amendment in the Sixth Republic, the National Assembly regained the right to investigate and audit the administrative organization. Although the president is not accountable to the National Assembly, as the administrative branch is represented by his ministers, disclosure of wrongdoings, corruption, and irregularities in the administration by the legislature through annual investigation and inspection is likely to be taken as a reflection on presidential leadership and hence serve as a constraint on the president.

These days opposition party leaders and assemblymen freely express their discontentment with and criticism of the way the president governs the nation. Opposition party assemblymen continue to offer critiques of the administration and use the assembly as an arena for debates on the forms that democracy should take. The media also enjoy freedom of expression in their scrutiny of the president.

Another source of constraint on presidential power is the fact that the ruling party is not likely to gain a majority of seats in the absence of a two-party system. Under the circumstances, the ruling party will have to form an alliance with at least one other party to establish a majority, meaning that presidential power will be curtailed by the need to compromise with an alliance party.

3. How do citizens influence or put pressure on the government?

(a) Corporatist control under the authoritarian regime. During the authoritarian era, citizens had limited opportunities to organize themselves into groups for the purpose of articulating and aggregating their interests. Those interest groups that existed – for example, the Korean Business Association, the Korean Federation of Labour Unions, and the Korean Teachers Association – were few in numbers, had been created by the government itself, and remained under its control. They were expected to support or cooperate with the government in the formulation and implementation of policies, and in return they received protection and benefits for their organizational activities. The administration used legal and other coercive means to discourage the formation of autonomous interest groups. Under such corporate control, interest groups had extremely limited capacity to negotiate with the government on behalf of citizens.

With the limitation of official channels through which citizens or interest groups could negotiate or bargain with the government to promote the interests for which they are ostensibly organized, these groups adopted unofficial methods of influencing, persuading, or pressuring the government. For example, the Korean Business Federation, which maintained a cordial relationship with the administration, sent petitions to government officials on policy formation that they wished to influence. Since the executive branch dominated the legislative process, it rarely consulted the National Assembly. Given the subordinate position of the Korean Business Federation, it usually had little effect on policy formation. The more prevalent method of interest articulation in the business world was for each business firm to approach the administration on an informal basis (personal connections), seeking preferential treatment with payment of various kinds – feasts, bribery, and commissions.

When the Korean Federation of Labour Unions was unable to protect factory workers, young female workers organized themselves within the factory on the work setting and negotiated directly with the owners and managers for wage increases, better working conditions, and more humane treatment. In promoting their interests, they invoked their constitutional rights.

Lay citizens tried to negotiate directly with candidates for or members of the National Assembly and sought personal favours in return for their votes. With little autonomy in the legislative chamber, the national assemblymen were unable to respond to their constituents' needs and requests regarding policy.

(b) The rise of pluralism

Opposition forces under the authoritarian regimes produced interest groups after democratization independent of government control, actively promoting their own interests. Enterprise unions organized by factory workers coalesced into larger industry-wide unions which then were united into a national-level union, the Korean Democratic Labour Federation. Faced with challenges from this new national labour union organization, the Korean Federation of Labour Unions (widely known as a pro-government organization) is trying to become a competitive, autonomous organization. It no longer relies on financial aid provided by the government. Even the Korean Business Federation is making efforts to become an autonomous organization. Both are increasingly voicing their criticisms of government economic policies and trying to have input into policy formation through channels other than the administrative bureaucracy – for example, the National Assembly, political parties, and mass media.

Outside of work organizations, numerous other groups are being formed for the purpose of promoting specific interests (women's organizations, farmers' organizations, etc.). With increasing concern about issues that affect everybody, such as air pollution, consumer protection, and the proliferation of nuclear weapons, citizens are now forming organizations oriented more toward the protection of public interests. They not only put pressure on both the National Assembly and the administrative bureaucracy to establish viable policies for properly managing these issues, but also increasingly contribute to policy by making specific proposals.

In pursuing their goals, they utilize all the channels open to them, official as well as unofficial. While they pursue all the parties involved in policy making – the president, his office of secretaries, the National Assembly, the administrative bureaucracy, and the mass media – through appeal, petition, letter writing, and demonstration, they also utilize what personal connections they may have with policy makers.

Korean citizens are no longer passive recipients of whatever benefits the government grants to them at its will or whim. They increasingly consider articulation and aggregation of their interests as their constitutional right, and they help one another to organize themselves into collective forces independent of corporate control by the government. In this respect, Korea is gradually becoming a pluralistic civic society – even though those patterns of particularistic interest articulation and aggregation established under corporate control by the authoritarian regime will continue to exist. And the personalist ethic will remain an important factor in the democratic political process with its emphasis on the person and mutual help. Both personalism and constitutionalism will coexist, adapting to each other.

VII CONCLUSION

Returning to the statement by Linz quoted at the beginning, it may be argued that South Korea has accepted democracy as a principle of legitimacy. Democracy has taken a firm root in the southern half of the peninsula. But, as became apparent above, the emerging South Korean polity is clearly not taking the same form of democracy that developed in the West. According to Pennock, "Historically . . . democratic theory is associated with individualistic theory. . . . Its ideal of liberty relates to the individual; and the means taken to secure it, franchise backed up by a series of individual rights, likewise reflects an individualistic philosophy."[27] Individualists contend that "Each individual knows his own interests best, [and] should be allowed to judge of himself" (Pennock 1979: 108), as his own conscience is the ultimate source of decision about what is right and wrong; "he himself is the one who can best be trusted to promote and defend it, and should be provided with a weapon (ballot) with which he could enforce his judgment and expression of individualistic self-reliance" (Pennock 1979: 103, 108).

The personalist, when he becomes a democrat, will no doubt concur with his individualist counterpart that each citizen is an independent being with a series of rights conferred by the constitution, that he is free to exercise these rights by himself, and that the government should ensure that these individual rights of the citizen are not violated by others. But personalist democrats are not likely to ignore one another or make their political decisions on their own. They will encourage consultation with or advice seeking from others in making decisions on political matters, and they will share information and lend moral support. Does the individual know his interest best? The personalist democrat is likely to think that the group decision is better, wiser, and safer than individual decision making. Within the close-knit circle, decision without group consultation would be regarded as offensive. Moreover, the network habitually works as an organizational unit. Often it becomes a matter of *uiri* to join others in the circle and do what they want to do. One may refuse to join others in a collective effort but risks offending others or being accused of betraying friends. With emphasis on mutuality, not on individual autonomy per se, personalist democracy might be able to avoid the widespread tendency among many citizens in individualist democracies to exclude themselves from political processes, including voting.[28]

27 J. Roland Pennock, *Democratic Political Theory* (Princeton, N.J.: Princeton University Press, 1979), p. 62.
28 Harry Eckstein, *Regarding Politics: Essays in Political Theory, Stability, and Change* (Berkeley: University of California Press, 1992), pp. 348–349.

Another difference between the democratic individualist and the democratic personalist would be that while the former stresses legalism, the latter focuses on the individual as a person. In individualist democracy, the rule of law tends to be emphasized, often at the expense of consideration for the individual as a person. In contrast, Koreans have traditionally followed the admonition by Confucius, "If you lead the people by regulations and order them by punishments, the people will evade these and have no sense of shame in doing so. If you lead them by virtue and order them through the rites, they will have a sense of shame and will correct themselves" [2:3] (quoted in de Bary 1998: 30). They have also developed ways of maintaining social order within the community without relying much on the authorities of local government. Should conflict situations arise, resolving them directly between the two parties or through mediation within the community is considered more desirable than going to court. Mediation is a cooperative enterprise to help parties heal the conflict and be reconciled to each other.[29] In the process of mediation, unlike in the law court, both parties may compromise their interests, but neither party comes out a loser. Personalists turn to law only as a last resort. The personalist democrat, by definition, becomes a rule-abiding citizen and yet he does not abandon his personalist orientation. The legalist outlook, as Father Bernard Haring, a Christian personalist, points out, "focuses mechanically on the legal situation, considering only one abstract principle at a time and with absolute loyalty to this one point," and "concerned only with barren formulations, not life and persons."[30] He goes on to say "Having lost contact with man in real life, he has lost contact also with values and with the sources of life and truth. Bare principles, or rather formulas, guide him and there is no consideration of how and why they were formulated or what human values originally justified those principles" (1971: 117). Like Aristotle, he claims that "every man-made law would become brutal and unjust if applied in all cases without regard for various forms of life" (1971: 117). If such legalism is more a product of an individualist orientation than of democracy in general, as is often assumed, then the personalist democracy is likely to develop a system of law with person regarding (reaching out to the inner being of the other as a unique person) an integral part of it. Personalism is widely considered to be antagonistic to legalism. When personalists commit themselves to public interests they become personalist-legalists. As the recent civic movement in Korea demonstrates, legalism does not necessarily replace personalism.

---

29 See the chapter by Albert Chen in this book.
30 Bernard Haring, *Morality Is for Persons: The Ethic of Christian Personalism* (New York: Farrar, Strauss and Giroux, 1971), p. 117.

An emphasis on person regarding and mutual help in the personalist ethic is also linked with sensitivity to others. If the democratic individualist thinks that democratic institutions are designed primarily for protecting and advancing the interests of individuals, the personalist democrat is likely to think of them in terms of the collectivity. The latter is more likely to think and act in other-regarding fashion (Pennock 1979: 117). "Americans," say Bellah and his associates, "define success in terms of the outcome of free competition among individuals in an open market. One is a success to the extent that one personally comes out ahead in a fair competition with other individuals."[31] Most of the Americans they talked to "would not deny the contributions others have made to their success in life; what they deny is the moral relevance of those contributions. It is only insofar as they can claim that they have succeeded through their own efforts that they can feel they have deserved that achievement" (1985: 198). Although South Korea is increasingly becoming a meritocratic society with an emphasis on individual ability and efforts, market competition will not discourage Koreans from seeking help from others. Koreans, in pursuit of private goals in the market, will endeavour to combine whatever they are capable of doing with whatever help they can receive from their relatives, friends, and acquaintances. Anyone who can help others is likely to aid those who need help out of a sense of personal obligation (Chang 1991: 119). Contributions made by others to individual success will not lose moral relevance. There remains, however, a question about how far other regarding will go in the personalist environment where those people near and dear count more than those people far and unrelated. But it may be conjectured that person regarding limited to personal or affective networks will be extended to strangers once the personalist is committed to democratic ideals.[32]

---

31 Robert H. Bellah et al., *Habits of the Heart: Individualism and Commitment in American Life* (New York: Harper and Row, 1985), p. 198.

32 I am greatly indebted to Bob Ratner for his critical comments and editorial assistance. Byung Young Ahn, Daniel A. Bell, Max Cameron, Ronald P. Dore, and Barrie Morrison read the manuscript and made numerous suggestions for revision for which I am grateful. Britanni Faulkes, Janis Bolster, and Patricia Woodsuff made it more readable by their careful editing. My thanks also go to the Social Sciences and Humanities Council of Canada for their financial support for my "Democracy in South Korea" project.

CHAPTER 5

A PRAGMATIST UNDERSTANDING OF CONFUCIAN DEMOCRACY

DAVID L. HALL AND ROGER T. AMES

PART I: JOHN DEWEY'S SECOND ASIAN MISSION

I A PRAGMATIC PROPOSAL

The widespread skepticism of both Asians and Westerners with respect to the realization of a Confucian-style democracy is rooted in two allied convictions. First, it is too much to expect that democratic institutions will be easily grown from seeds already present in Confucian soil. And second, the present institutional forms of Asian Confucianism and Western democracies are sufficiently distinct to preclude a marrying of the two. With respect to the importation of Western democratic institutions, there is little hope of detaching desirable democratic practices from the questionable economic and cultural forces that, in North Atlantic democracies, have too often mitigated the effectiveness of those practices. In sum, while there might be a strong interest on the part of many Confucian societies in adopting a democratic baby, there is justifiable concern about the continuing quality of its bathwater.

We believe that these skeptics have a strong case. Late-Western democracies are themselves fallen-away versions of their originally intended forms. Unquestionably, the importation of Western democratic institutions by non-Western countries has required the acceptance of economic and cultural forces that have little to do with democracy per se. Indeed, in instance after instance, no sooner is the Trojan Horse rolled through the gates than rationalized social, economic, and technological elements have escaped from it to do their work.

We certainly have our own doubts about the salutary effects of democratization movements in their present form. And, we are not altogether naive about the degree to which counterproposals of the sort we shall be making will bear fruit. Nonetheless, we hold that there is more to be gained from rehearsing the better of our possible futures than rendering what is now a likelihood that much closer to an inevitability by adding our assent to the presently most plausible consequence.

According to John Dewey, one of the two heroes of our essay, "a chief task of those who call themselves philosophers is to help get rid of the useless lumber that blocks our highways of thought and to make clear our path to the future." In that spirit we shall attempt to highlight what we hold to be the chief difficulties standing in the way of the development of a viable model of Confucian democracy and to suggest means whereby we might seek to remove them. This will, in part, require a search for non-Asian democratic resources that swing free of the most detrimental elements of "modernization" or "Westernization" or "Americanization" that so often accompany such resources. These elements that threaten persistent Confucian sensibilities include a legal formalism that mitigates the role of rituals as socializing processes; a concept of the autonomous individual that would negate the Confucian sense of the socially constituted self; a quantitative concept of equality that fails to note the qualitative distinctiveness of persons; an economic system that further exacerbates the pervasiveness of merely quantitative considerations of merit; a preoccupation with formal institutions as the determinative criteria for adjudicating social progress; and an insistence upon individual rights to the detriment of social responsibilities. In sum, the real consequence of presuming to import democratic institutions has been to promote an overall rationalization of social, economic, and political life that challenges both the form and dynamics of traditional cultures.

Our use of the expression "Confucian sensibilities" here is a deliberate attempt to reformulate the question "What *is* Confucianism?" that seeks an analytic understanding of this tradition to the methodological question "*How* does Confucianism work?" that pursues instead a narrative understanding of what is a porous, aggregating sensibility. We will argue that Confucianism like Deweyan Pragmatism might be better understood as a *way* of organizing and meliorating experience rather than as a potted ideology. That is, Confucianism is not *the* way, but is productive "way making." This approach to Confucianism would help explain the seeming lack of a severe separation between the momentum of an isolatable Confucianism and its transformation of whatever social and political forces it confronts, from Buddhism in the Song and Ming dynasties to liberalism in our contemporary historical moment.[1]

Following from this historicist understanding of Confucianism, our argument, elaborated in this essay, will be that American Pragmatism offers a productive cultural perspective in terms of which to engage the ideological and practical dynamics of Confucianism and democracy because it effectively side-

---

1 For a discussion of the desirability of redirecting this question, see Roger T. Ames, "New Confucianism: A Native Response to Western Philosophy," in *Chinese Political Culture*, edited by Hua Shiping (Armonk, N.Y.: M. E. Sharpe, 2001).

steps the obstacles we have just listed. In particular, the understanding of democracy found in the writings of John Dewey allows us to remain effectively untainted by the sometimes noxious precipitates associated with the dregs of the European Enlightenment, thus escaping many of the consequences of "modernization" and "Westernization." Specifically, Dewey's understanding of democracy in social and cultural rather than narrowly political terms prepares us to appreciate the manner in which democratic experiments in China, primarily associated with rural villages, are likely to have greater efficacy than would more self-consciously political efforts focused in the cities. Further, Dewey's transactional understanding of persons, along with his qualitative individualism, is rooted in a sense of the self as irreducibly social. His promotion of habit, habituation, and education provide sources for a positive evaluation of the constitutive role of rituals in a healthy society. His insistence that democratic institutions stand free of any particular form of economic system allows the importation of democratic institutions without having to accept their historically contingent connection with a strictly capitalist economic system. By rejecting an absolutist understanding of human rights – that is, by finding rights to be resourced in the particular historical community that grants them – Dewey provides a context for the rights debate that is far less threatening to the preservation and appropriate exercise of Confucian sensibilities.

Our contribution to the discussion of Asian democratization offered in this volume, then, is first and foremost an attempt to locate this important conversation about particular institutions and practices within a cultural vocabulary that, although certainly less formal and thus less demonstrable, is no less real or relevant than the specificities that might attend any rehearsal of pertinent case studies. In the absence of a sustained reflection upon those cultural values invested in different world views and alternative distillations of common sense, such a conversation can on the best of days be little more than competing monologues.

2 TWO MODES OF GLOBALIZATION

Except for a few late skirmishes and increasingly debilitating Pyrrhic victories on both sides, the dialectical struggle between the modernists and postmodernists has degenerated into a rather empty spectacle. Western (Anglo-European) philosophy owes its present vigor, not to a dialectical victory of the anti- or postmoderns over the promoters of the Grand Enlightenment Project, but to a transformation of conversational space within which viable intellectual engagements are taking place. That transformation is a consequence of *globalization* – a term that has taken on two competing senses.

The dominant sense is that associated, at the ideological level, with the dissemination of a rational and moral consensus born of the European Enlightenment and, at the practical level, rights-based democratic institutions, free enterprise capitalism, and rational technologies. In this sense, globalization is a synonym for modernization – which is itself thought to be synonymous with Westernization.

Discussing "postmodernism" within the context of this sense of globalization serves both to clarify and to relativize the notion. Postmodernity is a peculiarly Western event, if for no other reason than that modernity in its most effective senses is a Western invention.[2] And globalization construed as Westernization is, of course, a distinctly *modern* dynamic. The dialectical response of so-called postmodern thinkers to their received tradition advertises postmodernity as a set of counter-discourses that depend altogether too heavily upon their controlling narratives to serve the interests of non-Europeans.

As long as Western values monopolize the process of globalization, there will be a continuation of the expansionist, colonizing, missionizing impulses associated with the purveyance of liberal democracy, autonomous individuality, and rational technologies. But there are important signs that this modernist form of globalization is transmogrifying. At least in principle, there is no reason to understand globalization as either European expansion or American sprawl. For beyond the provincial, decidedly Western, sense of globalization, there is a competing meaning that recognizes the potential contributions of non-Western cultures. In this second sense, globalization simply refers to *the mutual accessibility of cultural sensibilities.*

Globalization as mutual accessibility retains one important connotation of "postmodernism" for the simple reason that a globalized world under this definition is radically decentered. The shift in world attention away from Europe and toward Asia; the dynamics associated with the complex relations of the Islamic and Christian worlds; the steady, if lumbering, emergence of Africa – all of these trends have provided practical illustrations of the irrelevance of a single narrative to account for past, present, or future events. Doubtless the Western processes of commodification and MacDonaldization will continue, but present globalizing dynamics may be vital enough to stand against even these dark forces. Contrary to the missionary dreams of Anglo-European statesmen and entrepreneurs, there may be a viable alternative to that form of globalization construed primarily as Western colonization.

---

2 For an extended discussion of the claim that modernity is a Western invention, see David L. Hall's *Richard Rorty: Prophet and Poet of the New Pragmatism* (Albany: State University of New York Press, 1997):29–47, and Hall and Ames, *The Democracy of the Dead: Dewey, Confucius, and the Hope for Democracy in China* (Chicago: Open Court Press, 1999):63–97.

In the West, becoming conscious of our world in a principled manner began with Hellenic speculation. Distinctly *self*-consciousness emerged with Modernity. Both self- and world-consciousness have reached their final flower in a putatively "postmodern" period that relativizes our forms of self- and world-consciousness by recognizing many viable patterns of self-articulation and just as many ontological visions of the way of things. In place of the desire to make the world in the rational and moral image of the Western Enlightenment, some so-called postmodern critics recognize that our name is Legion and that both we and our world are many.

The mutual accessibility of all cultures guaranteed in principle by this second sense of globalization carries the implication that, in the absence of a general consensus, the plurality of cultures and traditions must inevitably lead to local and ad hoc modes of negotiation. In place of the quest for a rational and moral consensus, there will be an increasing need for negotiation among alternative habits and sensibilities. In its most productive sense, global philosophy neither recognizes nor condones claims to any single controlling perspective or master narrative. There can be no consensual model of discourse. Rather, we are urged by our global context to acknowledge a vast and rich variety of discourses. We are thus drawn to the significance of local phenomena.

The term "global," while suggesting comprehensiveness, may in fact accentuate the fundamentally *local* character of objects and events. The model for understanding this second sense of globalization cannot be a consensual or universalist one that seeks common values or institutions across the globe. Rather, the model must be one that allows for the viability of local phenomena as *focal* in the sense that, while their objective presence may be altogether local, their influence is always potentially global in scope.

Under such conditions, there can be no avoidance of the primary facts of otherness and difference. The articulation of these differences leads inevitably away from universalist concerns and toward the articulation of productive intellectual contrasts. Differences heretofore were placed in the background of discussions, and family resemblances were held to be most crucial. Our post-cultural/multicultural age reverses the polarities – and difference now is thought to reign. In its most positive forms, difference is an emblem of tolerance, accommodation, and respect.

The interpretation of globalization as pan-accessibility and the foregrounding of the local or focal characteristics of forms of life support a strategy that allows us to maneuver around ideologies predicting a coming clash of civilizations. Such prophecies are predicated upon understandings of globalization as involving either competing universalist claims, or the resistance of an insular culture against such claims. The conflict of "Western" and

Islamic ideologies is an example of the former. The Chinese response to the threat of wholesale Westernization exemplifies the latter. A stress upon local sites of cultural engagement promotes a retail rather than a wholesale approach to cultural politics.

In sum, cultural politics is proceeding along two divergent paths. The first is the most recognizable in terms of processes of modernization associated with the extension of rationalized politics, economics, and technologies – all wrapped in the rational and moral consensus of the Western Enlightenment. The second form of globalization involves the recognition of the mutual accessibility of cultural forms and processes leading to ad hoc and local sites of negotiation aimed at the resolution of particular problems.

In the first sense of globalization, the term "Confucian democracy" is oxymoronic. Democratization is tantamount to Westernization – with all of the connotations of that term. Here, Confucianism is seen as a part of the rapidly fading world of traditional culture. And like the Cheshire cat, only its wan smile will be discernible in the New Democratic Age.

Hope for a combination of Confucian and democratic sensibilities depends upon the success of the second form of globalization – a sense that recognizes the potential benefits of mutual engagement in which both Confucian and democratic beliefs and practices are seen as valuable resources for the improvement of modes of togetherness.

3 IMPORTING DEMOCRACY: WHOLESALE, RETAIL, OR PIECEMEAL?

Processes of globalization that promote the mutual accessibility of cultural forms promise to relativize the dynamics associated with the extension of the rational sensibility of Western modernity. The increased rationalization of social, economic, and political life is to be resisted by the emergence of a shifting set of sites of intercultural engagement that eschew any overarching cultural norms. Such engagements are both local and ad hoc, aimed at resolving specific issues and problems rather than at realizing a rational consensus.[3]

Our first claim concerning the value of the discourse of Pragmatism as a means of engaging Confucianism and democracy is that the American Pragmatic tradition is at its core neither "Western," nor "modern," nor "American" in the dominant senses of these terms employed in both the Asian and the Western worlds. Though this fact is not widely recognized,

3 Thus, Western proponents of North Atlantic–style democracies ought not be greatly disturbed by the fact that issues of "human rights," "legal representation," "free elections," and so on, are seldom taken seriously on ideological grounds, but rather emerge in response to specific pressures both within and without Chinese society.

representatives of the American philosophical tradition from Jonathan Edwards through Emerson, James, Peirce, and Dewey did not share the problematic of the European Enlightenment. The strains of thought in America that gave rise to Pragmatism were grounded upon aesthetic rather than rational interests and the promotion of pluralistic rather than consensual concerns.[4] As William James noted, Pragmatism is "a method only" – a philosophical activity concerned with the engagement of specific problems arising within the sphere of public praxis.

As long as the Enlightenment search for a rational and moral consensus remained the philosophical dominant, American Pragmatism was neglected and allowed to remain on the margins of philosophical debate. Now, however, as the wholesale approaches of Western rationalism fall into disrepute, the decidedly retail methods of the Pragmatist seem to be in gradual ascendance. The American Pragmatic tradition offers an attractive resource for the engagement of Confucian and Western sensibilities on the subject of democratic ideals and institutions precisely because its intellectual goals and practices are not developments of the European Enlightenment and do not, therefore, share the features of modernity that would disqualify it as a possible connector with Asian sensibilities.

If sustained, our assertion that American Pragmatism is distinctly nonmodern may have both substantive and rhetorical consequences in discussions with Asian-resourced sensibilities. For, as long as modernization is equated with Westernization as it is generally construed, it will be resisted by the more traditional elements in Confucian societies – those very elements that would give the term "Confucian democracy" its most authentic resonance. Offering an interpretation of democracy that is not burdened by those aspects of modernity long rejected by proponents of distinctively Confucian societies is a most productive step.

Of equal importance, American philosophy as represented by voices such as Emerson, Whitman, and, later, Dewey is itself a marginalized tradition within America. For this reason, suggesting that we employ the resources of American Pragmatism in the interpretation of the import of democracy and its possible engagements with Confucianism is no more to promote "Americanization" in any narrow sense than modernization. This is true because the majority of American thinkers – including the interpreters of our American sensibility – have themselves, until very recently, peered at their own indigenous tradition through the lenses of Continental philosophy.

---

4 This claim is briefly considered in Hall and Ames (1999) and is discussed in detail in our forthcoming work, tentatively entitled *Peace in Action – America's Broken Promise*.

As a consequence, the resources of American philosophy have remained *un*-mined – or, even worse, have been *under*-mined, by misinterpretation.

The implication is that American Pragmatism is an essentially nonmodern, un-Americanized sensibility that bypasses the modern and expresses a heretofore marginalized strain of American ideals and practices. This means that it may be able to serve as a productive site of intellectual engagement within a global context. The pragmatic justification of this claim will be spelled out in greater detail in the remainder of this essay. Suffice it to say here that the distinctly American sensibility can be of crucial import in forthcoming global contexts for two principal reasons: First, unlike postmodernism, American thought is a *constructive sensibility* – not a counterdiscourse dialectically bound to the discourse of modernity. It offers a fresh start; one that is seasonally relevant to our global context. Second, the resonances between Asian and American sensibilities reckoned at the beginnings of our tradition by Emerson, Thoreau, Whitman, et al. offer promising possibilities for the Asian/Western dialogue that is sure to be one of the more important of the dynamics of future global discourse.

We recall that John Dewey attempted to introduce democratic beliefs and practices into Asia once before. He failed. The reasons for the eventual defeat of Dewey's programmatic reforms in China were largely associated with his refusal to take a wholesale approach to social problems in a period when it was wholesale or nothing. In spite of his radical reconstruction of the popular democratic ideal, Dewey was simply too moderate for a China in search of revolution. He took every opportunity to warn the Chinese against the uncritical importation of Western ideas (including, of course, his own), as well as the uncritical rejection of traditional Chinese values. Given the revolutionary temper of the times, however, it was perhaps inevitable that Marxism's generic ideology would overtake Dewey's decidedly piecemeal philosophy.

In his dealings with China as elsewhere, Dewey eschewed abstract principles and promoted concrete beliefs and practices as the only efficacious formative agencies of a society. Further, he insisted that totalizing processes – either economic or technological – were to be rejected. By contrast, there are presently many proponents of democracy who presume that democratic principles, laws embodying "right reason," as well as free enterprise capitalism and rational technologies as we know them, are a done deal that may be bundled and "shrink wrapped" for ready export. In his initial sojourn in China, Dewey was consistent in insisting that democracy is expressed in attitudes rather than laws and institutions and that the sort of democratic attitudes entailed by his vision of democracy are both gradually formed by, and reinforced through, education. This should serve as at least a point of reflection for any who would believe that heavy-handed efforts to democratize Asian nations, however sincere, will have much salutary effect. There are many potential exporters of Western democracy to Asia who seem satisfied that internal changes among urban entrepreneurs, or some influential intellectuals – or the pressure of other so-called democratic nations, or the demands of the world market – will work in a manner that Dewey's intelligent, patient, and altogether sensitive efforts did not.

We suggest that Dewey's second Asian tour faces much the same obstacles as the first. If he is thought to be underwriting ideas specifically identified with Western (read modern) values, his philosophy runs the risk of being rejected not once but twice, on two contrasting grounds. Traditional Confucians will ignore or reject him because they believe he is but another spokesperson for "Western" or "American" values, while the eager champions of a capitalistic version of liberal democracy – both Western and Asian – will reject him because he is (quite correctly) understood to represent a distinctly anticapitalist and resolutely communitarian form of democracy. There is not much hope that Dewey's communitarian views will persuade those already converted to the final virtues of a democracy motored by individual autonomy, free-enterprise capitalism, and rational technologies. Perhaps the more promising task at hand is to try to demonstrate to the more traditional of the Confucians that Dewey's philosophy holds the greatest promise for achieving a Confucian democracy in which central Confucian values are retained still largely intact.

If one merely extrapolates from past historical dynamics, there seems to be little choice but to accede to the forms of liberal democracy associated with the excess rationality of late-modern societies. Any hope that Dewey's second Asian journey will be more successful than his first lies in the fact that the four score years separating the two have seen a rather dramatic decline in the confidence shown toward generic ideologies. A space has opened, and the current trend is toward the transactional and the piecemeal. Citizens of a globalized and therefore localized world are becoming increasingly impatient with the thought of any general solution or universal plan. While we are far from realizing an "end of ideology," it surely seems that we now place much greater faith in the more modest intellectual efforts associated with ad hoc reforms.

In the following paragraphs of our essay we shall consider some specific issues with respect to which proponents of a Confucian democracy might benefit by appealing to the resources of Dewey's pragmatic model. Of course, to be consistent we must avoid any appearance of the simple reduction of Confucianism to Pragmatism. Ours is a distinctly modest, even bit-by-bit, approach that only seeks to indicate the usefulness of pragmatic resources in this or that particular instance.

4 LAW, HABIT, AND RITUAL

Other essays in this volume address in detail the distinctive role of law in Confucian societies and its application in particular institutions and practices. Such analyses must be qualified by a critical reflection on the distinctly pragmatic understanding of law and ritual as these strategies for social order are shaped by a central concern of pragmatic philosophy – namely, the cultivation of productive "habits." For, the pragmatic sense of "habit," in its dramatic contrast with the more mainstream Western philosophical understandings, establishes an intimate link with the distinctively Confucian dispositional understanding of the individual and social worlds.

In Anglo-European cultures, understandings of law developed within societies already characterized essentially as collections of individuals. Conceived as a defense against the exercise of despotic power, the rule of law quite rapidly developed in the direction of the protection of individual human rights associated with the limitation of governmental powers. The essential elements currently associated with the rule of law are constitutional guarantees for civil liberties (due process, equal protection), guarantees of the orderly transition of power through fair elections, and the separation of governmental powers. Together these comprise the fundamentals of a contractual relationship between rulers and citizens that prevents the latter from suffering abuses by the former.

The rule of law developed pari passu with the rights-based liberal ideology. Indeed, political liberalism today on some readings envisions the state as an increasingly neutral framework within which citizens may pursue their individual conceptions of the good life with a minimum of state interference. Such a framework is required, so the liberal argues, because of the pluralism of modern societies in which agreements on the meaning of "the good life" cannot be expected.

The different historical development of Asian Confucian nations precludes easy translation of the rule of law into a Confucian context. Confucian societies advertise neither an adversarial relationship between rulers and citizens nor a plurality of individual conceptions of the good life. The principal preconditions of the distinctive understanding of the rule of law in the West were not present, for example, in China. In China, law (*fa* 法) developed as a supplement to ritual action (*li* 禮) aimed primarily as the stipulation of administrative duties. Law developed alongside the development of the complex bureaucratic structure that served as the primary means of stabilizing Chinese society from the Han dynasty to the beginning of the twentieth century. With respect to what we in the West would term civil and criminal law, these regulations increased in number and application in periods in Chinese history in direct proportion to times when the observance of ritual propriety lost some of its efficacy as a binding force. Moreover, such laws were for the protection not of the citizen but of the community as represented in the persons of the rulers, and the "social order" these elites were enjoined to maintain.

Dewey's Pragmatism allows for an understanding of the role of law in society radically different from mainstream liberal theory. His understanding of the importance of custom and habit as forces of social cohesion resonates well with Confucianism. For, as radical as were Dewey's reformist ideas, he well recognized the determinative power of customs and habits, particularly when they function in support of circumstances that allow for the most relevant employment of intelligent action in the furtherance of community. A democratic community is comprised by individuals who are themselves constituted by distinctive social relationships and publicly recognized roles. These individuals realize their greatest satisfactions through roles and associations that are radically embedded in the customs and traditions of a society. Dewey recognized that one cannot simply choose to move beyond these customs and traditions. Thus, "the essential continuity of history is doubly guaranteed. Not only are personal desire and belief functions of habit and custom, but the objective conditions which provide the sources and tools of action . . . are precipitates of the past, perpetuating, willy-nilly, its hold and power."[5] It is important to understand that the "hold and power" of the past perpetuated by custom and habit is more than mere inertia. Far from construing the power of the past in terms of the "dead weight" of inertial forces, Dewey believed *habit* to be the essential condition of truly aesthetic experience. To understand the connection between habit and aesthetic experience, we must introduce a brief excursus.

We often think of habit in a negative manner as mere routine, or compulsively repetitive behavior, that we would alter if we but had imagination, creativity – or willpower. At a more formal level, we might entertain a more positive sense of habit as contributing to sound character and conduct. But, even here the concept is one most often associated with behavior that is somewhat "accidental" to the essential identity of an individual.

To grasp Dewey's alternative sense of habit, we may begin with senses of the term developed from the Ancient Greek. *Hexis* (habit) means "having" or "being in possession of." Early on, it also had the suggestion of both "condition" and "state." It was used to mean a natural or conditioned "tendency"

---

5 John Dewey, *The Public and Its Problems* (Athens, Ohio: Ohio University Press, 1927): 161–162.

of things – as the habit of a vine. Aristotle himself sometimes used *hexis* to refer to the natural or innate behavior of creatures.

If we combine the senses of habit as a state or condition and as a tendency, we arrive at the sense of the term found in the American Pragmatic tradition. Habit is disposition. Moreover, things do not have habits – they are habits. Habit is a mode of being. Dewey employs the notion of habit to establish a relationship between "having" and "being" that provides the core of his peculiarly aesthetic sensibility.[6]

This distinction, in fact, turns out to be one between two modes of "existing" – unmediated and mediated. Mediated experience entails the fact that being, in the mode of this or that essence, is made manifest through the particular beings of the world. Such experience is entailed by substantialist ontologies and cosmologies that make substance and form fundamental. Substances are known through forms or concepts either existing antecedent to the substances or abstractable from them. On the other hand, immediate experience requires that the particulars themselves be the objects of knowledge. Such particulars are "known" immediately in the sense that the experience of them is simply had. The structures that permit the having of experience are habits that dispose one toward that experience. Mediated experience requires one to grasp the essence of a thing as conceptually presented; aesthetic experience is simply *had*.

Scholars of Chinese thought have long noted that the Chinese lack a copulative sense of "to be" as "to exist." Rather, *you* 有 means "to have," "to be present." Whatever the translation of the Chinese *you*, it must be recognized that the concept privileges unmediated experience. Thus, if we allow for the importance of aesthetic understanding in defining the Chinese sensibility, it is plausible to assume that the notion of *you* as "having" is both a conditioning feature and a consequence of that mode of thinking. Being turns out to be habitual, dispositional. Being is *having*. As we shall elaborate in the discussion of the "enchanted world" of Confucius in Part II of this essay, it is this fact that connects the Confucian understanding of ritual activity (*li* 禮) with the Pragmatic understanding of habit.

5 INDIVIDUALITY, HIERARCHY, AND EQUALITY

The limitation of liberal individualism from the Confucian perspective is its challenge to a ritually ordered society in which the boundaries of one's person may be only vaguely delineated. Confucian selves are "individuated" as a

---

6 The pragmatic understanding of "habit" derives from the use of the term by the early American philosopher and theologian Jonathan Edwards. For a discussion of the centrality of the notion of habit and its contribution to the "aesthetic axis" of American thought, see our forthcoming work, *Peace in Action – America's Broken Promise*.

complex of constitutive roles and functions associated with their obligations to the various groupings to which they belong. A particular person is invested in personalized relationships: this son, this daughter, this father, this brother, this husband, this wife, this citizen, this teacher.

The identification of the person with roles is not in any sense a collectivist understanding. One does not begin with a separable sense of "self" which is then absorbed by or into a role. Rather, the roles are constitutive of what one in fact *is*. In the absence of the performance of these roles, nothing constituting a coherent personality remains: no soul, no mind, no ego, not even an "I-know-not-what." Thus, Confucianism is not a philosophy of self-abnegation in which "selflessness" is taken as a primary virtue. On the contrary, there is a palpable sense of not only personal identity but self-realization as well. The roles defining the person are ritually enacted. Again the resonance of Confucianism is with the pragmatic vision that assumes that individuals in a community will realize their greatest productivity through their distinctive roles and relationships.

The phenomenon of the radically individuated self is a rather late development within the Western tradition. In the beginnings of Greek culture, the tribal character of social organization effectively precluded a strong sense of otherness.[7] This sense increased markedly with the growth of cosmopolitan cities. In fact, as the word itself suggests, "civil-ization" was a process of "citi-fication." Attendant upon the rise of cities and of the commercial relations that sustained these urban centers, there emerged a strong distinction between the private and the public spheres. The separation of the intimate relations of the family from the more impersonal relations of public life enhanced the development of a sense of self-identity.

Things went quite differently in Asian Confucianism. Ancient China, for example, overcame the threat of the tensions and conflicts attendant upon ethnic and cultural pluralism by recourse largely to language rather than the process of urbanization as the medium for the transmission of culture. A class of Confucian literati emerged as official counsel to the imperial throne; a canon of classical works was instituted along with a commentarial tradition to promote Confucian doctrine as a national ideology; an examination system based upon these texts was introduced by the literati in the early Han. Throughout the two thousand years of imperial rule, a centralized and hierarchical bureaucracy perpetuated itself as a social and political infrastructure. Since the family was the model of all types of relationships, including the putatively "nonfamilial" relations obtaining among subjects, and between

---

7 See Alvin Gouldner, *The Hellenic World: A Sociological Analysis* (New York: Harper and Row, 1969):104ff for a discussion of the development of the Greek notion of the self.

ruler and subjects, there was little by way of an effective public sphere. Rather, social and political order was conceived in terms of mutually implicating radial circles, so that strong person, family, community, state, and cosmos are coterminous and mutually entailing. As such, the notion of "public" as contrasted with a distinct sphere of private life has had little relevance for Chinese society.

There is, however, a sense in which we might speak of the public sphere in China in much the same fashion as John Dewey defined it. For Dewey, the public consists of "all those who are affected by the indirect consequences of transactions to the extent that it is deemed necessary for those consequences to be systematically cared for."[8] Government consists in institutionally organized actions of those officers charged with the responsibility of overseeing these indirect consequences. In pluralistic societies the public sphere so defined is quite significant since there will be an indefinitely complex set of interactions accruing indirect consequences over which there must be concern. This may not be so evident in a more homogeneous, tradition-oriented society such as a ritually organized Confucian world.

One should not conclude that the attenuated public/private distinction in Confucian societies precludes conflicts between the claims of family and those of the larger community. In Confucian terms, these are typically construed with respect to notions of graduated loyalties. Obligations are first and foremost to the family – other loyalties are lesser priorities. In traditional Confucian societies, when disputes do exist between, for example, obligations to the ruler and to one's parents, these are handled in a distinctly ad hoc manner.

Confucian China has always constituted a political paradox. On the one hand, it has traditionally possessed a strong central government. On the other hand, the majority of the population has expressed the rather casual attitude that "the sky is high, and the Emperor is far away." We may resolve this seeming paradox by further articulating the rather attenuated sense of "public life."

The ritually organized community is shaped by custom understood as what Dewey has called "widespread uniformities of habit."[9] Rituals articulate these customs without requiring members of the community to develop individual habits. Insofar as one wishes to speak of a collective mind, it is, as Dewey asserts, "a custom brought at some point to explicit, emphatic, consciousness – emotional or intellectual."[10] As for examples in the more individualistic societies, the idea of a collective mind is usually regarded with some suspi-

8 Dewey (1927):15–16.
9 John Dewey, *Human Nature and Conduct* (New York: The Modern Library, 1957):58.
10 Dewey (1957):60.

cion. Mass religious movements, such as those associated with the Great Awakening of eighteenth-century European and American society, illustrate the power of focused habit to give rise to a group consciousness. More contemporary examples include the "collective consciousness" associated with the U.S. participation in World War II efforts.

In more individualistic societies, customs are not ends in themselves, but serve as the conditions under which individuals form their individual habits. In societies in which customs are less articulated through individual habits, the chances are greater that, under the pressure of novel events, collective consciousness will be manifest. This can lead to mob action. As Dewey observes:

> [In] a political democracy . . . thought is submerged in habit. In the crowd and mob it is submerged in undefined emotion. China and Japan exhibit crowd psychology more often than do western democratic countries . . . because of a nearer background of rigid and solid customs conjoined with a period of transition. The introduction of many novel stimuli creates occasions where habits afford no ballast.[11]

China's Cultural Revolution was one of the most dramatic manifestations of "crowd psychology" in recent history. The severity of the government's response to the 1989 Tiananmen protest was predicated upon the fear of a reversion to mob action. And the recent repression of the Falungong movement, seen from an internal perspective, is only the most recent example of the government taking social stability as its prime directive. The presence of a strong central government in China is a consequence of recognizing the potential for serious collapses of ritually sustained order during periods of transition.

In societies in which autonomous individuality is prized, violence and social disarray are most often threatened by individuals acting against other individuals. For example, while the Chinese government guns down far more of its citizens than does our government, we personally gun down far more of one another than the Chinese people do. Per capita, the United States suffers far and away more murder, more rape, and other forms of violence, and certainly more drug-related crime. As a consequence, we have a greater percentage of our population in prisons. There is no more justification for an individual murdering one of his fellow citizens out of passion, or from mere calculation of profit, than for a government such as that of the Chinese to murder its citizens deemed to threaten the social order. Both sorts of violence need be condemned. And remedies must be sought for both societal defects.

11 Dewey (1957):61.

Fear of the collapse of ritually sustained order exemplified in the Chinese government's reactions to Tiananmen and the Falungong movement is one of the primary reasons for the unpopularity of the dominant forms of liberal individualism. It is important to recognize, however, that American Pragmatism offers an alternative perspective on the meaning of individuality. The distinctiveness of Pragmatism as a philosophy of social engagement is most dramatically expressed in its understanding of "individuality." In contrast to the liberal democratic individualism that dominates modern Western thought, American Pragmatists such as George Herbert Mead and John Dewey have provided distinctly social characterizations of experience suggesting that the fullest form of human life is life together. Dewey claims that "assured and integrated individuality is . . . the product of definite social relationships and publicly acknowledged functions."[12]

Dewey took the presumed antithesis between the individual and society to be a consequence of an unwarranted assumption. That assumption is that if, as is the case in a liberal democratic society, individuals have the right to dissociate themselves from any particular grouping, one may conclude that this suggests that individuals may productively exist apart from any association whatsoever. But common sense instructs one that the antithesis of the individual and society is a false dichotomy. The right to dissociate ourselves from all groupings is, in fact, the "right" to cease having any meaningful existence as a human being.[13]

It is not enough to simply show that there are meanings of "individual" and "individualism" acceptable to both Confucian and pragmatic sensibilities. There are other apparent obstacles one must overcome. One of the most important of these is the belief that "hierarchy," as expressed in Confucian societies, is irreconcilable with democracy. This misconception is most telling, for it identifies democracy altogether too closely with understandings predicated upon discrete individualism and the purely mathematical notion of equality that follows from it.

The aesthetic richness required for the realization of a communicating community as the ground of democratic society cannot be achieved within a context defined by simple equality. Not only Confucianism, but Pragmatism as well, requires hierarchical relationships of parity rather than relations of

12 John Dewey, *Individualism Old and New* (New York: Capricorn Books, 1962):53.

13 If pressed, liberals might argue that the "right of association/dissociation" is referenced to particular associations construed individually and must not be taken to mean that an individual can exist meaningfully in abstraction for any association. The problem with such a claim would be that unless one qualifies in theory (in principle) the meaning of locutions such as the "right of free association" at the beginning of one's discussion – not simply in an ad hoc manner when forced to respond to a reductio ad absurdum argument – the effect is to have it both ways.

abstract equality. Only a society in which individuals stand in relationships that reflect the unique characteristics of their relevant roles and functions is a truly democratic society. According to Dewey: "Equality does not signify that kind of mathematical or physical equivalence in virtue of which any one element may be substituted for another. It denotes effective regard for whatever is unique and distinctive in each."[14]

In earlier times, democracy in America included the presumption of important inequalities with respect to knowledge, virtue, and the burdens of responsibility. Deference paid to teachers, the clergy, and public officials did not cancel the recognition of "equality before God and under the law." Persistent and widespread recourse to the attitude of deference in acknowledging excellence is one of the most effective means of preventing a democratic community from suffering the bland sameness associated with merely mathematical equality.

Equality, construed in individualistic terms, is a distinctly quantitative notion. Such an understanding promotes the conception of individuality as inviolate; it also mitigates the value of informal pressure and persuasion that can serve as alternatives to more coercive instruments for maintaining order. Autonomy so understood stands in tension with the non-egalitarian institutions of family, union, and academy that promote goods-in-common. The definition of persons as autonomous individuals militates against the notion of goods held in common.[15]

The Confucian project is to create community as an extended family. And family relationships are resolutely hierarchical. Ideally, the effects of hierarchy are meliorated by the processive conception of person. The performance of different roles and relationships enables persons to give and to receive comparable degrees of deference. Deference to my teachers will in due course place me in a similar relationship with my students. The roles of communal benefactor and beneficiary alternate over time. Hierarchy need not be as rigid and inflexible as it is often thought to be, and it need not entail the impoverishing shadow of coercion. Having said this, in even the best of Confucian societies, as was historically true in ideal Western societies (for rather different reasons), hierarchical assumptions have threatened the realization of equality for all. The treatment of women and minorities is the most obvious illustration of such inequality.[16]

14 Dewey (1927):150–151.
15 It is certainly possible that quite different individuals might share goods in common – most often by having quite different reasons for holding them to be goods. But this would be largely a contingent and accidental feature of any society. Moreover, the senses in which one holds things in common via rational consent and the holding of common goods at the level of attitude and affect are crucially distinct.
16 We have addressed the issue of women and minorities in Chinese and Western societies in Hall and Ames (1999):44–47 and 206.

For Dewey, the notions of "equality" and "individuality" are not a given but rather arise qualitatively out of ordinary human experience. Like "life" and "history," ordinary human experience is both the process and the content of interactions with social, natural, and cultural environments: "'Experience' ... includes *what* men do and suffer, what they strive for, love, believe and endure, and also *how* men act and are acted upon, the ways in which they do and suffer, desire and enjoy, see, believe, imagine – in short, processes of *experiencing*."[17] Individuality is the consequence of the myriad transactions that determine one's personal focus. Thus, "individuality cannot be opposed to association. . . . It is through association that man has acquired his individuality, and it is through association that he exercises it."[18] An individual so construed is not a thing, but an event, describable in the language of uniqueness, integrity, social activity, relationality, and qualitative achievement.

For Dewey, the human individual is a social achievement, an adaptive success made possible through the applications of social intelligence. Given the reality of change, this success is always provisional, leaving us as incomplete creatures with the always new challenge of contingent circumstances. And yet this success is progressive and programmatic. "We *use* our past experiences to construct new and better ones in the future."[19]

Like Confucianism, Dewey's Pragmatism invests enormously in the centrality of language (including signs, symbols, gestures, and social institutions): "Through speech a person dramatically identifies himself with potential acts and deeds; he plays many roles, not in successive stages of life but in a contemporaneously enacted drama. Thus mind emerges."[20] For Dewey, mind is "an added property assumed by a feeling creature, when it reaches that organized interaction with other living creatures which is language, communication."[21]

As we would expect, given Dewey's qualitative notion of individuality, equality is the active participation in communal life forms that allows one the full contribution of all one's unique abilities. Commenting on this departure from the common meaning of the term, Robert Westbrook allows that Dewey "advocated neither an equality of result in which everyone would be like everyone else nor the absolutely equal distribution of social resources."[22]

---

17 John Dewey, *Late Works*, 1899–1924, in 17 vols., edited by Jo Ann Boydston (Carbondale, Ill.: Southern Illinois University Press, 1981–1990)1:18.
18 "Lecture Notes: Political Philosophy, 1892," p. 38, *Dewey Papers*.
19 *Middle Works*, 1899–1924, in 15 vols., edited by Jo Ann Boydston (Carbondale, Ill.: Southern Illinois University Press, 1976–1983)12:134.
20 *Late Works*, 1:135.
21 John Dewey, *Experience and Nature* (New York: Norton, 1929):133.
22 Robert B. Westbrook, *John Dewey and American Democracy* (Ithaca, N.Y.: Cornell University Press, 1991):165.

Equality so construed is not an original possession. Again, attaching a most unfamiliar interpretation to a familiar term, Dewey insists that

> Equality does not signify that kind of mathematical or physical equivalence in virtue of which any one element may be substituted for another. It denotes effective regard for whatever is distinctive and unique in each, irrespective of physical and psychological inequalities. It is not a natural possession but the fruit of the community when its action is directed by its character as a community.[23]

In interpreting this passage, Raymond Boisvert underscores the fact that for Dewey, "equality is a result, a 'fruit,' not an antecedent possession." It is growth in contribution. Further, like freedom, it has no meaning in reference to a discrete and independent person and can only assume importance when "appropriate social interactions take place." In Dewey's own words, equality can only take place by "establishing the basic conditions through which and because of which every human being might become all that he was capable of becoming."[24]

In Dewey's democracy, the integrity of the individual would be a function of the coherence of a community of shared experiences. The fullness of the individual's experience can only be guaranteed by that community. A consequence of this recognition would be that the achievement of the principal rewards of individuals would be realized through their roles and the functions they perform, rather than through private pecuniary gain. Again we encounter the essentially *aesthetic* character of Dewey's vision. The individual is *particular*, but not *discrete*. Individuals are unique elements in a community where members serve in mutually satisfying ways to enrich the experiencing of one another. Interactive, participatory behavior is the mark of a viable democratic community, and this provides the context within which an individual is constituted.

Notions of freedom and autonomy take on radically different meanings for Dewey than for proponents of liberal democracy. Freedom is freedom-in-context in which actions and decisions are rendered effective by drawing upon experiential resources derived from shared existence. Dewey is concerned that freedom be efficacious, not abstract.

In the *abstract* sense we are free when there are minimal constraints precluding any particular action. In the *effective* sense of freedom, an individual is free only when conditions promoting a given action are present. Members of communities are responsible for maximizing their fellows' opportunities

---

23 *Middle Works*, 12:329–330.
24 *Late Works*, 11:168. For Raymond D. Boisvert's discussion, see *John Dewey: Rethinking Our Time* (Albany: State University of New York Press, 1998):68–69.

to make decisions and perform actions that, in turn, enrich the community. Further, in a democratic society, government officials are enjoined to promote these same ends. The enrichment of the community is not an end in itself. The individual, as a participant in the community, benefits from the enriching context. That benefit is shared with the community to the extent that resources for further enrichment of other individuals are augmented. The end of communal interaction is the enrichment of the individual.

For Dewey, autonomy would have to be construed from within the context of a communal understanding of experience. This would require that the moral obligations of individuals are not primarily to their individual consciences but to the communal context to which they belong. It is, after all, the individuals forming that community, who have authored both the content of that conscience and the means of maintaining one's integrity with regard to its claims. Being true to one's self is being true to the resources, capacities, and propensities that constitute the self-in-communal-context. *Being true* means nurturing the terminus a quo of the self (the community as experiential resource) as well as its terminus ad quem (the particular focus of the community). In effect, it means to understand the self as by no means separate from the communal context within which persons emerge as foci of experiencing.

Our discussion above has attempted to show that there is more than sufficient reason for Asian Confucians to take a second look at the thought of John Dewey. Not only does Dewey offer a distinctive alternative to more individualistic forms of political democracy, the specific differences between liberal political theories and his particular form of social democracy are precisely those that resonate with the constructive aspects of the Confucian understanding of society. In Part II of this essay we attempt to further elaborate our argument in terms of Dewey's alternative to the Weberian claims concerning the inevitable rationalization and "disenchantment" of the modern world. Dominant understandings of Asian democratization depend upon a notion of democracy accompanied by the rationalization of political institutions. As we shall see, Deweyan Pragmatism offers a model of democracy that would protect the productively nonrationalized elements of Confucian society and thus maintain a degree of "enchantment" of social life in the Confucian world.

PART II: DEWEY, CONFUCIUS, AND THE ENCHANTMENT OF THE SOCIAL WORLD

I JOHN DEWEY'S ENCHANTED WORLD

Were we to refer specifically to the dynamics of late-modern *Western* thought, we might benefit by substituting the term "post-cultural" for our present au

courant "postmodern."[25] After all, the concept of "culture" maintains its viability only if it is understood as a pattern of values and behaviors, a set of
usages, that operate beneath the level of conscious intent. The spheres of tradition and custom encompass the immediacies of life, those circumstances
requiring neither calculation nor reflection. Fundamentally, human culture
is the pre-rational, tacit, and implicit *lebenswelt*. It is a world of sedimented
feelings and practices requiring neither calculation nor reflection. As such,
culture is an "enchanted" world.

The history of the modern West is one of increasing awareness – expressed,
in Weberian terms, as demystification, secularization, rationalization, bureaucratization leading to "the disenchantment of the world." A comprehensively
rationalized, disenchanted world is effectively *post*-cultural. This is increasingly the character of the modern Western world. Globalization understood
merely as modernization would serve, in principle, to rationalize all competing sensibilities.

The important contrast running through our entire discussion thus far is
that of the increased rationality of social and cultural dynamics leading to
the disenchantment of human life, and the alternative to this rationalizing
dynamic found in the philosophy of Pragmatism. Rationalization, as Max
Weber noted, involves the depersonalization of social relationships and the
increased organization of technical means of controlling nature and society.
The resort to legal mechanisms rather than custom and tradition, the merger
of capitalism and technology, the appeal to abstract rights, and merely quantitative notions of individuality and equality are all aspects of the rationalization that Weber both celebrated and bemoaned. The gain is to be found
in increased efficiency – principally, in economics, politics, and education.
The loss is measured in terms of the loss of affective meaning associated with
the disenchantment of the social world.

John Dewey seems not to have read Weber until rather later in life, and he
offered only sketchy allusions to his central arguments. Partly for this reason,
Dewey interpreters have not generally been inclined to explore the degree to
which his thought serves as an alternative to Weber's assumptions of the
inevitable disenchantment of the modern world. However one judges its efficacy in the late-modern world, Dewey's distinctively *aesthetic* philosophy was
forwarded as an antidote to the very processes that Weber believed inexorable.

John Patrick Diggins has thematized the rather dramatic contrast between
the visions of Dewey and Weber in his *Promise of Pragmatism.*[26] Unfortunately,

---

25 "Post-cultural" is used in much the same sense by David L. Hall in his *The Uncertain
Phoenix: Adventures Toward a Post-Cultural Sensibility* (New York: Fordham University Press,
1982):363–365 and 393–395.

26 John Patrick Diggins, *Promise of Pragmatism* (Chicago: University of Chicago Press, 1994).
See especially chapter 1, "The Disenchantment of the World."

the contrast he makes presumes the standard tradition/modernity debate that Dewey's thinking effectively avoids. As a consequence, Diggins finds Weber's critique of science realistic and Dewey's (always qualified) enthusiasm for scientific inquiry altogether romantic and unrealistic. The priority Dewey gives to democracy over science is then simply dismissed as an "article of (misplaced) faith."[27] Diggins's misreading of Dewey is a consequence of his own immersion in the tradition/modernity problematic that leads him to believe that the greatness of modernity lies in the extent to which individuals and societies have allowed themselves to be guided self-consciously by a rational and moral consensus leading to increased freedom and autonomy. The disenchantment of the world through rationalization and bureaucratization is to be considered a problem only if it is "excessive" and overreaching.

It is a commonplace of modernist discourse such as that of Diggins to ignore the centrality of art and aesthetic experience in the formation and maintenance of a healthy society. Thus he cannot take seriously Dewey's discussion of the centrality of art as a means of the continual enchantment of everyday life.[28] The assumption is that concessions to the importance of art are little more than rhetorical flourishes. However, as Dewey insisted, it is not science but *art* that grounds the constructive activities leading to a democratic society and produces a communicating community.

> Common things, a flower, a gleam of moonlight, the song of a bird, not things rare and remote, are means by which the deeper levels of life are touched so that they spring up as desire and thought. This process is art. . . . Artists have always been the real purveyors of news for it is not the outward happening in itself which is new but the kindling by it of emotion, perception and appreciation.[29]

It is a sign of just how far along are the processes of rationalization leading to the disenchantment of the modern world, that the first response one is likely to have upon reading the above quote is "What in the world does a 'gleam of moonlight' have to do with democracy?" In fact, proponents of "enchantment" believe the connection to be both direct and important.

Thomas Jefferson's preference for the "enchantments," the affective bonding, associated with rural life as opposed to the lives of the Yankee trader, or "the occupants of the work-bench," is well known. In "Notes on the State of Virginia," he observes that the "corruption of morals in the mass of cultivators is a phenomenon of which no age nor nation has furnished an example.

---

27 Diggins (1994):42–43.
28 This crucial subject receives but one brief mention of a single page of Diggins's five-hundred-page work.
29 Dewey (1927):183–184.

It is the mark set upon those, who not looking up to heaven, to their own soil and industry, depend upon the casualties and caprice of customers." Looking to a common heaven, working with a common soil, establishes a commonality of experiencing that creates affective community, rather than the merely contractual modes of association bound by transitory "mutual interests" of an economic or political sort.

For Dewey, democracy and the educative processes meant to realize and sustain that democracy serve as the means whereby common affective experiences become effective agencies in society. "Democracy is the name for a life of free and enriching communion. . . . It will have its consummation when free social inquiry is indissolubly wedded to the art of full and moving communication."[30] Dewey's educational theory is dominated by the notion of communication. Effective communication is the communication of affective *feeling*. We do not begin with ideas. Nor do we begin in any simple sense with practices. "Learning by doing" – the cliché by which Dewey's form of education has been parodied and dismissed – is always a learning by *undergoing* as well. There is no doing without undergoing, no action without *passion*. Feeling both accompanies and is generated by educative activities. And, as all education is transactional, the aim of education is the creation of a *community of affect*. Such a community is the source and aim of a democratic society. And this *communicating community* is continually constituted by the enchantments of art and aesthetic activity.

It is important to recognize that "rare and remote" experiences individuate and separate. Experiences open to but a few create experiential elites of the sort associated with the effete aestheticism of a merely "cultured" class. Art dwells on the commonplaces capable of enriching every life. As a "communicating community," a democratic society ensures the common access to these commonplaces of life.

Dewey's aesthetic understanding is not without its distinctly spiritual component. Dewey employs the term "religious" to indicate "the sense of the connection of man, in the way of both dependence and support, with the enveloping world that the imagination feels is a universe."[31] Dewey's understanding of religion begins from social practices which, when they achieve a certain breadth and depth of meaning, reveal a religious sensibility that connects a cultured human community more profoundly to the natural world. Dewey's sense of religion requires no belief in a supernatural supreme being: "Nature, as the object of knowledge, is capable of being the source of constant good and a rule of life, and thus has all the properties and the functions that the Jewish-Christian tradition attributed to God."[32]

30 Dewey (1927):184.   31 *Late Works*, 9:36.   32 *Late Works*, 4:45.

In fact, although Dewey sometimes does refer to "God," any notion of a temporally prior, transcendent source and architect of the human experience, lawgiver and judge, is anathema to Deweyan Pragmatism. What Dewey wants to preserve of traditional theism is its "natural piety" as a sense of awe and wonder that encourages a humble attitude of cooperation with the natural complexity that surrounds us. It is religiousness in this sense that guarantees the enchantment of the human experience.

There is much in this idiosyncratic vocabulary of Dewey's that resonates with distinctly Confucian sensibilities: "experience" and *dao* (道), "consummatory experience" and *he* (和) (harmony), "individuality" and *ren* (仁), "religiousness" and *li* (禮), human nature and the processional *renxing* (人性) (human nature). Other points of convergence include the irreducibly social nature of human experience, the priority of situation to agency, the central importance of effective communication, and a human- rather than God-centered religious sensibility. On all these issues the ideas of Dewey and Confucius are joined in the effort to promote and maintain an enchanted world.

Critics are certainly correct in noting that Weber's fears have been more justified than Dewey's hopes. Weber's vindication, however, is more the result of refusing to attend to the Deweyan alternative than a consequence of circumstantial inevitabilities. Moreover, there is some reason to believe that, in its service to the development of a Confucian democracy, Dewey's thought may itself become additionally revitalized in the Western world. That is to say, the new variable in the historical equation – that of Confucianism – may shift the balance somewhat toward Dewey's understanding of democracy as a communicating community and away from Weber's concession to the inevitability of disenchantment and rationalization. In any case, if institutional democracies are to escape the strictures of Weber's "iron cage," they must proceed along lines similar to those charted by Dewey. The advantage here lies with Confucian societies since they are already shaped by an aesthetic rather than a rational dominant.

2 CONFUCIUS AND THE ENCHANTMENT OF THE FAMILIAR

Weber famously excepted Asian societies from his generalizations about the inevitability of rationalizing processes. Of course, were he theorizing today, he might wish to reconsider this exemption in the light of the current narrowed dynamics of globalization. The religious traditionalism predominating in Asian societies, which Weber thought to be intransigent, has begun to soften considerably under the pressure of Westernization. In particular, the hope that traditional values defining the Confucian sensibility might be isolated from the forces of secularization seems to have been in error. There are many informed and sometimes sympathetic interpreters of contemporary Asia who believe that, if present tendencies continue apace, what we recognize as Confucian culture might well be in jeopardy.

Indeed, a significantly rationalized Confucian society is difficult to imagine. Rituals (li 禮) are agencies of enchantment. They are means of allowing human transactions to take place at an unmediated, aesthetic level without the necessity of one having to "take thought." Rationalization of social forms is antithetical to Confucian li – and to the core of Confucianism itself.

In Confucianism, li are to be understood in terms of the controlling metaphor of "family" as a sphere of unrationalized intimacy. "The degree of love due different kin and the graduated esteem due those who are different in character is what gives rise to ritual propriety (li)" (Zhongyong 中庸 20). Speaking generally, it is the patterns of deference that constitute the family itself. The appropriate transactions among its members give rise to, define, and authorize the specific ritualized roles and relationships (li) through which the process of individual refinement is pursued. What makes these ritualized roles and relationships fundamentally different from rational rules or laws is the fact that not only must they be personalized, but the quality of the particular persons invested in these li is the ultimate criterion of their efficacy.[33]

The expression zhongyong (中庸), first found in the Analects and then elaborated in the text that takes this same term as its title, actually means a thorough attentiveness to the ongoing need to "focus the familiar." Zhongyong 1 states: "The Master said, 'Sustaining focus (zhong) in the familiar affairs of the day is a task of the highest order. It is rare among the common people to be able to sustain it for long.'" This Zhongyong version is reminiscent of Analects 12.1 in which "self-discipline (keji 克己) through full personal participation in li (fuli 復禮) produces authoritative conduct (ren 仁)": "If for the space of a day one were able to accomplish this, the whole empire would defer to this authoritative model. Becoming authoritative in one's conduct is self-originating – how could it originate with others?"

In reading the Analects, we have a tendency to give short shrift to the middle books 9–11 which are primarily a series of intimate snapshots depicting moments in the life of the historical person Confucius that reflect the habits of his daily life. Yet it is precisely these passages that are most revealing of the extent to which the appropriate behaviors of a scholar-

33 See Analects 3.3: "What has a person who is not authoritative got to do with observing ritual propriety? What has a person who is not authoritative got to do with the playing of music?"

official participating in the daily life of the court were choreographed: the slightest gesture, the cut of one's clothes, the cadence of one's stride, one's posture and facial expression, one's tone of voice, even the rhythm of one's breathing:

> On passing through the entrance way to the Duke's court, he would bow forward from the waist, as though the gateway were not high enough. While in attendance, he would not stand in the middle of the entranceway; on passing through, he would not step on the raised threshold. On passing by the empty throne, his countenance would change visibly, his legs would bend, and in his speech he would seem to be breathless. He would lift the hem of his skirts in ascending the hall, bow forward from the waist, and hold in his breath as though ceasing to breathe. On leaving and descending the first steps, he would relax his expression and regain his composure. He would glide briskly from the bottom of the steps, and returning to his place, he would resume a reverent posture.[34]

Such care in one's conduct, far from being reserved for court life, begins in the intimacy of one's home environment: "In Confucius' home village, he was most deferential, as though at a loss for words, and yet in the ancestral temple and at court, he spoke articulately, though with deliberation."[35]

The *Analects* does not provide us with a catechism of prescribed formal conducts, but rather with the image of a particular historical person striving with imagination to exhibit the sensitivity to ritualized living that would ultimately make him the teacher of an entire civilization. Take, for example, the following passage: "When ill, and his lord came to see him, he would not recline with his head facing east, and would have his court dress draped over him with his sash drawn."[36] This is an image of Confucius. It does not say that in all instances of being visited by a lord, one must behave in a particular way. Rather, it describes how Confucius found a way to express the appropriate deference and loyalty required of a relationship, even under the most trying of circumstances.

From these passages and many others like them, it should be clear that *li* do not reduce to generic, formally prescribed "rites" and "rituals," performed at stipulated times to announce relative status and to punctuate the seasons of one's life. The *li* are much more. The performance of *li* must be understood in light of the uniqueness of each participant and the profoundly local and focal project of becoming a person. *Li* involve an ongoing process of personal investment that, with persistence and effort, refines the quality of one's communal transactions. Rather than imposing some superordinate character

---

34 *Analects* 10:4.   35 *Analects* 10.1.   36 *Analects* 10.19.

upon this process, we might want to think of *li* as producing an achieved disposition, an habituated attitude, a posture, an identity-in-action.[37]

Referring to our discussion of Dewey's understanding of "habit" in Part I of this essay, we can understand how *li* promote unmediated, aesthetic, experience. We can further understand how inappropriate it is to think of *li* as a social mechanism that routinizes experience, effectively impoverishing it in the process. In fact, the Confucian reliance upon *li* is meant to achieve precisely the opposite. *Li* are intended as means of enchanting the everyday and inspiring the ordinary. Appropriately performed, *li* elevate the commonplace and customary into something elegant and profoundly meaningful. The focus on the familiar is an attempt to optimize the creative possibilities of the human community and to transform the patterns of everyday living into profoundly socioreligious practices.

Conversations among educated Chinese appeal to a core repository of discourse. Such conversations tend to be highly allusive, involving citations of classical texts and the employments of apothegms and proverbs common to the tradition. Such allusive interactions serve aesthetic, rather than strictly rational, ends. The effects of such aesthetic, allusive, communication is 1) to point away from individual personalities toward some commonly acknowledged cultural models, 2) to promote affective bonding by appeal to evocative rather than conceptual meanings, thus precluding raising to consciousness the precise reasons for any disagreements, and 3) to thereby preclude the otherwise meliorative exchange from degenerating into dissonance.[38]

To the extent that the term "propriety," entailing the cognate range of meaning of its root, *proprius* – "proper, appropriate, property" – is understood as "a making one's own," it is a felicitous translation of *li* that emphasizes the process of personalization. *Li* is thus a resolutely personal performance revealing one's worth to oneself and to one's community, a personal and a public discourse through which one constitutes and reveals oneself qualitatively as a unique individual, a whole person. Importantly, there is no respite; *li* requires the utmost attention in every detail of what one does at every moment that one is doing it, from the drama of the high court to the posture one assumes in going to sleep, from the reception of different guests to the proper way to comport oneself when alone; from how one behaves in formal dining situations to appropriate extemporaneous gestures.

37 See an extended discussion of ritualized living in Roger T. Ames and David L. Hall, *Focusing the Familiar: A Translation and Philosophical Interpretation of the* Zhongyong (中庸) (Honolulu: University of Hawaii Press, 2001).
38 One might reflect here how much more civil was our Western democratic life when Homer, the Bible, and Shakespeare formed the core curriculum.

Another way of underscoring this claim that the proper observance of *li* entails a full awareness of and responsiveness to the complexity and range of human interdependencies is to explore the role that *li* has as the primary subject of "study (*xue* 學)" in the classical texts. In fact, it is *li* that actually *constitute* the range and determinate pattern of one's own person, projecting and extending an identity outward against the indeterminate boundaries of one's world. When Confucius repeatedly celebrates a profound commitment to learning (*haoxue* 好學)[39] and describes his favorite student Yan Hui in the same terms,[40] he goes on to define the content of this "learning" as the personal refinement accomplished through ritualized living. The cognate, paronomastic relationship between "studying (*xue* 學)" and unmediated "feeling (*jue* 覺)" is of course relevant here. While the written culture might be an ancillary element in this education, recording as it does the narratives of cultural exemplars and the defining events of their lives, far more central is the actual authentication of *li* in "feeling" the familiar affairs of one's day.

"Familiar" is a deliberate choice of a term here because it shares the same root as, and thus evokes the notion of, "family" which is at the center of the Confucian socioreligious experience. In rehabilitating the "familiar" nature of *li*, we have to allow that the radial focus for observing ritual propriety in the "familiar" affairs of the day lies with the family. The *Zhongyong* 20 underscores the relationship between family and its extension as social and political order: "In general there are nine guidelines in administering the world, the state, and the family, yet the way of implementing them is one and the same." *Analects* 1.2 explicitly states that *dao* (道) itself – the emerging way of conducting oneself as a human being – emerges out of the achievement of robust filial relations: "Exemplary persons (*junzi* 君子) concentrate their efforts on the root, for the root having taken hold, the way (*dao* 道) will grow therefrom. As for filial and fraternal responsibility, it is, I suspect, the root of authoritative conduct (*ren* 仁)."

The family as an institution provides the model for this optimizing process of making one's way by allowing the persons who constitute it to both invest in and get the most out of the human experience. The underlying assumption is that persons are more likely to give themselves utterly and unconditionally to their families than to any other human institution. Promoting the centrality of family relations is an attempt to assure that entire persons without remainder are invested in each of their actions.

A second consideration in optimizing the creative possibilities of the community is the absence of a religion of transcendence. The power of the family to function as the radial locus for human growth is much enhanced when

---

39 *Analects* 1.14, 5.15, 8.13, 17.7.   40 *Analects* 6.3 and 11.7.

natural family and communal relations are not perceived as being in competition with, a distraction from, or dependent upon some higher supernatural
relations. It is from the family expanding outward radially that persons
emerge as objects of profound communal, cultural, and ultimately religious
deference. Beyond the achievement of an intense religious quality felt in the
everyday experience of their lives, these exemplary persons emerge as ancestors for their families and communities and as contributors to the ancestral
legacy.

The Hegelian picture of an Oriental despotism in which all authority lies
with the emperor reflects a common failure of Western interpreters to appreciate the extent to which *informal* social mechanisms such as "observing ritual
propriety (*li* 禮)" and the cultivation of a shame culture are conduits through
which the community effects its own order. This is precisely the point of
Analects 2.3: "Lead the people with administrative injunctions (*zheng* 政) and
keep them orderly with penal law (*xing* 刑), and they will avoid punishments
but will be without a sense of shame. Lead them with excellence (*de* 德) and
keep them orderly through observing ritual propriety (*li* 禮) and *they will
develop a sense of shame, and moreover, will order themselves.*" This passage gives
us an aspirational Confucian version of "noncoercive" guidance through full
participation in a ritually constituted community, a Confucian version of
"non-assertive actions (*wuwei* 無為)."

In the absence of an individual soul or essential nature, a human being in
classical Confucianism is ultimately an aggregate of shared, usually familial
experience. Ritual activity is a medium which ensures that this cumulative
experience is constantly refined and meaningful. Thus the human being is an
always "enchanted" being – and the social relationships focused by that being
are themselves processes of the continued enchantment of the world.

3 THE ISSUE OF RIGHTS

Contemporary China remains, even under "communism," a ritually constituted society, without even a rhetorical appeal to the belief in objective principles often associated with liberal reflections upon the issue of human rights.
The very idea of some regimen of human rights possessed prior to their being
granted by the particular society to which one belongs has never been an
assumption of Chinese rulers or peoples. But, as we shall see, this does not
mean that the Chinese are left without any guarantees of social or political
rights.

The real irony of the liberal approach to human rights is that even if it
were wholly defensible, the exclusive rhetoric of its presentation precludes
Chinese investment in its ideas and implications. After all, the consequences

of Western universalism for the Chinese have thus far been hegemonic and humiliating. And given the communal commitments of the indigenous Chinese notion of person, the values of autonomy, independence, and self-sufficiency espoused by liberal democracy would be seen not as ideals but as a particularly pernicious pathology.

In the recent rights talk, the Chinese have traditionally held, consistent with the pragmatic view, that "rights" are granted by society. Further, these rights are promoted through the sort of education meant to sensitize individuals to their importance both to individuals and to the overall harmony of society. Thus, in China there is less of a tendency to stress the strictly legal enforcement of rights. In fact, reliance upon the application of law, far from being a means of realizing human dignity, has been perceived as fundamentally dehumanizing since it leads to the impoverishment of mutual accommodation and compromises the particular responsibilities of the community to define what would be appropriate conduct.

It is also important to realize that the Chinese communitarian under-standing of rights tends to lead to the promotion of social *interests* over indi-vidual *rights*. The distinction between rights and interests mirrors the liberal distinction between the right and the good. The distinction provides some protection against collectivist arguments that would lead to the coercion of the individual in the name of some social good.

Rights are defined categorically in terms of moral principles. Interests, on the other hand, are associated with utility and social welfare. The moment social welfare is appealed to, the interests of the majority are thought to be sustained over those of the minority. Rights sometimes function to protect the individual against the majority. Appeal to interests tends not to allow for such protection. The goal in an interest-based society is not the protection of the individual, but the integration of individual interests with those of the group. This is a real roadblock to the development of a Confucian concep-tion of human rights. By making social harmony the goal, Confucianism does not seem readily consistent with any vision of human rights that would protect the individual against the majority. As Randall Peerenboom has observed: "Translating rights into the language of interests generally produces outcomes favoring state action and impinging upon individual pro-tections. When one weighs the interests of the individual against the inter-est of the many individuals, the community, the state, the many usually win."[41]

---

41 Randall Peerenboom, "Confucian Harmony and Freedom of Thought: The Right to Think Versus Right Thinking," in *Confucianism and Human Rights*, edited by Wm. T. de Bary and Tu Wei-ming (New York: Columbia University Press, 1998):251–252.

In a communitarian society, when social harmony collapses, the conse-quences are indeed most grave. For, in the absence of legal mechanisms pro-moting social stability and protecting the individual against the state and the majority, authoritarian actions by the government are all that remain. The present rapid transitions in China, therefore, are peculiarly troublesome since it seems inevitable that China will suffer from excess reliance upon actions of the central government. In spite of the imminence of this crisis, a careful and sympathetic look at the Chinese model might suggest that long-term solutions do not lie solely in the direction of increased legal resort, but to alternative nonlegal mechanisms.

The practical effectiveness of legal guarantees depends upon a significant degree of "social empathy" – the feeling that others are as deserving of legal protections as oneself. Honest reflection upon the status of minorities and the poor in liberal societies suggests that legal guarantees are hardly enough. The same is, of course, true in China. The egregious treatment of the Tibetans by the Chinese is a most serious case in point. Were we to face the issue squarely, we might be willing to recognize that since "human rights" are only guar-anteed to *humans*, the practical question is always "Who among us counts as a human being?" Pragmatically speaking, the Tibetans are denied the hon-orific "human being" by the Chinese – but so have been the Aboriginals by the Australians, African Americans by white America, Muslims by Christians (and vice versa) in Eastern Europe – and so on across the globe. It is an open question whether in America, for example, minorities and women have achieved more effective rights through the institution of legal mechanisms than would have been achieved by concentration upon the enlargement – through the agencies of a truly democratic education – of our practical under-standing of precisely who is fully human.

For the Pragmatist, there is less concern to "ground" any particular list of rights than there is to demonstrate their value in practice. The principal issue is not the specific belief in an antecedently existing individual as a bearer of this or that set of rights. It is, rather, the actual thick social practices of a society or community that validate or fail to validate the value of any set of beliefs. These thick practices are grounded in social empathy that extends the honorific "human being" as far as is possible through ritualized living.

So much of the liberal rhetoric concerning human rights amounts to little more than abstract theorizing about the need for every individual to be granted this or that right, with the communitarians' appeals to cultivating thick social practices being dismissed impatiently as Pollyannish utopianism. Dewey recognized this theoretical bias as a central problem of human rights discussions. It was his view that the more attention we pay to the imple-mentation of rights, and the less to abstract speculations concerning their status and content, the better off we would be. Wryly alluding to the French wag who observed that "the law prohibits both the rich and the poor from stealing bread," Dewey suggests that we see the problem of human rights as having "changed from that of seeking individual rights themselves to one of seeking the opportunity to exercise those rights."[42] Political theory has to be reoriented to inquire into ways in which individuals can get property, so that they can exercise the right of property ownership, instead of continuing to theorize in empty abstractions about the need for every person to be granted the right to own property.

Dewey's distinctly communitarian concerns are most clearly expressed here. Rights-based liberalism must be less concerned with the implementation of rights than the communitarian. Worrying over the fact that the "have-nots" de facto have less *effective* rights than the "haves" would tempt one to believe with the communitarian that second-generation rights, such as economic welfare, may actually precede the implementation of equitable first-generation rights. And no self-respecting rights-based liberal wishes to be so tempted.

4 RATIONAL POLITICS VERSUS ENCHANTED CULTURE: AN ILLUSTRATIVE COMPARISON

The central thread running throughout this essay has been the essentially Weberian contrast of rationalized "political" mechanisms and nonrationalized, "enchanted" operations of culture. Traditional democratic theories are both consequences of the processes of rationalization and agencies for the furtherance of institutional rationality. Our use of Deweyan Pragmatism as a possible counter to the disenchantment of the modern world has permitted us to bring Confucianism into a positive engagement with at least the communitarian wing of the proponents of Asian democratization.

It so happens that, as one might expect, the current trends toward democratization in Asia are represented by the forces of rationalization, on the one hand, and those of enchantment, on the other. In the following paragraphs we want to suggest how one might better understand and interpret the processes of democratization as they are presently playing themselves out in one Asian society. Although we focus on China, our comments have applications to other traditionally Confucian societies, certainly South Korea.[43]

---

42 John Dewey, *Lectures in China*, translated and edited by Robert Clopton and Tsuin-chen Ou (Honolulu: University of Hawaii Press, 1973):152.

43 See the chapters by Lew Seok-Choon and Chang Yun-Shik for more elaborate discussions of the ways in which "social empathy" is shaped in Confucian societies.

The popular media and the American Congress have no monopoly on what can fairly be referred to as "the demonizing of China." Although usually less strident, this indictment-in-search-of-an-issue attitude also has its counterpart within the Western academy. The profoundly negative and counterproductive affect of this posture with respect to the possibilities for Confucian democratization cannot be overstated. It encourages divisive tensions between those individuals who would pursue precisely that decidedly liberal democracy for China which we believe is anathema to traditional Chinese senses of social order, and an often insecure government that in this present period of transformation has taken the maintenance of social order as its prime directive.

We would suggest that the problem with this sort of critique of Chinese democratization is that it presupposes a distinctly rationalized political interpretation of democracy in which governmental institutions and decision-making processes are identified as the substance of a democratic society. If there is to be anything like an indigenous, Confucian democracy in China, this political approach must be replaced by one that is rooted in the fundamental operations of cultural values. To make this point, we shall contrast Michel Oksenberg as a prominent representative of the typically political method of assessing the possibilities for democracy in China with Kate Zhou and her distinctly cultural approach.

Michel Oksenberg has recently authored a "PacNet" essay entitled "The Long March Ahead." In this essay, Oksenberg first enumerates the many economic, social, and cultural obstacles that Chinese must clear in order to sustain China's upward direction in democratization, only to declare that such areas of concern are peripheral. In worrying over them, we are looking in the wrong place. According to Oksenberg:

> The biggest problem is neither economic nor social nor cultural. It is political: can the ruling Chinese Communist Party (CCP) reform itself and retain its relevance? Can the party, through self-reform, lead the nation through the major transitions that loom ahead? Or, will the party prove unable to meet the challenge, resulting in serious disruptions and setbacks in the modernization process?[44]

It is the CCP that is the "make it or break it" factor in China's march to democracy. Observing that even though China is not in imminent danger of disintegration, Oksenberg is concerned that "the party is in trouble. It is approaching the point where its decay will be irreversible. The 1980s and 90s have witnessed a severe erosion in the efficacy of the party's ideological

---

44 PacNet Number 45 (November 19, 1999) of Pacific Forum CSIS, 1001 Bishop Street, Honolulu, HI.

appeals, a weakening of its authority over other institutions, and the atrophying of its core apparatus. In many localities, the party is defunct."

In fairness to Oksenberg, he does not embrace the commonplace that China has achieved its astounding degree of economic reform without any significant political reform. Still, Randall Peerenboom observes that "after providing a lengthy list of reform initiatives," Oksenberg "acknowledges that political reforms have proceeded slowly and that China at its core remains a Soviet-Leninist state."[45] Oksenberg believes that the most important indicator of China's ongoing political reform is the formal structure of government. The elites are to be either blamed or credited for whatever changes occur in the quota of human liberty.

But most students of Chinese culture who have spent any time at all living in China over the past two decades have witnessed exponential changes in the liberties that attend the business of everyday life, not simply in the cities, but even more importantly in the countryside as well. If the CCP is the key factor and Oksenberg is right about its intransigence, what are we to make of this galloping transformation in the ways of thinking and living that are reshaping the habits of the day? And to what extent is an understanding of this sea change pertinent to an adequate assessment of the process of democratization?

The pragmatic perspective that requires arguments be made on behalf of practical relevance by no means enjoins an abandonment of cultural explanation. On the contrary, any attempt to ignore the broad range of cultural variables that might serve as guides or goads of action is distinctly unpragmatic.

Unquestionably, Oksenberg is correct in suggesting that events are often shaped by specific decisions relevant to concrete circumstances which may or may not involve explicit appeal to so-called cultural values. But it is crucial to note that the influence of cultural values does not have to be explicit to be important. Indeed, the specific effects of the enchanted world of culture are not easily reckoned with. Nonetheless, it constitutes the life-world to which political and economic actions must ultimately answer.

Individuals who accept political actions and decisions as the motors of social change are adverse to arguments that presume the importance of cultural values and institutions because they have already bought into the inevitable disenchantment of the cultural sphere consequent upon the rationalization of social life in late-modern societies. Edward Friedman notes,

---

45 Randall P. Peerenboom, *China's Long March Toward Rule of Law* (Cambridge: Cambridge University Press, 2002), citing Michel Oksenberg, "China's Political System: Challenges of the Twenty-first Century," *The China Journal*, No. 45 (2001):24–25.

"Political action can rapidly change the conditions that matter. . . . Politics changes faster than culture."[46] The presence of political pressure groups, or the unilateral decisions of a powerful leader, can effect at least short-term changes in spite of any cultural conditioning features appearing to work against them.

Politics, indeed, makes a difference. The rapidity with which China appears to be making the transition to a capitalist economy clearly suggests the power of economic interests and motivations. The point of the pragmatic culturalist is that while politics is faster, culture runs deeper – and has far greater long-term efficacy. Moreover, both politics and economics are cultural expressions whose power to effect change must be assessed alongside other cultural values. Economic and political approaches are largely focused upon governmental institutions. Cultural analyses, on the other hand, are concerned with a broad range of values embedded in social, ethical, aesthetic, and religious sensibilities in the everyday life of the people. The cultural approach permits us to recognize promising elements in Chinese society and culture that strictly political and economic analyses could easily overlook.

In our recent study of the prospects for democracy in China, *Democracy of the Dead*, we attempted to defend the explanatory principle that "everything is local" by challenging what we take to be the limits of political and socioeconomic accounts of the accelerating process of democratization that is presently taking place in China. We argue that in trying to interpret change in China, we are often influenced by our own prioritization of causal factors and end up looking in the wrong places. For example, we are inclined to fasten onto the intellectuals as a motive force in channeling and directing the floodwaters of democratic reform, forgetting that as elite (and often effete) "institutional intellectuals," they are, in important degree, complicit in the existing power structure and have a real vested interest in the status quo. Perhaps we need to look elsewhere. With the unstoppable rural influx into the urban centers having swelled to some 10–20 percent (100–200 million) of China's population and having altered irrevocably the human landscape of both country and city, we might do better to be looking to bottom-up, emergent pressures in explanation of democratic developments.

The anthropologist Elisabeth Croll argues persuasively for a much more nuanced and culturally sensitive understanding of "development" that was, during the communist era, driven by a collective dream of an imagined millenarian future. More recently, in an abrupt and painful awakening from a

---

46 Edward Friedman, ed., *The Politics of Democratization – Generalizing Asian Experiences* (Boulder, Colo.: Westview Press, 1994):4, 5.

dream that had darkened into an ideologically sustained nightmare, development has been driven by new ways of thinking about time and change.

> It is possible to identify a domestic space, domain or arena of relations which constitutes the peasant household and which is the locus of much of the rural development process. Indeed, what characterises the period of reform in the past decades has been the identification of development with the domestic sphere; it is the site where development is produced and re-enacted so that domestic organisation and activity is the centre piece of the rural development plan.[47]

We may also contrast the sort of analysis represented by Oksenberg's state-centered elite-focused approach with the account of the forces of change proffered by the political scientist, Kate Zhou. Deliberately substituting the term "farmer" for "peasant" to express a reassessment of the perceived locus of power, she argues that the reforms so evident in contemporary China were initiated in the countryside and have been successful not because of the deliberate policies of the CCP, but largely in spite of them. At best, the CCP that would take credit for the rising tide of recent development can only claim that it did not intervene to stop it.

In Zhou's book, *How the Farmers Changed China: Power of the People*, she traces the origins and energy of the most dramatic changes – economic, political, and cultural – to what she sees as the effects of informally tolerated relaxations in the locus of production at the local level. *Baochan daohu* 包產到戶 – the production and marketing by farmers of privately owned goods beyond their official quotas allowed at the local household level – was a seemingly minor innovation that had, and continues to have, cascading consequences. Zhou argues that the escalating process of reform, rather than trickling down into the countryside from policies enacted and enforced by power elites in the urban centers, was in fact the product of "a spontaneous, leaderless, non-ideological, apolitical movement (SULNAM)" that continues to induce restructuring at the macro levels of government. Importantly, Zhou does not set out to simply challenge political and socioeconomic accounts of reform in China, but to actually rewrite recent history from the farmers' point of view.

Although the issue of "democratization" is implicit in Zhou's earlier analyses of "development" in China, in her more recent work on civil rights it becomes the main theme of discussion. Her argument, building on and really going beyond the research of James Scott who first articulated the idea of the power of unorganized everyday resistance in Southeast Asia, is that civil rights are not given by those who run the formal apparatus of state, but are rather

---

47 Elisabeth Croll, *From Heaven to Earth: Images and Experiences of Development in China* (London: Routledge, 1994):x.

won slowly and surely by the people. And they are largely won through the informal and nonconfrontational transactions that take place in enchanting the everyday lives of the people as these doings and undergoings are played out in their schools, workplaces, and homes. It is the constant and unrelenting pressure of informal actions, including civil disobedience on a massive scale, that tests the tenacity of the formal structures, sometimes rendering them porous and malleable, and sometimes rendering them defunct.

Zhou's research looks to the changing conditions of the local and the everyday as they exert transformative effects on the global. Her project is entirely consistent with our suggestion that Confucian democracy as it emerges will have more to do with the degree of success that local groups have in slowly and quietly enchanting the routine habits of the day than with any dramatic pronouncements of central authority. It is precisely in the social, economic, and especially the cultural landscape of China that democratization will occur if it is to occur at all.

Is the demystification and disenchantment of the Confucian world unavoidable? If so, then the term "Confucian democracy" is, indeed, a contradiction in terms. We believe that the only hope in escaping the tradition/modernity dynamic encapsulated in the Weberian notion of rationalization is to appeal again to something like the pragmatic proposals we have been forwarding, since these proposals effectively swing free of many of the rationalizing processes Weber thought inevitable in the Western world. And we further believe that it is this pragmatic model of democracy that offers the only prominent exception to the processes of rationalization and secularization that are currently shaping democratization in Asian societies.

CHAPTER 6

THE CASE FOR MORAL EDUCATION

GEIR HELGESEN

In the primary and secondary school curriculum moral education is always mentioned before all other subjects, because the right way of living is more important than anything else. Learning to live as a member of society, as a civilized citizen, is the most important thing. In order to lead a civilized life, we need models, ideas and guidelines, and we need discipline. Our instruction aims at getting the children to think about these subjects, and the final goal is to lead them in the right direction, to lead them to behave as they were taught. That is why moral education always is mentioned first, even before Korean language.[1]

This is how a Korean schoolteacher underlined the importance of moral education in 1990, explaining something that for her was pretty obvious: If you fail to develop social skills, if you can't get along with your colleagues and friends, professional skills may be useless. In a Confucian country a person's human qualities (i.e., that he or she understands his or her role in society and performs in this role according to generally agreed upon norms) come first. This has had top priority in Korean education, and the schoolteacher expressed it quite clearly without making any reference to Confucius or Confucianism. This is probably the most significant aspect to note in a discussion of socialization and education as enculturation.[2] On what basis, however, do we claim that Confucianism prevails in Korea? Traditionally, filial piety and ancestor worship formed the moral axiom of society. This was ritualized and propagated by Confucian moral teaching, and this idea has moreover been transmitted to contemporary moral education. This much we know. But do we know whether Confucianism has survived as a moral creed,

---

1 Geir Helgesen, *Democracy and Authority in Korea: The Cultural Dimension in Korean Politics* (Richmond, Va.: Curzon Press, 1998), p. 169.
2 Enculturation is understood here as the process that imbues a people with their own culture, enabling them to operate naturally within it. In this sense, culture is not something people *have*, but something they *become*.

Table 1

Questionnaire Statement	Percent Agreement
A leader should care for the people as parents for their children	89
We can leave everything to a morally upright leader	75
The objective of good government is to maintain harmonious social relations	91
The ideal society is like a family	87
The quality of the politicians is more important than laws and institutions	74
The moral and human qualities of a leader are more important than his ideas	85
A group of people without a strong leader means chaos	82
It is more important to have an outstanding leader than political democracy	58

still commanding power as a guideline for human action? The short answer is that leaders are still depicted as patriarchal figures and the state is still ideally seen as the extreme extension of one's family.

In a national sample survey conducted by Hyundai Research Institute in the spring of 2000,[3] an overwhelming majority of the respondents confirmed that Korean politics are still marked by a strong moral touch, and that this is the context within which leaders and followers operate (see Table 1). The response pattern in Table 1 confirms that attitudes which make sense in a Confucian context have strong support in present-day Korea. It is not suggested that each and every one of the eight items in the table is necessarily linked to "a Confucian mind." As will be revealed later in this chapter, apparently Confucian statements can also be endorsed outside East Asia. However, in Table 1 the eight statements taken together clearly support the view that "If a ruler himself is upright, all will go well even though he does not give orders. But if he himself is not upright, even though he gives orders, they will not be obeyed."[4]

It is thus here assumed that Confucianism has survived and still informs the mainstream political culture in Korea. This is not solely, but mainly, because it has been transmitted in the socialization process and, in addition, because it permeates modern education. Moral education is, however, a controversial issue in Korea's modern history. Because of the division of the

---

3 The survey was conducted for the Eurasia Political Culture Research Network (EPCReN), N:1000.
4 See *The Analects of Confucius* 13:6; D. Howard Smith, *Confucius* (London: Temple Smith, 1973 [1974]), p. 82.

country and the late advent of a democratic political system, moral education was in effect used as an instrument for "brainwashing." Teaching social morality was mixed with politics, of which the most clear and obvious component was anticommunism and anti–North Korea propaganda. Notwithstanding the good reasons for this ideological component, it undermined the legitimacy of the subject of moral education. The fact that military governments exploited traditional morals, mixing them with political propaganda in order to justify their monopolization of political power, damaged the whole concept of moral education – albeit not necessarily the results of these efforts.

The advent of a new political regime in South Korea and the positive changes in relations with the former enemy up north mean that the political "brainwashing" element of moral education is now obsolete. But, has moral education become altogether outdated? Is it just a conservative means of socializing new generations according to the traditional values and norms? Is putting moral education to good use in transferring conceptions of right and wrong from one generation to the next through child-rearing and education antimodern, reactionary, perhaps even downright impossible, in this era of electronic mass communication?

The educational authorities in Korea might well answer in the affirmative. They have now prepared a reform for implementation in 2003 which will reduce the number of hours spent in formal moral education classes. This reform is a change deemed necessary by modernizers in this era of globalization. Apparently, they view moral education as backward and parochial, a dead weight holding back the modernization process. Korea and its people, in their opinion, need to become more open-minded and future-oriented.

Educational reforms have been abundant in modern Korean history. In the Korean cultural context, in which formal education is perceived as the very process which transforms one into a human being, in which this education is the most legitimate route to social advancement, and in which the authorities have always regarded education as a means of guiding people toward the prescribed behavior, educational reforms are obviously pivotal. Reforms are usually deemed to be necessary precursors of social change, but in reality they are often the product of changes that have already taken place. Not that there is necessarily a direct link between change and reform, but reforms presented as essential may actually prove to be no more than ill-considered adjustments to negative changes. In this chapter it will thus be argued that the planned educational reform may be counterproductive to its stated purpose: to prepare Korea and its people for whatever the future may bring – and at the moment, globalization is what most people see as the future.

Until recently, political socialization "naturally" took place within a geographical entity called a nation-state, in which the political authorities in charge defined the rules and regulations of social and antisocial behavior. The content of political socialization reflected political and ideological priorities and beliefs, but it was not independent of the general values and norms transferred from past to present, from generation to generation. Political socialization was related to a particular place and time and aimed at contributing to the shaping of the ideal citizen regardless of class distinctions. The changes now taking shape on the horizon apparently raise the question of whether it still makes sense to pursue the creation of "the ideal citizen." Alternatively, perhaps the authorities have convinced themselves that the qualities which will be needed in the future will be fundamentally different from those cherished in the past.

What changes in the social environment in Korea motivate the authorities to suggest a downscaling of moral education? To answer this question one has to look at *globalization*, the buzzword of contemporary political debates.

WHERE ARE WE HEADING?

The term *political development*, which used to denote a societal movement toward what were perceived as better times, has nowadays been replaced with the term *globalization*. In the globalization process, development is dissociated from politics. In our time, development seems to have become an ongoing process to which both politicians and everyone else has to adjust. What does it mean that the world is "globalized"? To summarize a general definition, it means increasing convergence and interdependence of national economies and of the international scope and availability of markets, distribution systems, capital, labor, and technology. What then are the non-economic consequences of globalization?

Zygmunt Bauman, a renowned sociologist who has dealt with the human consequences of globalization, has compared the present world situation with that of an airplane high up in the sky, in which the passengers, after having traveled for hours, suddenly discover that there are no pilots in the cockpit.[5] This easy-to-imagine (and for frequent flyers frightening!) illustration might be an exaggeration of the feelings of the ordinary citizen, but nevertheless it touches on a question in the contemporary world which is basic, existential, and difficult to answer: "Where are we heading?" It goes without saying that this question is decisive in the field of political socialization.

Another famous contemporary sociologist, Anthony Giddens, suggests that we, as citizens of the world, accept our fate; for no matter what we do (according to him), change is already sweeping the world, leaving no room for those who believe that it can be stopped and reversed. On the other hand, warns

---

5 See the Danish daily *Information*, February 10, 2000.

Giddens, globalization should not run amok, but should be controlled. He sees both fundamentalism and resignation as dead-ends in politics, and to avoid either pitfall he suggests "a democratization of democracy."[6] To accomplish this we need to understand what is happening around us and then to develop a *cosmopolitan society*. This may turn out to be as risky as it sounds beautiful.

One problem with such broad philosophical speculations on our era and the changes that we experience (and on which we must take a stand, whether we understand them or not), is that real people, real life, flesh and blood, emotions, and places have all disappeared from the discourse. So, too, has empirical evidence. We may all be acquainted with "cosmopolitan" people, exotic "globe-trotters" and famous scholars who are at home in any academic setting. But what about the rest of us? Can we truly say "I'm home wherever I happen to be"? Honestly, one might begin to fear that in this case *everywhere* would mean just about the same as *nowhere*. What kind of world would that produce?

It is difficult to take the concept of "world development" seen from a grass-roots perspective and deal with it convincingly, giving ordinary people a voice to express themselves with regard to these things. One way to attempt this, albeit incomplete and rather crude, is to conduct surveys. In a recent survey that we conducted in Denmark,[7] one statement read as follows: "The ideal society is like a family." This survey is being used as part of a comparative East-West study, and this was one of our typically "East Asian statements." To our surprise, 75 percent of *Danish* respondents agreed to this statement. I think it safe to comment that when people compare the ideal society to a family, it is hardly the "family of man" that they have in mind. It is rather a parent-child relationship, in which emotional bonds secure the functions of the family, regardless of the greater or lesser disagreements of daily life. The family may be regarded as the ideal model for society by a small European country in the final year of the twentieth century, but what is the social reality?

Anthony Giddens is one of the main architects of the ideology of or theoretical platform for the so-called New Labor in England, which is spreading to most of the other countries in Europe. This new political ideology can be seen as one of the strongest tools for undermining the view of politics as "the art of making things possible." Instead, politics has become "the art of making sense of the inevitable," a tool to convince people that there is no other possible solution, no realistic alternative, to what *is*. Giddens mentions

6 Giddens's book is entitled *Runaway World* (London: Profile Books, 1999), and it is this concept that has inspired the thoughts expressed in this chapter.
7 A representative survey using a panel of 1,400 respondents. Data not yet published.

two possible pitfalls in contemporary world politics – fundamentalism and resignation – but there is a third (which he may have failed to notice simply because he has already fallen into it). The third is to rationalize the current situation, to impart reason and acclaim to whatever is deemed inevitable. In Giddens's own country, the Tony Blair project is said to have reinvigorated England, and it is true that a massively advertised political optimism brought a young, not-too-dogmatic social democrat to power after years of conservative misrule. Today we read, however, that the proportion of those living in poverty is, in relative terms, higher in England than it is in the United States. While we might congratulate America, I am afraid that there is more reason to pity England, and in this case Mrs. Thatcher is probably not the only one to blame. What is good for the moneymakers has not turned out so well for the poor – and that is both a social and a moral problem. To merely accept it is an example of exactly the kind of resignation against which Giddens warns.

One of Giddens's observations is that the West has become *detraditionalized* and that the rest of the world is also becoming increasingly so. Traditions, that is, basic values and norms, were once rooted in past practice and imbued in people living in particular areas. The new trend observed by Giddens is the *invention* of "traditions," constructed "traditions" used to rationalize changes in behavior or any behavior at all. Such "traditions" are no longer linked to space or time and are absolutely not products of history. They are linked to particular phenomena or behavior and can be used by individuals all over the globe – a perfect "culture" for a globalized world which hails individual freedom as the most precious aspect of human life.

It is claimed that "[g]lobalization is the direct consequence of the expansion of European culture across the planet via settlement, colonization and cultural mimesis."[8] This also seems to be Giddens's position. As he says, globalization is "led from the West, bears the strong imprint of American political and economic power, and is highly uneven in its consequences" (Giddens 1999: 4). Whether it is an expansion of European culture or something else is not clear. What is clear is that people – first and foremost young people – cannot remain unaffected by whatever targets them as consumers in a global market.

Zygmunt Bauman offers a classic sociological interpretation of why the world is "running away." On the creation of wealth, Bauman says, "The old rich needed the poor to make and keep them rich. That *dependency* at all times mitigated the conflict of interest and prompted some effort, however tenuous,

---

8 Malcolm Waters, *Globalization* (New York: Routledge, 1995), p. 3.

to care. The new rich do not need the poor any more. At long last the bliss of ultimate freedom is nigh."[9]

With the globalization of the economy, the local area with its binding – although unequal – social relations in production and distribution has lost its meaning. The need to care, no matter what, is not a necessary consideration when the entire world is the area of interest. Among the problems Bauman underlines are the widespread fear and uncertainty that people feel about globalization. In his interpretation, people fear that globalization will change the meaning of *community*, both local and national community. Judging from Bauman's description of how wealth is acquired within a global context and of how this dissolves the bonds between "capital" and "labor," this fear is certainly well grounded. Instead of going along with the "inevitable," Bauman argues for a *reintroduction of politics*, but how can this be made possible?

GLOBALIZATION, UNCERTAINTY, AND DEMOCRACY

One particularly important aspect of globalization in relation to political matters is the way the phenomenon affects us and our understanding of the outside world, and how this in turn affects our actions. If globalization – or the many discussions of globalization in general – make people uncertain about the future, then this uncertainty is a reality and must be dealt with as such. If survey research, supported by findings in psychiatry[10] and psychology, reveals that there is a kind of existential insecurity among people which stems from globalization, then there is a real problem – and not only for the people who feel insecure. If people feel that things are getting out of hand and connect this feeling to globalization, then the problem has grave political consequences.

If people feel helpless and politically alienated, eliminated from the decision-making process, they will obviously not fulfill their roles as informed participants in a democratic polity. Their natural reaction will be a loss of interest in political matters and a retreat into personal, private spheres of interest.

Time won through a retreat from active interest and participation in society is generally used for consumption of entertainment. Instead of trying to grasp reality through information, more and more people prefer – or feel forced – to forget about reality and passively take in televised entertainment.

9 Zygmunt Bauman, *Globalization: The Human Consequences* (Cambridge: Polity Press, 1998), p. 72.
10 Paek Sang-chang, then chairman of the Korean Psychiatric Association, warned in 1984 against the psychopathological consequences of Korea's Westernization.

A growing number of satellite and cable TV channels offer nothing but entertainment. Commercial channels are at once agents for sale and consumption and creators of all kinds of needs and desires. The promotion of movie stars as ideal models affects the lifestyle of passive onlookers and perhaps also their world view. Through soap operas and series, certain kinds of ideas, values, and norms are promoted, characterized by oversimplified emotions and stereotypical characters designed to attract the highest possible number of viewers. The effect of the entertainment industry can easily be gauged by observing fashion trends promoting *individualistic uniformity*. The paradox is that while people see themselves as the creations of their own individual wills, they have in reality created a media-dictated figure following strict prescriptions from the fashion industry. Some modernizers see this as "freedom from the cloak of tradition," "unlimited possibilities in an open world," et cetera, but they have actually just exchanged one cloak for another.

Does it matter whether people follow tradition or prefer modern things, whether they are oriented toward local taste and costume or prefer foreign or "global" trends? Yes, it matters. When ideas and values are spread through TV via satellite, "localities are losing their meaning-generating and meaning-negotiating capacity" (Bauman 1998: 2). When "the centres of meaning-and-value production are [today] extraterritorial and emancipated from local constraints," the question is whether this affects the way in which the human mind and body relate to local environments, including local social relations. In a Danish book on "the faces of globalization,"[11] the author Sven Bislev refers to a Turkish writer Oram Pamuk, who observed how stereotypical body movements seen on TV shows affected the way in which local Turkish farmers walked and used their bodies. Similar observations have been made in India (Bislev 1999: 105–106). A keen observer could probably reveal the same sorts of changes taking place in Korea or in any other country that receives standardized (usually American-made) "junk" entertainment. The problem with allowing television and other electronic and digital media to take over the role of conveying ideas, values, and norms – a role once held by other means – is that the mass-produced stories they present are seldom created with the intent of promoting good, decent, or even tacitly acceptable values. They are produced so as to be salable to as many TV channels as possible. Therefore, most series for kids and young people can be termed "junk" entertainment. Implicit to this viewpoint is, of course, the opinion that young people need (but do not receive) moral direction.

Perhaps the way that young people walk, or what they wear, eat, or drink, is not so important. But if their own community loses its role as the center

---

11 See Sven Bislev, *En Ny og Stoerre Verden? Globaliseringens Ansigter* (A New and Bigger World? The Faces of Globalization) (Copenhagen: Fremad, 1999).

of production of meaning and value, then what role remains for the local community? And how will people now and in the future relate to, manage, preserve, renew, and develop their local social and political environment?

THE EMOTIONAL COMPONENT OF DEMOCRACY

Democracy – basically the idea of the people's power – can hardly be realized without a sense of belonging. It is not realistic to expect political participation by people who do not care, but it is reasonable (and based on plentiful experience) to expect that people who share a feeling of belonging will care for each other and for their community. It is simply hard to envisage any democracy without local roots or at least a shared set of values. Some sort of political community in which there is a shared general understanding of reality seems to be a logical prerequisite for that highly advocated political system known as democracy. In other words, without a shared *political culture*, democracy can only be realized on a formal, institutional level.

Before "globalization," democratic politics invited participation and rallied efforts toward the realization of ideas and dreams. The pursuit of development called for opinions and activism and created a competition based on attempts to reach the goal. In democratic polities, differences of opinion depended upon a basic general agreement. To word it somewhat dramatically, the agreement was formulated as follows: "I strongly disagree with your point of view, and I will fight for the opposite position. I will, however, give my life for your right to maintain your point of view and to fight for it."[12] This overstatement of the terms of the agreement has been chosen to underline the fact that democracy presupposed not only broad-mindedness and mutual respect but actually also a feeling of being "in it together," of being in the same boat.

This feeling did not occur just because a country happened to be democratic. It arose out of socialization and education in the family and in public institutions. It was an expression of the belief that society is made up of socialized *human beings*. An unsocialized individual was not a full-fledged human being and could not fill a position as part of the society. This is written in the past tense since it is doubtful whether this collectivist attitude holds the same power in the new world. It might be worth considering that this "dialogue-democracy" was just as typical for European social democracies as was the welfare idea. But this was way before "New Labor."

12 This sentence has been attributed to Voltaire, who, by the way, was perceived as the leading "sinophile" of the French Enlightenment thinkers. See John James Clarke, *Oriental Enlightenment: The Encounter Between Asian and Western Thought* (London: Routledge, 1997), p. 44.

One might at this stage see a parallel between this criticism of the effects of globalization and the situation in British textile production when machinery was introduced and the laid-off workers attacked the weaving mills. Admittedly, there is a little anti–high-tech feeling invested in this chapter, but it may actually be high time to ask whether every invention enabling us to travel, communicate, produce, eat, et cetera, more, longer, and faster is inherently good, necessary to develop, and worth having and using! This is an important reason for the critical approach, but not the main one.

The main reason why globalization, understood as *runaway world*, is frightening is that it has undermined politics on all levels, taking the power out of politics. This is why globalization might turn out to be a much more effective enemy of democracy than the totalitarian ideologies of the recent past ever were. Some have realized the danger. In France they have imposed certain limits on foreign- (read American-)made programs on TV in order to protect national interests (and, yes, their own TV and film industry). A French militant peasant group recently dismantled a McDonald's burger bar, placed it in boxes in front of the town hall, and asked the local authorities to have it shipped back to the United States. Neither of these actions may curb globalization, but both have met with more sympathy than condemnation among the "locals."

Even large organizations, some of which might even be seen as engines of globalization, are nevertheless increasingly (and for dubious reasons?) interested in culture. Almost ten years ago, the Director of the World Bank's Africa Department at the time[13] pointed out that development failures in Africa frequently could be explained by "the lack of a viable cultural framework [that] erodes national self-confidence and leads to social fragmentation with westernized elites and poor, alienated majorities."[14] Recently, World Bank president James Wolfensohn expressed similar views, saying that he doubts whether development is at all possible if a country's culture is not preserved.[15]

REASONABLE CONTINUITY AND SENSIBLE CHANGE IN MORAL EDUCATION

In Korea, globalization became a relevant topic for the Kim Young Sam administration to tackle, and a strategy for the country's *active participation in the globalization process* was developed.[16] The succeeding administrations seem

---

13 His name was Ismaïl Serageldin.   14 See UNESCO SOURCES, No. 25, April 1991.

15 Interview with the Norwegian magazine *Bistandsaktuelt*, No. 8, November 1999, p. 3.

16 An example is "The Segyehwa Policy of Korea Under President Kim Young Sam," an official pamphlet published by the Korean Overseas Information Service, 1995.

to be following up on this, restructuring Korea's economy according to present global demands. Restructuring is, however, not only something going on in economic spheres. In late 1998, one could read about the "new intellectuals' movement" in Korea designed to produce *permanent changes in people's cultural attitudes*. By favoring creativity over schooling and innovation over hierarchy, the movement's aim was said to be to "de-Confucianize" Korean public life.[17] This may prove a tremendous challenge and also one that could turn out to be counterproductive to the reason behind the formation of the movement, which was *to strengthen Korea in the globalization process*.

In the past, traditionalists held power until Korea lost its independence. The traditional state ideology and social morality had then for more than half a millennium been almost the same – and very much influenced by Confucianism. To some extent one could say that, from the time Korea lost its independence and until very recently, issues dealing with social, political, and ideological ideas have been confined within a rather restricted frame of discussion. North Korea is, of course, the extreme case, but even in South Korea alternative ideas had a limited scope. The radicals' role was left for the young generation to play, especially the students. And student radicalism in South Korea has been legendary.

Dealing with socialization, especially the political part of it – tensions between generations, quarrels between parents and children – has probably always been a part of the developmental process. In the West this was perceived as natural, albeit regrettable. Ancient Greek philosophers spoke of the unruly younger generation. Socrates (470–399 B.C.) complained about the contemporary youth. He said that they were only interested in luxury, that they misbehaved and lacked respect for authority, and that they showed no respect for old people and loved empty twaddle instead of decent work. This was around twenty-five-hundred years ago, and since then it has only gotten worse! In China Confucius – like his followers of different schools in the rest of East Asia – has been particularly interested in avoiding conflicts. Education and enculturation have been the way; tutoring and self-discipline, moral behavior performed as ritual, and reverence for age and tradition have been the message; and social harmony the goal.

Korea's modernization after the war has been marked by conflicts between two viewpoints on political socialization, one perceiving the traditional culture as an obstacle and the other viewing traditional values and norms as a necessary, even positive, point of departure. This does not mean, however, that groups of modernizers opposed separate groups of traditionalists. Usually

---

17 This was reported in *Newsreview*, December 19, 1998, and commented upon by columnist Robert J. Fouser in his regular contribution, "Cultural Dimensions," pp. 14–15.

the two viewpoints have been present side by side as competing notions *within* most Koreans' minds. The practice of moral education has also been marked by these two positions. In the curriculum, social morality was basically Confucian, using the ideal patriarchal, hierarchical family as the point of departure and explaining all other social relations within the same contextual frame. Ideally, this framework was meant to extend to the national level and the president as its head. At the same time, when politics and civic studies were introduced to the curriculum, the liberal version of democracy, as idealized in American political ideology, became the model. It is evident that these two ideals – Confucian social morality and liberal democracy – contrasted with each other, and so, if moral education has had any effect at all on those who received it (in my understanding it has and still does), the outcome might be the formation of divided minds. In his trend-setting article "The Clash of Civilizations," Huntington operates with the concept of "torn countries."[18] Divided minds may be the seeds of "torn societies."

In Korea, the existence of divided minds has been rationalized as a basically generational difference, a difference which means that it is only a question of time until the change is completed and the division resolved. Many observers, including social scientists, may however have overestimated the importance of obvious and often articulated differences in purely political viewpoints which are simply caused by the generation "gap." By focusing on generational differences (and hoping for change) they have overlooked the possibility that, beneath these political differences, there may lie a general agreement about more fundamental but less visible matters, that is, the basic values and norms which lay the foundation for the overall political orientation.

This was what we found when we conducted value surveys in Korea in 1990 and 1995.[19] Among people belonging to the urban, educated elite, about 90 percent agreed on the following four statements:

1. Politics mainly depends on good morals and a humanistic attitude.
2. A better future depends on the social morality in society.
3. Democracy is seeking harmonious social relations.
4. The ideal society is like a family.

There were no significant differences in views between younger and older respondents, no differences due to social status, educational background, or sex. Moreover, all these respondents were strongly in favor of *democracy*, 95

18 Samuel Huntington, "The Clash of Civilizations?" *Foreign Affairs* Vol. 72, No. 3, 1993, pp. 42–45.
19 See Helgesen, *Democracy and Authority in Korea*; 1990 survey 500 respondents, 1995 survey 838 respondents.

percent of the respondents in both surveys saw *people's participation* as essential to democracy, while 98 percent and 99 percent respectively agreed to the statement "Without respect for human rights, there is no democracy" (Helgesen 1998: 75). This suggests that both central traditional values and a Western-type understanding of democracy command support.

The question is whether these two attitudes mix well. In the abovementioned surveys the following statement was also tested: "The ideologies and lifestyle of the West, such as individualism and materialism, threaten to destroy the Korean society" (Helgesen 1998: 128). Large majorities agreed to that statement, 85 percent in 1990 and 78 percent in 1995. This negative statement about "the West" might be of a sort that invites the "right" answer. The response to the following statement indicates, however, that the above response is meaningful: "It is necessary to maintain our ancestor worship tradition even in the waves of modernization." In 1990 the rate of agreement was 89 percent, and five years later the rate of agreement was 88 percent. Thus, there is a strong and probably lasting support for some basic, traditionally rooted values among those interviewed in the two surveys.

Presenting these survey results as contradictory is, of course, the present author's responsibility. However, this does not imply that they are seen as expressions of the same kind, having the same function as guidelines for people's daily lives. It is probably easier – and more common – to support the idea of democracy and exhibit undemocratic conduct in daily life than it is to accept the idea of ancestor worship and demonstrate openly unfilial behavior in front of one's grandfather.

If the strong support for traditional values and norms which surfaced in the survey results bears generalization to the overall population, perhaps the only rational and reasonable thing is simply to accept this state of affairs. Instead of trying to uproot those values which are based on Confucian morality, simply to take them at face value as given may have to be the necessary point of departure for any modernization strategy. This might prove to be more realistic and effective, and it might even open up for necessary adjustments and modernization(s) of a widely accepted (political) culture.

A MORAL EDUCATION DESERVING THE LABEL

Upon what should a revitalization of moral education be built, in order to be loyal to cultural roots and, at the same time, reform oriented? Does Confucianism articulate any universally valid values and norms that could or should be included in a modern moral education curriculum? Without laying claim to expert knowledge of Confucianism, one thing which appears to be central to the philosophy, as well as accepted by most people, is the importance of family relations. They are considered important for the well-being of the individual and the functioning of society. Confucianism, more than any other social philosophy, has contributed to a rationalization of this relationship. Ideally, family relations are seen as the basic pattern to be extended to all social relations. By teaching a social morality which stresses proper rituals based on the emotional pattern people recognize from family life, Confucianism may well have something to offer a "runaway world." The following example, a text from a seventh-grade moral education textbook, may illuminate the argument. The story conveys the agony of a young father of two sons experiencing his own father's final days. At his father's bedside, in the hospital, he begins to realize what ancestor worship really is:

> I feel to the bottom of my heart that my flesh and blood are something that came from my father. This person on whom I am laying my hand is my father, who brought me into the world. He is a part of my flesh, and that part of me is dying.
>
> Until then I had felt that my father was a different being, but this time, looking at him in front of me, I felt that we really were one body – just like a new cactus stuck to the stem of the old one. I came to understand how my father felt about me, his son. I came to understand his heart. My father who brought me into this world is dying. . . . I feel as if my father is with me in my heart.

Any father – or any son already past his childhood – could easily relate to this story. A more powerful emotional illustration than life and death and the inescapable movement from one to the other hardly exists. If there is one it must be love – love that originates from the binding emotions between mother and child – without which any other love is made difficult and painful.

It is beyond the scope of this chapter to suggest in detail what aspects a modern, reformed Confucian moral education should include. The basic, almost revolutionizing, point would be to promote the feminine side of the teaching (which certainly already exists to some extent in the texts and certainly in practice). This must be brought to life and included in the curriculum. Some scholars who emphasize gender inequality in Confucian societies have long argued that, to gain societal recognition and power equal to that of the opposite sex, women must abandon their position in which they in actual practice head the family and go out to challenge the male power hegemony on the societal scene.[20] Copying the emancipation struggle of women in the Western world – leaving families in ruins; children unguided

---

20 See Cho Haejoang, in Walter H. Slote (ed.), *The Psycho-Cultural Dynamic of the Confucian Family: Past and Present* (Seoul: International Cultural Society of Korea, 1986).

and disoriented; and a growing number of individuals of both sexes socially and politically alienated – might not be a very good idea, though. Instead of promoting a masculinization of the female sex, a reformed Confucianism could femalize society. Taking the mother-child dyad as the point of departure for all social relations and elevating the social emotions stemming from this primary relationship to the level of a general norm would pose a very strong challenge to the atomizing forces of individualism which characterize the current stage of globalization.

An important point is that this would have positive implications for the endangered political system known as democracy. A system based on trust and mutual respect would probably profit from a feminization of social relations. To have a positive effect on the political sphere, the link between social norms and political ideals should be acknowledged and made clear. This might not be particularly easy, however. There are at least two aspects that create obstacles for such a rational position. The one is that in Korea moral education and democracy have never been seen as interconnected phenomena. The other is that "democracy," when propagated, has always been taken for granted as being of the *liberal* sort, with the *individual* citizen as its point of departure. This is obviously difficult to combine with the *social* morality expressed by Korean Confucianism.

This contradiction is reflected in a recent study focusing on moral education policy in South Korea. Reed and Choi found that "When the textbooks discussed Confucianism, stressing the paternalistic role of government by metaphorically casting the government in the role of the 'father,' [these] teachers made the point to their students that Confucian ethics were fundamental to Korean family life but had no place in a democratic system of government."[21] The authors point out that teachers' intentions can alter or subvert the content of the curriculum. Another question is whether the educational authorities have a clear stance with regard to the obvious contrast between the propagated social morality and the political culture of liberal democracy.

The above-mentioned authors claim that Korean education in the era of globalization still reflects a concern for cultural identity and historical experience (Reed and Choi 1999: 10). They also find among their respondents a strong sense of *cultural rootedness*, but a weak understanding of diversity and multiculturalism (Reed and Choi 1999: 12). If the authors are right in claiming that "traditional values were an essential part of being Korean" (Reed and Choi 1999: 17), what good does it then do to try to uproot these values? It

---

21 Gay Garland Reed and Sheena Choi, *Confucian Legacy, Global Future: Values Education Policy in South Korea*, Working Paper 1999, p. 6.

will only make Koreans feel less Korean. Do the Korean political authorities really believe that their citizens will then automatically feel more "cosmopolitan"?

The schoolteacher quoted at the very beginning of this chapter was asked to review her opinion now, ten years later. Her reaction was as follows:

> Basically I would say the same today. To learn how to live as a human being is more important than anything else. There is a new trend, however, marked by parents who believe in a democratic or open education at home as well as in the schools. Even though I can see some advantages to this idea, I must say that often, children do not receive proper guidance in how to behave in public. In the schools these days, teachers spend a lot of time and energy just on calming the children down. I know that creativity and the ability to learn for oneself may be important in the future, but to live in the correct way as a human being is still the most important thing, more important than anything else.[22]

One wonders how many teachers in Korea, not to mention in the world at large, would nod in agreement to this statement. What about parents? When Korean parents (as well as parents in most other "developed" countries) turn to a more open and "democratic" way of child rearing, they do it for the good of their children. Or at least, so they believe and hope. But are they right? Or are they just blindly accepting the push of – globalization? Does this revised way of thinking among young parents and teachers stem from a fear of being insufficient, of being unable to give the children what they need as ballast so that they can eke out an existence in an uncertain future?

I think this is the case. Would it not be a more responsible approach for parents, teachers, and educational authorities in Korea to accept *and appreciate* the Koreanness of Koreans and redefine the political goal as *social* rather than *liberal* democracy? And in a similar (but not the same) way for parents, teachers, and authorities in all other countries of the world? To be aware of and seriously consider the meaning of one's culture and build the organizational structures of society, the political system, in line with collectively accepted social values and norms would be a first step in reintroducing politics and challenge the market-based globalization.

The collective ethos of the Korean culture might fit better into a more communalistic, solidarity-oriented democratic ideology. The consecration of a maternalistic family, which promotes the qualities of caring and sharing, would be a fundamental tool in a Confucian reformation. By keeping familism as the basis, continuity is secured. Shifting the focus from the father to the mother would give an appreciation of the actual situation in most fami-

---

22 Verbal communication, September 25, 2000.

lies. This would be a clear modernization of Korean familism. Finally, if the female – or rather the motherly – priorities could be promoted and partly replace the traditional patriarchal system, a Confucian reformation would certainly gain speed. It would still be a mammoth task, a project requiring long-term political socialization. But it would be less of a "social engineering" project and more of an effort to build on the strengths of continuity and self-confidence, while meeting the challenges of globalization.

PART II

CONFUCIAN PERSPECTIVES
ON CAPITALISM

CHAPTER 7

CENTER-LOCAL RELATIONS

CAN CONFUCIANISM BOOST DECENTRALIZATION AND REGIONALISM?

GILBERT ROZMAN

Debates about the revival of Confucianism over the past two decades stem from at least four causes: 1) a sense of spiritual vacuum in East Asian societies, and the claim that the individual and community can regain their moorings; 2) a rise in nationalism and regime survival strategies backed by the claim that strong states are justified by tradition; 3) resistance to globalization and the spread of Western culture in a dynamic region which believes that its economic success should be matched by cultural success; and 4) a response to increasing economic integration within East Asia to create a more stable foundation for regionalism within a context of globalization. Diverse strands in the Confucian tradition are used to buttress different claims. The most basic split is between those with a rearguard mission to use group orientation, community responsibility, and nationalism to resist globalization, and forward-looking voices who draw on the past as well as the realities of our changing world to shape the process of globalization through a cosmopolitan self, heterogeneous communities, and open regionalism. The former equate Confucian traditions with centralization or with strict control through groups working closely with the center, while the latter, after a century of nationalism, are struggling to reaffirm the decentralized roots of the tradition.

This essay champions the idea that by finding positive messages in the history of their region the peoples of East Asia can ease their transition into the twenty-first century. It shines the spotlight on "decentralization" as a fundamental ideal of Confucianism, although not an explicit tenet.[1] Through recognition of this concept, nations could achieve greater balance between

---

1 For a history of the struggle between Confucian values favoring the dispersion of the official elite, the integration of urban and rural sectors of life, and other aspects of decentralization against the exploitation imposed on the Chinese population by conquering dynasties including the Mongols, see F. W. Mote, *Imperial China 900–1800* (Cambridge, Mass.: Harvard University Press, 1999).

local and national power and encourage regional cooperation. By looking back
to the history of East Asian countries, we can make the case that Confucian
ideals justified limitations on central power, encouraging social solidarity
below to balance controls from above. While Confucianism failed to adapt to
new circumstances by systematizing multiple levels of local power and
encouraging regional identities across national boundaries, an innovative revitalization of its ideals may further those goals. In turn, shared regional ideals
bolstered by market-oriented decentralization would stimulate new forces of
economic development.

China, Japan, and Korea urgently face a new wave of invigoration of local
government and civil society. In previous waves they achieved major advances
in economic development and personal rights. Most spectacular were the
results in Japan following the Occupation reforms and in China after the
Third Plenum of 1978. Yet, these were times when foreign models gained
sudden popularity and Confucian national traditions came under assault. The
case has not yet been made clearly that there are indigenous roots for genuine
decentralization – a balance of levels of administration and social vitality –
without raising the dreaded specter of disunity or chaos. We do not yet know
whether each of the nations of the region will be willing to use its historical
memory of Confucianism to advance a new model of localism and multilevel
development as part of East Asian regionalism and compatible with globalization. The first step is to clarify why history justifies "open, decentralized,
Confucian regionalism."

At times of revulsion over the effects of overcentralization, reformers have
been tempted to equate it with the mainstream traditions of Confucianism.
This occurred when tradition-laden institutions squelched local initiative
after the arrival of the West and remains a prevailing impression of why
reform took so long.[2] It happened again when aspiring centralizers buttressed
their excessive authority with appeals to Confucianism, while reigning in
localism that had tried to seize new opportunities in the collapse of the old
regime. After World War II the repudiation of centralization as Confucian
grew most intense under the onslaught of communist revolution, American
democratization, and postcolonial liberation. In the 1980s Chinese trumpeted
market reforms and the transfer of power downward at all levels. Although
the anti-Confucian campaigns of the Cultural Revolution were over, it was
convenient to place the blame for "two lost decades" on the legacy of Confucian authoritarianism, which Mao had merely revitalized.[3] Later leaders

2 In the PRC this is the usual argument. See Zhao Jihui et al., *Zhongguo Ruxue shi* (Beijing:
Zhengzhou guji chubanshe, 1991), pp. 808–853.
3 Zhengyuan Fu, *Autocratic Tradition and Chinese Politics* (Cambridge: Cambridge University
Press, 1993).

made an about-face in favor of Confucian authoritarianism as part of "Asian values" that speed growth while assuring social order,[4] again linking tradition to state dominance. In the 1990s first Japan then South Korea suffered a shock to expectations born of their economic miracles. Critics called for decentralization, charging that administrative guidance and other traditions have to be uprooted along with the mind-set behind them.[5] One message kept appearing: Confucianism means centralization and stifles initiative.[6]

We can also find countercurrents in the literature on excessive centralization in East Asia. Historically, Confucianism was contrasted, above all, to Legalism, which represented unlimited authority of the state backed by fixed rules imposed by officials. Leaders who set a good example often reminded individuals that Confucianism offered instead humane rule on the basis of moral suasion.[7] It linked center to locality through the brokerage of an elite steeped in moral education.[8] Tu Wei-ming and William Theodore de Bary have debated the presence of community as an intermediate stage between family and state in Confucian thought, recalling the suggestions of Gu Yanwu and other Neo-Confucians of the need for this intermediate level.[9] In Japan Confucianism reached its peak of influence in the Tokugawa era, when the country was divided into more than 260 quite autonomous domains.[10] This is not what we expect from a doctrine of centralism. When democratic reforms came in the late 1940s the Japanese people eagerly embraced them. Postwar institutions such as a weak prime minister and the *ringi* system of consultations in organizations before decisions are taken suggest a process different from what is usually seen as centralization. When Chinese copied the Soviet command economy tensions quickly arose. From the time of the Great Leap Forward observers argued that China split from the Soviet model because it lacked the centralized traditions of a tsarist system.[11] Later comparisons of

4 Edward Friedman, "A Democratic Chinese Nationalism?" in Jonathan Unger, ed., *Chinese Nationalism* (Armonk, N.Y.: M. E. Sharpe, 1996), p. 178.
5 T. J. Pempel, *Regime Shift: Comparative Dynamics of the Japanese Political Economy* (Ithaca, N.Y.: Cornell University Press, 1998).
6 For one of the strongest attacks, see Muramatsu Ei, *Jukyo no doku* (Tokyo: PHP Institute, 1992).
7 Wm. Theodore de Bary and Tu Wei-ming, *Confucianism and Human Rights* (New York: Columbia University Press, 1998).
8 Ito Abito, "Higashi Ajia no shakai to jukyo," in Mizoguchi Yuzo et al., eds., *Kosaku suru Ajia* (Tokyo: Tokyo University Press, 1993).
9 Wm. Theodore de Bary, *The Trouble with Confucianism* (Cambridge, Mass.: Harvard University Press, 1991), pp. 96–101.
10 Martin Collcutt, "The Legacy of Confucianism in Japan," in Gilbert Rozman, ed., *The East Asian Region: Confucian Heritage and Its Modern Adaptation* (Princeton, N.J.: Princeton University Press, 1991).
11 Franz Schurmann, *Ideology and Organization in Communist China* (Berkeley: University of California Press, 1968), pp. 195–219.

successful Chinese economic reforms in the 1980s and 1990s and failed Soviet ones invoked traditional differences again.[12] Repeatedly, a distinction was drawn between centralization and the real import of Confucianism.

To clarify questions of decentralization this essay specifies multiple levels of administration and authority. It places primary emphasis on the urban hierarchy as a framework for understanding center-local relations.[13] Comparisons focus on China and Japan with brief mention of Korea. Coverage is divided into three periods: 1) premodern historical development, where most attention is placed because it is where we must locate the tradition; 2) the transition from the 1840s to the 1940s, where we briefly show the decline in key elements of the tradition; and 3) the 1950s through the 1990s, when we see both further barriers and elements of the tradition resurrected. The final section assesses the potential for decentralization in Confucian terms, a combination of ideals and practices loosely linked to a set of texts. Our approach is not to quote from the classics, in which little is said directly on the subject, but to uncover how the tradition was interpreted in practice and to place evolving center-local relations in a context of evolving ideals.

CONFUCIANISM AND PREMODERN CENTER-LOCAL RELATIONS

Each country experienced long eras of division before the Confucian world view was adopted. Reacting against persistent warfare, leaders embraced this world view as a means of administrative regularization. Confucius had insisted that moral officials well educated in managing society through rituals and family solidarity could reduce the costs of administration.[14] History proved him right. At least eight dynasties or eras in China, Korea, and Japan (during a combined time span of under three thousand years when national leaders firmly championed Confucianism) achieved remarkable stability of two centuries or longer. Indeed, except for the invasions of Mongols and

---

12 Minxin Pei, *From Reform to Revolution: The Demise of Communism in China and the Soviet Union* (Cambridge, Mass.: Harvard University Press, 1994); Gilbert Rozman, "Stages in the Reform and Dismantling of Communism in China and the Soviet Union," in Gilbert Rozman, ed., *Dismantling Communism: Common Causes and Regional Variations* (Baltimore, Md.: Johns Hopkins University Press, 1992), pp. 15–58.

13 At a minimum, this means distinguishing four levels: 1) communities with face-to-face relations, 2) district-level cities, 3) provincial-level cities, and 4) the national-level city or cities. For each level we can consider whether the resources were there to balance other levels and whether autonomous decision making took root.

14 T. R. Reid, *Confucius Lives Next Door: What Living in the East Teaches Us About Living in the West* (New York: Random House, 1999), pp. 91–126.

Manchus the Confucian eras of the past millennium all maintained remarkable social order without being overthrown until the intrusions by the West. This achievement depended on much more than a virtuous ruler, a well-socialized elite, and close observance of rituals by the masses. While actual behavior often fell far short of the ideal, the stability of Confucian states required also a balance of power between central control, middle-level transmission and flexibility, and lower-level initiative. In essence, this was a recipe for decentralization without denying an important state role.

In the early stages of applying Confucian ideals in China, Korea, and Japan, administrative methods prevailed, while market forces were undeveloped. Periodic markets were limited to administrative centers, which operated as outposts for collecting taxes and keeping order with few commercial functions. In societies with low levels of literacy and mobility Confucian beliefs spread largely to the elite. Under these circumstances, the country was inevitably ruled indirectly, through local, walled district seats in China or even bypassing cities through estates in much smaller Japan. Indeed, both Korea and Japan borrowed heavily from China when its elite was already deeply Confucian, but they did not embrace Confucianism fully until society had matured well beyond these early stages. Even when they did, it made sense to concentrate on family opportunity and elite moral independence as limited means to decentralization.

As societies grew more complex, the challenge of governance changed. We see the transition from administrative to commercial forms of integration from the eighth century in China, then in Korea, and about five hundred years after China in Kamakura Japan.[15] In each case, the transition reached fruition, giving way to a stable pattern of central-local relations for the final premodern centuries. At least four social changes suggested the need for new forms of decentralization during this transition. First, instead of tightly controlled urban life with designated market areas, commerce was free to take place periodically in thousands of transportation junctures and in urban locations more convenient for exchange with the countryside or for daily consumption. In China as population growth continued the marketing hierarchy grew as well, reaching thirty thousand settlements around 1800 and climbing toward forty thousand in the mid-nineteenth century. In Japan, there were fewer markets relative to population, but the total exceeded one thousand. Correspondingly, the urban system was reorganized in response to forces from below. The proportion in cities and substantial marketing communities

---

15 For a discussion of the commercial revolution and the most thorough treatment of premodern Chinese cities, see G. William Skinner, ed., *The City in Late Imperial China* (Stanford, Calif.: Stanford University Press, 1977).

was roughly 17 percent in Japan and barely 6 percent in China.[16] In both cases, however, decentralization meant relying more on market mechanisms and working through a more complex urban hierarchy. Unlike European countries where state building largely followed commercial development,[17] East Asian states faced the challenge of drawing on the vitality of local economies and societies to revitalize already powerful states and to unleash the potential for more dynamism. This happened more in Japan than in China.

Second, changes in elites posed a separate challenge for decentralization. In Confucian states elite males became overwhelmingly literate. By late premodern times they were studying in schools or with tutors when young, preparing for examinations (or for scrutiny in Japan as to worthiness for bureaucratic service) as they matured, planning ahead for resources to improve consumption in a commercial society, and forming networks that could, if allowed to expand, challenge national authority. China responded to this social transformation by institutionalizing imperial examinations across the entire breadth of the country, socializing young men by controlling their education, and co-opting them by channeling their career aspirations into government service.[18] Of course, the elite found ample rewards in these changes. Social networks of degree holders who had passed one or another level of the exams were the non-economic glue that joined villages and marketing towns to the district capitals where magistrates were posted. Drawing on a very different feudal elite, Japan's lords gathered their own retainers as a separate samurai elite around them in castle towns. They too were inculcated through Confucian texts to reinforce their loyalty and improve their new bureaucratic service. Japan depended on an educated elite to serve as bureaucrats and to expand the range of networks linking officials to all types of communities. Song Neo-Confucianism, adapted beyond China in the Chosŏn and Tokugawa eras, sought to change society, including improvement of local administration, through reconstructing the bureaucracy and transforming elite attitudes.[19] While it accompanied a new process of integration

16 Gilbert Rozman, *Urban Networks in Ch'ing China and Tokugawa Japan* (Princeton, N.J.: Princeton University Press, 1974); and Gilbert Rozman, *Urban Networks in Russia, 1750–1800, and Premodern Periodization* (Princeton, N.J.: Princeton University Press, 1976), pp. 244–262.

17 Charles Tilly and Wim P. Blockmans, eds., *Cities and the Rise of States in Europe, A.D. 1000 to 1800* (Boulder, Colo.: Westview Press, 1994).

18 Benjamin A. Elman, *A Cultural History of Civil Examinations in Late Imperial China* (Berkeley: University of California Press, 2000).

19 Martina Deuchler, *The Confucian Transformation of Korea: A Study of Society and Ideology* (Cambridge, Mass.: Harvard University Press, 1992), p. 90.

of elites and some municipal engagement with signs of an emerging civil society,[20] it did not address systematic reform of the levels and functions of government.

Third, East Asian societies faced the challenge of relations between the top leader and his close associates and the various layers of officials. As population increased and societies grew more complex, government bureaucracies expanded. Many of these officials served outside the national administrative center. As commercialization advanced, elites became better informed and organized, including merchants who strove to apply Confucian principles.[21] As masses gained new knowledge and concerns about outside forces such as price changes, it was increasingly essential to station more officials in more locations. Other premodern states reorganized urban-rural ties too, but they varied in the degree of power entrusted to various levels. In comparison, China entrusted more power to the localities, but insisted on the "insignificance of subordinate officials."[22] F. W. Mote argues that even in the Ming period under a native Chinese dynasty the bureaucratic system became bogged down in procedures and forms, while imperial power rose inordinately. If the village community kept alive local government rooted in accepted standards of social behavior or normative controls built into the shared culture, neither it nor the intermediate levels of administration gained much power through decentralization from the imperial center.[23] Confucianism kept a check on central power without articulating a rationale for formal decentralization of power within the state bureaucracy. As in the changes in education, China led the way in trying to force local invigoration into narrowly defined channels.

A key question for decentralization was the transfer of authority to the level below the center with sufficient autonomy to respond to regional diversity but not so much as to fragment the country through wars and protectionism. In China it was a struggle to establish the circuit above the district level and, even more, to divide the country into provinces. When the number of provinces settled down as eighteen in the Qing dynasty, these units lacked much power. Chinese decentralization failed at the level of the province, sustaining a pattern of overcentralization of administration from the Mongol-led Yuan dynasty, boosted by the Ming dynasty and again by suspicious

20 Frederic Wakeman, Jr., "The Civil Society and Public Sphere Debate: Western Reflections on Chinese Political Culture," *Modern China*, Vol. 19, No. 2, April 1993, pp. 108–138.

21 Richard John Lufrano, *Honorable Merchants: Commerce and Self-Cultivation in Late Imperial China* (Honolulu: University of Hawaii Press, 1997).

22 T'ung-tsu Ch'u, *Local Government in China under the Ch'ing* (Cambridge, Mass.: Harvard University Press, 1962), pp. 4–13.

23 F. W. Mote, *Imperial China 900–1800*, pp. 728–729, 750–754.

Manchu emperors.[24] Given the commercial evolution of the time, raising regional cities to populations of 300,000, 500,000, or more and the growth of provincial populations to 20 to 30 million or even 50 million or more, imperial fear of rebellion left an unresponsive top-down bureaucracy poorly equipped for change. In contrast, Japan achieved a higher level of urban concentration in three central cities, while recognizing a balance of power in which the lords in their castle towns wielded genuine authority.

Urban data reinforce these conclusions about center-local relations on the eve of modernization. At the district level Japan was far livelier than China. In comparisons of England, France, Russia, China, and Japan, I found that Japan with its concentrated authority in castle towns, many of which administered areas of 30,000 to 100,000 people, mobilized resources into cities of 3,000 to 10,000 people at a high rate. Daimyo in these cities held substantial power as well as resources. In China there was "a considerable circulation of goods limited to the confines of a single market" without corresponding development of district-level cities and leadership. Magistrates might find illicit incomes, but they had little policy-making power and few resources. As a counterweight to central dominance, in Japan the high percentage of the urban population in centers of 3,000 to 10,000 people revealed "development of local administrative centralization."[25]

In China imperial Confucianism concentrated on the authority of the emperor in the national capital, offering no rationale for strong authority at intermediate levels, while in Japan each lord in his own castle town buttressed feudal vassalage with Confucian teachings calling for loyalty.[26] Until 1868 the emperor in Kyoto lived in obscurity and the shogun in Tokyo (Edo) ruled as part of a collective and an elaborate balance of power with local lords. Yet, Chinese Confucianism supported other forms of decentralization, favoring family initiative and filial duty, while Japanese Confucianism concentrated more on loyalty. A set of ideas inherited from an earlier millennium and approved by powerful leaders justified critical forms of decentralization, even if they varied across the region. Indeed, parts of Southeast China became known for the vitality of their crafts and commerce, leaving traditions that could be invoked again in the 1980s and 1990s when village and township enterprises led the economy forward after centralization had been relaxed.

24 The case for overcentralization is made by F. W. Mote, "Political Structure," in Gilbert Rozman, ed., *The Modernization of China* (New York: The Free Press, 1981), pp. 78–106.
25 Gilbert Rozman, *Urban Networks in Russia, 1750–1800, and Premodern Periodization*, p. 252.
26 Gilbert Rozman, "Comparisons of Modern Confucian Values in China and Japan," in Gilbert Rozman, ed., *The East Asian Region*, pp. 111–154.

Chinese developed a sense of provincial identity between the district level and the center, as seen in the proliferation of merchant associations. Smaller in scale, Japan saw its provincialism beginning to erode. Yet, until the second half of the nineteenth century when growing weakness of the center and the emergence of new military organizations to deal with scattered threats allowed some usurpation of power, Chinese provinces did not gain any significant administrative autonomy. The mind-set of the bureaucratic elite did not offer a rationale in support of the power of provincial or district authorities, which were posted for ever shorter stints in office while serving outside their home provinces.[27] Since the time of Confucius it concentrated on the scholar-official offering his services to a single authority figure or on the emperor's appointment of virtuous bureaucrats who could convey his will in a humane manner, not on explicit measures for institutionalizing a balance of power within the bureaucracy. To be sure, there was awareness of the faults of overcentralization and discussion of ways to overcome it by reorienting the elite to leadership in local communities.[28] These efforts were not easy to compound through political integration at higher levels. Since commercial conditions allowed provincial cities to garner a large share of urban population, the absence of decision-making rights left a huge gap. For both Japan and China the weakness of authority at the level of cities that were not national centers but could have been regional ones (usually with 30,000 or more people) made it difficult to check future centralization. But Japan's tradition of domains with powerful castle towns, most of which were smaller than 30,000, did leave behind a proclivity to exercise power from below rather than impose unchecked authority as occurred within China's administration.

In Japan the growing importance of Edo and the large combined population of 1.8 million or more in Edo, Osaka, and Kyoto as cities of the shogun eased the way to Meiji centralization. Conditions favored Edo, such as a national market, an alternate residence system for all lords and many of the nation's samurai, and growing integration of Japanese culture through the central cities.[29] On a smaller scale, Seoul dominated the Korean urban hierarchy too. In China Beijing's total of close to one million was rivaled by several regional centers, and the emperor did not act to strengthen its leading role apart from political power and the imperial examination system. Indeed, given the continental scale of China, it would have been futile to do so.

27 Thomas A. Metzger, *The Internal Organization of Ch'ing Bureaucracy: Legal, Normative, and Communication Aspects* (Cambridge, Mass.: Harvard University Press, 1973), pp. 334–336.
28 F. W. Mote, *Imperial China 900–1800*, pp. 682–683.
29 Gilbert Rozman, "Edo's Importance in the Changing Tokugawa Society," *Journal of Japanese Studies*, Vol. 1, No. 1, Fall 1974, pp. 91–112.

Chinese centralization was uniquely tied to Confucian methods of integration, including a common education for aspirants to power or prestige and bureaucratic hierarchy. Fearful of rebellion, authorities brushed aside the need for new manifestations of decentralization. They bought stability at the price of dynamism.

Ordinary people, the vast majority of whom were peasants, gained new standing in late premodern times. The state recognized owner-cultivators as the backbone of society across East Asia. If in earlier times the peasants had only vague awareness of Confucian teachings, now a process of mass Confucianization occurred.[30] It began in China and eventually reached Japan, especially in the second half of the Tokugawa period, spreading through popular religion, formal education, and informal arts.[31] Although the means varied somewhat in China, Japan, and Korea, in all cases family rituals played a large role. The peasants of East Asia by the early nineteenth century had substantial rates of male literacy, often engaged in commercial agriculture and sideline activities on a large scale, and were capable of organizing to air their grievances. Governments approved lineage groups in China and village organizations in Japan to keep mass aspirations within acceptable channels. At times they also attempted to impose more artificial groupings of households such as the *baojia* system or *goningumi* for firmer control. But the prevailing pattern was tolerance for individual households taking the initiative. Over the centuries the state recognized that a more complex society demanded new forms of opportunity, struggling with the right means of decentralization to maintain control. Respect for family opportunity is the cornerstone of Confucian balance, in which rulers were taught that ideal governance means creating conditions in support of the well-being of the population as a whole.

By the first half of the nineteenth century Japan and China each had elements of decentralization, which provided some counterweight for excessive concentration of power. Yet, they also had signs of imbalance, in which initiative had been sacrificed for stability and vested interests. In the case of Japan, 260 domain cities effectively balanced the top level. Less in evidence were regional cities between the central cities and castle towns or local market towns and urban ward power to check castle town power from below. In the case of China, sandwiched between the top level of the capital and the dis-

---

30 Mizoguchi Yuzan, "Chugoku jukyo no 10 no asupekuto," *Shiso*, No. 792, June 1990, pp. 22–23.
31 Patricia Ebrey, "The Chinese Family and the Spread of Confucian Values," JaHyun Kim Haboush, "The Confucianization of Korean Society," and Martin Collcutt, "The Legacy of Confucianism in Japan," in Gilbert Rozman, ed., *The East Asian Region*, pp. 45–83, 84–110, and 111–154.

trict level with little opportunity to assert their interests were provincial cities. If some voices in places distant from the capital aired doubts about the stifling of local initiative, they had little policy impact. Limits on power were inherent in Confucianism and encouraged some degree of decentralization, but in East Asian societies more concerned with order than dynamism there were gaps in a multilevel hierarchy of cities and of power. This led to the bottom or middle levels being stifled. Well before the coming of the West, crucial elements of the tradition of decentralization had been suppressed or not been allowed to grow.

THE TRANSITION FROM THE MID-NINETEENTH TO THE MID-TWENTIETH CENTURY

Analysts of Japan choose the word centralization to characterize the reforms of the Meiji that transformed the country. It signifies restoration of power to the emperor, the buildup of powerful ministries in Tokyo, and the shift in power from the domains to the unified central government.[32] In the first thrust of reforms leaders argued not only was this a matter of copying the effectiveness of the West, it also meant applying Confucian principles more fully. Until 1945 centralization prevailed, long after the Confucian theme was ignored in a country eager to leave Asian backwardness to enter Western modernity. In return for accelerated modernization, Japan was left with a legacy of weakened initiative from below.

Until wartime controls were imposed in the 1930s, checks continued to exist on Japanese centralism.[33] Small enterprises predominated in a market economy. The urban hierarchy was somewhat skewed by the extraordinary growth of Tokyo and, after it, Osaka, but regional cities emerged after castle towns lost their autonomous local role and grew at varied rates in the more competitive atmosphere. What excess centralization existed by 1945 could be addressed without a fundamental restructuring of the entire society. Yet, empowering society through democratization would not suffice to make the prefectural cities a sufficient counterweight to Tokyo. Meiji developmentalism had sacrificed important roots of decentralization.

Students of China often bemoan the absence of centralization in the century before the communists seized power. John Fitzgerald notes, "The late Qing reforms devolved power from the center to the province and at the same time

---

32 Michio Umegaki, "From Domain to Prefecture," in Marius Jansen and Gilbert Rozman, eds., *Japan in Transition: From Tokugawa to Meiji* (Princeton, N.J.: Princeton University Press, 1986), pp. 91–110.

33 Bai Gao, *Economic Ideology and Japanese Industrial Policy: Developmentalism from 1931 to 1965* (New York: Cambridge University Press, 1997).

assisted in centralizing power from the locality to the province."[34] While this led to experiments with local self-government at the provincial and district levels, concern concentrated on how to restrengthen the center with support from lower levels. Given the legacy of late imperial China, the first requirement was to strip the center of its stranglehold on official decision making. Then it was necessary to build a multilevel system with a balance of power appropriate to regions very different in their modern exposure. If Shanghai's rise showed that in decentralized conditions China could build an engine of modernization, it failed to suggest how a country with Confucian ideals of benevolent rule could develop on the basis of a freewheeling mélange of commercial and foreign elements. The collapse of the old forms of centralization left community-level vitality functioning poorly.

Leninism appeared to answer the appeal for a new system of centralization. To Marxists it was possible to pigeonhole Confucian society as a form of feudalism, lacking in both centralism and mass organizations. They no longer had to worry about its lessons for overcentralization because a change in the ruling class from the landlords to the workers (in Chinese ideology, the masses) would supposedly assure democratic balance. In dialectical terms, Marxism-Leninism promised to resolve contradictions, including that between city and countryside. As discrepancies widened in real life, communist critics could accuse the Nationalist government of both excessive centralization repressing the masses and insufficient centralization failing to suppress the exploitation of the ruling class and warlords. The communist doctrine claimed to have an answer to problems of unbalanced center-local relations, but this panacea in fact would add to China's woes.

Militarists in Japan and communists in China left a distorted message about the meaning of Confucian traditions for decentralization. Both groups honed an ideology of rejection of the West and promised a new harmonious existence in which successive levels of authority worked smoothly together without interference from checks and balances. In Japan in the 1930s propagandists blended Confucianism with state Shinto into a smooth fit between filial piety, community solidarity, and benevolent imperial omnipotence.[35] While community togetherness (*kyodotai*) justified reliance on self-policing, there was no recognition of tension between levels that required checks on the center from below. In the case of communist ideology and base areas of

---

34 John Fitzgerald, *Awakening China: Politics, Culture, and Class in the Nationalist Revolution* (Stanford, Calif.: Stanford University Press, 1996), p. 165.

35 Samuel Hideo Yamashita, "Confucianism and the Japanese State, 1904–1945," in Tu Wei-ming, ed., *Confucian Traditions in East Asian Modernity: Moral Education and Economic Culture in Japan and the Four Mini-Dragons* (Cambridge, Mass.: Harvard University Press, 1996), pp. 132–154.

the revolution, the need for guerrilla war boosted local autonomy. In China unlike the conspiratorial seizure of power at the top in the Bolshevik Revolution, decentralized practices had scope for development. Yet, the ideology of democratic centralism combined with thought reform measures sharpened at Yanan party headquarters allowed local party cells to become only a means to an end. Leaders did not recognize checks from below. China was on its way toward another wave of overcentralization, sacrificing its local dynamic elements.

In the transition to contemporary times Japan urbanized rapidly, relying on a mix of centralization and a market-based society. Its castle town tradition of power below the center faded; for a civil society new balance was urgently needed. Opponents of further centralization appealed to Western democracy or Soviet socialism rather than Confucian decentralization. Meanwhile, China hardly urbanized at all, losing its strong center and failing to entrench local autonomy. With little trust in decentralization, Confucianism's association with balance among levels slipped from consciousness.

THE DUAL POSTWAR MODEL: THE ROLE OF CONFUCIANISM AND DECENTRALIZATION

In the first quarter century after Japan and China applied a new model of development, Confucianism was anathema, a label for backwardness and stifled initiative. While the term appeared primarily as a negative epitaph, it does not mean that the past legacy had no impact on center-local relations. In Japan prefectural administrations may not have been able to do much about the gathering centralization in Tokyo, but they could form coalitions in the Diet to guarantee fiscal dispersions, including vast pork-barrel funding. Despite little autonomy, they played a large role in budget deficits, waste, corruption, and, eventually, growing stagnation and malaise. No wonder many officials and business interests in Tokyo feared that decentralization would only strengthen forces hostile to a new wave of globalization and market-oriented reforms. Despite lots of idealistic writing about the new "localism,"[36] it is mostly associated with protectionism.

In China provincial leaders also fared poorly in influencing policies in the center. The Soviet model continued operating along with radical campaigns imposed uniformly across the country. Yet, as divisions at the top widened, provincial powers were able to press for more self-reliance in finances and economic operations. We can identify the absence of a strong centralizing tradition in Confucian economic thinking as a limiting factor in Soviet-style

36 Kaneko Zenjiro, *Shin chihoshugi* (Tokyo: Gyosei, 1994).

centralization. Cycles of centralization-decentralization-recentralization pre-vailed.[37] In the 1970s there was much talk of a new model of center-local relations in China with great advantages for equitable modernization and a solid foundation in Maoist ideology,[38] but it was quickly repudiated. The urban model failed because of one-sided emphasis on production, an exces-sive urban-rural gap, and the absence of small town growth to promote local development.[39] Given the hostility to the market and to interest groups rep-resenting society, there was no way for decentralization to become a positive force for change until the Maoist era had ended.

By the end of the 1970s the pendulum had swung somewhat away from attacks against Confucianism, while interest in decentralization was mount-ing. For Westernizers and leftists the need for transferring power from the center still meant that Confucianism needed to be uprooted. But there were a growing number of others who looked to the past of their own country for reform ideas. Many were staunch traditionalists desperately seeking to stem the tide of modernization diluted in Westernization. They advocated stronger communities to save Japanese villages left nearly empty from continued out-migration or to revive lineage groups after communist radicalism had stripped them of their assets and genealogies. Others were guardians of vested interests, who reacted to the concentration of the most modern sector along the Pacific coast in China and Japan by demanding a transfer of power to inland governments as a way to obtain more benefits or resources from the state. But calls for decentralization also revealed sincere appreciation for reviving elements of premodern times associated with Confucian social prac-tices as appropriate to a new era. There was hope of reducing dependence on a single dominant capital city, as in olden times of self-reliance. Many said that a rapidly aging society requires revitalized communities.[40] In short, a proper state, acting in accord with tradition, must leave adequate resources and authority to lower levels of administration.

In the 1980s and 1990s China and Japan were moving from the first postwar model derived from borrowing and reactions against it. Public debate in both countries saw decentralization as a vital objective. Of course, with China's old system fully discredited, the need for fundamental reforms was compelling from the start. In the case of Japan, realization of the urgency of

---

37 Shiping Zheng, *Party Versus State in Post-1949 China: The Institutional Dilemma* (Cam-bridge: Cambridge University Press, 1997), p. 215.

38 Lawrence J. C. Ma and Edward W. Hanten, *Urban Development in Modern China* (Boulder, Colo.: Westview Press, 1981).

39 William L. Parish, "What Model Now?" in R. Yin-Wang Kwok et al., eds., *Chinese Urban Reform: What Model Now?* (Armonk, N.Y.: M. E. Sharpe, 1990), p. 4.

40 Sakata Tetsu, *Chiho toshi, jiritsu, bunken e no michi* (Tokyo, 1995).

decentralization rose in stages, the most significant of which occurred in 1993 when proponents of local power helped to engineer the end of the postwar political order. Despite the new consciousness, much more is needed.

In Japan advocates of a new balance of power aimed at reducing the power of Tokyo chose the term *"chiho bunken"* (local decentralization),[41] a response to *"haihan chiken"* (abolish the domains and decentralize) of the early 1870s when the prefectures were established. A new reform in the late 1880s stabilized their number and designated municipalities while sharply reducing the number of towns and amalgamated villages in a three-tier hierarchy. Through a new radical redistribution of power among levels, including sharp reductions in the number of units at the second and third levels, reformers aim to forge a new balance favorable to local responsibility rather than simply depending on Tokyo, people's active participation to counter growing apathy, a new social welfare society with more satisfaction from leisure and retirement, and economic efficiency.

The past served as an inspiration in Japan, although its meaning was contested. After all, the domains had enjoyed a great deal of autonomy. Their abolition had started Japan not only on the path to modernization, but also on a line toward militarism and overcentralization. In the year 2000 Tokyo, and even more the Tokaido megalopolis with close to half of the country's population along several hundred miles of coast, holds so much power (central government offices, company headquarters, cultural resources, educational magnets, etc.) that the rest of the country is left far behind. The best chance for spurring other centers with some competitive capacity is to build a new capital city and designate in place of the forty-seven prefectures a much smaller number of regional cities. The *Yomiuri* newspaper has proposed about twelve.[42] Along with forming a counterweight to central power in regional cities, most proposals advocate consolidation of towns and municipalities at the third level from more than three thousand to roughly three hundred. In this way, a structural basis for decentralization may be created. But without an intellectual rationale for how such reforms can lead to a more just society and effective economy, plans that were recently heralded as part of the "big bang" are bogging down.[43] So far, nationalists turn to State Shintoism and reformers to Western democracy, leaving discourse about the possible positive side to Confucianism virtually absent from Japanese discussions.

In China too there remains much to do in institutionalizing decentralization. Many worry that it leads to fragmentation or to the danger of many

---

41 Jijitai kenkyusha, *Chiho bunken* (Tokyo: Jijitai kenkyusha, 1993).
42 Yomiuri shimbunsha, *21 seiki no koso* (Tokyo: Yomiuri shimbunsha, 1997).
43 Gilbert Rozman, "Backdoor Japan: The Search for a Way Out Via Regionalism and Decentralization," *Journal of Japanese Studies,* Vol. 25, No. 1, Winter 1999, pp. 3–31.

"small kingdoms." In this reasoning, the main task is to recentralize commensurate with great national power. Others charge that the problem is not too much centralization, but ad hoc decisions without a balanced strategy. However successful the economic results over the past twenty years, the problems are formidable. Levels of development differ greatly, which is often seen as a consequence of unfair advantages to some areas. Usually analysts emphasize the fiscal system and the extractive capacity of the Chinese state in stressing how decentralized China has become. As Dali Yang explains, other factors favor the center such as a powerful communist party norm against factionalism. He concludes his discussion of central-local relations by arguing that growth under authoritarian rule will end and "the Chinese will have to grapple with the constitutional issue of how to reconstitute political power and authority on sounder moral foundations."[44]

Pressures for reform are quickening in China. Local protectionism now must face more openness and transparency from China's World Trade Organization (WTO) entry. In the process of combating corruption and regularizing reform, China is likely to take a fresh look at the levels and functions of its administrative system. Already there are plans to ease registration of recent migrants to small cities. A long-term slowdown in the economy is continuing, forcing a new wave of reforms. At the same time, the question of what follows communist ideology still hovers over China. A vacuum exists in conceptualizing what sort of society China is becoming. Given the rise of nationalism and the likelihood of continued rivalry with the United States, that vacuum is likely to be filled by searching in China's past. Decentralization involves identifying intellectual ideals as well as implementing structural reforms. Along with South Korea, China is the most likely advocate of Confucian traditions for both domestic reform and regional cooperation.[45]

NEW REFORMS AND THE RELEVANCE OF CONFUCIANISM

At the beginning of the 1990s four strands of optimism combined to suggest a renaissance of Confucianism as part of East Asian regionalism.[46] First, it was assumed that East Asian nations would continue their dynamism, over-

---

44 Dali Yang, "Reform and the Restructuring of Central-Local Relations," in David S. G. Goodman and Gerald Segal, eds., *China Deconstructs: Politics, Trade, and Regionalism* (London: Routledge, 1994), p. 90.
45 Gilbert Rozman, "Can Confucianism Survive in an Age of Universalism and Globalization?" *Pacific Affairs*, Vol. 75, No. 1, Spring 2002, pp. 11–37.
46 Mizoguchi Yuzo and Nakajima Mineo, eds., *Jukyo renessansu o kangaeru* (Tokyo: Taishukan shoten, 1991).

taking Western nations including the United States and giving a boost to Asian values. Second, there was hope that Sino-Japanese relations would gradually improve, and the states would forge a bond not only through economics but also by recognizing a shared Eastern civilization. Third, plans turned to local areas bypassing the central government to form decentralized networks, again extending from commerce to culture. Fourth, as Europe and North America announced regional blocs, East Asians explored proposals for regionalism.

Idealists searched in Confucianism for an integrating force to make regionalism a reality.[47] Such views spread in the People's Republic of China (PRC) first to associate China's future with successful economic transitions throughout the rest of the region (except North Korea) and later as a means to try to draw Taiwan's leaders back from flirting with new hybrid identities to separate their island from the mainland. By embracing decentralization as a principled path to development and regionalism, China can enhance its moral authority. So far, talk of "one country, two systems" suggests walling off diversity through one form of decentralization, but not welcoming it as strength for the whole country. Above all, there must be a shift to respect for guaranteed political and cultural rights consistent with the separate interests and identities of Taiwan and also of other parts of the country. In Japan too there was a surge of interest in finding a common identity with Asia, followed by disappointment that cooperation was largely limited to economic ties. Support for Confucianism linked to localism remains a means for Japan to assert its Asianness and its trust in peoples of the region. Such linkage would help avoid an overemphasis on cultural explanations that overlook necessary structural explanations, as seen not only in Chinese nationalistic reasoning but also in much of the *nihonjinron* thinking in Japan.[48] In 2001 new nationalist textbooks dismayed Japan's neighbors, but Japan's leaders kept trying to give new life to the search for regionalism.

It is important to view Confucian ideas as more than an equivalent to religious and ethical principles. While comparisons of Confucianism and Christianity cover many themes, including attitudes toward society and the individual, they usually overlook the ways value systems and religions were used in state building.[49] In China for two millennia and in Korea and Japan

---

47 Li Shengping, in Fang Litian and Bi Jundu, eds., "Dongya ruxue yu Dongya yishi," *Ruxue yu Zhongguo wenhua xiandaihua* (Beijing: Zhongguo renmin daxue chubanshe, 1998), pp. 131–146.
48 Tsuneyoshi Ryoko, "Bunka to shakai kozo: Nihonjinron no hikaku shakaigakuteki kosatsu," *Shiso*, January 1992, pp. 51–67.
49 He Guanghu and Xu Zhiwei, eds., *Duihua: Rushidao yu Jidujiao* (Beijing: Shehui kexue wenxian chubanshe, 1998).

(especially during their final premodern eras) leaders took Confucianism as a basis for social control and harmony. Even when policies did not derive from doctrine, they could often be justified by it. Confucius himself had made questions of the leader's relations to society a matter of the highest significance. As in the United States where states' rights and federal government power are issues of foremost national concern, matters of decentralization in East Asia lie at the heart of questions of national identity and legitimacy. As long as they are treated as policies of pragmatism or of foreign borrowing, their importance for national identity is bound to be overlooked.

Historically, elite Confucianism, which provided a moral compass for society, and mass Confucianism, which focused on the family, stood apart from the cult of state power in East Asia (imperial Confucianism in China). Combined, elite and mass Confucianism justified a limit to state power through local communities. Rarely did Confucian-led regimes challenge the right to localism, although they sought to limit its forms and any potential for it to evolve into rebellion. As assumptions of elitism yielded to calls for democracy and families lost functions to modern institutions through modernization, the relevance of Confucianism has been difficult to link to social institutions. It is time to make the implicit Confucian acceptance of localism an explicit statement about the role of community as defender of tradition. The Confucian element is strong encouragement for local identity and initiative, as the central state clears away obstacles to individual and family strategies for educational, entrepreneurial, and knowledge-based success.

In the 1990s present-day Confucianism became confused with Asian values, which was championed by ruling powers to support elements of authoritarianism over civil society. Implicit in this outlook is the notion that Confucian ideals are intertwined with nationalism rather than regionalism and even less internationalism. Each nation resists outside forces by insisting on its uniqueness as reflected in its state's central power to impede individual rights and a full range of open markets. There was even talk of the countries with Asian values finding common cause in state-centered regionalism.[50] It may be possible to enhance regionalism based on local values and networks without artificially relying on state manipulation. If the people are the true bearers of Confucian traditions, let them form their own ties through more open national borders. As intraregional trade accelerates, decentralization could bring the region together culturally as well. A first step is the formation of hierarchies of cities across borders, as can be seen in the Hong Kong-

---

50 Daniel A. Bell, David Brown, Kanishka Jayasuriya, and David Martin Jones, *Towards Illiberal Democracy in Pacific Asia* (New York: St. Martin's Press, 1995).

Taiwan-Guangdong-Fujian natural economic territory. Urban functions and populations increasingly depend on a division of labor that respects no borders. This is what has happened elsewhere on the globe. After all, European urban networks have been forming across national borders for at least five hundred years and provided the basis for postwar integration. Beyond economic pragmatism, a new respect for Confucian decentralization could reinforce this process. Regionalism holds out the promise of a counterweight to state power as the engine of economic development and a revival of local initiative through networks no longer dependent on nationalist power centers. After Singapore, China, Japan, and South Korea began serious discussions in the year 2000 on currency cooperation, a free trade area, and economic regionalism, hopes for an economic payoff were rising. The context of WTO economic integration was taken for granted in this new boost to regionalism. If in 2001 cooperation was set back both by bilateral problems in the region and the policies of the new Bush administration, it was likely to advance again in accord with growing economic ties.

Neither China nor Japan has yet found a cultural rationale for invigorating decentralization. By rediscovering the Confucian meaning of localism as a balance to centralism, each may find that starting point. In both cases this perspective could breath new life into the struggle to balance central power with local power and social vitality. In the case of China, the idea of Confucian localism could also be advantageous for making the case that Beijing respects Taiwan's right to autonomy and accepts a common Confucian tradition with the Chinese on Taiwan based on something other than Confucian nationalism. In Japan's case, it would strengthen the claim that Japan is part of Asia and favors regionalism that does not impose a vertical structure. By combining the themes of Confucianism as a venerable tradition of decentralization and Confucianism as a search for values drawing a new region together, East Asian nations would be sending a message of cooperation to each other. They would be asserting to the rest of the world that they have something in common besides geography and would shape the global agenda not through suspect Asian values but through a decentralized balance of localism, nationalism, regionalism, and globalism capable of earning international respect.

If we look back at the second half of the twentieth century we should have little trouble associating Confucianism with decentralization. From the standpoint of comparative modernization, we find a history of three systems in competition. Anglo-Saxon liberalism, dominant in the West, glorified individualism. It went a lot further than decentralization in challenging the power of the state and even the enduring organization with strong claims on its members. Soviet-launched socialism insisted on the supremacy of the state, rejecting decentralization in favor of vertical hierarchies under firm control. Whatever adjective one chooses from the litany of "familyism," groupism, paternalism, or corporatism, East Asian societies clearly contrast with these two ends of the spectrum.

Whether they started with a postwar infusion of individualism or state socialism, Confucian societies gravitated to a community-centered approach. They gained new dynamism through a wave of decentralization, but the process is far from complete. The centralization of state socialism has collapsed, and Anglo-Saxon individualism has appeared triumphant, especially after Japan fell into stagnation and the Asian financial crisis arose. But agreement that we have entered an age of globalization does not mean that we should assume an age of homogenization of societies. A new wave of decentralization remains on the agenda in East Asian societies. It is likely to lead to a loss of the state buffer against ever more foreign influences. Yet, it can also lead to newfound vigor from local and regional influences. Decentralization deserves to remain a priority as East Asian societies search for a new model of development.[51] Alone it offers hope, as long as the forces of corruption and protectionism do not twist it in their interests.

Decentralization also offers hope as the most promising mechanism for regionalism. To date, regional ties remain fragile with little cultural rationale and scant progress. Proposals for closed regionalism to counter U.S. influence endanger the gains achieved through trans-Pacific economic and security ties and the creation of APEC and WTO. Yet, that does not mean that regionalism must be rejected. Through agreeing on a shared agenda of "open, decentralized, Confucian regionalism," China, Japan, and South Korea could breathe new life into the way each of them develops and create a vision of how the past brings them together as they expand cooperation for the future. The tradition of Confucianism is shared across East Asia. How odd it would be for this tradition to be revived in one or another country and yet fail to spur a desperately needed regional identity. Indeed, the danger of nationalistic Confucianism would be with us if one country chose to boost ideas of the past without recognizing their shared relevance across the region. Instead, economic regionalism could excite new exploration of shared Confucian traditions, which would stimulate fresh thinking about networks bridging local areas and renewed hopes for decentralization. In our era of the Internet and economic globalization, decentralization must become an invitation for cross-national ties. In East Asia the Confucian tradition looms as an important means to achieve these ties.

51 Gilbert Rozman, "Decentralization in East Asia: A Reassessment of Its Background and Potential," *Development and Society*, Vol. 31. No. 1, June 2002, pp. 1–22.

CHAPTER 8

AFFECTIVE NETWORKS AND MODERNITY

THE CASE OF KOREA

LEW SEOK-CHOON, CHANG MI-HYE,
AND KIM TAE-EUN

I INTRODUCTION

Over the past four decades, South Korea has transformed itself from a poor agrarian economy into one of the leading industrialized nations of the world. During the same time period, it also underwent a successful transition to democracy. However, one of the seeming anomalies of this otherwise rapid and apparently thorough transition to modernity is the continued presence of strong "affective networks" (*yuangu jituan* 緣故集團). Indeed, one of the most striking characteristics of modern Korean society is the intricately webbed nexus among state/nonstate and official/non-official sectors. As was clearly revealed during the Asian financial crisis of 1997, many hitherto successful Asian economies, including that of South Korea, were characterized by strong state-business ties and business-to-business ties which went beyond the kind usually found in modern capitalist economies. Such characteristics had been the subject of much scholarly debate during the 1980s when they were hailed as the essential ingredients of the vaunted "developmental state" or "East Asian economic model." However, now they are being thoroughly criticized as the stuff of "crony capitalism," responsible for continued lackluster performance of most Asian economies in recent years.

The policy recommendations that have been forthcoming and the reforms undertaken since 1997 in South Korea have for the most part focused on dismantling the now discredited economic model, with a special emphasis placed on eradicating "cronyism" and affective networks that permeate the society. The assumption, explicit or otherwise, is that cronyism is not only inefficient but also characteristic of a premodern agrarian society and as such will disappear as modernization and rationalization of the society continues. Others admit that they were indeed responsible in some ways for the astonishing growth East Asian economies experienced in the past, but then go on to say that they have no place in the future as these economies advance to the next level of development by adopting more market-oriented business practices, or the "global standard."

However, despite the best efforts of many, the "affective networks" of South Korea hardly seem to be in decline. Even though some business practices that overtly cater to cronyism have been done away with, South Korean society and politics are still beholden to "affective networks." The problem is twofold. On the one hand, the network society has served Koreans very well in achieving their prized goal of economic development. Despite the recent economic crisis, the efficiency and efficacy of the network society for both economic and political purposes have yet to run their course. On the other hand, the Korean tendency to form and treasure affective networks derives from a world view deeply rooted in Korea's history, tradition, and philosophy, namely, Confucianism.

What then is the solution? If we continue on the assumption that the affective network is simply a remnant of a bygone era and, as such, something to be gotten rid of as quickly as possible, the fight will be a long one. If we argue that the only way to upgrade the economy and consolidate democracy is to do away with affective networks, nothing short of a complete transformation of the Korean world view and way of life will do. Of course, the majority opinion is precisely that. However, it is perhaps time to reevaluate some of the assumptions behind such recommendations. It is also timely to retrace and rethink the role of the affective network in South Korea's process of modernization and for its future. Could it be that the network society is efficacious not only in the short run but also for a fully industrialized democracy? Could it be that the affective network is more than just a crude "functional equivalent" of more "rational" and "advanced" means of organizing and ordering society, the economy, and politics?

Answers to such questions require us to question some of the most basic and cherished assumptions of modern economics and politics. Time and again we are faced with the "anomaly" of East Asian countries seemingly defying the "laws" of modernity and the assumptions undergirding them. Then again, such events as the East Asian financial crisis of 1997 and the continuing decline of some of East Asia's formerly mighty economies "confirm" our suspicions that something was indeed "rotten" in East Asia. We then can return to the old comforting sense that the assumptions and theories of modern social sciences are correct and universally binding after all. However, in this essay, we would like to challenge such assumptions, once again, by arguing that the affective networks so characteristic of South Korea are here to stay for much longer than most of us anticipate and that there are reasons, not only historical, cultural, and philosophical, but also economic, social, and political, to support our view.

2 MODERN MANIFESTATIONS OF
AFFECTIVE NETWORKS

Affective networks in Korea are based upon three factors: blood ties, school ties, and regional ties. Korean businesses are (in-)famous for the way in which they are family based. Most of the largest *chaebols* (conglomerates), including those most internationally competitive such as Samsung, Hyundai, and LG, are still controlled by members of the founder's family, usually brothers, sons, nephews, and grandsons. The importance of blood ties is even greater for smaller companies. Whereas the largest conglomerates make some effort, albeit usually halfheartedly, to adopt global standards by being less obvious about favoring members of the founding family, the smaller companies feel no such compunction. In fact, for most Korean businessmen (and women), the most important motivation for building their businesses is to pass it on to their children as part of their "patrimony."

Affective networks based on school ties are especially important in government and politics. The graduates of elite schools and universities dominate the political and economic sectors to a degree rarely witnessed in other societies. The highest echelons of the Korean bureaucracy have traditionally been occupied by members of the "KS," graduates of the elite Kyunggi High School and Seoul National University. Since the abolition of the high school entrance examination in 1974, the importance of elite high schools has diminished somewhat, but the dominance of Seoul National University within the government bureaucracy continues unabated to this day. Little wonder, then, that every schoolchild in Korea and their parents, dream of being accepted at Seoul National.

Indeed, Korean zeal for education is inextricably linked with the Korean penchant for forming affective networks, as school ties have always been one of the most important ways to form such networks. As such, there is a fierce competition to get into better schools, one of the surest ways of climbing up the social ladder. Elite colleges and universities are preferred as much, if not more so, for their alumni networks as for the quality of education they have to offer. This results in an infamously competitive college entrance examination system, in preparation for which many Korean families invest exorbitant amounts of resources, financial and otherwise. The importance of school ties as a basis upon which to build affective networks explains the ubiquitous alumni organizations and meetings. Most Koreans attend on a regular basis the meetings of the alumni organizations of their elementary, middle, and high schools as well as those of their colleges, graduate, and postgraduate programs. In recent years, the Internet has become a new medium for building and strengthening school ties in Korea. One of the most successful

Internet companies in Korea is one that specializes in locating long lost school friends and building up alumni networks in cyberspace, one indication that the affective networks are not necessarily incompatible with modern technology and society. In fact, if anything, at least in this case, the most modern technology and the most traditional aspects of Korea are mutually reinforcing.

In many cases, school ties combine with regional ties, the third factor most often used by Koreans to form affective networks. For example, former presidents Chun Doo-hwan and Roh Tae-woo were classmates at the military academy, and it was during their administrations that many of their classmates occupied important posts in the government. But, it was also during this period that the clique popularly known as the "TK" group came to dominate Korean politics and the economy. The "T" stood for Taegu, the name of the city from which most of them hailed. The "K" stood for Kyungbook High School, the elite high school in Taegu. During President Kim Young Sam's administration, the highest echelons of Korea's power elite were populated by the "PK" group where the "P" stood for Pusan, the home city of its members, including the president himself, and the "K" for Kyungnam High School, the elite high school in Pusan. With the accession of President Kim Dae Jung, graduates of Mokpo High School and people from his province, Chollanamdo, were clearly in the ascendancy.

Since the transition to democracy, regional sentiments have played an increasingly important role in Korean politics. In fact, it could be argued that regionalist sentiments enabled the first "turnover" of government to the opposition in the presidential election of 1997, when Kim Dae Jung was elected. Kim Dae Jung was able to win the presidency only because, in addition to the overwhelming support that he got from his home region of Honam, he was also able to rally to his side the sentiments of another region, namely the Chungchŏng region and its erstwhile leader Kim Jong-pil, who also had grievances against the Yŏngnam region which had dominated Korean politics till then. If such change of regime is the stuff of democratic consolidation, as it clearly is, then regionalism was a major force behind democracy in Korea. Although regionalism was indeed used as a means to maintain power by authoritarian regimes in the past, it also made possible for Korea to take another important step toward consolidating democracy.

Most analysts of the Korean political scene would agree that regional sentiments have only been exacerbated during Kim Dae Jung's presidency and that they were one of the decisive factors in the 2002 presidential election. Some rather cynical observers have noted that the "progressive" outlook for which the people from the Honam region have been celebrated is in reality nothing but a reaction to politics dominated by the people from Yŏngnam.

Given that the pattern of behavior of the Honam government follows the identical regionalist route for which the previous governments were severely criticized, their erstwhile progressivism seems to have been just another form of regionalism in disguise.[1]

Given the importance of affective networks, it is little wonder that Koreans invest significant amounts of time and energy attending innumerable social gatherings such as weddings, funerals, and alumni meetings, as well as more traditional social groups such as *kye* (*qi* 契, a traditional traditional Korean way of saving among close friends), *hyanuhoe* (*xiangyouhui* 鄉友會, social gatherings of people from the same hometown), or *jongchinhoe* (*zongqinhui* 宗親會, an extended family reunion). This is in sharp contrast to the conspicuous lack of commitment to and involvement in the voluntary citizens' groups or "civic organizations" deemed essential for a thriving democracy.[2] Although many Koreans would gladly pay U.S.$10 for a round of drinks for "old buddies," few are willing to pay even half that amount in fees and dues to citizens' groups. Even in the smallest localities, town elite gatherings – such as *"palgakhoe"* in the city of Jinju, the American Armed Forces Air Base Golf Club in the city of Kunsan, and other social clubs, such as the Lions Club, the Junior Chamber of Commerce, and the Rotary Club – function as the focal points of affective networks linked by blood, school, and regional ties. A broadcasting company once conducted a survey of over forty citizens' groups in the country and every single one of them acknowledged that there exists a local power group in their region based on family, school, and regional ties.[3]

The importance of affective networks and their tendency to compete for political power through myriad interlocking channels lead Koreans to place a great deal of importance on politics and the central government as the only means to address their grievances, political or otherwise.[4] According to a survey,[5] among the one thousand respondents, 26 percent chose political reform as the foremost task for the state, and many believed that politicians were the most responsible for the economic crisis of 1997. The flip side of

1 See Lee Kap-Yun, *Elections in Korea and Regionalism* (Orum [in Korean], 1998); see Lew Seok-Choon and Shim Jae-Bum, "Two Bases of Reform Movement in the Korean Society: Class Consciousness and Regional Discrimination," *Regionalism and Regional Conflict in Korea* (Sungwonsa [in Korean], 1990).

2 See Lew Seok-Choon and Yong-Min Kim, "Goal Displacement of Civil Organizations in Korea: With Special Reference to 'Citizens' Coalition for Economic Justice' and 'People's Solidarity for Participatory Democracy,'" *DongSuh YonKu* [in Korean], 12(2), 2000.

3 See Yang Sang-Woo and Cho Sung-Kon, "A Survey on NGOs: *Toho* (Local Power Elites) Are Present Everywhere," *Hankerye 21* [in Korean], May 27, 1999.

4 See Gregory Henderson, *Korea: The Politics of the Vortex* (Cambridge, Mass.: Harvard University Press, 1968).

5 See Um Tae-Seok, "Rooted Political Consciousness of Korean People," *Forum 21* [in Korean], Fall Issue 1997.

this is that the state is expected to intervene in such problems as corporate restructuring and business-labor relations usually deemed the purview of economic actors or the market. Korean society as a whole and each regional/local society in particular are "narrow societies" in the sense that they are center-oriented societies in which each individual strives to reach the center through various "human channels" (Lim H.-J., 1999).[6] For example, it is often noted that presidents of the student bodies at colleges and universities simply view their position as a means to enter mainstream politics. The same criticism is often leveled at leaders of various nongovernmental organizations and civic groups, as many end up in political parties.[7] As a result, a genuine civil society outside and independent of the state does not exist in Korean society.

As such, politics is identified with the state and government of a particular regime or institution (Lim H.-J., 1999); and this explains the Korean tendency to solve problems through abrupt changes in the persons in charge rather than through institutions and procedures. The oft-quoted phrase "human relations (or personnel managements) are everything" is a reflection of such a view. When a problem emerges, the person in charge is blamed for his/her lack of qualifications and bad character, and an extraordinary person, a leader, with the ability to solve all the problems is sought. Rather than developing and debating policies and institutional measures to remedy governmental and political shortcomings, Korean politicians would rather involve themselves in building new networks. This explains the weakness of political parties in Korea which have short life spans and are almost wholly dependent on a particular political leader who is the focal point of a giant affective network. Even President Kim Dae Jung, the champion of Western-style democracy, has single-handedly founded and dissolved almost a dozen political parties in his lifetime.[8]

6 See Lim Hyun-Jin, "The State and Ruling Structure: Center-Oriented Power," *A Structural Analysis of Korean Society* (Daewoo Academic Collection, Arche [in Korean], 1999).

7 See Kim Seong-Kook, "Structural Instability of the Korean Civil Society and the Formation of Citizen Power: With a Focus on New Social Movement," *Understanding the Korean Society with Structural View* (Daewoo Academic Collection, Arche [in Korean], 1999).

8 Of course, affective networks are not exclusive to Korea. As summarized in Table 1, business organizations in East Asia are based on various forms of affective networks (Gary Hamilton, W. Zeil, and W.-J. Kim, "The Network Structure of East Asian Economics," in Stewart Clegg and Gordon Redding, eds., *Capitalism in Contrasting Cultures* [Walter de Gruyter, 1990]), even though the system of corporate governance varies from country to country. In Taiwan, family-oriented small and medium-sized enterprises comprise the majority, whereas most Japanese enterprises are organized under *keiretsu* and subcontract relationships characterized by simultaneous horizontal and vertical relations. Korean enterprises, for their part, are organized in a patriarchal and strictly vertical manner (Gary Hamilton and N. W. Biggart, "Market, Culture, and Authority: A Comparative Analysis of Management and

Table 1. *Institutionalization of Affective Networks in East Asian Business Organizations*

	Cultural Sphere	Economic Sphere	
Korea	Familism, affective network, groupism, paternalism	*chaebols* (conglomerate)	A hierarchically arranged large-scale network of enterprises
Japan	"	Academic cliquism, paternalism	*keiretsu* (line) (subcontract relation)	A horizontal connection among big enterprises and a vertical connection between big enterprises and small and medium-sized enterprises
China	"	Familism, *guanxi* (關係, relation)	鄉鎮企業 *xiangzhenqiye* (township enterprise)	Various forms of non–state-owned corporate organizations, existing both in rural and urban areas, owned and managed by farmers' groups
Taiwan	"	家族企業 *jiazuqiye* (family enterprise)	A corporate organization based on noncontract relations among family members

3 PREVIOUS STUDIES ON AFFECTIVE NETWORKS

In recent years, an increasing number of scholars have been looking into affective networks by applying the theories of "social capital" or organizational analysis of social institutions. Studies that analyze regionalism utilizing these new approaches, for the most part, define regionalism as a version of factionalism, particularism, or "mob mentality." As such, it is regarded as the manifestation of an underdeveloped political process.[9] Some understand regionalism to have been produced as part of a political strategy, especially since the 1960s when authoritarian governments were seeking ways to maintain their grip on power. It is argued that President Park Chung Hee's regime fomented regionalism as a way to garner support from his home region for his repressive regime. Others argue that the authoritarian government accused the people of Honam of inciting regionalism when in reality they were simply trying to express their grievances against the government's economic policies that overtly favored the Yŏngnam region. Even the pro-democracy movement led by Kim Dae Jung and many of his followers, who happened to be from the Honam region, was portrayed by the government as nothing more than an expression of regionalist sentiment.[10]

Organization in the Far East," in Stewart Clegg and S. Gordon Redding, eds., *Capitalism in Contrasting Cultures* [Walter de Gruyter, 1990]; Lew Seok-Choon, "Confucian Capitalism: Possibilities and Limits," *Korea Focus*, 5[4], 1997, pp. 80–92). In China, *xiangzhen* (鄉鎮) enterprise is an example of business organization formed by extended regional connections based on a conception of the traditional Chinese family (*jia* 家) (Lew Seok-Choon and Kim Tae-Eun, "Development of Chinese *Xiangzhen* enterprise [*xiangzhenqiye* 鄉鎮企業] and the Restructuring of Family [*jia* 家]," delivered at the Autumn Seminar of the Association of Rural Sociology, 1999). These business organizations and systems of enterprises have been responsible for the explosive economic growth that the region has experienced over the past four decades as the "institutional isomorphism and embeddedness between business organization and cultural context found in East Asia has been advantageous to rapid growth by reducing transaction costs" involved in economic activities (Oliver Williamson, "Transaction Cost Economics," in Richard Schmalensee and Robert Willig, eds., *Handbook of Industrial Organization*, Vol. 1 [Amsterdam, 1989]; Chang H.-J., "The Political Economy of Industrial Policy in Korea," *Cambridge Journal of Economics*, 17, 1993, pp. 147–148). East Asia has successfully responded to the pressure from the capitalist world economy by building up the "social capital" (James Coleman, "Social Capital in the Creation of Human Capital," *American Journal of Sociology*, 94, July 1998; Robert Putnam, "Bowling Alone: America's Declining Social Capital," *Journal of Democracy*, 6[1], 1995) needed for the development of capitalism and democracy.

9 See Kim Moon-Jo, "Formation and Characteristics of Regionalism," *Present Korean Society* (Nanam Press [in Korean], 1993); Son Ho-Chul, "Reality and Means to Surmount Regional Conflict: The Fourteenth Presidential Election and Beyond," *Korean Politics in Transitional Era: Creation and Criticism* [in Korean], 1993.

10 See Choi Jang-Jip, "Ruling Ideological Function of Regional Sentiment," *A Study on Regional Sentiment* (Hakminsa [in Korean], 1991); Jung Keun-Sik, "Unequal Development, Regionalism, and the Change in Discourse on Regions," *A History of Modern Korea and*

According to studies that adopt rational choice theories,[11] trust in private networks rather than in the law and institutions made positive contributions to rapid industrialization. It is argued that an individual's decision to rely on affective networks is rational in the sense that they help reduce uncertainty and transactional costs in a sociopolitical environment characterized by instability and uncertainty: "when uncertainty of system is high, affective networks provide trustworthy membership with predictable conduct. Therefore, people employ network as a means to reduce uncertainty" (Kim Y.-H., 1996: 106). The preference for affective networks, then, was the result of strategic choices made by rational individuals under particular constraints. Affective networks based on "primary" ties can provide the sense of trust essential for the exchange of various kinds of political and economic resources when other institutions are underdeveloped. During social upheavals the social cost of establishing trust can rise to such levels that the cost of official contracts are higher than those incurred by transactions based on personal trust. Accordingly, people are able to gain access to scarce resources most effectively and efficiently by conducting their transactions through affective networks.

Yet another approach regards affective networks as the result of changes and distortions brought about by the "developmental state" through its active intervention in the market. Traditional familism of the past, affective and communitarian, arose from the labor intensive agrarian environment. However, during the industrialization process, it was transformed into an instrument for the maximization of narrowly perceived family interest, exclusively defined, to survive and win in the new fierce capitalistic competition. The developmental state intervened in the market by allocating scarce resources according to its own design, thus creating and maintaining massive inequality in the distribution of social wealth. In this process, individuals had to engage in a battle for survival, a battle to become the beneficiaries rather than the victims of the policies of the developmental state. In an environment that lacked procedural or institutional mechanisms that ensured fairness and equal opportunity, everyone attempted to gain access to the

---

Social Change: Literature and Intellectuals [in Korean], 1997; Choi Seok-Mann, "Theoretical Formation and Methodology for Uniting Confucian Ideas and Democracy," *Thoughts of Eastern Society* [in Korean], 2, 1999. Regionalism is evident in Korean politics, and scholars take different academic approaches and stances on regionalism depending on where they come from. They could be grouped into adhering to either the "hegemonic regionalism" of Yŏngnam or the "progressive or resistant regionalism" of Honam (Hwang Tae-Yun, *A Country of Regional Hegemony* [Moodang Media (in Korean), 1997]; Nam Young-Shin, *A Study on Regional Hegemony* [Hakminsa (in Korean), 1992]).

11 See Kim Yong-Hak, "Network and Transactional Cost," *Social Criticism*, 14, 1996; Kim Sun-Up, "Network and Affectivism," *Present Korean Society* (Nanam Press [in Korean], 1993).

powers that be through the affective networks at their disposal.[12] The affective networks were the only game in town when new ones, more befitting the changed circumstances, had not yet been properly developed.

In a similar vein, others have argued that rapid industrialization dissolved traditional communitarian ties without substituting a new principle of social integration to replace the old one. As a result, only a "lawless jungle" emerged in which individuals were forced to depend on primary inner groups or affective networks (Kim S.-U., 1993). Still others have argued that the reason affective networks became so important was because people relied on them as a counterweight to the sense of dislocation and alienation they experienced in the newly rising urban and manufacturing centers which offered only temporary and anonymous relationships.[13]

The assumption common to these analyses of the affective networks in Korea is that they are nothing more than expressions of parochial interests, nepotism, and other forms of premodern "irrationalism" (*wuli* 無理), obstructing modern, rational, and hence universal institutions and standards. As such, what is called for is unceasing effort to replace the "narrowly defined and closed connections" with "general and open networks."[14] Another assumption common to these analyses is that "premodern" agrarian societies have affective and communitarian social relations while "modern" industrialized ones are competitive and guided by rational regulations and principles: "a demand for structural clearness and fairness of competition will gradually put pressure for change on the existing balance of a connection-oriented society. Therefore, market competition will replace existing connections in social and political sectors as well."[15] Affective networks function effectively during the transitional phase when rational organizations that can generate true public trust and effective and efficient means of resource mobilization and allocation are lacking.

4 ALTERNATIVE VIEWS ON AFFECTIVE NETWORKS

As we have seen, affective networks seem to be firmly rooted in Korean society. As such, they are also one of the keys to understanding the logic of

---

12 See Kim Dong-No, "Lack of Legitimacy of the State and the Distortion of Everyday Life," *Phenomenon and Perception* [in Korean], 21(1), 1997.

13 See Song Bok, "Conflict Among Regions," *Conflict Structure of the Korean Society* (Kyungmoonsa [in Korean], 1997).

14 See Kim Yong-Hak, "Measures to Build Network for High Trust Society," *Policy Forum* [in Korean], 1997.

15 Lee Jae-Hyuk, "Possibility of Dynamic Structural Theory: A Feedback Mechanism Between Action and Structure," *Social Structure of Korea and Local Society* (Seoul National University Press [in Korean], 1999a), p. 49.

contemporary Korean society. However, their existence directly contradicts some of the basic assumptions of the modernization theory which claims that the traditional community is necessarily weakened as industrialization increases social mobility among different social stratifications. That is why most analysts seem to agree that the affective networks will soon disappear as the market economy and democracy take further root in Korea. If they fail to disappear as expected and hoped for, then it is imperative that every effort be made to eradicate them as quickly and thoroughly as possible. However, as of yet there is no clear-cut reason why affective networks should be viewed in such an unrelentingly negative light in the context of a modern society. It is unclear whether the influence of affective networks will necessarily decrease as society develops, or whether they will continue to exist and perhaps even be strengthened under certain circumstances.

For example, affective networks lower the cost of supervision and provide economic efficiency. They are highly effective means for monitoring and controlling behavior: "When a person is recruited by a company through recommendation or connection, he/she tends to work harder not to disappoint those who recommended him/her and to secure his/her position within the network of personal relations provided by that connection."[16] Again, "connections by blood (family), region, and/or school working in reality are all means to reduce transactional cost. If horizontal and vertical connections are correlated with already existing affective network[s], they create a strong trust" (Kim Y.-H., 1996: 111).

The claim that competition among network groups leads to conflicts and is always counterproductive, while the existence of many civic organizations and interest groups will ensure more rational and reasonable resolutions for conflicts of interests, does not seem to hold water either, at least in the case of Korea. Korean labor unions, and other more recently formed interest groups modeled after modern Western ones, do not necessarily lend themselves to peaceful resolution of disputes. If anything, they seem to have exacerbated the vehemence and violence which accompany many disputes that have arisen in Korea in recent years. The claim that modern Western-style organizations reduce transactions costs cannot be taken as a given.

Another common assumption is that affective networks are essentially "private" organizations and hence in fundamental conflict with "public" civil society: "a well-balanced connection-oriented society will diminish civil society while the collapse of the connection-oriented society will strengthen civil society" (Lee J.-H., 1999a: 50). However, where can citizens who wish to participate in institutionalized voluntary activities learn to make rational

16 See Lew Seok-Choon, *Munhwa Ilbo* [in Korean], March 30, 1999.

decisions and acquire a strong sense of political identity? In many cases, the family, the quintessential affective network, functions as the realm in which we receive socialization and acquire our basic dispositions and beliefs as citizens. Cohen and Arato acknowledge the importance of the family and argue that the following belong within the spheres of civil society: family or nonofficial groups and voluntary organizations that provide diversity and autonomy of lifestyle; cultural and communication systems; spheres for private self-development and ethical choice; and general law and fundamental rights that are needed to divide private life from the public sector.[17] In this regard, there is no intrinsic reason why families and other affective networks cannot function as the training ground for a sense of public life and citizenship.

The most problematic aspect of affective networks most often referred to is that they block outsiders from accessing their resources, and unfairly so: "If a group of actors forms an exclusive clique . . . it would become more effective in the short run. However, in the long run, it is bound to have an ill effect on all, that is to say, it will ultimately lead to inefficient distribution of resources in the society and cause institutional mistrust."[18] That is, "as reciprocity in the groups and personal trust created by cliquish connection accumulate on an exclusive basis, trust on general others outside the in-group or 'the rules of the game' which should generally be applied are inevitably damaged. Such groups damage fairness of competition and diminish possibility of productive transactions, eventually bringing about inefficiency in the distribution of resources" (Lee J.-H., 1999a: 49).

Affective networks create social networks and relations not through impersonal contracts based on overt calculations of self-interest but through voluntary agreements among participants, thus strengthening interpersonal ties and furthering efficiency in certain transactions. The downside is that the trust characteristic of the relationship among the in-group members cannot easily be extended to those outside the group or to the level of general trust. In fact, these two aspects of affective societies are likely to coexist in most cases. However, one of the issues most often overlooked in discussing both positive as well as negative effects of affective networks is the fact that, in many cases, affective networks lack clear boundaries between outer and inner groups.

Thus, the biggest problem of affective networks is seen as the existence of an "exclusive inner group" (Lee J.-H., 1999a: 47). However, in reality, indi-

---

17 J. Cohen and A. Arato, "Politics and the Reconstruction of the Concept of Civil Society," in Sang-Jin Han, ed., *Marxism and Democracy* (Institute for the Study of Social Culture [in Korean], 1989).

18 Lee Jae-Hyuk, "Political Economy of Social Control: Norms, Customs, and Exchange," *Understanding the Korean Society with Structural View* (Daewoo Academic Collection, Arche [in Korean], 1999b), p. 236.

viduals can and do belong to not just one but several affective networks simultaneously. A typical Korean belongs to numerous alumni associations. He or she typically belongs to numerous *hyanuhoes* (*xiangyouhui* 鄉友會, social gatherings of people from the same hometown) simultaneously, ones based on people from the same village (*myŏn*), *kun* (county), or *do* (province), among others. Ultimately, they all belong to the community of the Korean people. Even the family has porous boundaries as it extends beyond the nuclear family composed of parents and their children to include not only members of an extended family such as aunts, uncles, and cousins, but also everyone with the same "choronyms."[19] Also, one's family on both father's and mother's sides, as well as in-laws, could typically be included in one's "family" (Lee K.-Y., 1998).

In this respect, a boundary that divides inner and outer groups is highly flexible. In contrast, many of the networks or groups characteristic of modern societies tend to be much more exclusive with clear-cut boundaries. For instance, if an individual is a member of a certain class, he/she cannot be a member of another class simultaneously. Also, if he or she belongs to a particular political party, he or she cannot belong to another political party at the same time. A similar case can be made in regard to civic groups. In the West, if one participates in the activities of a particular voluntary association, he/she is likely to stay and devote most of his/her life to that group. On the other hand, a typical Korean belongs to many different groups and organizations because he/she regards the organizations as another means to participate in a new affective network or extend preexisting ones. Hence, the more prominent one is, the more likely that he/she has multiple memberships in several organizations but is not necessarily dedicated to the activities for which these organizations were formed. As of yet, there is no objective method for comparing the functional against the dysfunctional aspects of affective networks in a society.

5 CONFUCIANISM AND AFFECTIVE NETWORKS

The persistence of affective networks in Korean society cannot, however, be explained solely in terms of its rationality or efficiency in the context of rapid industrialization. Affective networks continue to exert their influence on Korea because they receive powerful ideational support and reinforcement from Neo-Confucianism which provided the normative foundations for Korean politics and society during the past five centuries. In order to understand the theoretical as well as normative bases of affective networks in Korea,

19 See Hahm Chaibong's chapter in this volume.

we must look into the theory and history of Neo-Confucianism in Korea, however briefly.

Neo-Confucianism refers to various new interpretations of Confucianism that arose during the Song dynasty in China, which saw a great revival of this ancient school of thought and government. The most dominant of these Neo-Confucian schools was the one articulated by Zhu Xi and it was his take on Confucianism, called *xing-li-xue* (性理學), which was imported by the founders of the Chosŏn dynasty in late fourteenth-century Korea. One of the most striking features of Neo-Confucianism was the emphasis that it placed on the importance of the family or the clan. Zhu Xi had made clear and elaborate provisions, both theoretical as well as institutional, for the reconstruction and strengthening of the institution of the family. The clan, or the family writ large, was the institution of choice for Zhu Xi just as it had been for Confucius, because it was where filial piety, loyalty, trust, and other values essential for the affective society idealized by Confucius could flourish. As a sociopolitical institution, it provided the sense of continuity, permanence, and identity that the highly bureaucratized, impersonal, and commercialized society of imperial Song could not. For Neo-Confucians who followed in Zhu Xi's footsteps, the family was as important as the dynasty. The dynasty, or the state, was where one's sense of loyalty and public service lay. Neo-Confucian scholars thought the purpose of their education and self-cultivation was public service, mostly by serving in the imperial bureaucracy. The state thus provided them with a sense of achievement as well as prestige, wealth, power, and honor. However, the family, or the clan, was the other pillar of a Confucian scholar-bureaucrat's self-identity and the object of his loyalty, expressed in terms of filial piety. It was in the family that one learned the most basic and fundamental values of Confucianism, including a sense of justice, trust, affection, order, and propriety, the Five Cardinal Principles. It is only after one has mastered these values and rules of propriety that one can then go out into the world as a truly "public" person.

In modern Western political discourse, home provides the space where emotional connection and ties are cultivated and strengthened among close companions. It also functions as a shelter from the impersonal public sphere.[20] In Confucianism, however, home is where moral discipline and the training of a public person are carried out, and accordingly, ties that bind the family, relatives, and other affective networks are considered public in nature rather than private (Duncan, 1998: 19). Home is the public sphere in which one is taught one's rights and duties, responsibility, and power.[21]

20 John Duncan, "The Problematic Modernity of Confucianism: The Question of 'Civil Society' in Chosŏn Dynasty Korea," Preliminary draft, 1998, p. 13.

21 See Lew Seok-Choon and Kim Tae-Eun, "Development of Chinese *Xiangzhenqiye* Enterprise (鄉鎮企業) and the Restructuring of Family (*jia* 家)."

Confucians viewed public and private spheres to be in harmony rather than in conflict.

The Confucian "citizen" thus produced is able to make the clear distinction between the public and the private, just as his/her Western counterpart does. In fact, like the ancient Greeks, the Confucian citizen clearly privileged the public over the private. The difference is that the distinction is not based upon a family-state dichotomy. It is possible to act in a "public" (*gong* 公) and just manner in the household just as it is possible to do so in public: "Master Zeng said: 'Be circumspect in funerary services and continue sacrifices to the distant ancestors, and the virtue (*de* 德) of the common people will thrive.'"[22] Or, "Where exemplary persons (*junzi* 君子) are earnestly committed to their parents, the people will aspire to authoritative conduct (*ren* 仁); where they do not neglect their old friends, the people will not be indifferent to each other."[23] Conversely, it is possible to act in a "private" (*si* 私) and hence self-interested manner in the family as well as in the public realm. Again, the family is the realm in which one is taught the values of the public (*gong* 公). In fact, the training for the public starts with self-cultivation (*xiushen* 修身) and the sense of the public thus acquired is then expected to be applied and practiced in the realm of the state and the world. This is the philosophy expressed in the famous opening lines of *The Great Learning*, one of the *Four Books* of Neo-Confucianism:

> The ancients who wished to illustrate illustrious virtue throughout the kingdom, first ordered well their own States. Wishing to order well their States, they first regulated their families. Wishing to regulate their families, they first cultivated their persons. Wishing to cultivate their persons, they first rectified their hearts. Wishing to rectify their hearts, they first sought to be sincere in their thoughts, they first extended to the utmost their knowledge. Such extension of knowledge lay in the investigation of things.[24]

What we have then, in Confucianism, is a philosophy of the public that does not follow or respect those dichotomies essential for the concept in the Western tradition, namely, "individual versus group," "state versus civil society," and "public versus private sectors." As we have seen, this does not mean that it lacks a sense of the public as opposed to the private. Confucians are able to make the distinction between "cronyism" and a "just" order. It is just that they are not neatly distinguished along the dichotomous lines so dear to Western political discourse.

---

22 *Analects* 1:9, translated by Roger T. Ames and Henry Rosemont, Jr, *The Analects of Confucius: A Philosophical Translation* (New York: Ballantine Books, 1998), p. 73.
23 *Analects* 8:3.   24 *The Great Learning* 1:4.

In fact, it is the particularly strong sense of the "public" over the "private" among the Korean public that has brought about the repeated prosecution and jailing of high-ranking government officials, army generals, and politicians, including former presidents, and businessmen, including founders of major conglomerates. It is the Confucian sense of the public that has been the force behind the resistance against authoritarian rule and the yearning for democracy. It is also this sense of the public that undergirds the seemingly endless series of "reforms" that we have seen in Korean politics, including market-oriented ones. "Civil society" in Korea also gains its theoretical impetus as much from the Confucian sense of the public as from the theories of civil society imported from the West in recent years.

To be sure, this is in no way to say that the Chosŏn Confucians or their descendants were able to maintain and practice such fine distinctions all the time. Chosŏn Confucians and modern-day Koreans have had more than their share of bouts with corruption arising from the neglect or conscious manipulation of the fine distinctions between the public and the private. However, it is to say that Koreans continue to be influenced by the Neo-Confucian terms of discourse which provide the opportunities for abuse and corruption of the values that they prescribe as well as the normative standards from which to criticize such abuses. Moreover, it is to say that the importance Koreans place on the family and other affective networks is not the result of their inability to make the distinction between the public and the private, as some have argued, but the result of a world view that operates on values and assumptions different from those of Western political discourse.

6 CONCLUSION: AN ALTERNATE MODERNITY?

Most scholars until now have regarded networks as transitional features of the Korean society, the side effects of a temporary social malaise brought about by rapid economic growth, or the lingering features of the premodern era soon to disappear. However, affective networks do not simply appear to be premodern practices or anomalous remnants of a bygone era soon to disappear. Studies that regard affective networks only as a "functional alternative" to better institutional means fail to give due recognition to the effectiveness and even compatibility of affective networks with modern society and underestimate their durability.

Moreover, as we have seen, families and clans were of central importance in the organization of society in traditional Korea. In particular, the Neo-Confucianism that was adopted as the "state religion" during the Chosŏn dynasty put family and clans on equal footing with the state. Confucianism also continues to provide normative justifications for practices that in modern

Western terms can easily be regarded as cronyism and nepotism. Given that Korean society is still highly influenced by Confucian values, it is little wonder that the importance of families, clans, and networks based on blood ties continues to this day.

Perhaps the question that needs to be asked is not how and how soon these networks can be replaced with more rational ones, but how it is that they not only have produced astonishing growth in the past but also continue to do so in the present. What is behind such practices that seem to defy the logic of increasing industrialization and democratization? How was it that South Korea was able to record remarkable economic growth and political progress while social practices often described as "disease," and "transitory evil practices" continue to coexist and sometimes even grow? How should we interpret the existence and persistence of diverse and strong affective networks during and after unprecedented economic growth and radical social change? Could it be that Koreans have developed new organizational and institutional resources and societal logic? Could it be that they have found in their tradition resources that can also be put to good use in a modern society? If the remarkable progress of capitalism and democracy in South Korea is inseparably linked to and made possible by such networks, perhaps it is indeed the case that the relationship between affective networks and modernity is more than one of a functional equivalence of a passing variety.

CHAPTER 9

CONFUCIAN CONSTRAINTS ON PROPERTY RIGHTS

DANIEL A. BELL

I INTRODUCTION

Confucius, as we know, stressed rule by moral example and opposed heavy-handed governmental control. Mencius extended this bias against state intervention to the economic realm. He suggested that anything beyond a taxation level of "one in ten" is "morally wrong" (III.B.8, Lau).[1] Minimal taxation would also have desirable economic consequences: "Tend the fields of grain and flax well, tax their yield lightly, and the people will be prosperous" (7A.3, Dobson). The government, he added, should refrain from fixing the prices of goods under exchange. Since people understand that different things have different value, the prices of goods should be primarily determined by means of people's judgment of the worth of goods:

> That things are unequal is part of their nature. Some are worth twice or five times, ten or a hundred times, even a thousand and ten thousand times, more than others. If you reduce them to the same level, it will only bring confusion to the Empire. If a roughly finished shoe sells at the same price as a finely finished one, who would make the latter? (3A.4, Lau)[2]

I would like to thank Hahm Chaihark and Kim Uchang for written comments on this essay and project participants for helpful oral comments on earlier drafts of this paper. I owe special thanks to Chow Siu Tak for outstanding research assistance and Song Bing for help with the Chinese language sources. The Research Grants Council (Hong Kong) provided a grant that allowed for research on this topic.

1 In this essay, I rely on one of three translations of Mencius: W. A. C. H. Dobson's translation of *The Works of Mencius* (London: Oxford University Press, 1963), which is helpfully organized by themes; D. C. Lau's complete translation of *Mencius* (Hong Kong: The Chinese University Press, 1984), Volumes 1 and 2, which includes the accompanying Chinese text; and the extracts translated by Wing-Tsit Chan in his edited work *A Source Book in Chinese Philosophy* (Princeton, N.J.: Princeton University Press, 1963). The translator is indicated in parentheses following the quoted passage.

2 Judging by the context of this passage, Mencius raises this example to oppose the "way of Hsu Tzu," an emperor who did his best to level all differences of status and hierarchy (e.g.,

Nor should the state levy import duties: "At the frontiers, travelers should be inspected but not taxed" (2A.5, Dobson). Mencius, in short, argues that restrictions on trade and high taxes result in the demoralization and the pauperization of the people.[3]

Mencius did not have much luck translating his ideas into practice, but his views eventually had practical consequences. As early as the Han dynasty (202 B.C.–9 A.D.), Chinese rulers began to heed Confucian warnings about the negative effects of state intervention in the economy. The famous Debate on Salt and Iron records a dispute on economic policy between Confucian literati and Legalist officials that took place in 81 B.C. The Confucians favored abolishing government monopolies in the vital industries of iron, salt, liquor, and coinage of money, on the grounds that this system forced the people to use inferior products and enriched a tiny class of corrupt officials and powerful racketeers. The Legalists replied that government control of vital industries was necessary to protect the people from exploitation by unscrupulous private traders.[4] The Confucians eventually won the debate and most government monopolies were abolished.[5]

There is no doubt that Confucians would also oppose Soviet-style planned economies. Does it follow, however, that "Confucians require a private-property economy"?[6] Not quite. There are possibilities between the extremes of total state control and a libertarian-style property rights regime. As we will see, Confucian prescriptions for the economy lie somewhere in this

by sharing the work of tilling land with his people). Just as prices of goods will (should) vary with their quality, so people's roles should vary according to their quality. For our purposes, it is interesting that Mencius takes it for granted that the government should not standardize prices regardless of quality – if only Mao et al. had brushed up on their Mencius before imposing crude forms of communism!

3 See Miles Menander Dawson, *The Ethics of Confucius* (New York: G.P. Putnam's Sons, 1915), p. 206.

4 The debate also turned on security matters. The Legalists argued that state control of vital industries was necessary to secure government revenues and thus to maintain defensive warfare against the surrounding tribes who threatened the empire, whereas the Confucians argued that China should make peace with its neighbors and be content to remain safely within its traditional boundaries.

5 See the extract in Wm. Theodore de Bary et al., *Sources of Chinese Tradition* (New York: Columbia University Press, 1960), pp. 218–223.

6 Ruiping Fan, "Confucian and Rawlsian Views of Justice: A Comparison," *Journal of Chinese Philosophy* 24 (1997), p. 443. The Confucian requirement of a private-property regime is meant to contrast with John Rawls who "wants his theory of justice to be consistent with either privately-owned or publicly-owned economy" (ibid., p. 442). Fan, however, tends to read Mencius through the lenses of contemporary libertarianism – overlooking, for example, Mencius's discussion of the well-field system (see section 3 of this chapter). In my view, Mencius is neither a right-wing liberal (or libertarian) nor a left-wing liberal (or Rawlsian). Rather, Confucian values justify distinctly nonliberal constraints on property rights.

intermediate zone. Confucians do oppose state control of the economy, but they also defend values that justify constraints on private property rights.

2 ON THE SELECTION OF FEASIBLE AND DESIRABLE CONFUCIAN VALUES FOR MODERN SOCIETIES

But which Confucian values should one appeal to? How does one select values from the complex and changing centuries long Confucian tradition, interpreted differently in different times and places and complemented in sometimes conflicting ways with Legalism, Daoism, Buddhism, and more recently, Western liberalism? In this essay, I employ the following criteria.[7]

First (and most obviously), I select values that bear on the topic of property rights. This leaves out many Confucian values, such as the meritocratic selection of scholar-officials, that may still be worth defending today but are not relevant for this topic.

Second, I limit myself to the values espoused and defended by the two "founding fathers" of Confucianism: Confucius and Mencius.[8] *The Analects of Confucius* is, of course, the central, founding text in the Confucian tradition, and any plausible interpretation of Confucianism must draw to some extent on the sayings of Confucius. Mencius, who elaborated and systematized Confucius's ideas, is the second most influential figure in the Confucian tradition.[9] The philosophy of Mencius became the orthodoxy in Imperial

---

7 I do not mean to imply that present-day Confucians should necessarily follow these criteria for selecting Confucian values. My only claim is that these criteria can generate results that shed some light on the potential clash between Confucian values and property rights in contemporary societies. Some of these criteria may be of more general applicability, but no doubt there are also other ways of selecting Confucian values for modern societies and it is important to leave room for this possibility.

8 A recent book has controversially argued that Confucius himself did not say most of the things attributed to him in *The Analects*, and one prominent scholar of Chinese history even doubts that Confucius ever existed (see Charlotte Allen, "Confucius and the Scholars," *Atlantic Monthly*, April 1999). Some Sinologists hold that stories about Mencius's life are largely legend (see W. A. C. H. Dobson, *The Works of Mencius* [London: Oxford University Press, 1963], pp. xii–xiii). In this chapter, I do not need to take sides in such disputes. What matters (for my purposes) is that the two classic Confucian texts – *The Analects of Confucius* and *The Works of Mencius* – have been transmitted in more or less intact form for well over two thousand years and continue to command a great deal of moral and political authority in contemporary East Asian societies.

9 Xunzi (c. 310–210 B.C.) is sometimes held to be the third "founding father" of the philosophy known as Confucianism. Xunzi, however, is a controversial character because he is also "blamed" for being a major influence on Legalism (Confucianism's main ideological competitor in Chinese history), with the consequence that he "was excluded from the Confucian orthodoxy" (Shu-hsien Liu, *Understanding Confucian Philosophy* [Westport, Conn.: Greenwood Press, 1998], p. 55). For this reason, I do not discuss the works of Xunzi in this essay.

China from the Song onward, and still today he is "regarded as a fountain-head of inspiration by contemporary Neo-Confucian philosophers."[10] Thus, basing one's interpretation of Confucianism on Confucius and Mencius is, arguably, the least controversial starting point.[11]

Third, I exclude Confucian values that have been explicitly repudiated by contemporary Confucian intellectuals.[12] East Asian political leaders such as Lee Kuan Yew have also invoked Confucian values, but critics argue that these leaders seem to be motivated primarily by the need to justify their authoritarian rule in the face of increasing demands for democracy at home and abroad rather than by a sincere commitment to the Confucian tradition. Whatever the truth of these accusations, one can avoid controversy by limiting one's focus to values that have not been criticized by Confucian philosophers and social critics. These Neo-Confucians typically reject such (apparent) classical Confucian values as the inherent superiority of men over women, the complete exclusion of commoners from the political decision-making process, the three-year mourning period for deceased parents, or the idea that "Heaven" somehow dictates the behavior of political rulers. Passages in *The Analects of Confucius* and *The Works of Mencius* that seem to lend themselves to these views have been either reinterpreted or relegated to the status of uninformed prejudices of the period, with no implications for contemporary societies.[13]

Fourth, I limit myself to Confucian values that contrast in some way with Western liberalism. Contemporary Confucian intellectuals often endorse values that are consistent with liberal-democratic norms – more precisely, some liberal ideas and practices have been invoked to complement and enrich Confucian values.[14] But skeptics may reply that liberal Confucians – in their

10 Ibid.

11 Once again (see note 7) I do not mean to imply that this is the only way of generating feasible and desirable Confucian values for modern societies (e.g., other contributors to this book fruitfully turn to Neo-Confucianism for inspiration).

12 For a discussion of contemporary Confucian intellectuals, see Liu, *Understanding Confucian Philosophy*, epilogue. Needless to say, I do not mean to imply that I have surveyed the thoughts of all contemporary Confucian intellectuals and my claims here may need to be further qualified.

13 See, e.g., Chan Sin Yee, "Gender and Relationship Roles in Confucius and Mencius," *Asian Philosophy*, Summer 2000. Chan argues that Confucius and Mencius did not argue in favor of the biological inferiority of women (in contrast to Aristotle) and that the central values of Confucianism do allow in principle for the equal participation of women in education and politics. The passages in *The Analects of Confucius* and *The Works of Mencius* that seem to justify the subordinate status of women, according to Ms. Chan, can be attributed to the purely contingent, uninformed prejudices of the period. See also Chan Sin Yee's chapter in this book.

14 For example, Confucius and Mencius both argued that the ruler must gain the trust of the population, but neither drew the implication that democratic elections are the best means

zeal to oppose authoritarianism – are sanitizing their own tradition, that is, picking and choosing among Confucian values according to whatever fits with the best of contemporary liberal-democratic norms. Thus, it is important to respond to the potential objection that Neo-Confucians defend the values of Confucius and Mencius on purely strategic grounds, because they are seen as means to promote Western-style liberal democracy in East Asia. For this purpose, I tried to identify – where relevant – areas of actual and potential conflict with liberal-democratic norms. The only real way to "prove" that Confucian norms have independent value, after all, is to show that Western liberal-democratic norms do not automatically have priority in cases of conflict (from the perspective of contemporary Confucian intellectuals). No doubt there are also substantial areas of overlap with Western liberalism, but that is not my concern in this essay.

Fifth, I focus on Confucian values that still inform – at least in part – the practices and institutions of countries in the East Asian region.[15] If one can plausibly point to some contemporary manifestations, this might help to respond to the potential objection that classical Confucian values are no longer influential in contemporary societies. But since I also want to leave room for the possibility that Confucian values can provide a critical perspec-

---

to achieve this end. Thus, contemporary Confucians need to draw on the Western liberal-democratic tradition for the purpose of implementing a crucial Confucian value.

15 For an account of precisely how and when the values espoused in "high culture" Confucian texts came to exert widespread influence in the East Asian region, see Gilbert Rozman, ed., *The East Asian Region: Confucianism and Its Modern Adaptation* (Princeton, N.J.: Princeton University Press, 1991). Rozman notes that the process took several hundred years: "Only in the second millennium after Confucius' death in 479 B.C. did the practices that had become closely identified with his teachings become widely disseminated among the Chinese people, and even in the third millennium diffusion continued but remained incomplete. In Korea the Confucian legacy was introduced later and did not spread widely until the fifteenth century. In Japan mass acceptance of Confucian principles was accelerated in the eighteenth and nineteenth centuries" (ibid., pp. viii–ix). Of course, it can be argued that Confucian values were undermined in the twentieth century, most notably by a Chinese Communist Party that did its best to extirpate every root and branch of the Confucian world view. But more than one scholar has argued that long-entrenched Confucian habits continued to provide the background assumptions and values even during the darkest days of the Cultural Revolution (see, e.g., Donald Munro, *The Concept of Man in Early China* [Stanford, Calif.: Stanford University Press, 1969], pp. 165–167). More recently a Neo-Confucian revival movement has recently taken shape among East Asian (and some foreign) scholars and social critics (see, e.g., Tu Wei-ming, "Confucius and Confucianism," in *Confucianism and the Family*, eds. Walter H. Slote and George A. Devos [Albany: State University of New York Press, 1998], p. 33). Even the Chinese Communist Party has now "rectified" its previous anti-Confucian stance, as it is increasingly relying on Confucianism to buttress its ideological rule (see Randall Peerenboom, "Confucian Harmony and Freedom of Thought," in *Confucianism and Human Rights*, eds. Wm. Theodore de Bary and Tu Wei-ming [New York: Columbia University Press, 1998], p. 236).

tive on political views in the East Asian region, I do not want to argue that Confucian values are currently manifested in their *most desirable form* in contemporary East Asia. There may well be different interpretations of Confucian values, or different combinations of Confucian and other values, that are more defensible than the status quo.

Let us now turn to the actual content of Confucian values. I will discuss two values that meet the criteria noted above: (1) the overriding value of basic material welfare and (2) the value of care for needy family members. Moreover, I will suggest that these Confucian values continue to exert moral and political influence in East Asia and that any property rights regime in the region[16] is likely to be shaped by "Confucian characteristics."

3 THE OVERRIDING VALUE OF MATERIAL WELFARE

According to *The Analects*, the government has an obligation to secure the conditions for people's basic means of subsistence and intellectual/moral development. In cases of conflict, however, the former has priority:[17] "The Master was on his way to Wei, and Ran Qiu was driving. The Master said: 'So many people!' Ran Qiu said: 'Once the people are many, what next should be done?' – 'Enrich them.' – 'Once they are rich, what next should be done?' – 'Educate them.'" (13.9).[18] This does not mean the blind pursuit of a higher GNP. The main obligation is to help the worst-off:[19] "I have always heard

16 Of course, one may ask why worry about the topic of property rights in the region? My assumption is that some form of capitalism is here to stay for the foreseeable future and any realistic defense of economic arrangements in East Asia needs to take this fact into account.

17 It could be argued that this is "merely" a theoretical point, since in actual fact social and economic rights never conflict with civil and political rights. Most notably, Amartya Sen has argued that no substantial famine has ever occurred in any country with a democratic form of government and a relatively free press (Amartya Sen, "Human Rights and Economic Achievements," in *The East Asian Challenge for Human Rights*, eds. Joanne R. Bauer and Daniel A. Bell [Cambridge: Cambridge University Press, 1999], p. 92). In the case of avoiding severe malnutrition, however, the record is not so clear – e.g., authoritarian China seems to be doing better on this score than democratic India.

18 See Joseph Chan's chapter for a different translation of this passage. Unless otherwise indicated, I rely on Simon Leys's recent translation of *The Analects of Confucius* (New York: Norton, 1997). This translation has been criticized, however, for occasionally extrapolating from the original text to make Confucius seem like an exponent of modern liberalism. In cases of doubt I checked Leys's translations against other recent translations and against the original source (with the help of Song Bing).

19 The reader will pardon the use of anachronistic terminology. My point is to suggest that Confucius (if he were around today) may well have endorsed something like Rawls's difference principle. Confucians, however, might dispute Rawls's assumption that basic liberties should have priority over the fair distribution of material goods in cases of conflict – and here lies one basic contrast with liberalism. In Western societies, as Will Kymlicka

that a gentleman helps the needy; he does not make the rich richer still" (6.4; see also 16.1).

Mencius echoes these concerns. People must be educated so that they can develop their moral natures. First, however, the government must provide for their basic means of subsistence:

> [The people] will not have constant hearts if they are without constant means. Lacking constant hearts, they will go astray and fall into excesses, stopping at nothing. To punish them after they have fallen foul of the law is to set a trap for the people. How can a benevolent man in authority allow himself to set a trap for the people? Hence when determining what means of support the people should have, a clear-sighted ruler ensures that these are sufficient, on the one hand, for the care of parents, and, on the other hand, for the support of wife and children, so that the people will always have sufficient food in good years and escape starvation in bad; only then does he drive them towards goodness; in this way, the people find it easy to follow him. (1A.7, Lau; see also 3A.3)

There is no point promoting moral behavior if people are worried about their next meal.[20] Thus, the government's first priority is to secure the basic means of subsistence of the people.

This does not necessarily translate into opposition to the free market. Absolute private property rights might still be justified on the instrumental grounds that they have the consequence of securing the basic means of subsistence of the people. Mencius, however, does not take this line. While he opposes high taxes and restrictions on commerce that lead to economic inefficiency, he explicitly argues that the state can and should control the distribution and use of land to secure people's means of subsistence.[21] And how

---

notes, "the assumption that civil and political rights should have priority is widely shared. . . . As a result, the disputes between Rawls and his critics have tended to be on other issues. The idea that people should have basic liberties protected is the least contentious part of his theory. . . . Some people reject the idea of a theory of fair shares of economic resources, and those who accept it have very different views about what form such a theory should take" (*Contemporary Political Philosophy: An Introduction* [Oxford: Clarendon Press, 1990], p. 54). *A Theory of Justice* has been translated into Chinese (three times), and many of the disputes center around the protection of basic liberties; the idea that people should have a fair share of economic resources is the least contentious part of his theory. This may be, arguably, a residue of the Confucian tradition that prioritizes the fair distribution of material goods.

20 The importance of food as a precondition for moral behavior is vividly expressed by means of the character *he* (和), or "harmony." The character is composed of two parts: (禾), meaning "grain," and (口), meaning mouth. In other words, a decent supply of food (grain in the mouth) underpins social harmony and (conversely) the absence of food leads to conflict (see Tan Huay Peng, *Fun with Chinese Characters: The Straits Times Collection* [Singapore: Federal Publications, 1980], p. 147).

21 It is interesting to note that Thomas Hobbes similarly allowed for state intervention if the distribution of property works in such a way that people are physically endangered by

does the government realize this aim? Mencius proposed his now-famous "well-field system":

> Humane government must begin by defining the boundaries of the land. If the boundaries are not defined correctly, the division of the land into squares will not be equal, and the produce available for official salaries will not be fairly distributed. Therefore oppressive rulers and corrupt officials are sure to neglect the defining of the boundaries. If the boundaries are correctly defined, the division of land and the regulation of salaries can be settled while you sit.
>
> Although the territory of T'eng is narrow and small, there must be gentlemen (rulers and nobles) and there must be country men. Without gentlemen, there would be none to rule the country men, and without country men, there would be none to support the gentlemen. I would ask you to divide land in the remoter districts into nine squares and to designate the central square (cultivated by eight families) as "aid" (tax), and in the central parts of the state, to let the people pay for themselves one-tenth of their produce.
>
> From the chief ministers on down, [each family] should have fifty *mou* as sacrificial land, and an additional twenty-five *mou* for each additional male. When there are deaths or moving from one house to another there will be no quitting of the district. In the fields of the district, those who belong to the same nine squares will render friendly service to one another in their going out and coming in, aid one another in keeping watch, and sustain one another in sickness. In this way, the people will live in affection and harmony. Each "well-field" unit is one *li* square and consists of nine-hundred *mou*. The center square is public field. The eight households each privately own a hundred *mou* and together they cultivate the public field. Only when the public work is done may they attend to their work. (3A.3, Chan)

This might seem like a rather rigid set of guidelines for establishing boundaries of land within states, but Mencius notes that "these are the outlines of the system. As to modifying and adapting it, it is up to you and your ruler" (3A.3, Chan). The important point is for the state to maintain a relatively equitable distribution of land at the local community level, to allow individual households to make productive use of land for their families, and to qualify farmers' rights to the produce of the land in order to ensure that enough food is supplied to the nonfarming classes. These principles, Mencius suggests, will secure basic material welfare for all members of the state.

Chinese rulers did subsequently adapt the principles of the well-field system to their own circumstances. In the early Tang dynasty, land was owned

---

it and members of the commonwealth do not have access to material necessities (see Richard Tuck, *Hobbes*, in *Great Political Thinkers* [Oxford: Oxford University Press, 1992], pp. 184–186).

by the state and distributed by it to peasant families, roughly in accordance with the well-field system. The system of state ownership eventually broke down, however. By the Song dynasty there were many landownership patterns,[22] including some forms of private ownership. The state did, however, maintain some control on the sale and purchase of land in order to secure people's basic means of subsistence. In the Ming and Qing dynasties, the state protected peasants against subsistence uncertainties by means of local community granaries. As R. Bin Wong notes, "the explicit logic of community granaries put responsibility for the creation and maintenance of these institutions in the hands of local people. The state's willingness to depend on the gentry and others to promote local grain reserves assumed a basic commitment to subsistence security as a key element in social stability."[23]

Of course, the Chinese Communist Party put an end to "Confucian" principles of land distribution, by abolishing all forms of local community autonomy and household responsibility for farming and forcing farmers to work for state-owned communes. Far from enriching the people, however, this system led to massive inefficiencies.[24] In 1978, Deng Xiaoping launched a rural land reform program that can be seen as a "reversion" to principles informing the well-field system.[25] State-owned communes were replaced by the household responsibility system. In this system, "individual households in a village are now granted the right to use the farmland, whereas the village cooperative, as the village-based governing body, retains other rights associ-

---

22 See Joseph P. McDermott, "Charting Blank Spaces and Disputed Regions: The Problem of Sung Land Tenure," *Journal of Asian Studies*, Vol. 44, No. 1, November 1984, pp. 13, 33–34.

23 R. Bin Wong, "Confucian Agendas for Material and Ideological Control in Modern China," in *Culture and State in Chinese History*, eds. Theodore Huters, R. Bin Wong, and Pauline Yu (Stanford, Calif.: Stanford University Press, 1997), p. 307. It is also worth noting that the Qing penal code secured the "right to food" by punishing local officials who failed to provide aid to the needy (see Joseph Chan's chapter). In this sense, the "right to food" really was a "right" in the modern sense, i.e., a legally enforceable norm.

24 Most obviously, it has been estimated that over twenty million Chinese died in famine in the late 1950s and early 1960s. Arguably, however, this famine was due to the faulty policies of the Great Leap Forward, not to the commune system. It can be further argued that at least the commune system succeeded in feeding most, if not all, Chinese people (other than in the period of famine noted above), which is an improvement upon what preceded the rule of the Communist Party (I thank Ci Jiwei for these points). On the other hand, one can argue that the Chinese Communist state could have done even better at feeding its people if it had implemented the Deng/Mencius agricultural reforms earlier.

25 Needless to say, I do not mean to imply that Deng and his reformers were directly motivated by the desire to restore Mencius's well-field system. It is worth noting, however, that Mencius's well-field system was explicitly praised in secondary schools in mainland China at the time of Deng's reforms (I thank Song Bing for this information), which suggests that the Communist Party leadership was aware of, and perhaps inspired by, Mencius's ideas at the time that they were thinking about agricultural reforms.

ated with ownership."[26] Farmers have an obligation to supply a quota of produce (which typically occupies one-sixth of the household's land) at a fixed low price to the state, but beyond that they are allowed to keep and sell the produce on the open market.[27] This system has been widely credited with underpinning China's rapid economic development (and the consequent improvement of the material welfare of the people) since that time.[28]

It is also worth noting that the four "Confucian tigers" (Korea, Taiwan, Hong Kong, and Singapore) have all significantly curtailed property rights in land, notwithstanding a commitment to free market principles. Taiwan and South Korea both engaged in massive land distribution programs after World War II (in part due to American pressure), which has underpinned the relatively egalitarian economic development since then. The Singapore government expropriated land shortly after independence and used it for industrial development and public housing[29] (today, 85 percent of Singaporeans live in quasi-public housing). The Hong Kong government technically owns all land in the territory, and much of it has been set aside for public housing projects (today, approximately half of Hong Kong residents live in public housing, and the Hong Kong government is the world's largest landlord).

This is not to suggest that there is a direct causal link between the sayings of Mencius and contemporary patterns of land distribution in East Asian states – no doubt other factors such as national defense, the requirements of power, pragmatic economic considerations, and ad hoc improvisation also played a role. But Confucian values that justify constraints on landownership

26 Xiao-Yuan Dong, "Two-Tier Land Tenure System and Sustained Economic Growth in Post-1978 Rural China," *World Development*, Vol. 24, No. 5 (1996), p. 915.

27 R. H. Folson, J. H. Minan, and L. A. Otto, *Law and Politics in the People's Republic of China* (St. Paul, Minn.: West Publishing Co., 1992), p. 254.

28 Some free-market economists, however, have blamed this two-tier land tenure system for the problems in land allocation and in land-specific investment observed in postreform China. Xiao-Yuan Dong, however, argues that their proposed solution – full land privatization – is unlikely to provide a solution to these agricultural problems (Dong, "Two-Tier Land Tenure System and Sustained Economic Growth in Post-1978 Rural China"). If, however, it can be shown that absolute private property rights in land is the best mechanism to secure the "right to food," then presumably Confucians would endorse this solution.

29 Kevin Tan notes that "the constitutional right to own property and to receive fair compensation for state acquisition of such property, embodied in Article 13(1) of the Malaysian Federal Constitution as it applied to Singapore, was deliberately left out of the postindependence Constitution" to allow the government to acquire land to secure the economic rights of the people (Tan, "Economic Development, Legal Reform, and Rights in Singapore and Taiwan," in *The East Asian Challenge for Human Rights*, eds. Joanne R. Bauer and Daniel A. Bell [New York: Cambridge University Press, 1999], p. 268). It would be interesting to find out if Lee Kuan Yew et al. were motivated by Confucian considerations.

were influential throughout East Asian history, and contemporary decision makers concerned with securing the basic material welfare of the people can and do draw on background Confucian values to justify constraints on private property in a way that would not be nearly as compelling in cultures largely untouched by Confucianism. It is difficult to otherwise explain the lack of opposition to constraints on property rights in East Asia, even in societies (such as Hong Kong and Korea) that allow for open dissent and contestation of the government's policies.

Let us now turn to the second Confucian value that justifies constraints on property rights. Libertarian or "capitalist-style" property rights usually refers to maximal alienation of property as well as identification of property with the individual.[30] This section has argued that the right to own and transfer (landed) property was limited by the government's responsibility to secure the people's basic material welfare, and the following section will argue that Confucian ownership rights are vested in the family, not the individual.

4 THE VALUE OF CARE FOR NEEDY FAMILY MEMBERS

A basic assumption of Confucian ethics is that the moral life is possible only in the context of particularistic personal ties.[31] For the general population, the most important relationship by far is the family. As Ruiping Fan notes, "Familial relationships are so important that they assume three out of five basic human relations [emphasized by] Confucianism. It is a Confucian moral requirement that one should take one's family as an autonomous unit from the rest of society, flourishing or suffering as a whole."[32]

Within the family context, individuals owe each other certain obligations. Most important, economically productive adults must care for needy family

---

30 See H. F. Schurmann, "Traditional Property Concepts in China," *Far Eastern Quarterly*, No. 4, 1956, p. 507.

31 Mencius explicitly attacked Micius (i.e., Mo tzu), who "speaks of 'loving all equally' as though the family did not exist" (3B.9, Dobson). This does not, however, rule out the possibility of sympathizing with strangers. Quite the opposite – the family may be a springboard for the natural emotion of sympathy that is eventually extended to all human beings, as in Mencius's famous example of noninstrumental compassion for a baby about to fall into a well (2A.6, 3A.5).

32 Ruiping Fan, "Self-Determination Versus Family-Determination: Two Incommensurable Principles of Autonomy," *Bioethics*, Vol. 11, No. 3/4, 1997, p. 317. Fan draws on the Confucian idea of "family self-determination" to explain the fact that in East Asia both the patient and family members must reach an agreement before a clinical decision can be made (as opposed to Western societies, where a competent patient typically has the final word regarding medical decisions). See also Pang Mei Che, "From Virtue to Value: Nursing Ethics in Modern China," Ph.D. thesis, Dept. of Philosophy, University of Hong Hong, 1999, esp. chapters 1, 3, 7.

members. This obligation is literally "beyond choice." From the political standpoint, as Mencius points out, it means that the government should try to ensure that economically productive members of families have sufficient means of support "on the one hand, for the care of parents, and, on the other hand, for the support of wife and children" (1A.7, Lau). The value of caring for children is widely shared in other cultures, but Confucianism places special emphasis on filial piety, the care for elderly parents. Quite simply, we are not free to neglect elderly parents. As Confucius said:

> Lord Meng Yi asked about filial piety. The Master said: "Never disobey."
> As Fan Chi was driving him in his chariot, the Master told him: "Meng Yi asked about filial piety and I replied: 'Never disobey.'" Fan Chi said: "What does that mean?" The Master said: "When your parents are alive, serve them according to ritual. When they die, bury them according to ritual, make sacrifices to them according to ritual." (2.5; see also 1.2, 2.6, 2.8, 4.19, 19.17)

Filial piety is not simply a matter of providing material comfort to aged parents: "Zixia asked about filial piety. The Master said: 'It is the attitude that matters. If young people merely offer their services when there is work to do, or let their elders drink and eat when there is wine and food, how could this ever pass as filial piety?'" (2.8; see also Mencius, 6B.3). The only real test of filial piety, Confucius seems to imply, is the willingness to serve elderly parents even when this requires sacrificing one's own interests. Confucius does allow for exceptions in extreme circumstances,[33] but in most cases people

---

33 Most notably, Confucius says that adult children should not *blindly* obey their parents. Confucius said: "In serving your father and mother you ought to dissuade them from doing wrong in the gentlest way" (14.18); see the discussion in Joseph Chan, "A Confucian Perspective on Human Rights for Contemporary China," in *The East Asian Challenge for Human Rights*, ed. Joanne R. Bauer and Daniel A. Bell (New York: Cambridge University Press, 1999), pp. 223–224. But see Mencius, 4B.30, who seems to advocate blind obedience to parents' wishes.

It is also assumed that people are somehow reciprocating for the love and care given earlier by their own parents. In response to a disciple who suggests a one-year mourning period (instead of the traditional three-year period), Confucius says:

> "The reason a gentleman prolongs his mourning is simply that, since fine food seems tasteless to him, and music offers no enjoyment, and the comfort of his house makes him uneasy, he prefers to do without all these pleasures. But now, if you can enjoy them, go ahead!"
> Zai Yu left. The Master said: "Zai Yu is devoid of humanity. After a child is born, for the first three years of his life, he does not leave his parents' bosom. Three years mourning is a custom that is observed everywhere in the world. Did Zai Yu never enjoy the love of his parents, even for three years?" (17.21)

This suggests that the obligation to care for elderly parents may not apply in cases where parents neglected their caring duties earlier (but for an argument that filial piety is an unconditional obligation that allows for no exceptions, see John Schrecker, "Filial Piety as a Basis for Human Rights in Confucius and Mencius," *Journal of Chinese Philosophy*, Vol.

must subordinate their own desires for the sake of serving their elderly parents.

Filial piety is also meant to take precedence over competing moral obligations. Mencius condemns those who are "selfishly attached [to] wife and children" (4B.30, Dobson) – instead, people should be particularly mindful of the "greatest" duty of all, the duty to one's own parents (4A.20). And both Confucius and Mencius argue that care for elderly parents should take priority over public duties in cases of conflict.[34]

In short, Confucians argue that productive adults have an obligation to care for needy family members, with special emphasis upon the need to care for elderly parents.[35] Barring exceptional circumstances, these duties have priority over both (narrowly defined) individual self-interest and competing moral obligations. These duties have been implemented in various ways by East Asian states, but I will discuss one means – the practice of joint family ownership – that contrasts with the liberal emphasis on individual ownership of property.

In traditional Chinese society, property was considered owned by the family, not the individual. The family clan lived together and pooled family property, and it was assumed that economically productive members of the family would fulfill their duties of care for needy family members within this context.[36] The practice of joint family property, which "existed in China for at least two millennia,"[37] also carried certain legal implications. According

24, 1997, pp. 402–404). It is interesting to note that Singapore, which explicitly (legally) enforces the right to be cared for by adult children, allows for exceptions where parents neglected parental duties earlier (e.g., if the parent did not provide material security for their children or resorted to extreme physical punishment).

34 Confucius famously argued that a son should cover up for a father who stole a sheep, and vice versa (13.18). Mencius went so far as to praise a sage-king who abdicated the empire for the sake of protecting a parent who had committed murder (7A.35, Dobson; see also *The Analects*, 13.18). Contemporary Confucians do not go to this extreme, but no doubt most would argue for more commitment to family duties, even if this involves sacrificing some involvement in voluntary organizations in civil society and some commitment to the duties of citizenship. In other words, commitments to the family and other communities often conflict in practice, and members of Confucian societies would typically draw the line closer to the former, in comparison with most Westerners. For some empirical evidence, see Daniel A. Bell, David Brown, Kanishka Jayasuriya, and David Martin Jones, *Towards Illiberal Democracy in Pacific Asia* (Houndmills: Macmillan/St. Antony's College, 1995), pp. 24–26.

35 A Straussian political theorist may be tempted by the argument that Confucians went out of their way to stress filial piety precisely because it is the least natural of the family-centered caring relationships (i.e., the one that requires the most ongoing, conscious, and effortful commitment).

36 Note that there may be significant overlap between the two Confucian values identified in this essay and they may not always be easy to distinguish in practice. For example, the duty to aid needy members of the family is one of the ways of securing the "right to food" identified in the previous section.

37 H. F. Schurmann, "Traditional Property Concepts in China," p. 510.

to law, junior members of the family could not be accused of stealing, but only of appropriating (for their own use) family property.[38] As late as the Qing dynasty, family property could not be divided when parents and grandparents were still alive: "If sons or grandsons should divide up family property during the lifetimes of their parents or grandparents, they will be punished by 100 blows with the heavy bamboo stick."[39]

Contemporary societies in East Asia, do not, of course, resort to physical punishment to enforce bans on the division of family property. But the duty to share one's property with one's parents is still legally enshrined in some East Asian states. In Singapore, for example, parents above sixty years old who cannot support themselves can appeal to the Tribunal for the Maintenance of Parents to claim maintenance from their children. Legal sanctions can be counterproductive,[40] however, and some East Asian societies prefer to rely on more indirect methods to secure the "right" to be cared for by adult children — for example, Hong Kong offers tax breaks and housing benefits to those who care for their elderly parents. In either case, however, the assumption that the government can constrain an individual's property rights for the sake of helping his or her elderly parents is not a matter of sharp political controversy in East Asia.

The constraints on property rights are even more striking when we look at an individual's right (or lack thereof) to dispose of property after his or her death. In traditional China, testate transfers by will rarely existed, as there was little room left for individual discretion.[41] In 1931, the Nationalist Party of China promulgated the Civil Code of China, which was an explicit attempt to modernize Chinese law and do away with the injunction against household division. It was divided into five parts, and the last part dealt with succession. On the face of it, the new Civil Code encouraged the "Western" idea

---

38 Ibid., pp. 511–512.

39 Qing code, No. 87 (quoted in Philip C. C. Huang, *Civil Justice in China: Representation and Practice in the Qing* [Stanford, Calif.: Stanford University Press, 1976], p. 25).

40 According to social workers in Singapore, most needy elderly parents would rather make do on their own or live on charity than ask the Tribunal for help, because it hurts their pride to have their children ordered to support them and to have family matters discussed in front of strangers ("They prefer charity to forcing children to pay," *Straits Times* [weekly edition], April 10, 1999, p. 5). There have also been reports that some adult children who once gave freely to their parents (the law that makes it mandatory to provide financial support for elderly parents was passed in 1995) now ask for receipts, just in case the government comes to check on them — one can imagine the impact this has on the amount of trust informing family relationships.

41 See R. H. Folsom, J. H. Minan, and L. A. Otto, *Law and Politics in the People's Republic of China* (St. Paul, Minn.: West Publishing Co., 1992), p. 281, and Louis B. Schwartz, "The Inheritance Law of the People's Republic of China," in *Law in the People's Republic of China*, eds. R. H. Folsom and J. H. Minan (Dordrecht: Kluwer Academic Publishers, 1989), p. 470.

of "disposal by the testator of his property by will."[42] Most notably, women were given equal rights of succession for the first time.[43] Like Western-style common law, the free disposal of property was constrained by the need to maintain young children. However, the Civil Code of China also maintained traditional Confucian limitations on the disposal of property. It specified a detailed ranking of family members who were entitled to a share of the inheritance, including "parents" and "grandparents."[44] Moreover, needy family members who were dependent on the support of the deceased during his or her lifetime also had rights of succession, with the precise details to be sorted out by "the family council."[45] In short, the intergenerational transfer of property through bequest and inheritance was constrained by the Confucian value of care for needy family members, including elderly parents (and grandparents). An individual was not free to neglect these obligations, even after his or her death.

Surprisingly, perhaps, inheritance practices in "communist" China also embody traditional Confucian ideas about inheritance. On April 10, 1985, the National People's Congress promulgated the first inheritance law in the history of the People's Republic of China. Like the 1931 Civil Code of China, the Inheritance Law was meant to challenge patriarchal practices and emphasize individual autonomy. Women were given equal rights of inheritance and the law allows for inheritance by will. Under inheritance by will, however, the decedent's choice is constrained by the requirement that he or she must provide for heirs who are elderly, infirm, or under age.[46] Moreover, heirs who abandon or maltreat the decedent with serious consequences forfeit their right of inheritance. The Inheritance Law also provides for intestate succession (i.e., the deceased dies without a will), to be accomplished through statutory inheritance. In this case, traditional ideas regarding the disposal of property also operate. Article 10 specifies that an estate is inherited first by spouse, children, and parents, then by siblings, paternal grandparents, and maternal grandparents. Statutory heirs are also subject to important exceptions, based on the relative financial needs of the heirs and the extent to which

---

42 William S. H. Hung, J.D., *Outlines of Modern Chinese Law* (Shanghai: Kelly and Walsh, 1934), p. 197.
43 Previously, property was divided equally among all sons following the death of parents, and daughters had a secondary right of succession.
44 Hung, *Outlines of Modern Chinese Law*, p. 198. Note that this was not a matter of individual will – the ranking overrides the deceased's preferences.
45 Ibid., p. 203.
46 It is interesting to note that the common law in Hong Kong makes it mandatory for part of an inheritance to be used to support disabled members of the family, even if they have been explicitly left out of the deceased person's will (see Lusina Ho's chapter for more details on the Hong Kong laws of inheritance).

the heirs have fulfilled their obligation to provide for the decedent (article 13). As Louis Schwartz notes, these exceptions are self-consciously drawn from traditional Confucian ideas about the family as the basic welfare unit of society:

> Chinese legal scholars emphasize that the failure of family members to support one another is both immoral and illegal. Article 13 continues "with the force of law" the traditional Chinese practice of providing for one another within the family. In this sense, mutuality of obligations and benefits may be analogized to the traditional practice of enforcing Confucian ethical principles (*li* 禮) with law (*fa* 法).[47]

From a contemporary Confucian perspective, in short, the intergenerational transfer of property through bequest and inheritance should be constrained by the need to provide aid for less well-off members of the family, including children and aged parents. One cannot justly (and legally, it turns out) disinherit needy members of the family, and potential heirs forfeit their inheritance rights if they failed to fulfill their obligations to the deceased during his or her lifetime.[48]

It might be argued that there is nothing particularly distinctive about the Confucian system of family-based property rights. Social-welfare states in the West, for example, often treat property as a "family-based" resource in divorce cases, with children and former spouses (but not elderly parents) having rights to property. Some Civil Law codes (as in Quebec) also secure the "Confucian" right to be cared for by adult children (though the extent of enforcement is questionable).[49] Still, it is difficult to think of modern societies outside

---

47 Louis Schwartz, "The Inheritance Law of the People's Republic of China," p. 477. Schwartz notes that this Inheritance Law, which reinforced the role of the family as the basic welfare unit in Chinese society, "parallels the reemergence of the family as the basic production unit in China (at least in the countryside)" (ibid., p. 478). Technically speaking, land cannot be inherited, but "article 4 of the Inheritance Law permits the inheritance of the right of possession and use of land pursuant to a land contract. Inheritance of land contract rights flows from the constitutional right of citizens to enter into contracts to engage in private economic activity. The right to inherit land contract rights under Article 4 creates a strong incentive for peasants to make investments in the land they work" (ibid., p. 472).

48 This assumes that the property was justly acquired in the first place – or at least, that it was not appropriated in ways that current generations consider to be unjust. For example, conquered territory cannot justifiably be passed down to descendants. As Confucius said, "Zang Wuzhong, having occupied Feng, requested that it be acknowledged by Lu as his hereditary fief. Whatever may be said, I cannot believe that he did not exert pressure upon his lord" (14.14). It is not made explicit, but Confucius leaves open the possibility that the original inhabitants have rights to the conquered land, or at least, more rights than the occupier's descendants.

49 I thank Gary Bell for this information.

East Asia that similarly emphasize, in both law and public morality, the duty to regard property as an asset of the whole family, including elderly parents. East Asian societies have incorporated "individualistic" conceptions of property rights to a certain extent, but they still draw the line closer to "family-based" property rights in comparison with their liberal Western counterparts.

5 APPLICABILITY IN NON-CONFUCIAN SOCIETIES?

To what extent are Confucian values realizable in societies that have not been shaped by the Confucian tradition? More grandly, perhaps, could Confucian values ever command international legitimacy? Let us review the two values surveyed in this essay and assess the potential for "export" to non-Confucian societies.

From a Confucian standpoint, the government's first priority is to secure the basic means of subsistence of the people, and this obligation has priority over civil and political rights in cases of conflict. Property rights in particular must be constrained by the need to secure the basic material welfare of the people. To this end, Mencius suggested the well-field system, which involves state intervention to claim a share of produce to secure the basic means of subsistence of nonfarming members of the state and intervention to secure an equitable distribution of land at the local community level. Beyond that, however, individual households have the right to make productive use of land and sell their produce on the free market. Alternative distributions of property rights are (in principle) acceptable if they more effectively secure the end of improving the basic material welfare of the people. However, the well-field system has been influential in Chinese history and it continues to be relevant in the contemporary era – Deng Xiaoping's rural land reform program represents (in effect, if not in theory) a "return" to Mencius's well-field system, and it has led to a dramatic improvement of material welfare in China. Any challenge to principles informing the well-field system would therefore need to (sur)pass a high bar of historical and present-day success.

Needless to say, the overriding value of basic material welfare and Mencius's idea for implementation would be more applicable in (primarily) agricultural societies. The lessons for North Korea and Vietnam – both "communist" countries with Confucian characteristics – are obvious.[50] But there is no reason why these societies need to be distinctly Confucian or Chinese-influenced – certainly Mencius believed that his principles were universaliz-

---

50 Vietnam is self-consciously looking to the Chinese experience with agricultural reform as a model for its own reforms.

able[51] – and non–East Asian societies could well experiment with Mencius's well-field system. China has shown that it is possible to move from communist-style collectivism to this Mencian mixture of private and public property, which could provide guidance for reform in communist states such as Cuba.

We also discussed the Confucian value of care for needy family members, including children and elderly parents. This entails granting property rights to families rather than individuals, since it is assumed – and legally enforced, if need be – that economically productive persons find it easier to aid less well-off members of their families under a system of joint family property. In principle, Confucians would endorse alternative distributions of property rights that more effectively secure the value of care for needy family members. In East Asia, however, contemporary decision makers have opted to maintain some Confucian-style property rights. In comparison with their Western counterparts, Asian governments go out of their way to use different combinations of legal sanctions and financial incentives that facilitate the realization of the "right" of elderly parents to a share of the family property – and there is little, if any, opposition to these policies in society at large. Moreover, it is noteworthy that the Nationalist Party of China (i.e., the KMT), the Chinese Communist Party, and the Hong Kong government – notwithstanding radically different political ideologies – have all passed laws that curtail the freedom of individuals to disinherit needy members of their families. The worry, presumably, is that more individual-centered property rights would undermine, rather than promote, the Confucian value of care for needy family members.

To the extent that other societies worry about the corrosive effects of liberal individualism on family life, they might well seek inspiration from the Confucian value of care for needy family members and its practical consequences. Feminist and communitarian thinkers in Western societies have written about the need to care for vulnerable members of the family,[52] and the Confucian idea of family-centered property rights (or variations thereof) can be considered as a means of promoting this desired end.

In sum, there is no barrier in principle to the universalization of Confucian values. If these values are given more international prominence and if it is widely felt that they help to remedy the defects of non-Confucian societies, they may also come to be universally shared (and implemented) one day.

---

51 Early Confucians did not (it seems) even contemplate the possibility that cultural differences might justify different normative and political standards.
52 See, e.g., Susan Moller Okin, *Justice, Gender and the Family* (New York: Basic Books, 1989), esp. chapters 4 and 7; and Amitai Etzioni, *The Spirit of Community* (New York: Crown, 1993), chapter 2.

CHAPTER 10

GIVING PRIORITY TO THE WORST OFF

A CONFUCIAN PERSPECTIVE ON SOCIAL WELFARE

JOSEPH CHAN

In recent years there has been a growing interest in exploring the social and political dimensions of Confucianism and their contemporary significance. There have been interesting works examining the compatibility between Confucianism on the one hand and civil liberties and democracy on the other. However, one set of issues has been left relatively unexamined: How would Confucianism deal with the issues of social welfare and distribution of resources in society? This essay is a modest attempt to partially fill the gap. It aims to discuss the principles and institutions of social welfare from the perspective of Confucian benevolence (*ren* 仁). The essay takes the view of Mencius (approx. 379–298 B.C.) on social welfare as a focus for discussion. Although all major classical Confucian thinkers (Confucius 551–479 B.C., Mencius, and Xunzi, approx. 340–245 B.C.) share similar views on this issue, it is Mencius who gives more thought to it. In addition, as we shall see, Mencius's thought on social welfare has influenced Confucian scholars and government policies in later dynasties. The first section of the essay reconstructs Mencius's view on people's responsibility to offer welfare assistance to the poor and needy. I shall argue that implicit in Mencius's view is the idea of a multilayer system of welfare assistance in which the family, social networks, and government all have specific roles to play. The second section examines how this multilayer system can be justified by the Confucian ethics of benevolence. Particular emphasis will be put on the limits as well as the attractiveness of this approach to social welfare issues. The third section formulates some general principles that capture the concerns of Confucianism and discusses one possible way to improve modern welfare mechanisms in light of those concerns.

I A MULTILAYER SYSTEM OF WELFARE ASSISTANCE

Classical Confucian thinkers all share the view that the most basic task of government is to relieve suffering and help people pursue material welfare.

For them, economic well-being even has priority over education in governing people.

> *Confucius*: Ranyou drove the Master's carriage on a trip to Wey. The Master remarked, "What a teeming population!" Ranyou asked, "When the people are already so numerous, what more can be done for them?" The Master said, "Make them prosperous." "When the people are already prosperous," asked Ranyou, "what more can be done for them?" "Teach them," replied the Master.[1]

However, the Confucian emphasis on securing material welfare for the people does not imply a nanny state that takes care of every aspect of people's lives from the cradle to the grave. The government's job is rather to provide the conditions in which people can make a living so that they can help their families and relatives if they are in need. For Mencius, the conditions sufficient for material sufficiency are not difficult to be had. The most important of them are light taxation and proper distribution of land.

> Mencius said, "Put in order the fields of the people, lighten their taxes, and the people can be made affluent."[2]

> "If Your Majesty practices benevolent government towards the people, reduces punishment and taxation, gets the people to plough deeply and weed promptly, and if the able-bodied men learn, in their spare time, to be good sons and good younger brothers, . . . serve their fathers and elder brothers, and outside the family, serve their elders and superiors, then they can be made to inflict defeat on the strong armor and sharp weapons of Ch'in and Ch'u, armed with nothing but staves."[3]

Mencius believes that poverty is largely caused by political misrule – heavy taxation, tight economic control, improper distribution of land, and confused land boundaries. When maladministration is redressed, however, people will make a good living out of their laboring; and when they have gathered enough material support for their families, they will have the free time to learn virtues and take care of their family members and the elderly.[4] In modern terminology, Mencius might be saying something like this: What

---

1 *The Analects*: 13.9 (see also *Mencius*, Book I, A: 7). Translation of *The Analects* is taken from *The Analects of Confucius: A Philosophical Translation*, translated by Roger T. Ames and Henry Rosemont, Jr. (New York: Ballantine Books, 1998). Ames and Rosemont note that Confucius's theme of placing economic well-being over education is carried "through both Mencius and Xunzi, and down to the priority of economic and welfare rights over political rights in the contemporary human rights discourse." See p. 254, note 209.
2 Ibid., Book VII, A: 23. Translation of *Mencius* is taken from D. C Lau, trans., *Mencius* (London: Penguin Books, 1970).
3 Ibid., Book I, A: 5. See also Book III, A: 3.   4 Ibid., Book I, A: 7.

the government should do is (1) ensure everyone has a job to maintain a living, (2) keep taxation low so that people can save their earnings, and (3) instill in people the virtue of caring for one's family and relatives so that they can help each other out in times of sickness or economic deprivation. Classical Confucians certainly did not envisage a full-fledged welfare state.

However, there are occasions when direct help from the government is necessary. For example, there is a group of people whom Mencius thinks should be given direct help from the government – those who are unable to help themselves and have no family to turn to for assistance. The following conversation between Mencius and King Hsuan of Chi is revealing:

> King Hsuan of Chi asked, "May I hear about Kingly government?"
>
> "Formerly, when King Wen ruled over Chi, tillers of land were taxed one part in nine; descendants of officials received hereditary emoluments; there was inspection but no levy at border stations and market places; fish-traps were open for all to use; punishment did not extend to the wife and children of an offender. *Old men without wives, old women without husbands, old people without children, young children without fathers – these four types of people are the most destitute and have no one to turn to for help. Whenever King Wen put benevolent measures into effect, he always gave them first consideration.*"[5]

This passages states clearly the idea that even when a government is doing all the right things to provide the conditions for people to be prosperous, there are always some people who are not able to make a living and have no family to fall back on – they are, in Mencius's words, the old men without wives, old women without husbands, old men without children, and young children without fathers. Mencius says that they are the most destitute and have no one to turn to for help. They should be given first consideration from the government. To use modern terminology, these are "the worst off" to whom government should give first priority.[6]

At this point we can construct a more systematic picture of the system of welfare provision which seems to be implicitly embedded in *Mencius*.[7] I believe the text endorses what I would call a multilayer system of provision of care and help in which the family, the village or commune, and the government all play a role. When one is in need, one should first turn to one's family for help. We have already seen the important role of family as a source

5 Ibid., Book I, B: 5. Italics added.
6 Which does not necessarily mean "absolute" priority as understood in John Rawls's *A Theory of Justice* (Cambridge, Mass.: Harvard University Press, 1971).
7 This might run the risk of giving a more systematic and tidy view than what can be found in the text. But I believe my interpretation has textual support, or at least it is not incompatible with the text.

of caring and help. The family is what may be called the first – most basic and important – tier in a multilayer system of help. But Mencius also envisages a network of *communal* relationships which serves as a second tier of help. When Mencius proposes a method of distribution of land – his famous idea of the "*jing* (井) system" or "well-field system" – he expects that the eight households which form the basic unit in a well-field system would perform the role of mutual aid. Mencius describes the *jing* (井) system in this way:

> A *jing* (井) is a piece of land measuring one *li* square, and each *jing* (井) consists of 900 *mu* (畝). Of these, the central plot of 100 *mu* (畝) belongs to the state, while the other eight plots of 100 *mu* (畝) each are held by eight families who share the duty of caring for the plot owned by the state. Only when they have done this duty do they dare turn to their own affairs.[8]

Now, Mencius says that people living in this well-field system are expected to offer mutual aid to each other: "Neither in burying the dead, nor in changing his abode, does a man go beyond the confines of his village. If those who own land within each *jing* (井) befriend one another both at home and abroad, help each other to keep watch, and succor each other in illness, they will live in love and harmony."[9] Strictly speaking, the idea of mutual aid need not presuppose a "well-field system." The idea needs only to presuppose a small community, a village or commune, in which people reside together and interact with each other on a regular basis. Our neighbors are our second tier caretakers, if our family members are the first tier. The idea of mutual aid among fellow villagers coheres well with another famous saying of Mencius: "Treat the aged of your own family in a manner befitting their venerable age and extend this treatment to the aged of other families; treat your own young in a manner befitting their tender age and extend this to the young of other families."[10]

The third tier in the multilayer system of welfare assistance is the government, which plays the role of some kind of last resort. There are two main occasions in which assistance from the government is necessary. The first occasion has already been mentioned: There are people who cannot help themselves and have no family to turn to. Mencius argues that the government

---

8 *Mencius*, Book III, A: 3. D. C. Lau writes the following to explain the notion of *jing* (井): "As can be seen from the sequel, when a piece of land is divided into nine parts, it looks like the Chinese character *jing* (井). Hence the system is known as *jing* (井)-fields. The common translation of the term as 'well-fields', being based on the accident that the word *jing* (井) means 'a well', is somewhat misleading, but I have kept it as it has become the standard translation" (p. 99).

9 Ibid.   10 Ibid., Book I, A: 7.

should give first priority to these people. But couldn't one turn to one's fellow villagers for assistance if there is no adult family member around to help? Why rely directly on the government? Why not first try the second tier? These questions are not considered by Mencius, and this is one issue that necessarily requires elaboration and extension of what is said in the text. One possible answer is that if a person – old or young – is unable to support herself and also permanently lacks adult family members to do so, then it would probably be too much of a burden for neighbors to support her for life. This is especially true if the neighbors are not well-off enough to do so. In an agricultural economy, production is heavily affected by contingent natural factors such as weather and fertility of land. There are times when peasants do not reap sufficient harvests to maintain a good life for themselves. So this second tier may not always be able to provide long-term, stable, and sufficient assistance to the old and young fellow villagers who have no direct family support.

This leads to the second main occasion in which governmental assistance is necessary. There are poor people who do not have enough even to plough their land, and there are people living in hunger because they do not harvest enough due to natural causes. If the number of these people is large, perhaps only a government can provide sufficient aid to them[11] Mencius suggests to King Hsuan of Chi that if he is on a tour of inspection in spring, he should "inspect ploughing so that those who have not enough for sowing may be given help"; and on an autumn trip he should "inspect harvesting so that those who are in need may be given aid."[12] In another place, Mencius explicitly says that a good government should prudently collect resources through taxation (in terms of money or goods such as grains) in good times so that it would have enough to help the most needy in bad times. He puts this point powerfully in his condemnation of King Hui of Liang:

> Now when food meant for human beings is so plentiful as to be thrown to dogs and pigs, you fail to realize that it is time for collection, and when men drop dead from starvation by the way-side, you fail to realize that it is time for distribution. When people die, you simply say, "It is none of my doing. It is the fault of the harvest." In what way is that

11 In principle, members of a community could establish a granary to support each other. But even this is not a safe guarantee, for sometimes an entire community, or all the communities in a region, would suffer, for a long period of time, from bad harvests and natural disasters. The idea of voluntary community granaries is explored in Wm. Theodore de Bary, *Asian Values and Human Rights* (Cambridge, Mass.: Harvard University Press, 1998), ch. 5. Their history, however, was not well documented. From a historical point of view, government-funded and managed community granaries were more prevalent than voluntary ones. See the discussion below.

12 *Mencius*, Book I, B: 4.

different from killing a man by running him through, while saying all the time, "It is none of my doing. It is the fault of the weapon." Stop putting blame on the harvest and the people of the whole Empire will come to you.[13]

Mencius thinks that a government that fails to assist those who die of starvation is morally responsible for their death. It is no excuse to blame a bad harvest owing to natural causes, because a responsible government should have prepared for the worst situation. Similarly, Mencius accuses the government of Duke Mu of Tsou of treating its people cruelly when it fails to help them in years of bad harvest and famine:

> In years of bad harvest and famine, close on a thousand of your people suffered, the old and the young being abandoned in the gutter, the able-bodied scattering in all directions, yet your granaries were full and there was failure on the part of your officials to inform you of what was happening. This shows how callous those in authority were and how cruelly they treated the people.[14]

Mencius's principle of giving special favor to the four classes of the needy and, more generally, the poor was put into practice in China. According to Chen Huan-Chang, the author of an important but neglected book published in 1911, *The Economic Principles of Confucius and His School*,[15] in the Song dynasty (A.D. 960–1279), the central government established a granary in each district for the storing of rice which came from the public land as a rent. Each of the four classes of people was given rice and sometimes food and clothes. In the Ming dynasty (A.D. 1368–1644), there were decrees to support the destitute. For example, in A.D. 1386, a decree was made to the effect that

> Among poor people, if the age was above eighty, five pecks of rice, three pecks of wine, and five catties of meat were given to each of them monthly. If the age was above ninety, one roll of silk and one catty of cotton were added to this amount annually. Those who owned some farmland were not given rice. To all the four classes – widower, widow, orphan, the solitary – six bushels of rice were given annually.[16]

Similarly, in the [Qing] dynasty, every district had an almshouse maintained by the government. Officials who failed to fulfill their welfare responsibilities would be punished. "According to the Law Code of the Tsing [Qing] Dynasty, if the officials do not support the four classes, the very sick person and the infirm and superannuated who need public support, they shall be

13 Ibid., Book I, A: 3.   14 Ibid., Book I, B: 12.
15 New York, Columbia University Press, 1911.
16 Chen Huan-Chang, *The Economic Principles of Confucius and His School*, Vol. II, p. 599.

punished with sixty blows of the long sick."[17] This demonstrates, Chen claims, that the Confucian idea that government has a responsibility to help the needy and poor "has been put into actual law, and its effects differ only because of the efficiency of administration."[18]

II ETHICAL REASONS FOR THE MULTILAYER SYSTEM OF WELFARE ASSISTANCE

Mencius believes in some kind of multilayer system of assistance for the needy. The system involves three layers – the familial, the communal, and the governmental, and in that descending order of priority. Notice that the text of *Mencius* itself does not explicitly indicate that special priority should be given to familial and communal assistance, or that governmental assistance is regarded as a last resort. But when we examine the ethical reasons for this multilayer system, this order of priority should become clear.[19] In the course of doing do, the limits of these reasons will also be discussed.

What are the reasons for such a multilayer system, as opposed to a nanny welfare state in which the government is the dominant caretaker? One of the reasons is, of course, historical: Governments in ancient China were simply not well enough developed in terms of their administrative and financial capacities to undertake the role of a full-fledged welfare state. But there are also important ethical reasons in Confucianism for favoring a multilayer welfare assistance system in which family and community are expected to take up essential welfare responsibilities. These reasons, as we shall see, still have relevance today. Let us discuss the family first.

1 THE FAMILY

The family is the most important social unit in Confucian ethics. This is the site where people develop and exhibit their most natural and immediate affection and love. Mencius says that young children naturally know love for their parents, and when they grow they will naturally respect their elder brothers.[20] If one needs any help at all, the most natural and appropriate source of help would be one's family, the prime site of affection and love. Moreover, for Confucians, it is one's ethical responsibility to take care of one's family members. Filial piety (*xiao* 孝), the most important Confucian virtue,

---

17 Ibid.   18 Ibid.

19 This statement will be qualified later. As we shall see, although *ideally* the second tier should be preferable to the third one from an ethical point of view, Confucians may not be so certain of their reliability as a source of welfare assistance.

20 *Mencius*, Book VII, A: 15.

consists of the duty to financially support and care for one's parents.[21] Similarly, parental love (ci 慈) requires parents to be kind to their young children and take good care of them.[22] If a son is able to provide care and help to his parents, it would be seriously wrong to shed his responsibility onto other people or the government. For this reason I believe Confucians would support the idea that welfare responsibility resides firstly on the family. Only when this first tier of help fails to deliver would the other tiers come in.

This idea seems to help explain two phenomena in some East Asian societies. The first is that, traditionally, Chinese people typically prefer to seek help from their family rather than from the government.[23] The second phenomenon is that China, Taiwan, and Singapore today have legislation to the effect that parents who are unable to support themselves have the right to be supported by their children who have come of age and are financially able to do so. The idea behind the legislation is not that the government has no responsibility to help the elderly. It is rather that from a Confucian point of view, caring for the elderly should rest first on the shoulders of their own adult children.[24]

2 SOCIAL NETWORKS AND RELATIONSHIPS

Social networks and relationships form the second tier of assistance. In Mencius's scheme, social networks refer to fellow villagers in the "well-field system" who reside together and work jointly in the common fields and separately in their own private ones. This proposal might not have clear implications in urban areas today.[25] But the idea behind it does. The fellow villagers in Mencius's time could well be our relatives, neighbors, friends, and colleagues today. In principle, they could "befriend one another both at home and abroad, help each other to keep watch, and succor each other in illness." From the perspective of Confucian benevolence, assistance coming from social ties should be preferable to governmental help. It comes with caring and concern, and it may be more effective because the caretaker understands the needs and problems of the one who seeks assistance. Also, it is an important opportunity for the caregiver to engage in virtuous activity and for both

---

21 Ibid., Book IV, B: 30; *The Analects* 2: 7. 22 *Mencius*, Book VI, B: 7.
23 See Lau Siu-kai, *Society and Politics of Hong Kong* (Hong Kong: Chinese University of Hong Kong Press, 1983).
24 For a more detailed discussion on the rights of the elderly from a Confucian perspective, see my "A Confucian Perspective on Human Rights for Contemporary China," in Joanne R. Bauer and Daniel A. Bell, eds., *The East Asian Challenge for Human Rights* (Cambridge: Cambridge University Press, 1999), pp. 235–236.
25 For implications in rural areas, see Daniel A. Bell's chapter in this volume.

parties to develop a valuable relationship. Confucian benevolence is expressed, and virtuous relationships developed and sustained, through the act of caring and concern.[26]

However, all this seems a bit idealistic, even if judged by Confucians' own ethical theory. The problem is that as an ethical theory Confucianism is uncertain and vague on what one may reasonably expect from one's neighbors and friends. It is true that for Confucians, one's care and concern for others should reach beyond the gateway of one's home. Mencius even explicitly asks us to "treat the aged of our own family in a manner befitting their venerable age and extend this treatment to the aged of other families; treat our own young in a manner befitting their tender age and extend this to the young of other families." Yet Mencius is equally explicit to warn us not to confuse benevolence with the Mohist doctrine of equal concern for all, which he heavily criticizes. For Mencius, it is natural and legitimate for a man to love his brother's son more than his neighbor's newborn baby.[27] And surely to treat my neighbor's father in exactly the same way as I treat my father, as Mozi asks us to do, would amount to a denial of my father.[28] Confucians believe in a graded love for people, not impartial concern for all.

There is another way to characterize the difference between Confucian and Mohist thinking on this issue. Mohist thinking seems close to the utilitarian notion of the ideal impartial observer, who tries to see things from an impersonal point of view and to treat people impartially. Confucian thinking, however, always starts ethical thinking with one's personal point of view, and then tries to imagine and infer other people's needs and wants from one's own. Confucius says that a benevolent person is one who "helps others to take their stand in so far as he himself wishes to take his stand, and gets others there in so far as he himself wishes to get there. The ability to take as analogy what is near at hand can be called the method of benevolence."[29] Benevolence is thus motivated, but also *limited*, by one's natural desires, and concerns, and imagination. The analogical method takes the personal point of view as the natural and trustworthy starting place for ethical reflection. It therefore has to allow much room for individual variation. As people's desires to receive help and their willingness to give vary greatly from individual to individual, it follows that there would be a great deal of indeterminacy as to how much one may legitimately be expected to help others and how much one may expect others to help. Confucius says that if there were a man who gave extensively to others and brought help to the multitude, this would no longer be

26 Mencius does not explicitly say this. But this is a clear implication of Confucian ethics.
27 *Mencius*, Book III, A: 5.   28 Ibid., Book III, B: 9.
29 D. C. Lau, trans., *Confucius: The Analects* 6:30 (Harmondsworth: Penguin Books, 1979).

a matter of benevolence. He would be a *sage (sheng)*.[30] Thus what we are certain of is only that benevolence requires more than familial love but much less than the ideal of a sage. Exactly where the requirement of benevolence should lie in between these two poles Confucianism has very little to say. Perhaps given its "method of benevolence," it is impossible to specify the degree of gradation of concern for different people outside of one's family.

The moral indeterminacy of benevolence is carried into Mencius's multi-tier system of assistance. Ideally, it would be best if social networks and ties as the second tier could play a vital role in the provision of welfare assistance. But Confucians cannot confidently say exactly how much mutual aid may be reasonably expected from this source.[31] This second tier is, therefore, not as reliable as the familial and governmental tiers which carry definite responsibilities as envisaged by Mencius.[32] This perhaps explains why there never seemed to be any law in traditional China which coercively compelled people to help their neighbors, whereas there were, and still are, laws enforcing filial piety in societies with a Confucian heritage. Confucian moral psychology may be more realistic than Mohist. Yet the indeterminacy that follows from this moral psychology prevents Confucians from giving a persuasive account of the ethical and institutional guidelines for mutual aid based on social networks and communities.

3 GOVERNMENT

All classical Confucian masters from Confucius to Xunzi hold that the foremost duty of government is to provide welfare assistance to its subjects and improve their material welfare. They also share similar reasons for assigning this task to government. But it is Mencius who gives the most explicit and strongest version of those reasons. First, Mencius holds a theory of politics that puts the people before those in authority.[33] Second, while the government has the responsibility to educate the people, this task cannot be effectively carried out if the people are seriously deprived of material resources to support their living.[34] Even a government which emphasizes moral education

---

30 Ibid.
31 For a related but somewhat different discussion of this issue, see David B. Wong, "Universalism Versus Love with Distinction: An Ancient Debate Revived," *Journal of Chinese Philosophy* 16 (1989): 251–272.
32 Unlike the second tier, the responsibilities of family and government are not vague. Adult children are expected to give all they can to help maintain their parents. The government is also expected to step in to provide for basic subsistence when other alternatives do not work.
33 *Mencius*, Book VII, B: 14.   34 Ibid., Book I, A: 7; Book I, A: 5.

needs to pay attention to the material life of the people. Third, the ruler is the person in a regime who has the heaviest responsibility to practice the way of benevolence. As benevolence is about showing care and concern for others, a ruler who is required to practice benevolence ought to care for the well-being of the people, albeit from a long distance.[35] Finally, to ignore the suffering of the people is to alienate oneself as a ruler from the people. A harmonious relationship with the people can only be sustained if the ruler identifies with the people and shares their happiness and suffering.[36]

It is important to note, however, that the above reasons are not sufficient for a complete account of a justification for governmental welfare responsibilities. The justification considered thus far assumes that the government is an independent actor which has its own resources to perform the welfare tasks. But even in ancient times a large part of the government's revenues in a monarchical regime had to come from taxation. This means that the burden of public provision of welfare has to be borne by the people as well as the ruler. The above straightforward justification for the government's welfare duties, therefore, turns out to be deceptively simple. It conceals a series of questions about the moral responsibility of fellow members of a political community to help each other.[37] Among the people, who has the responsibility to help others with whom they have no personal ties and relationships? Is it the rich? Or is it all the common people who can afford to pay tax? And why do they have such a responsibility? Is the responsibility justified by the Confucian theory of benevolence? But can the Confucian ethics of benevolence, which puts a great emphasis on personal relatedness, explain why I should bear the responsibility to help someone with whom I have no relationship and whom I have never met? If Confucianism is uncertain about the exact degree of moral responsibility one owes to one's neighbors and friends, would it be even more uncertain about one's responsibility to strangers and those who live far apart?

Some scholars even argue that Confucian ethics sees ethical responsibilities as arising *purely* from social relationships, such as familial relationships, friendship, and political associations. Benevolence is always about human relationships, as humanity is essentially relational. It follows, the argument goes, that Confucianism would find it hard to accommodate the idea that one

---

35 Ibid., Book I, A: 7.   36 Ibid., Book I, A: 2; Book I, B: 4.

37 To be fair, however, classical Confucians did not believe that the government's power to impose welfare taxation on citizens had to be ultimately based on citizens' moral duty to help others. On their view, the government may have an independent authority, based on parentalism, perhaps, to demand its citizens to help others. I don't pursue this line of justification because I believe it is difficult to justify government parentalism nowadays.

may have a moral responsibility to help a person with whom one has no particular relationship. However, I believe it is a mistake to take Confucian ethics as purely relation based. The Confucian view is that human persons are first and foremost agents capable of realizing benevolence, which means, among other things, that they have an ability or disposition to care for and sympathize with others.[38] Although the sites for the realization of benevolence are commonly found in personal relationships, there are nonrelational occasions when moral actions are also required by benevolence. A clear example is Mencius's well-known discussion of a child on the verge of falling into a well. For Mencius, if I am benevolent, I would be moved by compassion to save the child even though I have no personal acquaintance with the child or his parents. I would do this because of my concern for the suffering of a human person.

Some might object that the falling child example applies only when one *sees* a falling child. When one sees the child, there is some kind of "interaction" going on between the child and the one who then saves him. There is some kind of a "relationship." This objection seems to stretch the notion of relationship too far. A personal relationship does not begin instantly in the first moment of eye contact (arguably not even romantic first encounters). Moreover, even if it is the appearance of the falling child before me that arouses the benevolent heart in me and moves me to action, my compassion could be similarly triggered by my simple knowledge of the existence of people, whom I have not personally encountered, suffering out there. Benevolence also demands us to respond to this awareness. Confucians believe that benevolence is not confined to those personally known and can reach to all people within the "Four Seas" – everywhere in the world.[39] Later Confucians even talk about the benevolent heart being able to encompass nature and Heaven. This is not to deny that Confucian ethics favors a graded concern for all. Of course gradation implies that we should care more for our family and friends than for strangers. My point here is only to stress the potentially unlimited scope of benevolence. Benevolence motivates us and demands us to respond to our awareness that there are people in need, even if they are strangers to us and live far apart from us. Confucian benevolence can provide a moral basis for welfare entitlements.

38 This and the following few lines are drawn from my "A Confucian Perspective on Human Rights for Contemporary China," pp. 217–218.
39 *Mencius*, Book II, A: 6: "If a man is able to develop all these four germs [compassion, courtesy, shame, and a sense of right and wrong] that he possesses, it will be like a fire starting up or a spring coming through. When these are fully developed, he can take under his protection the whole realm within the Four Seas, but if he fails to develop them, he will not be able even to serve his parents." See also Book I, A: 7.

However, gradation creates moral indeterminacy, as we have seen earlier. While we are certain that benevolence demands us to respond to the suffering of strangers, it is not clear how much we ought to give to help them. What we may be more certain of, however, are some general points. Confucians would certainly agree that we ought to help when helping requires little sacrifice from us, and so Confucians would not have any problem accepting a minimal public welfare system that imposes only relatively minor burdens on people. However, Confucians would have reservations with a welfare system that puts such a substantial burden on people that they would find themselves unable to promote the welfare of their own family members. Moreover, they would have reservations with a system that tends to shift the primary responsibility of caring from the familial and social tiers to the governmental one.

III FROM PRINCIPLES TO INSTITUTIONS

Let us take stock. If our previous discussion is not far off the mark, Confucian ethics would endorse the following principles.

1 WELFARE ASSISTANCE SHOULD FIRST BE PROVIDED ON THE BASIS OF TIES OF FAMILY AND SOCIAL NETWORKS

We can give several points to support this principle.[40] First, family members have the primary responsibility to take care of each other. Second, family and social networks are often built on affection and care. Third, affection and care are genuine only if they are voluntary. A welfare assistance system has a better chance of manifesting the value of care if it is based on the voluntary commitment of the caregiver. Fourth, a family-based or community-based system can respond more effectively to the varying needs of different individuals than a system based on bureaucratic regulations. Finally, this system may have the desirable consequence of strengthening family and community ties.

2 WELFARE ENTITLEMENTS SANCTIONED BY GOVERNMENT SHOULD BE SEEN AS A FALLBACK SUPPORT

Governmental assistance is necessary when the familial and communal tiers break down. There are unfilial children and uncaring parents. There are communities that lack strong ties and mutual concern. An ethics of benevolence would not want the weak and vulnerable to be left behind. Confucian benev-

---

40 Some of these points can be supported by Confucian ethics. Some, like the last two, are just based on judgments about the probable effects of welfare systems.

olence demands that we help these people, and one way to do it is by supporting the government which acts as our agent. Similarly, governmental assistance is necessary when the first two tiers cannot provide sufficient assistance. Consider the example of care for the elderly. There are many aged people whose quality of life is dependent upon long-term care. But today adult children find it a heavy burden to take good care of their aged parents, as their jobs demand a great deal of time and energy and even women need to work to share the family expenses. So even filial children may not be able to help their parents as much as they want to. In this case, government-based social services would be very welcome and even necessary (if social networks cannot offer sufficient help).

3 WELFARE ENTITLEMENTS SYSTEMS SHOULD AVOID ENCOURAGING PEOPLE TO SHIRK THEIR PERSONAL RESPONSIBILITY TO CARE FOR THEIR FAMILY MEMBERS

While accepting a welfare safety net sanctioned by the government, Confucians would be worried by the growing trend of people becoming reliant on government. It has been noted that in Western welfare states, "too many people have come to think of their welfare, and their neighbors' welfare, as the government's problem."[41] Active governmental involvement runs the risk of encouraging people to shirk their personal and communal responsibilities. It may also "crowd out" the valuable voluntary charity groups and mutual aid associations that are so fragile in modern industrial society. Confucians want the government to provide the minimal safety net. But they also want to have a safety net package that induces people to contribute voluntarily and do so in the spirit of care.[42] (This preference can further be linked to the general tendency in Confucianism to rely more on people's voluntary actions than on government's sanctions and legal coercion.) Too often people assume that the end of personal responsibility means the beginning of governmental responsibility. But this is not true. We should, and can, tap the resources of the family, charity groups, voluntary associations, mutual aid societies, and the general public.

4 A PROPOSAL

But didn't I argue earlier that Confucian ethics suffers from a considerable degree of moral indeterminacy regarding the extent of moral responsibility

---

41 See David Schmidtz, "Mutual Aid," in David Schmidtz and Robert Goodin, *Social Welfare and Individual Responsibility* (Cambridge: Cambridge University Press, 1998), p. 64.

42 These are my extrapolations, which I believe are consistent with Confucian ethics, although they are not points made in Confucian texts.

we have toward our neighbors and strangers? Without a clear moral guideline, how do we know what to do? I believe we have to live with this theoretical uncertainty. But good *institutions* may reduce the uncertainty *in practice*.
The best way to deal with this is to create welfare institutions that can induce
maximal personal contributions from people and yet give them a choice to
decide whether to participate. A primarily voluntary scheme would reduce
the need to rely on extensive welfare taxation which, from a Confucian viewpoint, has an unclear moral basis. In what follows I shall consider how we
could improve the modern welfare mechanisms in light of the Confucian
principles reconstructed above.

The standard method of financing governmental social services in modern
welfare states is through involuntary taxation – either compulsory deductions
from monthly paychecks (as in many Western countries) or a one-off compulsory tax payment (as in Hong Kong). In paying taxes, most people do not
undergo a mental process that helps them think they are doing some good
for others. Instead, most of them just experience the pain of seeing their
money being forcibly taken away. In addition, the entire process is as impersonal as it is involuntary. Taxpayers do not know where their tax money goes,
and the welfare recipients do not know from whom they are receiving help.
The two groups of people seldom think of the existence of each other,
and present welfare mechanisms deliberately prevent them from having any
contact. The only agent they are in touch with is the government bureaucracy. In Hong Kong, for example, old people queue up in postal offices to
collect old age pensions from anonymous office clerks behind the bars. They
do not experience anything remotely close to caring and concern. Rightly or
wrongly, then, many taxpayers and welfare recipients feel victimized or
humiliated by the welfare state.

There must be ways to improve this situation. I propose one way to do it,
albeit a tentative one.[43] The core of this proposal is a new mechanism that
encourages people's voluntary participation and the active involvement of
charity and social welfare groups in the process. Instead of compulsory taxation, voluntary donation would be the major source of revenues. Instead of
bureaucratic agencies, voluntary groups would be encouraged to assume the
responsibility for delivering as many welfare services as possible. The central
aspect of the mechanism would be that each year when taxpayers receive their
tax forms, they would also receive a booklet prepared by a government (or

---

43 Another way, more suitable to the countryside than the urban city, is to try to provide an
environment in which communal mutual aid societies can survive and flourish. For stim-
ulating discussions of mutual aid societies in traditional China and Korea, see Wm.
Theodore de Bary, *Asian Values and Human Rights*, Ch. 5, and Chang Yun-Shik's chapter
in this volume, "Mutual Help and Democracy in Korea."

independent) agency which lists information about all the qualified (or certified) voluntary social services groups – information about whom they help, the programs and activities that assist them, a breakdown of what they spent in the previous year, and their projected costs for the coming year. Taxpayers would also be given an assessment of the efficiency of these groups. They would then be asked to choose one or more of these groups for voluntary donation. Taxpayers would, in return, receive tax breaks for their donation. In the entire process, the government would play mainly the role of a middle agent that provides trustworthy information and effective coordination. As for the social services groups which receive revenue from this process, they would be required to provide opportunities for taxpayers to visit their offices and ask questions about their work. It would be in the interest of these groups to make these opportunities attractive to taxpayers.

Would this proposal work? The proposal is based on two key empirical assumptions which, if true, would supply good reasons for the feasibility of the proposal. First, it assumes that people are to some degree altruistic. As Mencius says, people have a compassionate heart. We often experience something close to Mencius's falling child example: When we watch TV news about starving people, the deprived conditions of the handicapped and the blind, or people who suffer from chronic illness or homelessness, we are moved and feel the urge to help by making donations. However, this urge does not often result in actual action. The main reason – other than weakness of will – is that there is a problem of trust, and this is the second assumption. Since we do not have information about the groups which claim to help people and which request public donations, there is a risk that our money might not go safely into the hands of the needy. Note that this problem of trust is reducible to a problem of information – if we knew a group was doing well, we would not hesitate to donate. There is no free-riding problem here since, given the first assumption, people want to help whether or not others are helping. If the sacrifice is not substantial, they would want to do it because they would think they were doing the right thing and would feel good doing so. (I assume, of course, that the donation each person would be motivated to offer would be of an amount that he or she felt comfortable with.)

Now the government's role is precisely to solve the problem of information. The government collects information about the groups and assesses and grades their performance, just as a government inspects and assesses the hygiene of restaurants, or a government's own auditing department assesses the performance of other departments. Performance would be assessed in terms of how much of the donation received by a group goes to administrative costs and how much to clients, and the cost-effectiveness of their programs and activities. (If a public agency instead of a governmental department is performing the job, then part of the donation would go to financing of it.) Taxpayers would thus receive not only useful information that would motivate them to donate but also reliable information about the performance of the groups.

The government has another role to play as well. Since this mechanism relies on individual choice, it is likely that the distribution of donations would be uneven across groups, and hence it is possible that some needy people might receive little support. To address this problem, the government could take some money off the top of total donations to fill the needs of those categories of people. In addition, when choosing where their money should go, people could be asked to choose not individual groups as such but different aid packages that combine a whole range of groups.

This model of voluntary donation scheme is quite similar to the United Way in the United States.[44] As mentioned in its official statement, "The mission of the United Way movement is to increase the organized capacity of people to care for one another."[45] The United Way helps people in the United States through funding a vast network of volunteers and community service agencies (about 1,400 of them, called local United Ways). Each is independent, separately incorporated, and run by local volunteers. The United Way raises funds to support local agency service providers. In total, voluntary contributions to United Ways support approximately 45,000 agencies and chapters. For example, the organization raised US$3.4 billion in the 1997–1998 campaign and $3.2 billion in 1996, which was used for human services ranging from disaster relief, emergency food and shelter, and crisis intervention to day care, physical rehabilitation, and youth development. Each group receiving funds is a nonprofit, tax-exempt charity run by volunteers, and each submits to an annual, independent financial audit. Because of the vast network of volunteers and the simplicity of corporate payroll deduction, administrative expenses for the largest local United Ways average 13 percent of all funds raised.

The success of the United Way provides an empirical basis for the viability of the model I propose here. Both models work with similar aims and methods, except that the central agency in my model is the government or

---

44 I first heard of this organization from a passenger sitting next to me when I was flying United Airlines from Boston to Seoul to attend the conference at which this essay was to be presented. In a casual but intellectually charged chat, I was explaining to this passenger the main ideas of this essay and in particular this model of voluntary welfare. To my delight and distress, the passenger then immediately told me that the U.S. United Way was very close to my proposal. The passenger was an American IT businessman who happened to be interested in social sciences and, surprisingly, Confucianism.

45 *United Way of America*, http://national.unitedway.org/uwa.html.

a publicly authorized independent agency. The advantage of the latter over a private institution is that the public agency, precisely because of its source of authority, is able to express, in a symbolic way, public support for the importance of voluntary help and mutual caring.

However, the example of the United Way also shows that this kind of voluntary welfare scheme is not sufficient to meet the welfare needs of people. Realistically, it is likely that the model proposed here might not generate enough revenues to support a welfare safety net for all and thus the traditional method of governmental taxation would still be necessary. This proposed mechanism is not meant to replace taxation for welfare purposes. It only aims to diminish our need for it. Nevertheless, even within a compulsory taxation scheme, we could still create room for choice – for example, one would have the choice of giving 10 percent of one's tax contribution to a charitable group (or area) or an aid package.[46] This method, though compulsory in nature, does to some degree encourage taxpayers to reflect and deliberate on the needs of the needy.

To conclude, this model has a number of virtues. It is not unrealistically ambitious; it encourages people to share the plight of the unfortunate; it allows people to choose to help those they most care about; it promotes the development of voluntary social service groups;[47] and it increases the opportunity for interaction between the benefactor and the beneficiary and fosters a culture of care and benevolence.[48]

46 I thank Daniel A. Bell for this suggestion.
47 Today's charity groups, especially the small ones, do not easily survive precisely because of the information problem. They have to use a lot of manpower and revenue for fundraising and public relations. This proposed mechanism helps reduce the need for them to do so.
48 I thank Chan Sin-yee and Daniel A. Bell for helpful comments. My work on this essay was supported by a grant from the Research Grants Council of the Hong Kong Special Administrative Region, China (HKU/7129/98H).

PART III

CONFUCIAN PERSPECTIVES ON LAW

CHAPTER 11

MEDIATION, LITIGATION, AND JUSTICE

CONFUCIAN REFLECTIONS IN A MODERN LIBERAL SOCIETY

ALBERT H. Y. CHEN

In every society there is a wide range of alternatives for coping with the conflict stirred by personal disputes. Litigation is only one choice among many possibilities, ranging from avoidance to violence. The varieties of dispute settlement, and the socially sanctioned choices in any culture, communicate the ideals people cherish, their perceptions of themselves, and the quality of their relationships with others. They indicate whether people wish to avoid or encourage conflict, suppress it, or resolve it amicably. Ultimately the most basic values of society are revealed in its dispute settlement procedures.

– Jerold S. Auerbach, *Justice Without Law?* (New York: Oxford University Press, 1983), pp. 3–4

I INTRODUCTION

The nature, structure, and operation of the institutions for dispute settlement of every society are an expression of its culture, its philosophy, its world view, as well as its mode of social, economic, and political organization. It is well known that in traditional China, mediation rather than litigation was the preferred means of dispute settlement in ordinary civil disputes among the people.[1] The theory and practice of mediation have largely been shaped by Confucian philosophy. The system of mediation was also compatible with, and served well the needs of, the traditional society with its agrarian economy,

My research for this essay was supported by a grant from the Research Grants Council, Hong Kong Special Administrative Region, China (HKU/7129/98H).

1 It should however also be acknowledged that recent scholarship has revealed that the extent of the predominance of mediation over litigation in traditional China has probably been overemphasized in earlier scholarship, and that litigation did have an important role to play in, say, the Qing legal system: see generally Philip C. C. Huang, *Civil Justice in China: Representation and Practice in the Qing* (Stanford, Calif.: Stanford University Press, 1996).

kinship-based social structure, loose mode of central imperial rule, and emphasis on social stability rather than economic development.[2]

Modernity has ushered in the market, capitalism, individualism, materialism, consumerism, democracy, liberty, human rights, and the Rule of Law. The legal systems of traditional societies like China have undergone rapid modernization and Westernization so as to cope with the demands of modernity.[3] In the last decade of the twentieth century, China officially embraced the institution of the market,[4] and, in its constitutional amendment of 1999, declared the intention to build a socialist state based on the Rule of Law (i.e., the *Rechtsstaat* in German).[5] Efforts are being made to strengthen the court system and to train better judges and lawyers. More and more people are resorting to litigation as a means of dispute settlement. Is the traditional practice and philosophy of mediation becoming increasingly out-of-date as modernization proceeds? Is the old Confucian wisdom becoming increasingly irrelevant under modern and postmodern conditions? These are questions for us to ponder.

Interestingly, in contemporary studies of means of dispute resolution in the Western world, there is much discussion of the relative advantages and disadvantages of mediation and litigation as means of dispute settlement. In the last two decades, some major legal systems in the West, particularly in the United States, Canada, Australia, and Britain, have been promoting the use of mediation as a means of "alternative dispute settlement" (ADR).[6] Mediation is seen as much cheaper and usually less time-consuming than litigation. It also has the advantage of being able to preserve the social relations between the parties concerned or even to achieve reconciliation between them.

---

2 See, e.g., Liu Min, "The Traditional System of Mediation and Its Creative Transformation: A Legal-Cultural Analysis," *Shehui kexue yanjiu* (Social Science Research) No. 1 (1999) 58, reprinted in *Fali xue, fashi xue* (Jurisprudence and History of Laws) (China Renda Social Sciences Information Center) No. 3 (1999) 53.

3 On the developing legal system in mainland China, see Albert H. Y. Chen, *An Introduction to the Legal System of the People's Republic of China* (Singapore: Butterworths Asia, rev. ed. 1998). On the relationship between modernity and rights-based law, see Albert H. Y. Chen, "The Rise of Rights: Some Comparative Civilizational Reflections," *Journal of Chinese Philosophy* 25 (1998) 5.

4 On the relationship between law and the market economy, see Albert H. Y. Chen, "The Developing Theory of Law and Market Economy in Contemporary China," in Wang Guiguo and Wei Zhenying (eds.), *Legal Development in China: Market Economy and Law* (Hong Kong: Sweet and Maxwell, 1996) 3.

5 See generally Albert H. Y. Chen, "Towards a Legal Enlightenment: Discussions in Contemporary China on the Rule of Law," *UCLA Pacific Basin Law Journal* 17 (1999) 125.

6 See, e.g., Michael Palmer and Simon Roberts, *Dispute Processes: ADR and the Primary Forms of Decision Making* (London: Butterworths, 1998).

However, mediation has also been criticized as not being able to give effect to the rights of the parties concerned, or as resulting in such rights being unfairly compromised in the course of settlement by mediation. It has been argued that, compared to litigation, mediation is a lesser vehicle for enabling justice to be done and is inconsistent with the ideals of the Rule of Law, the legal protection of rights, and the legal struggle to build a better society.

This chapter is intended to contribute to our reflections on these issues. I will first describe the traditional Chinese approach, particularly the Confucian approach, to dispute settlement (section 2 of this chapter). Then, drawing upon the insights and achievements of modern liberal legal thought and practice, I will subject the Chinese tradition of mediation to a critical analysis (section 3). Finally, the inadequacies of modern liberal legalism and the enduring strengths of mediation will be considered (section 4) and an attempt made to integrate the best elements of the Confucian perspective on the one hand and the modern perspective on the other hand (sections 4 and 5). I hope to demonstrate that, in line with some scholars' call for the "creative transformation" of the Chinese cultural tradition in the course of China's modernization,[7] mediation as a traditional Confucian institution for dispute settlement can and should also undergo a creative transformation that will enable it not only to adapt to and survive in modernity and postmodernity, but also to make a positive contribution to, and to remedy some of the ills of, modernity.

2 THE CONFUCIAN TRADITION OF MEDIATION

In the *Analects*, "The Master said, 'In hearing litigation, I am no different from any other man. But if you insist on a difference, it is, perhaps, that I try to get the parties not to resort to litigation in the first place'" (XII.13).[8] This, then, is a clear and definitive statement from Confucius himself which sets out the Confucian view of litigation. A similar view can be found in the *Book of Changes*, in its text on the sixth double hexagram, called *song* (訟) (conflict): "*Song* intimates how, though there is sincerity in one's contention, he will yet meet with opposition and obstruction; but if he cherish an

---

7 The leading scholars in this regard are Lin Yü-sheng and Yu Ying-shih. See Lin Yü-sheng, "Radical Iconoclasm in the May Fourth Period and the Future of Chinese Liberalism," in Benjamin I. Schwartz (ed.), *Reflections on the May Fourth Movement* (Cambridge, Mass.: East Asian Research Center, Harvard University, 1972); Lin Yü-sheng, *Zhengzhi zhixu yu duoyuan shehui* (Political Order and Pluralistic Society) (Taipei: Lianjing, 1989), especially pp. 387–394; Yu Ying-shih, *Cong jiazhi xitong kan Zhongguo wenhua de xiandai yiyi* (The Modern Meaning of Chinese Culture from the Perspective of Value Systems) (Taipei: Shibao, 1983).
8 Quotations from *The Analects* in this essay are taken from D. C. Lau's translation: Confucius, *The Analects* (Hong Kong: Chinese University of Hong Kong Press, 2nd ed. 1992).

apprehensive caution, there will be good fortune, while, if he must prosecute
the contention to the (bitter) end, there will be evil."[9] Litigation is considered to be a negative social phenomenon because it is a deviation from and a
disruption of harmonious social relationships. The construction of a harmonious social order is one of the greatest Confucian ideals. This is the famous
vision of *da tong* (Grand Unity 大同, also translated as Great Community):

> When the Great Way was practised, the world was shared by all alike.
> The worthy and the able were promoted to office and men practised good
> faith and lived in affection. Therefore they did not regard as parents only
> their own parents, or as sons only their sons. . . . All evil plotting was
> prevented and thieves and rebels did not arise, so that people could leave
> their outer gates unbolted. This was the age of Grand Unity.[10]

According to the Confucian perspective, harmony is an unqualified good, and
"the rites" (*li* 禮) provide the means to this great end. According to the
Analects:

> Yu Tzu said, "Of the things brought about by the rites, harmony is the
> most valuable. Of the ways of the Former Kings, this is the most beauti-
> ful, and is followed alike in matters great and small, yet this will not always
> work: to aim always at harmony without regulating it by the rites simply
> because one knows only about harmony will not, in fact, work." (I.12)

It has been pointed out that harmony, including harmony in the cosmos,
harmony between humans and Nature, and harmony among humans, in fact
constitutes a common ideal for Confucianism, Daoism, and Legalism,
although they advocate different means for the realization of this ideal.[11] The
quest for harmony is thus one of the defining characteristics of the traditional
Chinese philosophical outlook, which is also powerfully expressed in Chinese
landscape paintings. And the traditional Chinese approach to dispute resolution in society is inextricably linked to this vision of harmony.

Apart from the philosophy of harmony, another reason why litigation was
viewed with disdain in traditional China is that the pursuit of material self-

---

9 The quotation is taken from James Legge's translation, republished in *Book of Changes*
   (Changsha: Hunan chubanshe, 1993) (The Chinese-English Bilingual Series of Chinese
   Classics).
10 This translation is taken from Wm. Theodore de Bary et al., *Sources of Chinese Tradition*,
   vol. 1 (New York: Columbia University Press, 1960) 176. The original text is in the
   opening portion of an essay on the "Evolution of Rites" (*Li yun*) in the Book of Rites (*Li
   ji*), one of the great Confucian classics.
11 See generally Zhang Zhongqiu, *Zhongxi falü wenhua bijiao yanjiu* (A Comparative Study of
   Chinese and Western Legal Cultures) (Nanjing: Nanjing University Press, 1991) chap. 8;
   Liang Zhiping, *Xunqiu ziran zhixu zhong de hexie* (Seeking Harmony in the Order of Nature:
   A Study of Traditional Chinese Legal Culture) (Beijing: Chinese University of Political
   Science and Law Press, 1997) chap. 8.

interest that underlies civil litigation was perceived to be inconsistent with the Confucian ideal of moral self-cultivation, character formation, and personal growth. As in other great religious traditions, Confucianism privileges self-restraint, the inner life, the incubation of virtues, and the subordination of natural desires and selfish material interests to higher moral demands: "The Master said, 'To return to the observance of the rites through overcoming the self constitutes benevolence'" (*Analects* XII.1). Benevolence (*ren* 仁) is the greatest virtue, and to realise it one has to "overcome the self." Overcoming the self necessarily involves recognising the distinction between "the moral" and "the profitable": "The Master said, 'The gentleman is versed in what is moral. The small man is versed in what is profitable'" (*Analects* IV.16). In quarrels and litigation, what motivates the parties would be "what is profitable," or material advantage (usually in the form of money, land, or other property interests), rather than "what is moral." From the Confucian perspective, the moral law requires one to live in harmony with other human beings surrounding oneself. In case of potential conflicts with others, the correct attitude would be that of self-scrutiny (to examine oneself to see what wrong one has done and what moral failings one should be responsible for), self-criticism, politely yielding (*rang* 讓) or giving concessions to others, complaisance and compromise, rather than to assert one's interests, claim one's "rights," and press one's case by taking the other party to court. Indeed, going to court would be an extremist act[12] that is inconsistent with the Golden Mean advocated by Confucius: "The Master said, 'Supreme indeed is the Mean as a moral virtue. It has long been rare among the common people'" (*Analects* VI.29). The duty of the enlightened Confucian scholar is, therefore, to teach the people the virtues and the moral law, so that they would understand what is exemplary and what is shameful behaviour: "The Master said, 'Guide them by edicts, keep them in line with punishments, and the common people will stay out of trouble but will have no sense of shame. Guide them by virtue, keep them in line with the rites, and they will, besides having a sense of shame, reform themselves'" (*Analects* II.3).

In Chinese history, an increase of litigation in society was usually interpreted as a sign of moral decline. A low litigation rate, on the other hand,

---

12 The extent to which Confucianism inclines against litigation is, however, open to debate. For example, the quote from Confucius at note 8 above may be taken as implying that litigation is justifiable in the final resort when other means of dispute resolution have failed. See the discussion on "the nonlitigious nature of Confucian society" in Joseph Chan, "A Confucian Perspective on Human Rights for Contemporary China," in Joanne R. Bauer and Daniel A. Bell (eds.), *The East Asian Challenge for Human Rights* (Cambridge: Cambridge University Press, 1999) 212 at 226–227. Chan refers also to *Analects* XIV.34: "Someone said, 'Repay an injury with a good turn. What do you think of this saying?' The Master said, 'What, then, do you repay a good turn with? Repay an injury with straightness, but repay a good turn with a good turn.'"

was regarded as evidence of good administration and of officials (acting in
the position of "parents of the people" [*fumuguan* 父母官]) successfully educating the people in the *li*. Local officials would be highly evaluated by their
superiors if there was little or no litigation in the regions under their jurisdiction, which indicated that people were living in harmony. Conversely, a
high litigation rate would reflect badly on the performance of the relevant
local officials, who should engage in self-criticism as to why they failed to
ensure that their subjects should adhere to the Confucian norms of self-
restraint and mutual deference.[13]

The Confucian ideal is therefore a society free of litigation (*wusong* 無訟).[14]
In practice, however, most people in society are not Confucian sages, and disputes do arise. The question then is how the disputes are to be resolved. One
possible response would be for the ruler to set up courts in which disputing
subjects can litigate and judges render judgment. In the English common
law tradition, this has precisely been the dominant response. Indeed, after
the Norman Conquest in the eleventh century, there was a gradual historical
process of the centralization of the administration of justice, in which the
king made the courts he established an attractive channel for dispensing
justice, and cases hitherto handled by local authorities were gradually
diverted to the royal courts.[15]

The traditional Chinese response to the same social problem of dispute
resolution was very different. The dominant Confucian philosophy requires
officials – instead of judging the dispute and imposing a binding judgment
on the parties – to mediate the dispute and search for a solution which is
agreeable to and voluntarily accepted by the disputants. The objective is to
use persuasion and education to make the parties rethink their original positions, to help them arrive at a settlement out of court, and hence to abandon

13 See generally Zhang Jinfan, *Zhongguo falü de chuantong yu jindai zhuanxing* (The Tradition
    and Modern Transformation of Chinese Law) (Beijing: Falü Press, 1997) 277–302; Fan
    Zhongxin et al., *Qing li fa yu Zhongguo ren* (Feeling, Reason, Law, and the Chinese) (Beijing:
    China Renmin University Press, 1992) 180–182.

14 See, e.g., the discussion on this point in Zhang Jinfan (n. 13 above) 277–283; Fan (n. 13
    above) 157–167; Zhang Zhongqiu (n. 11 above) 322–339; Liang (n. 11 above) chap. 8.
    It can however be argued that Confucianism accepts that litigation would still exist in an
    ideal society. For example, Mencius said to King Xuan of Qi, "Now if you should prac-
    tise benevolence in the government of your state, then all those in the Empire who seek
    office would wish to find a place at your court, all tillers of land to till the land in outly-
    ing parts of your realm, all merchants to enjoy the refuge of your market-place, all trav-
    ellers to go by way of your roads, and *all those who hate their rulers to lay their complaints
    before you*" (emphasis supplied). This translation is by D. C. Lau, *Mencius* (London: Penguin
    Books, 1970) 58 (Mencius IA.7). I am grateful to Daniel Bell for drawing my attention
    to this passage.

15 Derek Roebuck, *The Background of the Common Law* (Hong Kong: Oxford University Press,
    1988) chap. 5.

the litigation. The Chinese terms for this practice are *quansong* 勸訟 (beseeching the parties to drop the litigation) and *xisong* 息訟 (dissolving the litigation). The ultimate aim is the reconciliation of the disputants to each other and hence the restoration of the personal harmony and social solidarity that have been temporarily breached by the conflict.

Jesus said, "Blessed are the peacemakers" (Matthew 5:9). Chinese historical texts glorify officials who serve as peacemakers for disputants among their people. They range from legendary historical figures in the earliest period of Chinese civilization to scholar-officials in the Qing dynasty:[16]

(1) Shun was one of the greatest sage-kings of ancient times. Before he became king, he was an official. Peasants in the Lishan region often quarrelled over land boundaries, and fishermen in the Leize region also had disputes with one another. Shun went and lived in the two regions with the people there, talking to them, teaching, and enlightening them. After one year, things had completely changed, and the people in the two regions were all friendly to and willing to make concessions to one another. King Yao was so impressed that he chose Shun to be his successor.[17]

(2) Zhou Wen Wang was one of the greatest kings of the Zhou dynasty. He ruled so well that the peasants made compromises with one another regarding land boundaries, and the people respected and took care of the elderly. Nobles of feudal domains who had disputes with one another would go to Wen Wang for arbitration. In one case, when the disputing parties arrived at Zhou territory, they were so impressed by the harmony and mutual forbearance of its people that they felt ashamed of themselves, realising that the Zhou people would consider it a shame to quarrel over the kind of matter which they were now quarrelling about. They therefore decided to leave immediately and entered into a compromise.[18]

(3) When Confucius served as the principal justice official of the Lu state, he was good at persuading people not to litigate. Mutual *rang* 讓 (yielding, making concessions and compromises) was practised among the people.[19] In

16 Apart from the first two cases which probably belong to the realm of myths, the other cases mentioned below are probably true stories. Most of them were told by historians, although it cannot be denied that they also serve a didactic function.

17 The story was recorded in Sima Qian's *Shi ji* (History), *Wudi benji* (History of the Five Early Emperors). See the discussion in Zhang Jinfan (n. 13 above) 277–278; Fan (n. 13 above) 163–164; Cao Pei, "The Origins of Mediation in Traditional China," *Dispute Resolution Journal*, May 1999, pp. 32–35; T'ung-tsu Ch'ü, *Law and Society in Traditional China* (Westport, Conn.: Hyperion Press, 1980, reprint of original version, Paris: Mouton, 1961) 252.

18 The story was recorded in *Shi ji* (n. 17 above), *Zhou benji* (History of Zhou), and discussed in Fan (n. 13 above) 164; Zhang Jinfan (n. 13 above) 278.

19 The original source is *Kongzi jiayu*, *xiang Lu* and is discussed in Fan (n. 13 above) 181.

one case, a father was litigating against his son (probably charging the son with being unfilial). Confucius ordered them to be detained together. After three months, the father requested the case to be withdrawn. Father and son embraced each other, wept, and vowed never to litigate again. Apparently, the detention was intended to serve as a cooling-off period for the parties to reflect upon the matter. Confucius himself also reflected on his failure to educate the people properly which resulted in the suit being brought.[20]

(4) Han Yanshou, an official in the Western Han dynasty, ruled by virtue (*yide weizhi* 以德為治), and court cases declined in number in the region under his administration. In one case, two brothers litigated over land. Han was depressed by it and blamed himself for failing to educate the people. He left his office on the pretense of illness to reflect on his fault. Officials and gentry in the county were deeply moved and also blamed themselves. Members of the litigants' clan also felt guilty, and the brothers regretted what they had done. They settled the dispute and were determined never to quarrel again. Han then recovered from his "illness" and held a feast for the brothers to celebrate their reconciliation.[21]

(5) Lu Gong was an official in the Eastern Han dynasty. He ruled by moral education rather than punishment. In one case involving a land dispute, several predecessor officials had not been able to conclude the case. Lu talked to the parties and explained to them what was right and wrong in the matter. The parties thereupon withdrew the litigation, blamed themselves, and gave land concessions to each other. In another case, one borrowed an ox from its owner but refused to return it. The owner sued and Lu ordered the return of the cow, but the borrower still refused to comply with the order. Lu sighed and exclaimed, "education and moral cultivation has failed!", and wanted to resign from his post. His subordinates wept and tried to retain him, and the borrower repented and returned the ox.[22]

(6) Wu You was a county official in the Eastern Han dynasty. Whenever there was litigation among the people, he would first close his door to reflect

---

20 The story was recorded in *Xunzi, Youzuo* and discussed in Fan (n. 13 above) 186; Ch'ü (n. 17 above) 252–253.

21 The story was recorded in *Han shu* (History of Han), *Han Yanshou zhuan* (Biography of Han Yanshou) and discussed in Fan (n. 13 above) 181, 187; Liang (n. 11 above) 208; Zhang Jinfan (n. 13 above) 279; Ma Zuowu, "Gudai xisong zhi shu tantao" (An Inquiry into the Means of Terminating Litigation in Ancient Times), *Wuhan daxue xuebao: zheshe ban* (Wuhan University Journal: Philosophy and Social Sciences Section) No. 2 (1998) 47, reprinted in *Fali xue, fashi xue* (Jurisprudence and History of Laws) (China Renda Social Sciences Informaiton Center) No. 5 (1998) 46, at p. 49; Ch'ü (n. 17 above) 253.

22 The story was recorded in *Houhan shu* (History of the Latter Han), *Lu Gong zhuan* (Biography of Lu Gong), and discussed in Liang (n. 11 above) 208–209; Zhang Jinfan (n. 13 above) 279; Fan (n. 13 above) 181, 187–188; Ma (n. 21 above) 49; Ch'ü (n. 17 above) 254.

on his failure in educating the people. Then he would deal with the case by teaching the parties the relevant moral principles in an easily understandable manner, or by visiting their homes to persuade them to become reconciled with one another. Under his administration, litigation declined, because officials and ordinary people all cared for one another and would not defraud one another.[23]

(7) When Chou Lan was a minor village official in the Eastern Han dynasty, there was a Chen Yuan who lived together with his mother. The mother charged Chen with being unfilial. Chou was disturbed and believed that the problem was that the parties had not received sufficient moral education. He pointed out to the mother that she had been a widow and it had not been easy for her to raise the child. Why would she, in a sudden burst of anger, accuse her son of the most serious crime? The mother was moved, wept, and left. Chou then visited the home, drank together with the mother and son, and taught them the ethics of the family. The son repented and subsequently became a very filial son.[24]

(8) Wei Jingjun, a county magistrate in the Tang dynasty, also dealt with a case of a mother and a son litigating against each other. Wei told them that he was an orphan and had always envied those with living parents. He asked them why, having been "fortunate enough to be in the land of warm emotions," they would now come to this point? He also blamed himself for his failure as a magistrate as evidenced by this case. Both parties were moved and wept, and Wei gave them a copy of the Book of Filial Piety (*Xiaojing* 孝經) to study. Mother and son were filled with remorse and subsequently became a loving mother and a filial son.[25]

(9) In a similar vein, Kuang Kui in the Tang dynasty dealt with a case of brothers fighting over land. He gave them a copy of the poem "*Fa mu*" (chopping wood 伐木) in *Shijing* (the Book of Odes 詩經), personally recited the poem, and explained its teachings to them. They thereupon wept, became reconciled to each other, and understood that their struggle over land rights was extremely shameful.[26]

23 The story was also recorded in *Houhan shu*, *Wu You zhuan* (Biography of Wu You), and discussed in Fan (n. 13 above) 181, 187; Zhang Jinfan (n. 13 above) 279; Cao (n. 17 above) 32–33; Ni Zhengmao et al., *Zhonghua fayuan siqian nian* (Four Thousand Years of Chinese Law) (Beijing: Qunzhong Press, 1987) 414–415; Ch'ü (n. 17 above) 253.

24 The story was also recorded in *Houhan shu*, *Chou Lan zhuan* (Biography of Chou Lan) and discussed in Fan (n. 13 above) 186–187; Ma (n. 21 above) 48–49; Ch'ü (n. 17 above) 253.

25 The story was recorded in *Jiu Tang shu* (History of the Tang), *Wei Jingjun zhuan* (Biography of Wei Jingjun) and discussed in Liang (n. 11 above) 209; Ch'ü (n. 17 above) 253.

26 "*Fa mu*" is a poem which glorifies solidarity within the family, including the loving relationship between elder and younger brothers. For an English translation of the poem, see Bernhard Karlgren, *The Book of Odes* (Stockholm: Museum of Far Eastern Antiquities, 1974) 108–109. Kuang Kui's story is told in Liang (n. 11 above) 207; Fan (n. 13 above) 187.

(10) When Lu Jiuyuan, the famous Confucian scholar, was an official in the Song dynasty, he encouraged litigants to settle their disputes. Where the dispute was within the family, he would enlighten the parties with Confucian moral principles. In many cases the parties were so moved that they tore up their plaints and became reconciled with one another.[27]

(11) Lu Long was a magistrate in the Qing dynasty. Two brothers quarrelled over property and brought the case to his court. Instead of determining the question of property rights, he ordered the brothers to call each other brother repeatedly – the younger brother would have to say "elder brother" (*gege* 哥哥) to his elder brother, and the elder brother would have to say "younger brother" (*didi* 弟弟) to his younger brother. After fewer than fifty such exchanges, the brothers wept and wanted to end the litigation. In his judgment, Lu wrote that "in sharing the same breath and the same voice, nobody is as close as brothers; it is so stupid to harm such feelings of bone and flesh (*gurou zhi qing* 骨肉之情) for reasons of property external to one's body." And he ordered that all the property be under the management of the elder brother, and that the younger brother should assist the elder brother in managing it.[28]

(12) Kuai Zifan, another Qing magistrate, came across a case in which the complainant accused his aunt of beating him after he refused to lend her money. The injury he sustained was proved to be minor. He said to the complainant, "You are poor, but your aunt still wants to borrow from you. This shows that she is even poorer. If you take this case to court, not only will your aunt suffer, but you also have to wait in the city. Court staff will demand many kinds of fees from you, and your farm land will go to waste. Why should you endanger the livelihood of two families just to ventilate your anger?" He then gave the complainant some of his own money. The complainant was moved, wept, and withdrew the case.[29]

The stories above were recorded in history because they were deemed significant, and the behaviour of the officials concerned praiseworthy and exemplary. In these stories, we can see the Confucian ideal at work. The same ideal is also reflected in writings of Confucian scholars who urged people to give way to one another, to live in harmony, and to avoid litigation. For

---

27 This was recorded in *Song shi* (History of the Song), *Lu Jiuyuan zhuan* (Biography of Lu Jiuyuan) and discussed in Fan (n. 13 above) 194; Cao (n. 17 above) 33; Ni (n. 23 above) 415.

28 The story was recorded in *Lu Jiashu pandu* (Collected Judgments of Lu Jiashu) and discussed in Zhang Jinfan (n. 13 above) 280–281; Fan (n. 13 above) 188, 190; Cao (n. 17 above) 34.

29 The story was recorded in Kuai's work, *Wuzhong pandu* (Collected Judgments in Wuzhong) and discussed in Fan (n. 13 above) 194; Cao (n. 17 above) 33–34; Ni (n. 23 above) 415–416.

example, Zhu Xi, one of the greatest Confucian philosophers in Chinese history, wrote to urge community members to be friendly to one another. If there are minor grievances, they should reflect upon the matter deeply, try to compromise and reconcile their differences, and should never easily contemplate litigation. He pointed out that even if one is in the right, litigation is expensive and consumes one's energy. And if one loses the case, one would be punished.[30] Zhu also remarked that many cases involved only petty disputes over property and land but resulted in people hating one another or violating the principles of morality.[31]

Lu You, the famous Song poet, wrote to instruct his descendants that quarrelling and litigation are a shame on the household.[32] Wang Shouren, the leading Ming philosopher, promoted a kind of community compact among residents. He composed a Tablet of Rules for Ten Families (*shijia paifa* 十家牌法). One aspect of this is that every day members of each family should, in accordance with the Tablet, encourage and persuade one another to be virtuous. The aim is to build a fiduciary and harmonious community in which members realise that conflict and litigation are wrong. Wang taught the people to have a peaceful and forgiving heart and to avoid quarrels, to be patient and forbearing and to avoid litigation, to encourage one another in doing good and warn one another against doing evil, and to cultivate a social environment with virtues in which the spirit of the rites and of mutual complaisance reigns. He suggested that whenever a dispute arises within the subcommunity of ten families, members of the subcommunity should mediate it and attempt to reconcile the parties. The matter should go to the magistrate only if the mediation effort fails.[33]

Hai Rui, a scholar-official in the Ming dynasty famous for his loyalty, integrity, and competence in adjudicating litigated cases in a fair manner, nevertheless shared the Confucian view of litigation as an unhealthy social phenomenon. He wrote that the high litigation rate in the county Chunan was a sign of moral decline. People pursued their selfish interests and thought

---

30 See Liang (n. 11 above) 205, referring to *Zhuwengong wenji* (Collected Works of Zhuwengong), vol. 100.

31 See Liang (n. 11 above) 208, also referring to *Zhuwengong wenji*, vol. 100.

32 Fan (n. 13 above) 172, referring to *Lu You zhu xun* (Teachings of Lu You). See also Li Wenhai and Zhao Xiaohua, "'Yansong' xinli de lishi genyuan" (The Historical Origins of the Psychology of "Disliking Litigation"), *Guangming ribao* (Guangming Daily), March 6, 1998, p. 7, reprinted in *Fali xue, fashi xue* (Jurisprudence and History of Laws) (China Renda Social Sciences Information Center) No. 4 (1998) 45.

33 See generally Liang (n. 11 above) 205–206, drawing on volumes 16 and 17 of *Yangming quanshu* (Collected Works of Yangming); Fan (n. 13 above) 182. For the community pact, see also Wm. Theodore de Bary, *Asian Values and Human Rights: A Confucian Communitarian Perspective* (Cambridge, Mass.: Harvard University Press, 1998) chap. 5.

highly of those who made profits by defrauding others and those who litigated and won. Relatives no longer respected one another, and people did not
understand the virtues of faithfulness and harmony. He lamented the litigiousness of his time and noted that if the sages were here, they would not
be contented with merely adjudicating the cases but would find a way to halt
the litigation.[34]

The combination of Hai Rui's success as a judge and his conservative view
of litigation illustrates what Professor Philip Huang calls the "practical
moralism" of Confucian magistrates:

> It was "moralism" because of the insistence on the primacy of high moral
> ideals, but it was also "practical" because of their very pragmatic
> approach to the real problems of governance. . . . In the culture of the
> Confucian magistrate, moralistic outlooks and practical considerations
> were two coexisting realities. . . . [A]lthough in the moral culture of the
> magistrate, lawsuits over trivial matters [civil matters regarding debt,
> land, marriage, and inheritance] were not to exist at all, the practical
> culture of the office acknowledged the reality of such lawsuits and called
> for their unequivocal adjudication by law.[35]

Confucian magistrates generally agree that as far as civil disputes – what
Qing law called "minor matters relating to family (household), marriage, and
land" (*hu, hun, tiantu xishi*)[36] – are concerned, they should ideally be settled
by mediation, preferably mediation conducted at the community level by
neighbours, kin, elders, or gentry, or, if that fails, mediation conducted by
the magistrate himself. Adjudication by the magistrate would only be a last
resort when both kinds of mediation fail to persuade the parties to drop the
litigation and arrive at a settlement. As regards the difference between mediation and adjudication from the magistrate's perspective, the Qing official
Wang Huizu wrote:

> It was good for a magistrate to be diligent at hearing and adjudicat-
> ing a case [*ting duan* 聽斷]. But there are instances when he should not
> take to excess a black-and-white approach. The best way to restore

34 Liang (n. 11 above) 203, citing from *Hai Rui ji* (Collected Works of Hai Rui); Ma (n. 21
    above) 46; Zhang Zhongqiu (n. 11 above) 337–338.
35 Philip C. C. Huang, *Civil Justice in China: Representation and Practice in the Qing* (Stanford,
    Calif.: Stanford University Press, 1996) 203–204, 207. As regards whether Qing magis-
    trates practised "adjudication by law" or whether they decided cases on the basis of partic-
    ularistic considerations as applied to the unique circumstances of each case, the Japanese
    scholar Shiga Shuzo has a completely different view from Huang's. See the comment on this
    point in Liang Zhiping, *Qingdai xiguan fa: shehui yu guojia* (Qing Customary Law: Society
    and State) (Beijing: Chinese University of Political Science and Law Press, 1996) 18.
36 These can be contrasted with the "weighty cases" (*zhong an*) – mainly criminal cases –
    which were of serious concern to the state. See Huang (n. 35 above) 1, 6; Zhang Jinfan
    (n. 13 above) 286.

harmonious relations is the mediation of relatives and friends. While adjudication is done by law [*fa* 法], mediation is done by human compassion [*qing* 情]. When it is a matter of law, then there has to be a clear-cut position for or against. If it is a matter of human compassion, then right and wrong can be compromised some. The one in the right [*lizhi zhe*] can accommodate the feelings of a relative or friend, while the one in the wrong [*yiqu zhe*] can avoid the law of the court. . . . That is why mediators were established in ancient times.[37]

Much has been written about the system of community mediation as it was practised in the Qing dynasty.[38] It was a fairly effective system for the purpose of dispute settlement, given that courts were not a "user-friendly" institution in those days,[39] the culture and the government discouraged litigation, and for very practical purposes people needed to maintain amiable relationships with kin and neighbours in the face-to-face community (or *Gemeinschaft*)[40] in which they lived. The mediated settlement was "face saving" for both disputing parties, even where one party was shown to be in the wrong.[41] Indeed, such a party might be required to hold a feast for the mediator and all others concerned, or to pay for some other form of entertainment for the whole village. Such a joint participation in an enjoyable activity serves as a symbol of the reconciliation that has been achieved and of the disputants' reintegration into the community.[42] In many cases, however, the mediated settlement would provide for a compromise instead of demonstrating which party was right and which wrong.[43] Mediation would often be a "learning experience" for the whole village[44] and result in the reaffirmation of shared values and the strengthening of group cohesion in the community.[45]

37 This translation is taken from Huang (n. 35 above) 204. See also the discussion in Zhang Jinfan (n. 13 above) 286; Fan (n. 13 above) 195.
38 See generally Huang (n. 35 above); S. van der Sprenkel, *Legal Institution in Manchu China* (London: Athlone Press, 1977); T'ung-tsu Ch'ü, *Local Government in China Under the Ch'ing* (Cambridge, Mass.: Harvard University Press, 1962); J. A. Cohen, "Chinese Mediation on the Eve of Modernization," *California Law Review* 54 (1966) 1201.
39 Scholars have pointed out how unpleasant an experience it was for anyone to litigate in the courts and the physical, financial, and psychological risks which one would be exposed to. See Cohen (n. 38 above) 1212–1215; Fan (n. 13 above) 177; Li (n. 32 above) 46. Philip Huang however was of the view that the Qing courts were in fact quite accessible to disputants in civil matters and were regularly turned to for the settlement of civil disputes. See Huang (n. 35 above) 13.
40 See the discussion in Fei Xiaotong, *Xiangtu Zhongguo* (Rural China) (Hong Kong: Sanlian shudian [Joint Publishing], 1991) 5–11.
41 Huang (n. 35 above) 65.
42 Sprenkel (n. 38 above) 100, 115; Cohen (n. 38 above) 1219.
43 Huang (n. 35 above) 13, 68, 71; Sprenkel (n. 38 above) 114.
44 Fei (n. 40 above) 61.   45 Cohen (n. 38 above) 1224.

The following case furnishes an example of community mediation at work during the Qing dynasty. A widow brought a suit against her deceased husband's cousin, alleging that the defendant had illegally occupied her land. To prevent the litigation from developing and damaging the clan's reputation, six relatives intervened to mediate the dispute. They invited the parties to meet together (as the defendant was old, his son acted on his behalf) and looked at the land title documents. It was discovered that although the widow's deceased husband had once owned the land, he had mortgaged it to his cousin and had not been able to redeem the property before his death. The widow then understood that she had no lawful claim. But the relatives had sympathy for her and her children, and they persuaded the defendant's son to help her. He then agreed to convey the land to the widow free of charge. The conveyance deed was signed in front of the relatives, and the parties became reconciled. The relatives then jointly applied to the magistrate to terminate the litigation, and the magistrate gave his approval.[46]

3 A LIBERAL CRITIQUE OF CONFUCIAN MEDIATION

The liberal constitutional democratic state that has evolved in the West in modern times glorifies liberty, personal autonomy, equal human rights, fundamental freedoms, and the Rule of Law. Tradition has been subject to rigorous criticism, and much of it has been exposed as repressive, exploitative, suffocating the individual, and supporting social hierarchies that uphold illegitimate power, privilege, and domination. It is possible to argue from this modern liberal perspective that the Confucian theory and practice of mediation belong to this kind of discredited tradition and should be discarded by enlightened humankind. The following are some of the main strands of this critical view.

(1) First, it can be pointed out that mediation often produces outcomes that are unjust because of the inequality between the disputants in terms of power, wealth, status, knowledge, and influence. This point has been made even by scholars of the Chinese tradition of mediation who are not particularly ideologically oriented. For example, Philip Huang wrote that mediation "operated within a context of power relations":[47] "Mediated compromise worked best in instances of disputes among people of roughly equivalent

---

46 This case was recorded in the files of the criminal justice department of the Baodi County government in the Qing dynasty, which files are now in Archive No. 1 in Beijing. The case is described in Ni (n. 23 above) 414; Cao (n. 17 above) 33; Fan (n. 13 above) 192–193; Zhang Jinfan (n. 13 above) 290.

47 Huang (n. 35 above) 70. See also Zheng Qin, *Qingdai sifa shenpan zhidu yanjiu* (A Study of the Judicial System in the Qing Dynasty) (Changsha: Hunan Education Press, 1988) 224.

status and power; it could do little in the way of righting injustices against the powerless by the powerful. The emphasis on mediated compromise, in fact, could serve to excuse or cover up gross injustices."[48] He gave the example of the conflict-ridden relationship between the married-in daughter-in-law and her parents-in-law. Being a social inferior, the former would have no chance at all of obtaining redress against the latter by way of mediation, and in practice such conflicts would simply be suppressed.[49]

There are several reasons why mediation would be vitiated by power imbalance. First, the content of the settlement that is the product of the mediation process, like any agreement between parties reached at the end of a negotiation, depends significantly on the bargaining power of the parties. The weaker party may be forced by circumstances to agree to a proposed settlement (the question of "coercion" in mediation will be discussed below). Secondly, unlike modern litigation, procedural safeguards or due process do not apply to traditional mediation. There is institutionally nothing to guard against the mediator being biased against the socially inferior or weaker party. Thirdly, the principles of *li* that inform the traditional mediation system themselves prescribe hierarchical social roles and relationships, and are inconsistent with the modern liberal notion of equality before the law.

Liberals thus believe that modern legality can provide justice for all much more effectively than traditional Confucian-style mediation. Any aggrieved person can go to court, where judges impartially and faithfully apply the law which upholds human rights and social justice. Even the powerful in society are subject to the law, and judicial independence ensures that courts will give judgment against them if they have violated the law. And they will be bound by the court's judgment, whether they like it or not.

(2) A related criticism of mediation is that in practice it has often operated in a coercive manner and thus betrays the ideal of consensual settlement. Officials exercise state power and are in high positions of authority and prestige. When they conduct mediation and propose solutions for the resolution of a dispute, parties may find it difficult not to accept the proposed settlement. Similarly, in mediation conducted at the clan and community levels, mediators are usually respected elders, and thus their views are backed up by the public opinion of the community. There is therefore social pressure on the disputants to accept the settlement proposed by the mediators.[50] Hence der Sprenkel, in her oft-cited work on Qing legal institutions, suggests that the distinction between mediation and adjudication is not always easy to draw, and in circumstances where the mediators' authority is backed

---

48 Huang (n. 35 above) 68.   49 Huang (n. 35 above) 72–75.
50 Fei (n. 40 above) 61–62.

up by public opinion and group pressure, the mediators are actually playing the role of adjudicators:

> The form of intervention [by mediators] ranged from completely private mediation at one end of the scale to public adjudication at the other, the one shading into the other almost imperceptibly as public opinion was felt to be more strongly involved. . . . Theoretically at the point when private bargaining gives place to acceptance of formal group authority we are in the presence of law. . . . But as this progression is a continuum along the line of growing public opinion supporting the authority, it would be hard to draw a line at the point where law begins.[51]

(3) As discussed above, the Confucian view of disputes in society is that the mere phenomenon of the dispute arising is a bad thing, a sign of the failure of scholar-officials in the work of moral education of the people, and the disputants should be educated and persuaded to end the dispute by arriving at an amicable settlement. This presupposes a paternalistic conception of the state and can therefore be criticized as such from the liberal perspective. From this perspective, officials have no right to claim a morally higher ground than ordinary citizens. It would be wrong for the state to promote a particular conception of the good life, and its business should be limited to the maintenance of social order and the administration of justice on the basis of neutral rules of law. It is therefore not the business of officials to tell citizens that it is wrong to quarrel with one another or even to hate one another. The function of judges is to render a judgment on the facts of the dispute by applying the law laid down by the legislature elected by the citizens themselves, to determine who is in the right and who is in the wrong in the litigation, and not to educate the people on the importance of maintaining harmonious relations with one another, respecting one another, or loving one another.

(4) In the Chinese tradition, when officials or community leaders conduct mediation, they are acting as spokesmen of a set of shared values and norms accepted by the community at large, and they are appealing to the parties' conscience as shaped by these values and norms. That is why mediation has been understood as a didactic process, and why it is believed by anthropologists to contribute to social cohesion and solidarity in primitive, tribal, rural, or other small-scale societies in the nature of the *Gemeinschaft*.[52] Insofar as mediation presupposes the existence of a closely knit community with a high

---

51 Sprenkel (n. 38 above) 117–118.
52 See generally Richard L. Abel, "A Comparative Theory of Dispute Institutions in Society," *Law and Society Review*, Winter 1973, pp. 217–347; Hilary Astor and Christine M. Chinkin, *Dispute Resolution in Australia* (Sydney: Butterworths, 1992) 20–21; Richard L. Abel (ed.), *The Politics of Informal Justice, Vol. 2 (Comparative Studies)* (New York: Academic Press, 1982).

degree of consensus on applicable norms, it is inconsistent with the open and pluralistic nature of modern society in which the individual rather than the community is the sovereign.

(5) A common criticism – on the basis of common sense rather than liberal philosophy – which has been voiced against mediation is that mediation often means no more than "plastering over" the dispute,[53] making the parties compromise for the sake of making peace without regard to the right and wrong or justice and injustice of the subject matter in dispute. Harmony is obtained at the expense of justice, and the party who has been genuinely wronged gets less than his or her due. The legitimate interests and lawful rights of such a party are sacrificed for the sake of social order and stability. The balance between the individual's interest and the collective interest is improperly tilted toward the latter. From this perspective, litigation followed by adjudication by the court according to law is a better vehicle for the realization of justice in the sense of each person getting his or her due.

(6) One may go one step further and question whether it is right for the traditional Chinese and particularly the Confucianists to attach such a high value to harmony and order, and whether it is right for them to look down on litigation as evidence of lack of moral cultivation and of the shameless pursuit of selfish and materialistic interests. This traditional Chinese approach may be contrasted with the ancient Graeco-Roman view of litigation, justice, and law.[54] As early as in this classical era of Western civilization, the assertion of one's interests by way of litigation was accepted as morally and legally legitimate. There is nothing wrong with claiming one's due where others have unlawfully deprived one of one's due. The task of the court is to do justice according to law, and to arrive at a just resolution of the dispute. The task of the law is to define what interests and rights one may legitimately assert and to ensure that they will receive due protection. Hence the development of the civil law of Rome to levels of sophistication, which in turn paved the way for the modern theory and practice of the Rule of Law. The Western approach to the conflict of interests that inevitably arises in human coexistence may be regarded as more realistic than the traditional Chinese approach, which may be criticized as overly moralistic.

53 Stanley B. Lubman, "Dispute Resolution in China after Deng Xiaoping: 'Mao and Mediation' Revisited," *Columbia Journal of Asian Law* 11, No. 2 (Fall 1997) 229–391 at 291, 337, which also refers to the Chinese expression "*huo xini*," roughly meaning "plastering over" the dispute. See also Michael Palmer, "The Revival of Mediation in the People's Republic of China: (1) Extra-Judicial Mediation," in W. E. Butler (ed.), *Yearbook on Socialist Legal Systems 1987* (Dobbs Ferry, N.Y.: Transnational Publishers, 1988) 219–277 at 238: "important principles may have to be sacrificed in the effort to smooth matters over between disputants, and the methods of mediation are sometimes specifically referred to as 'unprincipled wishy-washiness.'"
54 For this contrast, see generally Zhang Zhongqiu (n. 11 above) chap. 8.

(7) The dominance of the discourse and practice of mediation in traditional China has hampered the development of Chinese law, particularly Chinese civil law, in the form of either legislation or case law.[55] It is well known that the provisions in the elaborate dynastic codes in Chinese history are mainly on criminal law and on administrative matters, and civil law on matters such as property rights and contractual relations was underdeveloped in comparison with the Western legal tradition. This in turn means that the traditional Chinese legal system was not able to provide the predictability and "calculability" for economic actors which Max Weber held to be the defining characteristics of the operation of "rational" modern legal institutions and necessary conditions for capitalistic economic growth.[56]

(8) Finally, the traditional system of mediation has been criticized by leading Chinese legal historians as a conservative force that sought to maintain the existing social order at the expense of freedom, exploration, and progress.[57] At the same time, modern liberals have argued that litigation can contribute to social reform in many important ways. Through litigation, existing social institutions that are unjust or repressive may be challenged, and judges have the power and responsibility to translate the promises and ideals of the law and the constitution into reality.[58] Court adjudication on the basis of evidence and reasoned arguments is one of the best examples of human reason at work.[59] Court judgments do much more than simply resolve the dispute in the case at hand; they also give expression to the public values that ought to be upheld and provide guidance for behaviour by the community at large.[60]

4 MEDIATION IN MODERNITY

Despite criticisms such as those set out in the preceding section, the theory and practice of mediation as a means of dispute settlement have not in fact

---

55 Zhang Zhongqiu (n. 11 above) 344; Cohen (n. 38 above) 1224.

56 See generally Albert H. Y. Chen, "Rational Law, Economic Development and the Case of China," *Social and Legal Studies* 8 (1999) 97.

57 Zhang Jinfan (n. 13 above) 300; Zhang Zhongqiu (n. 11 above) 339–341; Zheng (n. 47 above) 225.

58 Owen M. Fiss, "Against Settlement," *Yale Law Journal* 93 (1984) 1073; Owen M. Fiss, "Out of Eden," *Yale Law Journal* 94 (1985) 1669.

59 Owen M. Fiss, "The Social and Political Foundations of Adjudication," *Law and Human Behaviour* 6, No. 2 (1982) 121; Lon L. Fuller, "The Forms and Limits of Adjudication," *Harvard Law Review* 92 (1978) 353, reprinted in Lon L. Fuller, *The Principles of Social Order* (Durham, N.C.: Duke University Press, 1981) 86.

60 Edward Brunet, "Questioning the Quality of Alternate Dispute Resolution," *Tulane Law Review* 62, No. 1 (1987) 1 at 16; Marc Galanter, "The Day After the Litigation Explosion," *Maryland Law Review* 46 (1986) 3, 32–37.

been abandoned by modernity. On the contrary, mediation has enjoyed a new lease on life. In China itself, after the fall of the Qing and before the establishment of the People's Republic, both the Nationalist Government and the Communist Party had introduced systems of mediation in areas under their rule.[61] Mediation is still alive and well in both contemporary mainland China and Taiwan,[62] although the theory and practice of mediation have now become quite different from their premodern counterparts. Indeed, mediation is an element of the Chinese tradition that has successfully undergone a creative transformation in modernity.

In the West, particularly in the Anglo-American world, a movement to introduce means of "alternative dispute settlement" (ADR) started in the 1970s and 1980s, and its influence has steadily increased since then.[63] Mediation is recognised and promoted as one of the most important means of ADR, and there has also been interest in the cross-cultural study of mediation in general and in Chinese mediation in particular.[64] Many lawyers are expanding their practice to include mediation, and many institutions providing mediation as a professional or voluntary service have sprung up.

What are the limitations of litigation, adjudication, and justice according to law which, according to the preceding section, seem a superior vehicle of justice to mediation, particularly after the Enlightenment of humankind? What are the strengths of mediation that enable it not only to withstand the test of modernity in China but also to carve out an increasing space for itself in the West? In this regard, is there still value in Confucian thinking and practice relating to mediation?

Let us begin our inquiry with two important statements by American pioneers in the promotion of ADR. In 1982, Chief Justice Warren Burger,

---

61 See generally Palmer (n. 53 above); Stanley Lubman, "Mao and Mediation: Politics and Dispute Resolution in Communist China," *California Law Review* 55 (1967) 1284.

62 For the case of mainland China, see Palmer (n. 53 above); Lubman (n. 53 above). For the case of Taiwan, see Lin Duan, "Huaren de falü yishi: yi Taiwan 'tiaojie zhidu' de xiandai yiyi wei li" (The Legal Consciousness of the Chinese: The Example of the Modern Meaning of Taiwan's "Mediation System"), paper presented at the 4th conference on the psychology and behaviour of the Chinese organized by the Institute of Ethnology, Academia Sinica and Department of Psychology, National Taiwan University, Taipei, 29–31 May 1997; Zheng Zhengzhong, *Haixia liang'an susong fazhi zhi lilun yu shiwu* (The Theory and Practice of the Systems of Litigation on Both Sides of the Straits) (Taipei: Taiwan Shangwu, 2000) chap. 10, which provides a useful comparison between the mediation systems in mainland China and Taiwan. In the case of Hong Kong, mediation as an institutional component of the legal system is not as well developed as in mainland China and Taiwan (e.g., there are no mediation committees for dispute resolution in general at the neighbourhood level), but mediation is used and legally recognized in certain specific domains (e.g., family disputes, employer-employee disputes, complaints regarding sex discrimination).

63 See, e.g., Palmer and Roberts (n. 6 above).

64 See, e.g., Abel (n. 52 above) and the works cited in n. 62 above.

in his report on the state of the American judiciary, called on the legal profession to fulfil "its historical and traditional obligation of being healers of human conflict" and urged the American Bar Association to extend its efforts toward the spread of alternative dispute resolution.[65] In 1983, law professor Derek Bok, then president of Harvard University, criticized American law schools for training students "more for conflict than for the gentler arts of reconciliation and accommodations." He went on to write:

> Over the next generation, I predict, society's greatest opportunities will lie in tapping human inclinations toward collaboration and compromise rather than stirring our proclivities for competition and rivalry. If lawyers are not leaders in marshaling cooperation and designing mechanisms that allow it to flourish, they will not be at the center of the most creative social experiments of our time.[66]

These quotations underscore an important contrast between litigation and mediation as means of dispute settlement. Litigation is confrontational and adversarial and often exacerbates the conflict, while mediation is basically a cooperative enterprise to help the parties heal the conflict and be reconciled to each other. Given the way Confucianism privileges human relationships and social harmony, it is clear that mediation is much more consistent with Confucian philosophy than litigation. Thus the contrast between litigation and mediation corresponds to the contrast between Confucian philosophy and modern Western liberal legal thinking (what I would call "liberal legalism"), which, as the Marxist legal philosopher E. B. Pashukanis points out, is predicated on the members of modern bourgeois society being isolated possessors of private, egoistic interests.[67]

---

65 Quoted in D. Paul Emond, "Alternative Dispute Resolution: A Conceptual Overview," in D. Paul Emond (ed.), *Commercial Dispute Resolution: Alternatives to Litigation* (Aurora, Ontario: Canada Law Book, 1989) 1 at 5.

66 Derek Bok, "A Flawed System of Law and Practice Training," *Journal of Legal Education* 33 (1983) 570 at 582–583, reprinted in Palmer and Roberts (n. 6 above) 28; also quoted in Emond (n. 65 above) 5. The litigiousness of American society demonstrates the contradiction between the modern Rule of Law with its emphasis on the rights of the individual which can be legitimately asserted in litigation and the traditional Chinese Confucian conceptions of social and cosmic harmony and of mediation as a means for conflict resolution and the achievement of such harmony. For a radical critique of contemporary American legal culture and of the language of rights (leading to "a nation of enemies," in the author's own words), see Philip K. Howard, *The Death of Common Sense: How Law Is Suffocating America* (New York: Warner Books, 1996). For a more optimistic view, see Lawrence M. Friedman, *The Republic of Choice: Law, Authority, and Culture* (Cambridge, Mass.: Harvard University Press, 1990); Lawrence M. Friedman, *Total Justice* (New York: Russell Sage Foundation, 1994).

67 E. B. Pashukanis, "The General Theory of Law and Marxism," in H. W. Babb and John N. Hazard (eds.), *Soviet Legal Philosophy* (Cambridge, Mass.: Harvard University Press,

Why is it that litigation and mediation have such different effects on the conflict while both are means of terminating the dispute? The answer lies in the very nature of the two kinds of activities. Litigation results in a judgment given by the court which is imposed on and binding on the parties irrespective of their will. Usually one party wins and the other party loses the case. Before the judgment, each party and his or her lawyer must try their best to convince the court that they are right and the other party wrong. Conversely, the defining feature of mediation is that it is a process whereby the mediator facilitates a consensual settlement which both parties agree to accept voluntarily. Seeking to reach an agreement that meets the needs and interests of both parties is itself a cooperative venture. An agreement is, by nature, a meeting of minds, and such a mental convergence is itself conducive to the relationship between the parties because it presupposes a certain degree of mutual communication, understanding, and trust. What is lacking in litigation is real communication between the parties, because the structure of litigation only emphasizes communication between each party and the court. Thus one writer draws on Habermas's theory of communicative rationality to defend the practice of mediation and cautions against the "colonization of social life by legal adversarialism."[68] For in mediation, it is possible for the disputant to engage in a truly participatory mode of discourse that is noncoercive and that leads to a consensus based on shared values and common interests.

Other writers draw on the religious traditions of Judaism and Christianity for the purpose of advocating mediation as a superior alternative to litigation.[69] Reference is made to St. Matthew's Gospel:

> If your brother sins against you, go and show him his fault, just between the two of you. If he listens to you, you have won your brother over. But if he will not listen, take one or two others along, so that "every matter may be established by the testimony of two or three witnesses." If he refuses to listen to them, tell it to the church; and if he refuses to listen even to the church, treat him as you would a pagan or a tax collector.[70]

1951) at 155–156, discussed in Larry May, "Legal Advocacy, Cooperation, and Dispute Resolution," in Stephen M. Griffin and Robert C. L. Moffat (eds.), *Radical Critiques of the Law* (Lawrence, Kans.: University Press of Kansas, 1997) 83 at 84–86. Although there is some insight in Pashukanis's theory, it cannot be accepted in an unqualified manner. Modern legality is not only about the egoistic defence and pursuit of private rights and interests; it is also about the quest for justice. Much of public interest litigation and human rights litigation exemplifies this quest.

68 May (n. 67 above) 92.
69 Andrew W. McThenia and Thomas L. Shaffer, "For Reconciliation," *Yale Law Journal* 94 (1985) 1660.
70 Matthew 18:15–17.

The following text by the writers who refer to this biblical passage is worth
quoting at length, for it can be observed how much convergence there is
between Confucian thinking and Hebrew thinking:

> Thus, the procedure gives priority to restoring the relationship. Hebraic
> theology puts primary emphasis on relationships, a priority that is polit-
> ical and even ontological, as well as ethical, and therefore legal. And so,
> most radically, the religious tradition seeks not *resolution* . . . but *recon-
> ciliation* of brother to brother, sister to sister, sister to brother, child to
> parent, neighbor to neighbor, buyer to seller, defendant to plaintiff, *and
> judge to both*. . . . We see the deepest and soundest of ADR arguments as
> in agreement with us: Justice is not usually something people get from
> the government. And courts . . . are not the only or even the most impor-
> tant places that dispense justice. . . . Justice is what we discover – you
> and I, Socrates said – when we walk together, listen together, and even
> love one another, . . . justice is the product of piety, to be sure, but not
> piety alone; it is the product of study, of reason, and of attending to the
> wise and learning from them how to be virtuous.[71]

Some feminist thinkers have also rallied to the cause of mediation and the
ADR movement.[72] It has been argued that while men are competitive, aggres-
sive, and confrontational (as in litigation), women prefer to compromise and
to maintain a cordial relationship (as in mediation). Men think in terms of
abstract rights and general rules (which are what count most in litigation),
while women are more sensitive to context and the particular circumstances
of the case (which matter more in mediation). In mediation, human connection, relationship, dialogue, and empathy are valued, and these are seen to be
particularly consistent with the feminine element of humanity. Ironically,
even though Confucianism has been associated with patriarchy, these
allegedly feminist values are apparently also Confucian values.

Another interesting contemporary Western perspective on mediation is the
theory of the "transformative dimension" of mediation and its potential for
"citizen empowerment" and revitalization of the urban neighbourhood.[73] It
is pointed out that mediation promotes the participants' recognition of each

---

71 McThenia and Shaffer (n. 69 above), 1664–1665, 1666. Emphasis in original.
72 C. Menkel-Meadow, "Portia in a Different Voice: Speculations on a Women's Lawyering
    Process," *Berkeley Women's Law Journal* 1 (1985) 39; Janet Rifkin, "Mediation from a
    Feminist Perspective: Promise and Problems," *Law and Inequality* 2 (1984) 21, referred to
    in Astor and Chinkin (n. 52 above) 22.
73 See generally Robert A. Baruch Bush and Joseph P. Folger, *The Promise of Mediation:
    Responding to Conflict Through Empowerment and Recognition* (1994), an extract from which
    can be found in John S. Murray et al., *Mediation and Other Non-Binding ADR Processes*
    (Westbury, N.Y.: Foundation Press, 1996) 133–138; Edward W. Schwerin, *Mediation,
    Citizen Empowerment, and Transformational Politics* (Westport, Conn.: Praeger, 1995).

other as fellow human beings and their empathy and concern for the situations and problems of others. It can also restore to them an awareness of their own value, potential, and strength, particularly their own capacity for problem solving and managing human relationships. As such, it not only has a reparative effect on human relationships but can also change the participants for the better as human beings and contribute to their personal and moral growth. Indeed, it is said that mediation can be empowering not only for the disputants themselves but also for the mediators, particularly those who volunteer to work as mediators as a kind of community service. In contrast with the empowering potential of mediation, it is argued that litigation is disempowering because it is dominated by lawyers and judges, whereas in mediation the parties themselves are in control and they "own" their conflict themselves.

This brings us back to the essence of mediation itself as understood by the Confucianists and by modern jurists. In the Confucian stories of mediation, the typical pattern is that the conflict is brought to an end as the parties regret what they have done, repent, become reconciled to each other, and commit themselves to a new and better future. In other words, the human person undergoes a transformation as a result of the persuasion of the mediator. Nothing like this happens in the course of litigation, except that the party who wins the suit will feel gratified, victorious, and justified, and the loser feels disappointed, defeated, and humiliated. Thus the sets of human sentiments involved in mediation and litigation are very different from one another.

The point about the personal transformation that can take place in mediation has been well captured by the American jurist Lon Fuller in his account of mediation:

> the central quality of mediation [is] its capacity to reorient the parties toward each other, not by imposing rules on them, but by helping them to achieve a new and shared perception of their relationship, a perception that will redirect their attitudes and dispositions toward one another. . . . [T]he proper function of the mediator turns out to be, not that of inducing the parties to accept formal rules for the governance of their future relations, but of helping them [to accept] a relationship of mutual respect, trust, and understanding. . . . This suggests a certain antithesis between mediational processes, on the one hand, and the standard procedures of law, on the other, for surely central to the very notion of law is the concept of *rules*.[74]

74 Lon L. Fuller, "Mediation – Its Forms and Functions," in *The Principles of Social Order* (n. 59 above) 125 at 144–146. Emphasis in original.

The convergence of the Confucian view of mediation and the various strands of contemporary Western thought mentioned above that affirm the value of mediation as a means of dispute resolution that is alternative to litigation testifies to the timeless validity of some Confucian insights into human nature and the human condition. Although the Confucianists and, indeed, also the other schools of traditional Chinese philosophy, believe in harmony in society and the universe, they recognize that conflicts are inevitable in the real world. The question then is how human beings should cope with conflicts. The teaching of Confucianism is that it is better for the parties in the conflict to settle the dispute in a consensual matter, if necessary with the assistance of mediators. This is the solution that is more consistent with human dignity and social well-being than the alternative of a decision imposed on the parties by a judge backed up by the coercive powers of the state. Even if the matter fails to be resolved by mediation at the community level and comes before a judge, it is better for the judge to persuade the parties to accept a consensual settlement than for him to render a judgment that is binding on the parties by the force of law.

Here we see the familiar Confucian distinction between ruling by moral persuasion and conversion and ruling by power and coercion,[75] and the great respect for human dignity and human rationality that is implicit in the former. Also reflected in this thinking about conflict and mediation is the Confucian optimism about the goodness and conscience that is latent in each person, without which personal transformation in the course of education and persuasion would not be possible. The Confucian theory of mediation presupposes that human beings have the rational and moral capacity to reflect on what they have done and to change their minds about themselves and about others after listening to others' (including the mediators') views. Human desires can be altered, purified, or otherwise made subject to rational and moral control, and moral growth is possible. Indeed, many of the success stories of mediation in both ancient and modern times may be interpreted as case examples of moral growth.

The Confucian insight that still has a valid contribution to make to modern liberal society is therefore as follows. Mediation need not be relegated to second-class justice (e.g., for those who cannot afford to litigate) even in a society based on the Rule of Law administered by a competent and independent judiciary that enjoys the confidence of the people. In many situations, mediation can even provide a superior form of justice to litigation and

75 See generally Albert H. Y. Chen, "Confucian Legal Culture and Its Modern Fate," in Raymond Wacks (ed.), *The New Legal Order in Hong Kong* (Hong Kong: Hong Kong University Press, 1999) 505–533.

adjudication, in the sense that it is morally more desirable and better serves human needs and interests. Confucian philosophy can provide a defence of mediation that is at least as powerful as other contemporary Western theories of mediation.[76] And the long Chinese tradition in thinking about and practising mediation can be drawn on to enrich the modern understanding and experience of mediation.

This does not however mean that the criticisms of traditional mediation from the modern liberal perspective cannot stand. On the contrary, these criticisms are useful because they can assist in the creative transformation of traditional mediation, both for the purpose of improving it and rectifying its deficiencies, and for the purpose of adapting it to the new conditions of modern society. This leads us to the final section of this chapter.

5 THE "CREATIVE TRANSFORMATION" OF MEDIATION

Although the Confucian theory and practice of mediation are a valuable resource for modernity as demonstrated above, the same cannot unfortunately be said of the Confucian and the traditional Chinese attitude to litigation.[77] In a modern liberal society, litigation is a legitimate activity not only for the purpose of dispute resolution, but also for the purpose of protecting the lawful and legitimate rights and interests of persons, elucidating and publicizing the meaning of constitutional and legal norms which the democratic state has created or endorsed, generating principles and rules to guide social behaviour, and serving as a channel for social reform and progress. Parties and their lawyers have the right to present evidence and arguments in open court in accordance with procedural rules that guarantee due process. Judges have the obligation to decide cases in accordance with the law and the highest

---

76 In this chapter, I am not asserting that Confucianism can support a distinctively Confucian mode of contemporary mediation that is different from mediation as theorized and practised in the contemporary Western world. I only argue that from the *philosophical* point of view, Confucian philosophy can provide a theoretical justification for mediation that is at least as effective and powerful as contemporary Western theories.

77 The title of this chapter is "Mediation, Litigation, and Justice: Confucian Reflections in a Modern Liberal Society." My thesis is that when Confucianists living in a modern liberal society reflect upon the tradition of Chinese Confucian mediation, they would agree that this tradition has a valuable role to play in the contemporary world, but it should also undergo a "creative transformation." I am not in this chapter engaged in a critique of modern liberal society from a Confucian perspective, as I myself accept the basic tenets of liberalism and believe that China ought to embrace a Confucian version of liberalism: see my article "The Political Thought of Twenty-First Century China," in Joseph C. W. Chan and Man-to Leung (eds.), *Zhengzhi lilun zai Zhongguo* (Political Theory in China) (Hong Kong: Oxford University Press, 2001) 12–25 (in Chinese).

constitutional ideals of the liberal constitutional democratic state, and to justify their decisions by providing full legal reasons. This kind of Rule of Law has never existed in traditional China, and there is a consensus in China today that this is what China needs to develop in the course of modernization.

The "creative transformation" of mediation means that the traditional thinking and practice regarding mediation need to be revised in the light of the modern understanding of the Rule of Law. It must be recognised that progress is possible and has indeed occurred in human history: For example, the modern liberal constitutional democratic state which practises the Rule of Law is a superior form of political and legal organization to the traditional imperial-bureaucratic state in China. The Chinese people need more than what tradition can offer – which however does not mean that what tradition can offer is not valuable and important. The Chinese people should treasure their cultural heritage and can benefit tremendously from it, but they also need modern human rights, modern democracy, and modern justice according to law.

Thus in the modern society which China is building, as in the modern or postmodern society in the West, mediation has a positive and useful role to play, but not as the predominant mode or the officially preferred mode of dispute resolution. As the concept of "alternative dispute resolution" implies, mediation should properly be regarded as one of the alternatives to litigation for the purpose of dispute resolution. This means that even though there is much that is insightful and timeless in the Confucian view of mediation as a means of dispute settlement, the Confucian view of litigation should be regarded as largely obsolete and inconsistent with the modern understanding of the Rule of Law. And the modern liberal conception of rights, litigation, adjudication, and justice is much more persuasive to people living in modern conditions than the Confucian view of litigation.

It should be acknowledged that most of the points made in the liberal critique of traditional Chinese mediation as constructed above in this chapter are indeed valid and should be taken seriously, even though they should not be taken as implying that mediation should be completely abandoned in a modern liberal society. Traditional mediation should undergo a creative transformation so as to preserve what is valuable and timeless in it on the one hand, and to change and improve itself on the other hand so as to address the valid concerns of liberalism.

For example, it should be ensured that mediation is noncoercive and does not in any way diminish the parties' right to litigate the matter in court. This means that every effort must be made to ensure that there is no social or institutional pressure on the disputants to agree to any proposed settlement in the course of mediation. Settlement must be truly consensual, and the process leading to the settlement must be such that the parties are not subject to any coercion. The parties thus retain the right to seek justice before the court if no solution acceptable to both sides can be agreed to. A corollary of this is that the court system must be made accessible, legal knowledge must be widely disseminated, and legal aid must be provided for the indigent, so that litigation is a really viable alternative to mediation.

The principle mentioned above that no form of coercion should be used during the process of mediation is self-evident. It is however arguable whether disputants should be required, at least in the context of certain types of cases, to undergo mediation *before* they can initiate legal proceedings in court. Mediation enthusiasts would say that people who might otherwise refuse to submit their dispute to mediation will be able to appreciate its benefits once they have actually experienced it at work; hence the imposition of submission to mediation as a condition precedent for the right to sue in court can be justified. On the other hand, it can be argued that the Rule of Law requires direct access to justice according to law as administered by the courts; the imposition of a condition precedent regarding mediation is an undue restriction on the citizen's right to litigate; in any event it would be a waste of time and resources to compel parties to go through the mediation process if at least one party finds the very idea of mediation objectionable and would not have submitted to it but for the condition precedent mentioned above.

It seems that it would be difficult to give a definite answer to this question that would be applicable to all cases that would otherwise go before the courts. The answer to the question depends significantly on an empirical rather than philosophical point: How likely is it that a party who is "compelled" (by the condition precedent) to undergo mediation will drop his or her resistance to mediation in the course of experiencing it and freely agree to a settlement at the end of the mediation process? If there is evidence to demonstrate that in a particular kind of dispute such likelihood is sufficiently high, then the imposition of the condition precedent may be justified. However, what is "sufficiently" high for this purpose would depend on how much one values the right and freedom to litigate without being subject to any condition precedent regarding mediation.

In the creative transformation of traditional mediation, the problem of "power imbalance" in mediation must also be seriously addressed.[78] If the parties are to come to a genuine consensual settlement, they must be able to negotiate on the basis of mutual equality. They must have relatively equal

---

78 See generally Astor and Chinkin (n. 52 above) 105–109; Jack Effron, "Alternatives to Litigation," *Modern Law Review* 52 (1989) 480 at 493–495.

bargaining power. Disparity in financial resources, in social power, and in information possessed will often mean that the negotiation cannot be genuinely uncoerced. Hence mediation may not be appropriate in situations of acute power imbalance, and it may be necessary for public policy to specially facilitate and promote the use of litigation in such situations.

There may also be other types of cases in which mediation and private settlement should not be encouraged.[79] It has been suggested that disputes involving constitutional and other public law issues or major questions of public policy are more appropriately dealt with by the court system than by mediation. This is because whereas judges are trustees of the community entrusted with the power and responsibility to make and enforce public norms of behaviour in a system of open justice (involving public trials and publicized judgments with reasons), mediation is not similarly subject to public scrutiny and accountability. The community as a whole has an interest in such questions of public law, which have ramifications extending beyond the dispute between the actual parties of the case.

What, then, are the types of cases for which mediation is particularly suitable? Fuller suggests that they are those in which the intermeshing of the parties' interests is such that they have an incentive to collaborate in mediation, those in which regulation by impersonal rules focusing on acts (as distinguished from persons – Fuller points out that whereas mediation is directed toward persons, legal rules are oriented toward acts) or formally defined rights and wrongs may not be appropriate, or those involving human associations which depend on spontaneous and informal collaboration.[80] Thus divorce cases are the best example. However, mediation has also been used in the West widely beyond the context of domestic relations, for example, in the areas of small claims, traffic accidents, consumer grievances, petty crimes, labour relations, minorities' relations, education, housing, environment, intellectual property, and construction.[81]

The question of the types of cases in which mediation is most likely to work is closely related to the question raised above of what are the circumstances, if any, in which disputants may legitimately be required to undergo mediation before they can litigate the dispute in court. Since divorce cases

---

79 See generally Harry T. Edwards, "Alternative Dispute Resolution: Panacea or Anathema?" *Harvard Law Review* 99 (1986) 668; Emond (n. 65 above) 1–25; Hiram E. Chodosh, "Judicial Mediation and Legal Culture," *Issues of Democracy* 4, No. 3 (1999) 6 (electronic journal <*http://www.usia.gov/journals/journals.htm*>).

80 Fuller (n. 74 above) 147–149.

81 See generally Chodosh (n. 79 above); Nancy T. Gardner, "Book Review on *Mediation: A Comprehensive Guide to Resolving Conflicts Without Litigation*," *Michigan Law Review* 84 (1986) 1036; Richard Delgado et al., "Fairness and Formality: Minimizing the Risk of Prejudice in Alternative Dispute Resolution," *Wisconsin Law Review* (1985) 1359.

furnish the best example of situations for which mediation rather than litigation is particularly appropriate, it may not be unreasonable to require parties to produce evidence that they have attempted to resolve the matter by mediation before allowing them to bring matrimonial proceedings in court.[82] There is also evidence that mediation is widely used and fairly effective in handling disputes arising from agricultural production and housing matters in mainland China,[83] and in automobile accident claims and housing matters in Taiwan.[84] These are therefore matters for which "mandatory" mediation (before litigation) might be appropriate.

Finally, the creative transformation of traditional mediation would entail the abandonment of the paternalistic role of the mediator and the overly moralistic elements of mediation. Modern mediators play the role of facilitators of communication between the disputants. They are there to help the parties and not to lecture to the parties.[85] They can no longer draw directly on the Confucian norms of self-restraint and moral cultivation and urge the parties to give up their interests and rights. But as discussed above, personal transformation and moral growth in the course of mediation is still possible and can still serve as a noble ideal at least in some types of cases. Through dialogue, through reflection, human beings can still learn to become better and wiser human beings. Reconciliation is not an impossible dream.

The theory and law of mediation in both contemporary mainland China and Taiwan in fact already exemplify the creative transformation of mediation along the above lines.[86] For example, in mainland China, three

82 In Hong Kong, solicitors who commence matrimonial proceedings on their clients' behalf are required to certify whether they have already drawn their clients' attention to the availability of conciliation/mediation services for marital problems. See Athena N. C. Liu, *Family Law for the Hong Kong SAR* (Hong Kong: Hong Kong University Press, 1999) 127, 139. In 1999, the Hong Kong judiciary introduced a pilot scheme to provide family mediation to divorcing couples. Practice direction 15.10 issued by the Chief Justice on April 10, 2000, requires solicitors advising clients on matrimonial proceedings to inform them of the availability of the family mediation service. At present, Hong Kong law does not go so far as requiring parties to have attempted mediation before matrimonial proceedings can be brought. However, Hong Kong law goes one step further in the domain of gender discrimination. Under the new Sex Discrimination Ordinance (enacted in 1995), a complainant who applies to the Equal Opportunities Commission for assistance in bringing court proceedings must have already undergone conciliation conducted under the auspices of the Commission (but such conciliation has failed to bring about a settlement). See sections 84 and 85 of the Ordinance.

83 Palmer (n. 53 above) 253.

84 Lin Duan, "Research Report on a Sociological Analysis of the Mediation System in Taiwan" (Department of Sociology, National Taiwan University, 1999; not yet published).

85 Emond (n. 65 above) 19–20; Gardner (n. 81 above) 1037; Robert A. Goodin, "Mediation: An Overview of Alternative Dispute Resolution," *Issues of Democracy* 4, No. 3 (1999) 13 (see n. 79 above). See also points (3) and (4) in section 3 above.

86 See the works cited in n. 62 above.

fundamental principles of modern mediation are often emphasized: mediation should aim at an outcome which is consistent with the law and with
state policies; submission to mediation must be entirely voluntary and coercion should not be used in any stage of the process; the disputants have the
right to go to court without first submitting the matter for mediation.[87]
These reflect an attempt to reconcile mediation with the requirements of the
modern Rule of Law, although it has been pointed out that in practice,
adherence to these principles is still far from perfect.[88] China still has a long
way to go in her march toward the Rule of Law. And as she travels, she will
carry with her "mediation" as one of the elements of China's cultural heritage
– not in its traditional form, but in a creatively transformed form.

Will the mediation system that emerges from the creative transformation
of China's traditional legal culture share with mediation in the Western world
the same universal features, or will there still be a specifically Chinese or
Confucian version of mediation? It is difficult to speculate on the long-term
solution to this riddle. As far as this historical juncture is concerned, the landscape of mediation, litigation, and justice in China is still very different from
that in the West. Because the Chinese legal system lags far behind the West
in its level of development, because the great majority of China's population
still live in rural communities, because the vast system of people's mediation
committees is actively sponsored by the state, and because the attempt by
judges to practise mediation even after litigation has commenced is officially

---

87 These principles are now provided for in article 6 of the Regulations on the Organization
   of People's Mediation Committees (1989). See the discussion in Palmer (n. 53 above) 259;
   Lubman (n. 53 above) 277–279; Lubman (n. 61 above) 1318.
88 The main problem is that coercive forces exist within the mediation process so that often
   parties are not really free to reject a settlement proposed by the mediators. The pressure
   to accept a settlement may come from different sources. For example, since the people's
   mediation committees (PMCs) in China are under the "leadership" of the judicial-
   administrative organs of the local government and the local court, and their chairmen are
   often leaders of villagers' committees or residents' committees, they are sometimes perceived as a component of state power to which people have to submit. The social relationships within state enterprises and rural society may also generate pressures to accept
   settlement by mediation. Furthermore, in many cases litigation is not a genuine alternative because legal services may not be easily accessible because of financial, geographical,
   or institutional constraints. Even in the context of mediation conducted by courts rather
   than by PMCs, complaints regarding coercion also exist. Apparently some judges put pressure on litigants to accept a settlement so as to avoid proceeding to adjudication, which
   would require a fuller investigation of the facts and a stricter application of the law, and
   would therefore be more time-consuming and professionally demanding. See generally Liu
   Guang'an and Li Cunpeng, "Minjian tiaojie yu quanli baohu" (Civil Mediation and the
   Protection of Rights), in Xia Yong (ed.), Zou xiang quanli de shidai: Zhongguo gongmin quanli
   fazhan yanjiu (Towards the Age of Rights: A Study of the Development of Civil Rights in
   China) (Beijing: Chinese University of Political Science and Law Press, 1995) 288, especially 307–326.

and legally sanctioned,[89] mediaton plays a much more important role in dispute settlement in China than in the West. Cases settled by mediation annually have consistently outnumbered those that go into the court system, although the ratio by which the former outnumbered the latter has declined over the years as the legal system has developed.[90] Among the latter type of cases, the majority are still settled by judges acting as mediators without proceeding to formal adjudication.[91] Thus, as two Chinese scholars conclude their in-depth study of mediation in contemporary China:

> Compared with state administrative mechanisms and judicial mecha-
> nisms, mediation as a mechanism for the protection of rights at the grass-
> root level of Chinese society has some clear advantages in resolving
> disputes and protecting citizens' rights. . . . Mediation is common in the
> life of the Chinese people; it has a long historical tradition, a firm basis
> among the people and advantages of a general nature. . . . Because medi-
> ation has the advantages of being simple, flexible, generally applicable
> and relatively autonomous from the State, it will remain a major means
> for dispute resolution and the protection of citizens' rights in Chinese
> society.[92]

89 Chapter 8 of the Law of Civil Procedure of the PRC expressly provides for mediation conducted by the courts. For this kind of "judicial mediation," see Lubman (n. 53 above)
   334–343; Michael Palmer, "The Revival of Mediation in the People's Republic of China:
   (2) Judicial Mediation," in W. E. Butler (ed.), *Yearbook on Socialist Legal Systems 1988*
   (Dobbs Ferry, N.Y.: Transnational Publishers, 1989) 145.
90 Liu and Li (n. 88 above) 293, 307–308; Lubman (n. 53 above) 282–283, 298.
91 Liu and Li (n. 88 above) 317; Lubman (n. 53 above) 335.
92 Liu and Li (n. 88 above) 326 (my own translation). For a more pessimistic view of the
   future of mediation in China, see Fu Hualing, "Understanding People's Mediation in Post-
   Mao China," *Journal of Chinese Law* 6 (1992) 211.

CHAPTER 12

TRADITIONAL CONFUCIAN VALUES AND WESTERN LEGAL FRAMEWORKS

THE LAW OF SUCCESSION

LUSINA HO

Whatever insights there are in the classic writings of Confucianism, the substantive content of Confucian values lies in their concrete and distinctive influences on political and legal institutions in society. Accordingly, the aim of this chapter is to consider how, in relation to the Law of Succession, Confucian values have been or could be given effect through concrete legal institutions that are comparable to those in established Western legal systems.

The law of succession provides a very good window through which to examine the impact of Confucian values, in that inheritance systems are often a function of family structures and cultural values in a society, and are often used by the state to encourage or discourage certain forms of relationships and behavior.

This chapter comprises two theses. The first, descriptive, thesis is to identify the extent to which existing succession laws in predominantly Chinese communities are the result of Confucian influence. It will seek to look for unique features in these laws that can only be justified by Confucianism. In the event that this strong claim cannot be established, it will also consider the weak claim as to whether such features can be said to have resulted from the influence of Confucian values on the minds of the legislators.

Accordingly, the laws in several predominantly Chinese communities[1] will be compared to those of their Western counterparts, namely, those of the Western jurisdictions upon which the correspondent Chinese laws are closely based. For example, the chapter will focus on the laws of Hong Kong (in comparison to those of England, its former sovereign) and the laws of

---

1 This chapter will not consider Chinese customary laws, as they are preserved mainly to accommodate feudal – as opposed to Confucian – family practices. Moreover, a claim based on modern succession laws rather than diminishing customary law and practice would be more significant.

Taiwan and mainland China (in comparison to those of Western civil law jurisdictions, especially Germany). The Western jurisdictions serve as "controls" to help highlight unique Chinese (and hopefully Confucian) features.

The distinction between the strong and weak claims is significant, not only to determine the precise extent of Confucian influence, but also for a pragmatic reason as follows. If only the weak claim can be established, namely, that the "Confucian" laws may also be justified on liberal grounds even though they are the result of Confucian influence, such laws would still appeal to Western countries which do not necessarily subscribe to Confucianism and so will more likely be "exported" to non-Chinese communities.

The second, prescriptive, thesis seeks to draw upon the laws and practices in the jurisdictions surveyed in order to postulate how one may construct a law of succession upon a Confucian foundation that can at the same time be accommodated in a Western technical framework and the social conditions of a modern Asian society. In the context of succession law, the challenges presented by a modern Asian society are the need to allow greater scope for testamentary freedom (including the freedom to disinherit certain heirs), to recognize that female descendants should have equal rights to inheritance as their male counterparts, to take into account the rise of nuclear families, and to incentivize the younger generation to look after the elder generation through positive encouragement.

A preliminary point that needs to be made is that the inquiry conducted in this chapter relates to the substantive law rather than the dispute resolution procedures (for example, mediation or litigation) of inheritance regimes. This is to keep the inquiry within reasonable length and, more fundamentally, to recognize that the choice of procedures is often motivated by mixed concerns of costs and efficiency, and not necessarily the need to maintain harmony as championed by Confucian teachings. In any event, effective dispute resolution procedures for inheritance disputes also largely depend on clear guidance in the substantive law.

I CONFUCIAN VALUES IN FAMILY AND SOCIAL LIFE

In this section, I shall sketch the values in classic Confucianism in relation to family and social life. The classic teachings of Confucius and Mencius are focused on mainly because, in the context of family and social ethics as opposed to, say, political institutions, there is relatively less controversy as to their applicability to modern life. Nevertheless, it will also be argued that some of these values should be reinterpreted to suit the conditions of modern society.

1 BENEVOLENCE AS THE BASIS OF MORAL VIRTUES

In the Confucian system of ethics, benevolence (*ren* 仁) is the most important moral quality of a gentleman (*jun zi* 君子). It is the fundamental basis that gives rise to all virtues (*de* 德).[2] These virtues include, in the family context, filial piety (*xiao* 孝), reverence (*jing* 敬), fraternity (*di* 弟), and kindness (*ci* 慈).

Confucius has defined benevolence as the love of one's fellowmen.[3] While this cryptic saying does not offer a very complete description,, the Master has elaborated that such "love" is graduated,[4] "beginning with one's family members and extending by degree out into one's society."[5] For instance, he says: "A young man should be a good son at home and an obedient young man abroad . . . and should love the multitude at large."[6] The idea is more clearly explicated in *The Doctrine of the Mean*: "Benevolence is the characteristic element of humanity, and *the great exercise of it is in loving relatives.* . . . The *decreasing measures of the love* due to relatives . . . are produced by the principle of propriety."[7] This is reinforced in *The Analects* by the statement that the basis of benevolence is filial piety and brotherly fraternity: "Being good as a son and obedient as a young man is, perhaps, the root of a man's character."[8]

Such a conception of benevolence as graduated love that begins with filial piety can be explained by the quasi-feudal political structures of the time. Confucius had great preference for the rituals and political system of the Zhou dynasty. During that period, governance was built upon blood relations and lineage, and the ruling class was comprised of members of an extended family. Moreover, as only the eldest son of the principal wife could inherit the father's political status, and with it power and wealth, harmony in the family was concomitant with political harmony and stability. Filial piety and brotherly fraternity were stressed above all else. As it says clearly in *The Analects*: "It is

2 Ma, Zhen Duo, *Ren, ren dao: Kong zi de zhe xue si xiang* (Ren – The Way of Man: The Philosophical Ideas of Confucius) (Beijing: Chinese Academy of Social Sciences, 1993) p. 84.

3 Confucius, *The Analects*, translated by Lau, D. C. (London: Penguin, 1979) (hereafter "*The Analects*") XII:22: "Fan Ch'ih asked about benevolence. The Master said, 'Love your fellow men.'"

4 Hall, D., and Ames, R., *Thinking Through Confucius* (New York: State University of New York Press, 1987) p. 120.

5 Ibid.   6 *The Analects*, I:6.

7 Confucius, *The Doctrine of the Mean*, in *The Four Books*, translated by Legge, J. (Beijing: The Commercial Press Ltd, n.d.) (hereafter "*The Four Books*") v. 5 (emphasis added).

8 *The Analects*, I:2. See also Ebrey, P., "The Chinese Family and the Spread of Confucian Values," in Rozman, G. (ed.) *The East Asian Region – Confucian Heritage and Its Modern Adaptation* (Princeton, N.J.: Princeton University Press, 1996) Chapter 1.

rare for a man whose character is such that he is good as a son and obedient as a young man to have the inclination to transgress against his superiors; it is unheard of for one who has no such inclination to be inclined to start a rebellion."[9] Now that political and family structures in modern society are not intertwined in the same way they were in feudal Chinese societies, it should be uncontroversial that Confucian virtues in family life should be pursued for their own sake and not as a political instrument. In the context of inheritance law, this should involve equal treatment of all siblings, rather than inheritance of the family estate by the eldest male of the family alone.

2 VIRTUES IN FAMILY LIFE

(a) Filial Piety (Xiao 孝) and Reverence (Jing 敬)

References to filial piety in classic Confucianism require not just looking after the physical needs of the parents,[10] but also showing reverence to them.[11] In a stable and nonmobile agrarian society, filial piety might mean carrying on exactly as one's father did,[12] or not traveling too far afield when one's parents are alive.[13] Nowadays it might be more appropriate to leave behind such requirements.

Instead, filial piety could simply be invoked to impose a moral (and maybe legal) duty to provide maintenance and emotional support to parents. As such, a Confucian society would differ markedly from a liberal society, in that in the latter each generation *only* owes a duty to look after the following

---

9 *The Analects*, I:2. See also *The Great Learning* (*The Four Books*) IX:1: "What is meant by 'In order rightly to govern the state, it is necessary first to regulate the family,' is this: – It is not possible for one to teach others, while he cannot teach his own family. Therefore, the ruler, without going beyond his family, completes the lessons for the state. There is filial piety: – therewith the sovereign should be served. There is fraternal submission: – therewith elders and superiors should be served. There is kindness: – therewith the multitude should be treated." And see Confucius's response to a question as to why he did not participate in formal government: "Filiality! Simply extend filiality and fraternity into government" (*The Analects*, II:21).

10 *Mencius* (*The Four Books*) XXX:2: "There are five things which are said in the common practice of the age to be unfilial. The first is laziness in the use of one's four limbs, without attending to the nourishment of his parents. The second is gambling and chess playing, and being fond of wine, without attending to the nourishment of his parents. The third is being fond of goods and money, and selfishly attached to his wife and children, without attending to the nourishment of his parents . . ."

11 *The Analects*, II:7: "Tzu-yu asked about being filial. The Master said, 'Nowadays for a man to be filial means no more than that he is able to provide his parents with food. Even hounds and horses are, in some way, provided with food. If a man shows no reverence, where is the difference?'" See also *The Analects*, II:8.

12 *The Analects*, IV:20.   13 *The Analects*, IV:19.

generation(s).[14] However, in the former, the children *also* owe a duty to look after their own parents in old age.[15] In such a society, there would be an extra source of support for providing for the elderly.

(b) Fraternity (Di 弟)

In classic Confucianism, fraternity between brothers involves the submission of the juniors to their superiors: "There is fraternal submission: – therewith elders and superiors should be served."[16] This notion of fraternity reinforced the authority of the eldest male heir as head of the family. In an ancient agrarian society, such authority was crucial to the functioning of an extended family as a unit of production and consumption. Nowadays, with the emergence of nuclear families as units of consumption rather than production,[17] the justification for submission to superiors does not hold anymore. Fraternity should accordingly be interpreted as involving mutual love and respect between brothers (as well as sisters). A feudal inheritance system that favors only the eldest males should rightly be replaced by egalitarian distribution between all issue, whether male or female. In a similar vein, the paradigmatic "family," for defining inheritance rights, should be the nuclear family rather than the extended family that includes next of kin, unless the deceased has no issue of his own.

3 THE EXTENSION OF FAMILY VIRTUES TO SOCIAL RELATIONSHIPS

(a) Kindness (Ci 慈)

According to classic Confucianism, benevolence begins but does not stop at home. A gentleman is supposed to extend family virtues to social life generally and in treating the common people. Thus, it is said: "The gentleman is reverent and does nothing amiss, is respectful towards others and observant of the rites, and all within the Four Seas are his brothers."[18] Perhaps Mencius best captures the idea as follows: "Treat with the reverence due to age the elders in your own family, so that the elders in the families of others shall be similarly treated; treat with the kindness due to youth the young in your own

14 Save for the indirect support to the elder generation by way of tax contributions and state pensions.
15 Fei, Xiao Tong, "The Issue of Maintenance of the Elderly in Changing Family Structures" (author's translation), in Fei, Xiao Tong (ed.) *Fei Xiao Tong Xuan Ji* (Selected Works of Fei Xiao Tong) (Tian Jin: Tian Jin People's Press, 1988) p. 467.
16 *The Great Learning* (*The Four Books*), IX:1.   17 See above n 15.   18 *The Analects*, XII:5.

family, so that the young in the families of others shall be similarly treated."[19] In sum, benevolence can be manifested at the outermost level of social relationships as treating people with kindness.[20]

To sum up, the Confucian values referred to in this chapter as informing succession law are those based on classic Confucian teachings on family and social virtues, but revised to exclude features closely tied to the needs of an agrarian society. These antiquated features include, for example, the preeminence of the eldest male, discrimination against female ascendants and descendants, and the use of the extended family as a paradigm unit of heritance.

II SUCCESSION LAWS

Having identified the moral values that might shape succession laws, I shall now pursue the descriptive thesis of this chapter, namely, to compare the succession laws in various jurisdictions to see how far they contain features that can only be justified by, or can be explained as having been influenced by, Confucian values.

The laws shall be compared according to the following questions: First, in the absence of a will, who is entitled to inherit the deceased's properties, in what order of preference, and to what are they entitled? Second, how far could the deceased leave a will to disinherit such heirs?

1 INTESTATE SUCCESSION

As intestate succession involves applying rules devised by the state to distribute a deceased's properties when he fails to leave a valid will, there is much scope for the state to implement its views on political philosophy. Accordingly, this area of law is also of particular interest to a Confucian legislator.

In this subsection, I shall compare how various jurisdictions resolve the three main questions in intestate succession: Who is entitled to inherit? In what order of preference? And to what are they entitled? Then, in light of this comparative survey, I shall consider how far Confucian values have influenced the laws in predominantly Chinese communities.

(a) The Existing Law

(i) WESTERN CIVIL LAW JURISDICTIONS. In Germany,[21] the following heirs are entitled to succeed the deceased in the following order of priority:

---

19 *Mencius (The Four Books)*, VII:12.   20 *The Great Learning (The Four Books)*, IX:1.
21 BGB ss1924–6.

1. descendants of the deceased (i.e., children, grandchildren, and great-grandchildren);
2. parents of the deceased and their descendants (i.e., brothers, sisters, nephews, and nieces of the deceased);
3. grandparents of the deceased and their descendants (i.e., uncles, aunts, and cousins of the deceased);
4. great-grandparents of the deceased and their descendants; and
5. the system continues until there are no more eligible relatives.

An heir in a higher priority takes the estate to the exclusion of those entitled under a lower priority. In other words, it is only when there is no heir in a higher priority that the heirs in the next priority are entitled. An heir also takes to the exclusion of those descendants entitled through him, that is, succession is *per stirpes*. Within the same rank, the heirs enjoy equal shares. Switzerland[22] and Austria[23] have adopted a similar system, except that they cut off the class of statutory heirs at the third degree and the fourth degree[24] respectively. The laws in France[25] and Italy[26] are also variations on the same theme.

The entitlement of the surviving spouse is separately provided for, and her inheritance depends on the persons that she is sharing the estate with: the more remote the relatives, the greater the spouse's share. For example, in Germany, she takes one-half of the estate if she is sharing with those entitled in the first priority; but the whole of the estate if there are no relatives in the first and second priority, and no grandparents. This might seem quite unfavorable to the spouse, but on the deceased's death she has already taken a substantial portion upon cessation of the matrimonial property regime. Only properties that belong exclusively to the deceased devolve for intestate distribution.

A few preliminary observations are in order: First, the primary basis for intestate succession is blood relationship or marital status.[27] Among those related by blood, descendants are generally preferred to ascendants. For example, grandchildren and great-grandchildren rank in the first priority, whereas equally remote ascendants such as grandparents and great-grandparents rank only in the second and third priority respectively.

---

22 Arts 457–9, CC.   23 s731 ABGB.
24 In Austria, great-grandparents are entitled to succeed, but not their descendants.
25 In France, the surviving spouse is classified as an heir of the fourth degree only since 1958. For details, see Revillard, M. L., "France," in Hayton, D. (ed.) *European Succession Law* (Bristol: Jordan, 1998) Ch. 7 at para. 7.59.
26 Arts 565–6, 581, CC.
27 The laws are progressively treating adopted and illegitimate children in the same way as natural children.

Second, the needs of the heirs or others are at least implicitly relevant to intestate succession, in that the heirs also overlap to a great extent with those who are entitled to statutory rights of maintenance from the deceased. For example, article 329 of the Swiss Civil Code makes an explicit link between the heirs' statutory rights of maintenance (vis-à-vis the deceased) and their rights to inheritance. Section 1969 (1) of the German Civil Code also provides that as regards the members of the deceased's family who belonged to the deceased's household and were maintained by him, an heir is bound to maintain them for the first thirty days after the accrual of the inheritance.[28]

Third, the merits of the heirs are also relevant to their rights of inheritance. For example, under the German Civil Code, where the descendants' duties to maintain the testator rank ahead of those of the ascendants,[29] they also enjoy a prior claim to inheritance. Similarly, an heir may become "unworthy to inherit" if she has committed egregious misconduct,[30] unless she was pardoned by the deceased.[31]

(ii) CHINESE CIVIL LAW JURISDICTIONS. Generally speaking, Taiwanese law adopts an approach similar to German law: The spouse enjoys a comparable entitlement;[32] the heirs are, in the following order of priority:

1. Descendants of the deceased;
2. Parents of the deceased;
3. Brothers and sisters of the deceased; and
4. Grandparents of the deceased.[33]

However, according to section 1149 of the Civil Code, a person (who is not necessarily an heir) who was maintained by the deceased should receive a discretionary share of the estate, subject to the views of the relatives, the degree by which he was maintained, and other relationships.

In mainland China, the class of heirs is even smaller. They are, in the following order of priority:

---

28 BGB s1969(1).   29 BGB s1606 (1).

30 BGB s2339: "if the heir has wilfully killed or attempted to kill the testator, has wilfully prevented the testator from making or revoking a will, has, by fraud or unlawful threats, induced the testator from making or revoking a will, or has been guilty of a relevant offence in respect of a disposition under the will. However, the grounds do not include the heir's dereliction of his statutory duty to maintain the deceased. This factor is only relevant in depriving him of his compulsory portion."

31 BGB s2343.   32 Art 1144, CC.

33 Art 1138, CC. Note that unlike in Germany, the collateral ascendants and descendants (uncles, aunts, nephews, nieces, and cousins) are excluded, but there is predominant opinion that the class of heirs recognized in German law is too large anyway.

1. Spouse, children, and parents of the deceased;
2. Brothers, sisters, and grandparents of the deceased.[34]

However, the PRC's Law of Succession contains several far-reaching provisions: First, article 12 provides that widowed sons or daughters-in-law who have principally maintained their parents-in-law will be heirs in the first priority. Second, article 13 provides that the *prima facie* principle of equal distribution between heirs in the same priority is subject to the following: (a) heirs who lack the capacity to work and have special difficulty in maintaining themselves should be provided for; (b) heirs who have principally maintained or lived with the testator may receive a larger share; and (c) heirs who have the ability to maintain but did not maintain the testator shall receive a lesser share or none at all. Third, and lastly, article 14 provides that persons who are not heirs but who (a) lack the capacity to work and a source of income, and were dependent on the deceased for maintenance, or (b) have provided more maintenance to the deceased, may receive an appropriate share.

These provisions evidence significant qualifications to the primary principle of determining inheritance on the basis of blood relationship and marital status, in that inheritance would be granted or withheld depending on the needs and merits of the heirs.

(iii) WESTERN COMMON LAW JURISDICTIONS. The justification for the rules in England is the putative intention of the deceased, in other words, how the deceased would have preferred to distribute his estate had he drawn up a will of his own.[35] A survey was conducted to collect the public's views on intestacy rules which indicated that most people would, on intestacy, prefer to leave the whole of the intestate's estate to the surviving spouse.

Accordingly, the rules were reformed in 1995 to give primary protection to the surviving spouse. She has a first claim to the estate and her share depends on whether the deceased leaves any issue who attain the age of eighteen or marry under that age, a parent, or a sibling of the whole blood or issue thereof that attain eighteen or marry under that age. At the minimum, where the deceased leaves issue, the surviving spouse takes all the personal properties, a fixed net sum (adjusted from time to time at a level sufficient to purchase an average dwelling house), and a life interest in one-half of the balance of the residuary estate. At the maximum, where none of these competing heirs exists, she takes the entire residuary estate. Thereafter, those enti-

---

34 Law of Succession of the PRC, art 10.
35 English Law Commission Report No. 187, "Family Law: Distribution on Intestacy" (1989) para 24; Working Paper No. 9, para 212. Hong Kong Law Reform Commission, Topic 15, para 7.3.

tled in the following order of preference are: children, parents, brothers and sisters of the whole blood (and their issue), brothers and sisters of half blood (i.e., step-siblings), grandparents, uncles and aunts of the whole blood, and uncles and aunts of half blood. The heirs of a higher priority inherit to the exclusion of those in a lower priority.

The above rules were fixed and certain so as to achieve efficiency in the administration of intestate estates. They leave little scope for detailed consideration of the individual needs of the heirs or any deserving individuals. Thus, the rules on intestacy are supplemented by the Inheritance (Provision for Family and Dependants) Act, which allows certain individuals to apply to the court, within six months of the death of the testator, to claim a discretionary award for reasonable financial provision.[36]

Apart from the deceased's spouse[37] and children,[38] any person who immediately before the deceased's death was being maintained by him may apply for financial provision (the so-called any person clause); after 1995, the right was extended to cohabitees.[39] However, parents are not specifically provided for; they would have to qualify under the any person clause, which has been invoked to make provision for a sister[40] and the mistress[41] of the deceased. Similar legislation can be found in Australia, Canada, and New Zealand, the latter most of which pioneered this area of law by enacting the Testator's Family Maintenance Act in 1906.

(iv) A CHINESE COMMON LAW JURISDICTION. In Hong Kong, both the intestate succession rules (amended in 1998)[42] and the discretionary rules on family provision (amended in 1995)[43] are closely modeled upon the English rules described above, save that as regards the law of family provision, the correspondent Hong Kong legislation specifically identifies certain categories of applicants. For example, a parent, an adult child, or a sibling of half or whole blood who was maintained by the deceased immediately

---

36 The applicant needs to prove that the will, or the rules on intestacy, or the combination of both, fail to provide him with a reasonable financial provision.
37 As well as a former spouse who has not been remarried.
38 As well as a stepchild who was "treated by the deceased as a child of the family."
39 Certain conditions apply: one must be "living in the same household as the deceased, and as the husband or wife of the deceased, during the whole of the period of two years ending immediately before the date when the deceased died."
40 *Re Wilkinson* [1978] Fam 22; *Re Viner* [1978] CLY 3091.
41 *Malone v. Harrison* [1979] 1 WLR 1353.
42 Intestates' Estates Ordinance 1998 ("IEO"), Cap 73, Laws of Hong Kong.
43 Inheritance (Provision for Family and Dependants) Ordinance 1995 ("IPFDO") Cap 481, Laws of Hong Kong. Note, however, that the latter piece of legislation had not taken into account the 1995 amendments made to its English model.

before his death;[44] a child of the deceased who is, by reason of some mental or physical disability, incapable of maintaining himself; and a concubine[45] may apply to the court for provision from the estate.

The legislation then sets out specific guidelines in relation to each of these categories of applicants.[46] For example, in relation to a parent, the court shall consider the age of the applicant and the contribution made by the deceased toward his or her needs.[47] Accordingly, both the English and Hong Kong law reforms sought to respond to the changing conditions of society. The former took a bigger step in extending inheritance protection to cohabitees, whereas the latter removed the differential treatment between sons and daughters, albeit also continuing to accommodate to social phenomena arising from the practice of concubinage (which was abolished only in 1971).

(b) Confucian Influences?

In all jurisdictions considered, intestate succession is based primarily upon blood relationship and marital status, and then the merits and needs of the heirs. They differ only in the degree of weight placed upon these (sometimes) conflicting considerations. Nonetheless, do the differences – such as the apparently greater emphasis on merits and needs in mainland China – evidence Confucian influences?

In the author's view, in a majority of cases, the differences in the rules per se are ambivalent. For example, the mere fact that a son is given a greater share because he has furnished maintenance to the testator could be based on the policy of encouraging filial piety, but could equally be based on the liberal justification of requiring the testator to reciprocate the son's maintenance. Similarly, the limited weight attached to the needs of the heirs in some jurisdictions could be due to differences in legislative techniques – jurisdictions that put a high premium on efficiency, simplicity, and certainty may prefer to keep detailed considerations of the financial needs of the heirs to a self-contained discretionary scheme. England is a good case in point.[48] It could also be founded upon the state's belief that it has an adequate social welfare system to cater to the needy.

---

44 IPFDO, section (3)(1)(b)(iv), (vi), and (viii).
45 The legislation includes "a male partner by a union of concubinage."
46 IPFDO, section 5.   47 IPFDO, section 5(3).
48 See Sherrin, C. H., and Bonehill, R. C., *The Law and Practice of Intestate Succession*, 2nd edn. (London: Sweet & Maxwell, 1994) p. 374; Law Commission Working Paper No. 42, pp. 215, 252; Law Commission Report No. 52, p. 10.

Accordingly, where intestacy is concerned, the proper inquiry as to the presence of Confucian influence should be twofold: First, how did the legislature devise the rules? Did it seek to reconstruct the testator's intention as to the distribution of his estate, or did it simply base the rules upon independent moral principles, and are those principles distinctly Confucian? Second, irrespective of the justification offered by the legislature, are any of the contents uniquely Confucian, that is, are they explicable only by Confucian norms and not other moral principles?

(i) THE LEGISLATURE'S JUSTIFICATION. At one extreme, England (and Hong Kong) clearly justify their intestacy rules on liberal grounds; whereas at the other extreme mainland China bases its rules on independent moral principles and unique Chinese virtues. Taiwan and other civil law jurisdictions stand somewhere in between.

In England, as mentioned above, the intestacy rules were based on the presumed intention of the testators as revealed in a public survey.[49] Hong Kong simply followed in the footsteps of its sovereign (at the time), in that a similar survey was also conducted, though the Hong Kong Law Reform Commission deliberately departed from English law in a few places to accommodate local Chinese culture. This overwhelming emphasis on the intention (and autonomy) of the citizens is characteristic of a liberal society and nonintervention by the state, in that intestate succession rules are perceived as playing the facilitative function of laying down a set of rules that enable citizens to pass their properties according to the manner that they would have preferred. Ideally, therefore, intestate distribution broadly accords with their wishes such that in most cases it would not be necessary for a citizen to draw up his own will. The state does not make any judgment upon independent moral principles on how the properties should be distributed.

It is true that these intestacy rules, which are based on the deceased's putative intention, are qualified by the court's discretion to award reasonable financial provision to the deceased's family and dependants. To that limited extent, these jurisdictions are acting upon independent moral principles; yet it remains to be seen whether these principles are Confucian.

In contrast, in mainland China, the rules on intestate succession make no reference to the presumed intention of the testator. Five basic principles have been identified as justifying the Law of Succession: the protection of the citizens' rights to inherit private property,[50] equal rights of inheritance

---

49 Of course it might be argued that the surveys were not carefully conducted, as per Sherrin, C. H., and Bonehill, R. C., above n 48, p. 24, though this does not affect the claim in this essay.

50 Only this principle is explicitly endorsed in article 1 of the Law of Succession of the PRC, which states as follows: "This Law is enacted pursuant to the Constitution of the People's

between men and women, mutuality in rights and obligations, harmony and mediation in the administration of the estate, and finally maintenance of the elderly, the young, and the needy.[51] The last of these principles was particularly emphasised by the draftsmen when introducing the draft of the law to the legislature; they also attributed this principle to traditional Chinese values.[52] Similarly, it has been claimed that section 1149 of the Taiwanese civil code, allowing a discretionary award to the nonheirs who were maintained by the testator, helped promote traditional Chinese values.[53] Again, the issue as to whether these principles really are Confucian will be deferred to the next subsection.

Taiwan and Western civil law countries lie somewhere between these two extremes. On the one hand, there is no explicit attempt to reconstruct the putative intention of the testator. On the other hand, there is enough support for the view that blood relatives and spouses enjoy rights of inheritance on intestacy on the ground that: (a) as family members they often have helped the testator to accumulate his wealth; and (b) as dependants of the testator they need or can legitimately expect his maintenance.[54] However, any further speculation as to whether these principles were adopted because the deceased would have adopted the same principles is likely to be futile.

(ii) UNIQUE CONFUCIAN INFLUENCES? Interestingly, all of the predominantly Chinese communities considered have claimed that certain features in their rules on intestacy are influenced by traditional Chinese cultures or values. These features are: (a) in all three communities, there are special provisions for needy persons or heirs that might be more far-reaching than those of their Western counterparts;[55] (b) in mainland China, those entitled in the first priority include not just the spouse and children of the deceased, but also his parents; and (c) in mainland China, inheritance (or a greater share of it) may be granted or withheld depending on whether the claimant has furnished maintenance to the deceased.[56]

Republic of China with the view to protecting the rights of citizens to inherit private property."

51 See Liu, C. M., *Zhong-guo min fa xue: cai chan ji cheng* (Beijing: China People's Public Security University Press, 1990) p. 44.

52 Wang, H. B., "Explanation Relating to 'The Law of Succession of the People's Republic of China (draft)'" (author's translation) (1985), collected in He, S., and Xiao, S., *Ji cheng fa gai yao* (Beijing, 1986) p. 219. The Legislatures did not elaborate whether these traditional values derived from the teachings of Confucius.

53 Chen, Y., *Min fa ji cheng* (Taipei: San Min Publication House, 1989) p. 131.

54 Ibid., pp. 5–6.

55 Civil Code (Taiwan), art 1149; IPFDO, s3(iv)–(vi); Law of Succession of the PRC, art 13 (first para); art 14.

56 Law of Succession of the PRC, art 13 (second para), art 14 (last subclause).

Special Protection for the Needy. The rules in Hong Kong do differ from their English model, in that they make specific reference to parents who were maintained by the deceased immediately before his death and specifically require the court to take into account the level of maintenance provided by the testator himself. At first blush, this seems to support the presence of Confucian influence. However, the mere fact that parents are specifically protected is not distinctly Confucian: They are so protected by forced heirship rules in most Western civil law countries anyway. And the protection could be based on a policy to assure permanent possession of family wealth,[57] rather than a policy to promote filial piety.

Moreover, on close examination, the Hong Kong rules are actually "anti-Confucian," though probably not deliberately so. This is because to qualify for the award, the parents need to prove that they were being maintained by the deceased immediately before his death.[58] Thus, ironically, an unfilial son who has never maintained his parents would in effect bar any such claims on his estate and leave his parents in dereliction.

It is contended that this might be the unintended consequence of an unsuccessful legislative attempt to adapt the "any person" clause in English law to Confucian values. The original basis of that clause is that a dependant of the testator has, as against the testator, a legitimate expectation to continue to be provided for and so has a moral claim on the estate regardless of what the will says.[59] Accordingly, the English legislation does not place the parents in any special position and requires every applicant under the "any person" clause to prove prior maintenance.

The Hong Kong legislators might have sought to offer better protection to the parents by making specific reference to them and attaching special guidelines thereto. However, this attempt to graft Confucian norms onto legislation founded upon a different philosophical basis backfired. In fact, the Hong Kong Law Reform Commission recommended that the parents' right to apply should not be qualified by the requirement of prior maintenance by the children,[60] but this was not adopted by the legislature and no explanation was given.

Turning to Taiwan and mainland China, there are (a) rules which allow a nonheir who was formally maintained by the testator to claim a discretionary award from the estate,[61] with the mainland Chinese rule further imposing

---

57 Most prominantly in France, see discussion on the reserved portion (réserve héréditaire) in Revillard, M. L., above n 25 at para 7.4.
58 The guidelines require the court to take into account the amount of such maintenance – presumably the more the maintenance the higher the judicial award.
59 *Parry & Clark: The Law of Succession*, 10th edn. (London: Sweet & Maxwell, 1996).
60 Law Reform Commission, Topic 15, para 14.10.   61 Art 1149, CC.

the precondition that the claimant lack the capacity to work and a source of income;[62] and (b) in mainland China, a rule requiring that at the discretion of the estate, the needs of a destitute heir who lacks the capacity to work should be provided for.[63]

Insofar as the rules about needy nonheirs are only applicable to those who were maintained by the deceased, they fall into a similar category as the Hong Kong rule for parents' provision discussed above. While such rules could be attributed to the Confucian virtue of kindness, they could equally be attributed to the liberal justification that through prolonged maintenance the testator has generated sufficient legitimate expectation on the dependant's part to give rise to a duty of maintenance on himself (and after his death on his estate). Also, as explained above, such a clause can operate in an anti-Confucian manner. In fact, in other clearly non-Confucian countries, a similar, probably more far-reaching rule has been adopted. For instance, under the Russian Civil Code, a nonheir who was maintained by the deceased for more than a year and who lacks the capacity to work can share equally with the heirs of the second priority.[64]

The rule requiring protection for the needy heir is equally ambivalent, especially in light of the presence of similar rules in other jurisdictions. For instance, the family provision legislation in England (and Hong Kong) stipulates, in much the same breath, that a child of the deceased who is, by reason of some mental or physical disability, incapable of maintaining herself, may apply for reasonable financial provision. Arguably, the absence of similar provisions in civil law countries is due to the fact that those who have the right to statutory maintenance are in the same order of priority as those who have the right to succeed.[65]

Parents Included as Heirs in the First Priority. The fact that the parents of the deceased are heirs in the first priority has often been claimed by Chinese commentators[66] (and also law draftsmen)[67] as uniquely based on traditional Chinese values. Such an approach is indeed consistent with the Confucian emphasis on filial piety, which involves at least providing financial support for the parents. However, this would only support the weaker thesis that such laws can be explained by Confucian values, which were in the minds of the

---

62 The Law of Succession of the PRC, art 14 (first subclause).
63 Ibid., art 13 (second para).
64 Russian Civil Code, 1964, art 532. See also Swann, P. T., "Russian Intestacy Law" 8 *Tulsa J Comp. & Int'l L* 133 (2000); Foster-Simmons, F., "The Development of Inheritance Law in the Soviet Union and the People's Republic of China," 33 *Am J Comp L* 33 (1985); Tay, A., "The Law of Inheritance in the New Russian Civil Code of 1964," 17 *Int'l & Comp L Q* 472 (1968).
65 See art 329, Swiss Civil Code.   66 See above, n 51.   67 See above, n 52.

legislators. It does not establish the stronger thesis that the law is uniquely justified by Confucianism alone, because exactly the same rule can be found in the Russian Civil Code,[68] which can hardly be said to have been influenced by Confucianism.

Conduct of the Claimant in Providing Maintenance to the Deceased. The intestacy rules in mainland China provide quite an intricate system whereby inheritance is granted or withheld depending on whether the potential heir has furnished maintenance to the deceased. For instance, inheritance would be granted as follows: (a) If a widowed son or daughter-in-law has furnished maintenance to his or her parents-in-law, he will be treated as an heir in the first priority;[69] (b) if a nonheir has furnished maintenance, he may be granted an appropriate share;[70] and (c) if an heir has principally maintained or lived with the deceased, he may be granted a greater share. Conversely, (a) an heir who has, in the extreme case, abandoned the deceased, loses his right of inheritance;[71] and (b) if he has the ability to but fails to furnish maintenance to the deceased, he might not receive any share or may receive a lesser share.

Both positive and negative incentives are employed here, by rewarding those who discharge their duties of maintenance, or act beyond the call of duty, and by taking away the rights of those who breach their duties. The values promoted (or enforced) may be the Confucian virtues of filial piety and kindness. However, taking away the inheritance rights of those who fail to discharge their duties of maintenance is not unique. Article 531 of the Russian Civil Code provides exactly the same; it is also one of the grounds that deprives a German heir of his compulsory portion (which the testator could not deprive him of), though not his statutory inheritance on intestacy.

In comparison, the granting of inheritance rights (or greater discretionary shares) to those who furnish maintenance, and the special treatment of widowed sons and daughters-in-law in the PRC, are very unique indeed.[72] In particular, none of the other countries surveyed use the rules on intestacy to reward good behavior as the PRC does; beyond blood relationship and marital status, they would only grant inheritance on the bases of dependency or need. These features may, again, be attributed to Confucian influence, in encouraging help for the elderly and the young,[73] and thus facilitate the realization

---

68 Art 532.

69 The Law of Succession of the PRC, art 12.

70 Ibid., art 14 (second subclause).

71 Ibid., art 7(4).

72 See Foster, F. H., "Linking Support and Inheritance: A New Model from China," 1999 *Wisc LR* 1199 (1999); "Towards a Behavior-Based Model of Inheritance? The Chinese Experiment," 32 *UCDLR* 77 (1998).

73 Another predominant feature of the PRC inheritance system is the "5-guarantee system" prevalent in rural areas, whereby an individual may enter into a contract of "inheritance

of the Utopian state whereby: "The elderly can depend on, and the young are cared for."[74]

Thus far, we have established the weak thesis that the positive incentives provided by intestacy rules in mainland China to those who have furnished maintenance to the deceased are unique and are the result of Confucian influence on the minds of the draftsmen. However, this does not in itself mean that the strong thesis is also established, for it is equally plausible to explain such rules on liberal grounds and as reflecting the special social structure of Chinese society. It could be said that having received regular and substantial benefits from the claimants, the deceased would, if given the chance to draw up a will, have reciprocated and in any case should reciprocate. This justification is consistent with liberalism, in that mutual assistance between individuals would promote their autonomy.

That this non-Confucian reasoning is also operative at least in the minds of the law enforcers is borne out by a decision of the People's Court of Ruichang City, Jiangxi Province, applying article 14 of the succession law. In *Ke Yuyue v. Ke Yuji*,[75] the court invoked this article to grant one of the eight rooms of the disputed premises to the defendant who was not a statutory successor[76] of the deceased but who had contributed to his funeral expenses. In granting this right, Judge Wang significantly reasoned as follows:

> In this case, . . . the defendant had made a significant contribution to the funeral expenses of [the deceased]. Furthermore, he had difficulty in getting accommodation. Following *the principle of reciprocity of rights and obligations* and with a view to the enhancement of the unity and stability of society, the people's court decided that the defendant be allotted a portion of the estate.[77]

Likewise, the fact that widowed sons and daughters-in-law are singled out for inheritance rights can also be justified by the particular social culture and

and care" with her collective society promising to leave the society all her properties in her will in return for care and accommodation by the society during her life. Such contracts take precedence over the individuals' wills and intestacy rules. For details, see Liu, C. M., above n 51 at 494–502. Insofar as the legal framework of the 5-guarantee system is based on inheritance contracts, which protect autonomous individuals who assume responsibility through promises, it cannot be seen as an example of Confucian law making. Similar protection for inheritance contracts can also be seen in civil law jurisdictions. See, for example, BGB, s 2274–2302.

74 *The Book of Rites: Li Yun.*
75 [1991] 2 *China L Rep* 116.
76 The defendant had been adopted by the deceased, though he lived with his natural parents and so was held by the court not to be in a foster relationship with the deceased and his wife.
77 Above n 64, Foster-Simmons, at 118–119 (emphasis added).

structure of China, in that: (a) as China is still in the process of transition from an agrarian society based on extended families to an industrial society based on nuclear families, such a rule would rightly encourage the widowed spouses to look after the parents-in-law; and (b) as it is relatively uncommon in traditional Chinese culture for widowed female spouses to remarry, such a rule would encourage them to live with the parents-in-law and be integrated into that extended family.

To sum up, in this section the author has examined the special features in the intestacy rules of three Chinese communities against those of their Western counterparts, and argues that though some of these rules were purportedly based on traditional Chinese (perhaps Confucian) values, they are either not unique or can be explained by liberal justifications as applied to the social conditions of Chinese communities.

2 LIMITS TO FREEDOM OF DISPOSITION – FORCED HEIRSHIP AND FAMILY PROVISION

The preceding section deals with the default rules of succession when the deceased fails to provide a valid will. What if the deceased did provide a valid will but he purported to disinherit his heirs? To what extent does the law respect his testamentary freedom?

The answers to these questions depend on two types of rules: first, the so-called forced heirship rules which provide that certain rights of inheritance cannot be curtailed by will; and second, rules that grant provisions for the family and dependants of the deceased irrespective of what the will says. While forced heirship rules are more commonly adopted in *civil law* countries (such as those in Continental Europe), family provisions are preferred by *common law* countries (such as England and former or present Commonwealth jurisdictions). However, the goals are the same.

Such rules provide better evidence of the influence of nonliberal policies than the rules on intestate succession. For they trump the intention of the testator, a deceased who has left a will, in that a liberal society may prefer to respect his express indication of intention irrespective of what moral obligations he might owe to his family or dependants, whereas a nonliberal society would prefer to limit such freedom in order to enforce or encourage certain values. This section will survey the limits posed in different jurisdictions on testamentary freedom, identify the instances where the laws in the Chinese communities differ from their Western counterparts, and consider how far these differences are attributable to Confucian influence.

(a) The Existing Law

(i) COMMON LAW JURISDICTIONS. In general, the *common law* jurisdictions put primary emphasis on freedom of disposition. For a long time in England, there even was total testamentary freedom (supported by the church to enable charitable donations in its favor).[78] This freedom is now qualified by discretionary family provision discussed in the preceding section on intestate succession. Hong Kong simply follows the English position, subject to minor differences explained above. These rules trump the default rules on intestacy as well as the will.

(ii) WESTERN CIVIL LAW JURISDICTIONS. In all *Western civil law* countries considered, the forced heirship rules protect the immediate family of the deceased. For instance, in Germany,[79] Greece,[80] Italy,[81] and Switzerland,[82] if statutory heirs such as the descendants, surviving spouse, or parents of a testator are excluded by a will, they would still obtain a compulsory portion of the amount that they would have obtained on intestacy. The will would be invalid to that extent.

Forced heirship rights may be lost. In Germany, for example, a testator can disinherit a descendant or parent if, inter alia, she maliciously commits a breach of her statutory duty to furnish maintenance to the testator.[83] Such duties of maintenance are owed to needy relatives.[84]

(iii) CHINESE CIVIL LAW JURISDICTIONS. Turning to *Chinese civil law* jurisdictions, the equivalent rules in Taiwan are closely based upon those in Germany, save that the testator's siblings are also protected as "forced" heirs.[85] However, unlike in Germany, the failure to discharge one's duty to maintain the testator is not a ground for taking away such rights.[86]

---

78 See the Statute of Wills 1540, which first endorsed the freedom of disposition. Such freedom became total with the enactment of the Mortmain & Charitable Uses Act, 1891.

79 BGB s2303. There is a technical difference between inheritance as a compulsory heir and the compulsory portion in Germany, in that the latter only allows a claim of debt against the estate.

80 Art 1825(1)(b), CC. The compulsory portion is one-half.

81 ss536, 538 & 540, CC.

82 Arts 470, 471, CC. The compulsory portion "for a descendant [is] three quarters of his or her statutory share of inheritance; for each of the parents [is] one half; for the surviving spouse [is] one half."

83 BGB s2333(4); s2334.   84 BGB s1601; s1602(1).

85 Arts 1187, 1123, CC. The compulsory portion for siblings and grandparents is one-third, whereas that for the other heirs is one-half.

86 Art 1145, CC.

The equivalent rule in mainland China is rudimentary in comparison. Article 19 of the Law of Succession provides that a will shall reserve a "necessary portion" for the statutory heirs – spouse, children, parents, siblings, grandparents – if they lack both the capacity to work and a source of income. However, there are no guidelines as to what is "necessary."[87] As under German law, it also appears[88] that these (indigent) heirs will lose their rights if they deliberately kill the testator or other heirs in order to benefit from the inheritance, or if they abandon or seriously mistreat the testator.[89]

(b) Confucian Influences?

The salient features in forced heirship rules in the predominantly Chinese communities that may be attributable to Confucian influences are: first, all these jurisdictions specifically include brothers and sisters[90] in the protected class; second, in mainland China a compulsory heir must also lack the ability to work and a source of income in order to qualify for the necessary portion; and third, forced heirship rights in mainland China will be lost if the heir commits egregious misconduct against the testator or other heirs. These features shall be examined more closely to see whether they are unique, and if so whether they are only attributable to Confucian influences.

(i) SIBLINGS AS COMPULSORY HEIRS. The inclusion, in Taiwan, mainland China, and to a certain extent Hong Kong,[91] of the deceased's brothers and sisters as compulsory heirs is indeed unique. It may also be attributable to Confucian influence, in that the virtue of brotherly fraternity imposes an obligation on the testator to provide for his siblings and accordingly invalidates his attempt to disinherit them.

87 Section 37 of the Interpretation of the Supreme People's Court on the Law of Succession only elaborates that in the administration of the estate, such portions should be set aside first and the residue distributed according to the will.
88 The Law of Succession does not make this point clear. On the one hand, art 8 lists the situations in which the heirs lose their rights of inheritance; on the other hand, art 19 stipulates that indigent heirs are entitled to a necessary portion. It has not been clarified whether art 8 overrides art 19, or vice versa. However, legislative experience in other civil law countries suggests that even forced heirship could be lost in circumstances listed in art 8.
89 Ibid., art 8.
90 Classic Confucians may quibble about the inclusion of female siblings in the protected class, though insofar as liberal Confucians would have no qualms about it, this difference is irrelevant for the purposes of the present chapter.
91 The Hong Kong legislation makes specific references to brothers and sisters of the whole (as well as half) blood, though these claimants would still have to prove the presence of prior maintenance by the testator. To this extent, the rule suffers from the same problems discussed in the preceding section.

However, the same rule can equally be justified on grounds consistent with liberalism. The primary justification (which is acceptable to a liberal) for forced heirship is to enforce the testator's moral obligations to maintain those who depend on him for maintenance and so have a legitimate expectation to be provided for in the will.[92] Thus, most countries restrict the scope of beneficiaries to the immediate family to whom the testator owes statutory duties of maintenance.[93] Similarly, in England, family provision is only available to the immediate family;[94] beyond that, whoever applies for a provision has to prove the existence of prior maintenance. A secondary justification is to recompense those – such as the spouse – who have helped the testator build his wealth.[95] Applying these liberal justifications to the social structures of a traditional Chinese society wherein people live in extended families, it is reasonable to treat the brothers and sisters mutatis mutandis as the immediate family. In other words, in a Chinese community, the immediate family includes the siblings as well as the spouse, children, and parents. Accordingly, the unique rule in Taiwan and mainland China could be explained on liberal grounds and as reflecting the social conditions (especially the prevalence of extended families) of a Chinese society.

(ii) NEEDY HEIRS. At first blush, the requirement in mainland China that the compulsory heirs must also be needy appears to evidence Confucian influence. For the virtue of kindness requires giving priority to those who are more needy. However, this requirement is not unique. The Russian Civil Code contains a similar requirement and offers better protection to indigent heirs by guaranteeing them two-thirds of their statutory share.[96] The provision is

---

92 See Magliveras, K. D., "Greece," in Hayton, D., above n 25, chapter 9 at para 9.65. One of the factors the court must take into account under the English legislation is the obligations and responsibilities that the deceased had toward the applicant (and other beneficiaries): s3 (d), Inheritance (Family and Dependants Provision) Act, 1975.

93 Art 329, Swiss Civil Code; BGB s2303 for descendants of the deceased (remoter descendants and the parents of the deceased are not entitled to the compulsory portion insofar as the immediate descendants are entitled per stirpes [s 2309]).

94 Note, however, that the law does not also impose any requirement for the "dependants" to prove any financial needs. This might be due to the need for certainty and efficient administration of the law.

95 There is also a third reason, more relevant in the past, namely the (permanent) preservation of wealth within a family. France is the best case in point – the French Civil Code provides for compulsory portions for only the descendants and ascendants of the testator, not the spouse (Art 913, CC). Art 915 clearly states that: "In default of ascendants and of descendants, bounties by inter vivos or testamentary instruments may exhaust the totality of the properties."

96 Russian Civil Code, s535.

better explained by the practical need in socialist states to conserve the relatively small private estate for the needy.[97]

3 CONFUCIAN QUALIFICATION ON WESTERN SUCCESSION LAW?

In the final analysis, one has to retreat from the stronger thesis, that some of these rules can only be justified by Confucianism and so are the *unique* result of Confucian influence. However, the weaker thesis still stands, namely, that quite a few rules in the succession laws of predominantly Chinese communities have been purported to (and can) be explained as the result of the influence of Confucian values on the minds of the legislators. For example, the rules on the granting of inheritance rights to widowed sons and daughters-in-law who maintained the deceased, the special protection of the needy, the inclusion of siblings in the protected class, and the withholding of inheritance from heirs who deliberately failed to maintain the deceased, to name but a few.

Admittedly, only some of these rules – such as those protecting siblings and widowed sons and daughters-in-law – are unique. Moreover, they represent relatively insignificant qualifications to a typical succession law in any Western jurisdiction and are also a function of the disappearing traditional social structure in China. It is doubtful whether these rules suit the changing conditions of a modern Asian society. For example, with the increasing mobility of family members and the increase in number of nuclear families, it is difficult to justify granting compulsory heirship to adult siblings irrespective of their needs and relationship with the testator.

III CONCLUSION: CONSTRUCTING A LAW OF SUCCESSION ON CONFUCIAN NORMS

The limited and haphazard Confucian influences in the succession laws of the Chinese communities considered may be due in great part to the fact that some of these communities have adopted Western laws as a foundation and then simply tinkered with them to suit local values. For example, the rules in Hong Kong follow the English model, subject to minor (and poorly thought-out) tinkering, with the anti-Confucian consequence that the less filial the deceased has been, the less likely his parents will be able to claim maintenance provision from the estate.

To construct a law of succession that coheres systematically with Confucian norms, it is contended that these norms should be adopted as the basic

97 See He, S., and Xiao, S., above n 52, where such an explanation is strongly advocated.

philosophical foundation of the law. In other words, they should determine
the questions as to who is entitled, in which order of preference, and to how
much.

Starting from the fundamental principle that citizens should be encouraged to practice benevolence, which involves a graduated love depending on
the nature of the relationship, the order of this hierarchy of social relationships should correspond to the order of the rights of inheritance. Bearing in
mind also the increasing trend of nuclear families in modern Asian societies,
and the need for the clarity and certainty of the law, it is argued that succession law could involve the following two-tier structure.

First, on intestacy, after duly providing for the spouse, both the parents
and children[98] should be entitled to inherit in the first priority.[99] Grandparents, grandchildren, and siblings should be entitled in the second
priority, followed by uncles, aunts, nephews, and nieces in the third priority.
Only the spouse, parents, and children are entitled to a compulsory portion
which a testator cannot alter by will.[100] Both the rights to intestate succession and the compulsory portion will be lost if the heir commits egregious
misconduct or if he deliberately failed to furnish maintenance to the deceased.

Second, to compensate for possible injustice in individual circumstances
caused by this relatively inflexible set of rules and to provide positive incentives (or negative disincentives) for certain behaviors, the law should be
supplemented by a discretionary scheme that allows the following. A right
to apply for discretionary provision or a greater share of inheritance should
be available, in first priority, to needy heirs and needy nonheirs who were
being maintained by the deceased; and then in second priority, to those who
have furnished maintenance to the deceased.[101] Conversely, upon application
by disgruntled heirs, the court (or any relevant mediation agency) has the
discretion to downwardly adjust the share of those who have, without
reasonable excuse, failed to maintain the deceased. This discretionary scheme
should be applicable both on intestacy or if the testator left a will to disinherit the heirs.

98 As far as parents and children are concerned, there should be no distinction between
   natural and adopted relationships, or between legitimate and illegitimate relationships.
   The position of cohabitees demands a fuller investigation beyond the scope of this chapter.
99 This proposal differs from mainland Chinese law, which in practice gives the spouse a
   smaller share by requiring him to share equally with the children and parents; it differs
   from Taiwan, Hong Kong, and most Western laws, which place parents in the second
   priority.
100 The exact portion should be fixed by individual countries depending on the average size
   of their citizens' estates and at a level that provides for reasonable maintenance for the
   beneficiary.
101 This category includes both heirs and nonheirs, and the nonheirs are not limited to
   widowed sons or daughters-in-law.

This two-tier structure of succession law combines, on the one hand, the technical framework of the laws of common law jurisdictions to balance the conflict between clarity and flexibility, and on the other, the substantive norms as derived from a Confucian foundation, in order that such a proposed law would promote Confucian virtues as appropriately interpreted in light of the conditions of a modern Asian society.

CHAPTER 13

THE CONFUCIAN CONCEPTION
OF GENDER IN THE
TWENTY-FIRST CENTURY

CHAN SIN YEE

Throughout its long history, the Confucian conception of gender certainly has undergone many phases.[1] Most studies of the early Confucian conception of gender concur that it is *complementarity*, rather than subordination, that is emphasized in women's gender role.[2] And they often refer to two different bases for drawing the gender distinction: 1) the *yin-yang* (陰陽) correlation and 2) the *nei-wai* (內外) (inner-outer) distinction. Since I have already discussed the second distinction in detail in another essay,[3] I shall now concentrate only on the idea of *yin-yang* and examine its implications. In what follows, I shall first trace the historical development of the *yin-yang* distinction and discuss some of its implications. I shall then apply the implications

1 By "Confucian conception," I am referring to the conception discussed in *philosophical* Confucianism. By "philosophical Confucianism," I mean the system of thought expressed by the Confucian texts. Philosophical Confucianism is different from other types of Confucianism such as imperial Confucianism and popular Confucianism. Imperial Confucianism aims to reinforce the institution of rulership and promote the survival of China as an empire. Dong Zhongshu is a representative of this kind of Confucianism. Popular Confucianism refers to the practices of the family ethic, and its key supporters were local gentry who tended to bolster family and clan values at the expense of general benevolence toward strangers. For a discussion of these three types of Confucianism, see Donald Munro, "Introduction," in *Constructing China*, ed. Kenneth Lieberthal, Shuen-fu Lin, and Ernest Young (Ann Arbor: Center for Chinese Studies, University of Michigan, 1997).

2 See, for example, Richard Guisso and Stanley Johannesen, eds., *Women in China* (Youngstown, Ohio: Philo Press, 1981); Alison Black, "Gender and Cosmology in Chinese Correlative Thinking," in *Gender and Religion*, ed. Caroline Bynum, Stevan Harrell, and Paula Richman (Boston: Beacon Press, 1986); Liu Te-han, *Tung-chou fu-nu wen-ti-yen-chiu* (Taipei: Taiwan hsueh-sheng shu-chu, 1990); and Pao Chia-lin, *Readings in Chinese Women History* (Taiwan: Cowboy Publishing Ltd., 1979).

3 Sin Yee Chan, "Gender and Relationship Roles in the *Analects* and the *Mencius*" in *Asian Philosophy*, Summer 2000. The paper discusses the inner-outer distinction as a functional distinction: Males are primary in the outer (public/social) sphere, females are primary in the inner (domestic) sphere. I show how the distinction can be used to justify the subordination of women by excluding them from the Confucian ideal of *junzi* (君子). The paper concludes with a critique of that justification.

to the areas of politics, the workplace, the domestic sphere, and education. A comparison will be made between the Confucian and the feminist position on these issues. This essay will conclude with a brief discussion of the legal implications of the *yin-yang* distinction in a Confucian society.

As a preliminary matter, we should note that gender differences are distinct from sex differences. Sex differences pertain to physiological features related to procreation and biological reproduction. Gender differences, on the other hand, represent the social *interpretation* of sex differences. For example, while the ability to bear children is a feature of the female sex, being nurturing is a gender trait society attributes to females.[4]

THE *YIN-YANG* (陰陽) DISTINCTION

The polarity of *yin-yang* as the two fundamental cosmic forces that account for the myriad changes and events in the cosmos plays a significant conceptual role in both Neo-Confucianism and Neo-Daoism. The terms *yin* and *yang* originally referred to the weather conditions of being cloudy and sunny respectively. They were then extended to mean the northern and the southern sides of a hill (i.e., the shady and sunny sides) and coldness and warmth. In the Spring and Autumn periods (春秋時代) (722–481 B.C.) *yin* and *yang* were seen as two of the six cosmic forces.[5] They were fully established in the philosophical literature as two fundamental principles by about 300 B.C. and as principles of a cosmology that emphasized correlations after 100 B.C.[6] As cosmic forces, *yin* was associated with darkness, coldness, female gender, night, the moon, the earth, the directions west and north, the orientation right, behind and below, with softness and weakness, and with waning and death. *Yang* was associated with light, warmth, male gender, day, the sun, the heavens, the directions east and south, the orientation left, before and above, with hardness and strength, and with waxing and life.

The following things are of special interest when we discuss the relationship between *yin-yang* and the Confucian conception of gender. First, the discussion of *yin* and *yang* as cosmic forces never appears in the *Analects*, the *Mencius*, the *Great Learning*, and the *Doctrine of the Mean*. Hsu Fu-kuan also argues that in the part of the *Book of Changes* that can be attributed to

4 For a discussion of the concept of gender, see Ann Oakley, *Sex, Gender, and Society* (New York: Harper and Row, 1972).

5 The other four forces are wind, rain, dark, and light. The above discussion follows Hsu Fu-kuan's account of the development of the concepts of *yin* and *yang*. See Hsu Fu-kuan, *Chung-kuo jen-hsing lun-shi* (Taiwan: Tunghai University Press, 1963).

6 A. C. Graham, *Yin-yang and the Nature of Correlative Thinking* (Singapore: Institute of East Asian Philosophies, Occasional Paper and Monograph Series No. 6, 1986).

Confucius himself there is no mention of *yin-yang*.[7] In *Xunzi*, however, *yin-yang* is mentioned. For example:

> 1 Therefore, it is said that when Heaven and earth combine, all things are born, when *yin* and *yang* combine, all changes are produced, and when nature and conscious activity combine, the world is well ordered. (*A Discussion of Rites*)

Due to his pragmatism, Xunzi did not explore the cosmic forces of *yin* and *yang*. More references to *yin-yang*, however, are made in later nonphilosophical Confucian texts like the *Liji* (禮記). But *yin-yang* plays no significant role in early Confucian philosophical canons.

Second, even with the prevalence of the *yin-yan* polarity in the second century, it was not yet correlated with the gender of male and female. Lisa Raphals points out that in the pre-Han (before 206 B.C.) philosophical works, proximate and related treatments of *yin-yang* and man and woman (*nan-nu* 男女) occur only two times in the *Mozi* and *Huai-nanzi*.[8] But in *Mozi*, the terms *yin* and *yang* are not yet treated as the two fundamental cosmic forces. And in both *Mozi* and *Huai-nanzi*, *yin* and *yang* are not really correlated with females and males. For example:

> 2 When the sage kings transmitted (their knowledge), with regard to Heaven and Earth, they spoke of above and below. With regard to the four seasons, they spoke of *yin* and *yang*. With regard to human nature, they spoke of men and women. With regard to birds and beasts, they spoke of male and female (animals) and cock and hen. (*Mozi* 7/6/34–35)

Third, and more importantly, since *yin* and *yang* are always aligned with Earth and Heaven, it is quite obvious that *yin* and *yang* as two cosmic forces have always been seen as hierarchical. However it is their complementarity, rather than their hierarchical nature that is emphasized in the pre-Han Confucian texts. Passages in *Liji* provide evidence for this: "Therefore the rituals must originate from the Great Unity, [which] separates to become Heaven and earth, turns to become *yin* and *yang*, changes to become the four seasons . . ." (*Liji* 9:31). This, passage emphasizes the different components of the original unity, and *yin-yang* is one of the components.

The complementarity of *yin* and *yang* can also be seen from the fact that though *yin* is seen as the subordinate force, it is not denigrated as it sometimes is in Neo-Confucianism. For example: "Music comes from *yang*, rituals

---

7 Hsu, *Chung-kuo jen-hsing lun-shi*, p. 558. It should be noted that it is controversial whether Confucius himself authored part of the *Book of Changes*.

8 Lisa Raphals, *Sharing the Light* (Albany: State University of New York Press, 1998), p. 158.

come from *yin*, when *yin* and *yang* harmonize, myriad things are fulfilled" (*Liji* 11:5). Since rituals (*li* 禮) are of utmost importance in Confucianism, to conceive of *yin* as their source is indeed to accord *yin* a very respectable status.[9] Consequently, when males and females were aligned with *yang* and *yin* in early Confucianism, they were believed to be complementary as well.

It was in the *Chun-chiu fan-lu*, the work attributed to Dong Zhongshu (179–104 B.C.), that the alignment between *yin-yang* and female-male became codified and their hierarchical nature was stressed:

3 Things emerge and contract by following *yang*. All things end and begin by following *yang*. The rectitude of the three kings rose to its utmost in following *yang*. In this way it can be seen that they esteemed *yang* and demeaned *yin*. . . . Men, however mean, are in all cases *yang*; women, however noble, are all *yin*. (*Juan* 11, chapter 43, p. 290)

The practical implications of the denigration of the *yin*/female were clearly spelled out in the Han work, *Pai-hu-tung*:

4 Why is it that according to the rites, the man takes his wife, whereas the woman leaves her house? It is because *yin* is lowly, and should not have the initiative; it proceeds to the *yang* in order to be completed. *Yang* sings and *yin* harmonizes. Man leads and woman follows. (II (40)46a–b)

Using the *yin-yang* polarity as the basis, *Pai-hu-tung* formally codified the human hierarchies into the Three Bonds (*san-gang* 三綱): the bond between ruler and minister, father and son, and husband and wife. The three bonds later became the authoritative reference for guiding human relationships.

With the advent of Neo-Confucianism, the denigration of the *yin* force, and hence the female gender, was further accentuated. For example, Zhu Xi (A.D. 1130–1200) wrote, "Good and evil can be applied to describe *yin* and *yang*. It can also be applied to describe the male and the female."[10]

IMPLICATIONS

There are four implications we can draw about the *yin-yang* distinction: 1) it is a fluid distinction, 2) it does not imply according to males significant

9 Lisa Raphals disputes Graham's conclusion about the hierarchical nature of *yin-yang*. However her argument rests mainly on non-Confucian texts such as the *Ma-wang-tui* texts. Furthermore, the passages that support her position are too scanty compared with the voluminous descriptions of *yin-yang* in hierarchical correlative contexts such as Heaven and Earth, or above and below. Roger Ames also points out the complementarity of *yin* and *yang* in "Taoism and the Androgynous Ideal," in Guisso and Johannesen, *Women in China*.
10 See *Chou Lian-hsi chih* (Taipei: Commercial Press, 1973).

practical advantages such as power, 3) it implies gender essentialism, and 4) it assumes dynamism. Let us look at them in more detail.

1) YIN-YANG *AS A FLUID DISTINCTION*

It is a *fluid distinction* in the sense that there is no fixed rule in assigning weight to its features of complementarity and hierarchy. Certainly these two features can potentially create tensions. Yet strictly speaking, the two do not contradict each other. Complementarity implies mutuality and reciprocity, therefore exerting some constraints on the degree of hierarchy. Indeed, as seen above, different periods tended to emphasize differently one or the other of the two features. Consequently for the Ming and Song dynasties in which special emphasis on the hierarchical dimension was made, the oppression of women was very severe. Early Confucianism, on the other hand, focused on the complementary aspect, and women's status was relatively higher than in the later period.

2) *THE DISTINCTION DOES NOT IMPLY GRANTING MALES SIGNIFICANT PRACTICAL ADVANTAGES*

The basis of the hierarchical relationship between *yin* and *yang* is unclear. When we say that *yang* is a superior cosmic force to *yin*, what exactly do we mean? The judgment of superiority can be made on various grounds. For example, *yang* could be superior in the sense that it is more worthy. This may be because it plays a more major role in the cosmic functioning, or because its contribution is more significant. Or it could be superior because it is the leader and is directing and controlling *yin*. Alternatively, its superiority could be understood in the sense that it possesses a sui generis value. Unfortunately, the Confucians leave us no clear explanation of what constitutes the superiority of *yang* over *yin*. Even the Neo-Confucians, who had sophisticated discussions of metaphysics, did not seem to address the question. For example, Shao Yung (A.D. 1011–1077) said,

> 5 The interaction of activity and tranquility gives full development to the Way of Heaven and Earth. At the first appearance of activity, *yang* is produced. As activity reaches its limit, *yin* is produced. The interaction of *yin* and *yang* gives full development to the functions of Heaven.[11]

Note that this passage does not say that *yang* produces *yin*, though it asserts the temporal priority of *yang*. Furthermore, it is the *interaction* between the two forces that explains the functioning of Heaven.

11 Shao Yung, *Huang-chi ching-shih shu* (5:1b).

Given the ambiguity of the basis of the cosmic hierarchy of *yin-yang*, it is difficult to interpret its implications for gender hierarchy. As seen in passage 4 above, some Confucians would want to say that the superiority of *yang*, at least in the human realm, lies in its greater worth or virtue. This is because *yang* is active and takes the initiative. *Yin*, on the other hand, is passive. On this view, males therefore should lead and females should follow.

But this claim is unjustified, especially in the context of Confucianism. There are various types of leadership. A charismatic leader, for example, does not need to busy herself with initiatives and actions. Her charisma will influence people's choices and behaviors. The ideal Confucian sage-ruler is supposed to play the political role by doing nothing. He just needs to exemplify moral excellence and thereby transform the moral characters of his subjects (*Analects* 15:4). Leadership therefore seems to correlate with tranquility rather than activism. Consequently, if we follow the argument that *yang* is active, we should assign the leadership role to females rather than males in the context of Confucianism.

Perhaps we should say that the *yin-yang* distinction suggests impartiality toward males and females as leaders. Note that in the Chinese cosmology, *yin* and *yang* as cosmic forces are permanently undergoing different phases of development, and they *take turns in prevailing*. For example, day (*yang*) and night (*yin*) alternate. Whether this implies a strict alternation between male and female leaders is not something that we need to decide now.[12] What is important is that the barring of women from leadership is shown to be unjustified. But if men are not entitled to leadership just because of their superiority, perhaps the same can be said about other privileges like power and claims to resources. In brief, if the superiority of males does not mean that they have more merit, it is unjustified to reward them with special privileges that could be used to help them to secure a dominant position.

How about the interpretation of *yang*'s superiority as possession of a sui generis value? Should that kind of superiority carry special privileges in Confucianism? Interestingly, Confucianism does discuss the other bases of honors besides worth/virtue:

> 6 There are three things which are acknowledged by the world to be exalted: rank, age and virtue. At court, rank is supreme; in the village, age; but for assisting the world and ruling over the people it is virtue. (*Mencius* 2B:2)

---

12 As I shall discuss in more detail later, sometimes males can also be described as *yin*. For example, sons and ministers are *yin* roles as relative to the roles of fathers and rulers. Maybe a more tranquil and passive person possesses more *yin* elements. Hence the alternation between *yin* and *yang* need not imply a strict alternation of leaders of different sexes.

In this passage, we can see that, of these three bases of honor, the honor accorded to the virtuous is based on merit, and that of the nobility is premised on convention. The honor of the elders, on the other hand, like the superiority of the males, seems to be based on a sui generis value, that is, on a natural characteristic that by itself carries a value that is not grounded in any other value.

It is indisputable that Confucianism advocates veneration of elders: "The proper order between the old and the young cannot be abandoned" (*Analects* 18:7). Mencius even describes the ability to respect one's elder brother as innate (*Mencius* 7A:15). But we should be careful in interpreting the honor based on age:

> 7 Meng Chi-tzu asked Kung-tu Tzu, "Why do you say that rightness is internal?" Kung-tu Tzu said, "It is the respect in me that is being put into effect. That is why I say it is internal." "If a man from your village is a year older than your eldest brother, which do you respect?" "My brother." "In filling their cups with wine, which do you give precedence to?" "The man from my village.". . . Mencius said, ". . . You can then say, In the case of the man from my village it is also because of the position he occupies. Normal respect is due to my elder brother; temporary respect is due to the man from my village." (*Mencius* 6A:5)

> 8 There are honors bestowed by Heaven, and there are honors bestowed by man. Benevolence, dutifulness, conscientiousness, truthfulness to one's word, unflagging delight in what is good, – these are honors bestowed by Heaven. The position of a Ducal Minister, a Minister, or a Counselor is an honor bestowed by man. Men of antiquity bent their efforts towards acquiring honors bestowed by Heaven, and honors bestowed by man followed as a matter of course. (*Mencius* 6A:16)

Passage 7 points out that respect toward the elderly is a genuine feeling. However, age is not the only, or the decisive, factor in determining honor. For one respects one's elder brother more than a senior fellow, even though the latter is older than the former. (The hierarchy of respect is reversed only temporarily in some rituals.) In brief, familial relationship is a more important factor in determining honor. Moreover, the honor of age is not unconditional. Confucius calls someone who has not made any contribution and who refuses to die when old a pest (*Analects* 14:43).

In passage 8, the honor of the virtuous is prized above the honor of the nobility and described as the Heavenly honor. Thus we can infer that the honor of the virtuous is supreme among the three kinds of honors. More importantly, this passage shows that special privileges like power, leadership, and entitlement to resources should be the "natural" or the proper accompaniment only to the honor of the virtuous. Hence we can conclude that respect toward the elderly is not a very significant honor in Confucius. Age is relegated to other bases of honor such as familial relationships and virtues. It carries no entitlement to significant privileges. Perhaps the young should proceed and speak only after the elder one has done so, but this still does not mean that the young cannot be leaders of the old. The same can be said about males and females.

3) THE YIN-YANG DISTINCTION WHEN ALIGNED WITH GENDERS SUGGESTS A KIND OF GENDER ESSENTIALISM

By gender essentialism, I mean the idea that there are invariable or core characteristics that define that particular gender identity.[13] For example, it may be thought that aggressiveness is an invariable element constituting masculinity, and maternal instincts femininity. Since *yang* is associated with what is strong and active, and *yin* with what is passive and weak, when *yin* and *yang* become correlated with female and male, should the respective characteristics be seen as inherent in the genders, as the defining features of the genders? I disagree with Henry Rosemont's answer to this question. According to Rosemont, gender essentialism is not implied because *yin* and *yang* are relational terms:

> Nothing is either *yin* or *yang* in and of itself, but only as it stands relative to something else. An elderly man is *yang* with respect to an elderly woman, but *yin* with respect to a young man. . . . This relationality clearly militates against the view that the early Chinese thinkers are essentialistic in their accounts of women and men.[14]

In one sense, it is correct to say that *yin* and *yang* are relational terms. Dong Zhongshu also has a passage which has both sons and ministers described as *yin* in relation to their respective superiors – fathers and rulers.[15] However, there is no inconsistency in claiming the relationality of *yin-yang* while maintaining its suggestion of gender essentialism. That males can sometimes be in the *yin* position does not mean that it cannot be true that all males are *yang when compared* with females. Put another way, remember that *yin* and *yang* imply different characteristics or attributes. For example, *yang* = strong,

---

13 For discussion about the anti-essentialist stream in recent feminism, see Nancy Fraser, "Equality, Difference, Democracy: Recent Feminist Debates," in *Feminism and the New Democracy*, ed. Jodi Dean (Thousand Oaks, Calif.: Sage Press, 1997).

14 Henry Rosemont, Jr., "Confucian and Feminist Perspectives on the Self," in *Culture and Self*, ed. Douglas Allen (Boulder, Colo.: Westview Press, 1997).

15 Dong Zhongshu, *Chi-yi*, chapter 52. See Hsu, *Chung-kuo jen-hsing lun-shi*, p. 580.

yin = weak. Rosemont's conclusion seems to ignore the fact that many attributes can be understood in both the absolute sense and the relative sense. We say that a person is (physically) strong in the absolute sense when the person's physique and health condition exceed a certain threshold. On the other hand, we say that a person is (physically) strong in the relative sense, when the person is compared to another person weaker than himself or herself. In other words, the word "strong" when understood in the relative sense only means stronger. It does not imply having passed a certain threshold. Consequently, in Rosemont's example, since an elderly man is stronger than an elderly woman, he is *yang*. But he becomes *yin* when compared to a young man. This, however, does not mean that all males are not strong in the absolute sense, that is, all have reached a certain threshold that females cannot meet. Seen in this light, *yin* and *yang* still suggest the correlation of attributes, understood in the absolute sense, with gender: Males are strong and take initiative, females are weak and passive.[16]

Of course saying that *yin* and *yang* when aligned with genders suggest gender essentialism does not mean that males, for example, cannot be weaker than females under certain situations. Just as the southern side of a hill can be shadier than the northern side (because a huge building has blocked out the sunlight), an old and sick man is weaker than a young and healthy woman. But this does not refute the claim that males are stronger than females. For in those special situations, other interfering factors tip the balance. An old and sick man should be compared to his counterpart, that is, an old and sick woman, rather than a young and healthy one.

Note that I am not claiming that the *yin-yang* distinction *by itself* suggests gender essentialism. The idea is that the distinction when *aligned* with genders suggests gender essentialism. After all, if *yin* and *yang* are seen as strictly relational, and males are not seen as inheriting the characteristics of *yang* and females of *yin*, what would it mean to say that males are *yang* and females are *yin*? The alignment would be completely vacuous. Perhaps, the alignment should not have been made in the first place. Indeed, as I shall explain later, the alignment is not necessary and should be discarded. Nevertheless, we should note that the alignment was in fact made by Confucians in the past, and with the alignment, gender essentialism is suggested.

16 Another argument to the same conclusion runs as follows: The instantiation of *yin* and *yang* attributes is relative to contexts. In the context of interaction between people of different genders, males should be strong, females weak. In the context of interaction between people of different ages or different ranks, the senior person should be strong, the junior weak. Masculinity then can be defined as the ability to instantiate the *yang* attributes in the appropriate context.

Gender essentialism has normative implications: Any divergence from the presumed pattern would be seen as a deviation and, therefore, wrong or bad, or at least undesirable. A female who takes initiatives would be seen as transgressing against the pattern of *yin*, hence not behaving properly. More importantly, such essentialism would mean that alternative behavior patterns are impracticable for normal people, as people cannot transcend their natures. Education, upbringing, and conscious efforts may bring about some modifications, but the modifications would be very limited and set within the parameters laid down by nature.

4) THE YIN-YANG DISTINCTION ASSUMES DYNAMISM

As seen above, *yin* and *yang* are constantly undergoing changes and taking turns in prevailing. One may say, for example, that day (*yang*) is superior to night (*yin*), though the two take turns to prevail. Consequently, the *yin-yang* distinction should imply the room for the full development of both genders. It should also be recognized that their time of prevalence may be different, and that the two may even follow a cyclical pattern with each of the two genders following its own repeated path of eclipse and rise. For example, girls may excel over boys during early school years, men may be dominant in times when women are engaged in reproduction, and so forth.

Moreover, the dynamism implied by the *yin-yang* distinction can also imply pluralism in gender relationships. Since the *yin* and *yang* forces are always undergoing changes and differing in their relative strengths, their interactions would come in numerous ways depending on the particular combination of the relative strengths of the *yin* and *yang* forces. For example, the interaction between an adult woman and a male child would be very different from that between an adult man and an adult woman. Hence, not only would we expect that there be no set way about how male and female should interact, we should also expect that even for the same persons, there would be different interactive patterns over time, for example, changing ways of interactions between a mother and her child.

In brief, *yin-yang* is a fluid distinction that can be seen either mainly from the perspective of complementarity or mainly from the perspective of hierarchy. As a hierarchical polarity, its ground for hierarchism is unclear. Hence I have argued that no significant practical advantage, such as power, should be implied by the hierarchy. The distinction also seems to imply gender essentialism and dynamic interactions between genders which defy strict rules.

CRITIQUE

A critique of the *yin-yang* cosmology is beyond the scope of this chapter. We just need to note that the *yin-yang* distinction is an integral part of Neo-Confucianism. To a large extent, the metaphysics of Neo-Confucianism is structured around the *yin-yang* cosmology. The concept of the Great Ultimate (*Taiji* 太極) in Chou Tun-i's philosophy, for example, evolves around the *yin-yang* conceptions. Furthermore, the chief characteristics of the distinction are also coherent with many basic Confucian ideas. For example, the distinction implies hierarchy, which is rampant in many parts of Confucianism, such as the Five Relationships. The *complementarity* in the distinction also echoes the element of reciprocity in Confucian hierarchical relationships. While a father should love his son, the latter should obey his father. That *yin* and *yang* suggest different gender characteristics is also coherent with the Confucian idea of roles. Each person has a particular role to take, and each relationship has a distinctive kind of duty associated with it. A father's love toward his son is expressed in the form of affection, and a son's love toward his father in the form of respect. Hence it seems that we cannot dismiss the *yin-yang* distinction easily.

On the other hand, the essentialism implied by the *yin-yang* distinction is, to say the very least, problematic. Anthropological findings are full of reports of contrary roles and natures attributed to women by different societies. For example, among the Suku of Africa, only the women can plant crops and only men can make baskets. But among the Kaffa of the Circum-Mediterranean, only the men can plant crops and only the women can make baskets.[17] Similarly, women were traditionally seen as emotional and irrational in the West,[18] but not so in Confucian China. If so, what is the reason for thinking that the particular gender traits correlated with the *yin-yang* distinction accurately represent the essential characteristics of genders? Moreover, is there any way to prove that those attributes are results of nature rather than nurture?

APPLICATION TO GENDER ISSUES IN CONTEMPORARY SOCIETY

Perhaps one consideration in determining whether we can justifiably discard the correlation of the *yin-yang* distinction with gender is to look at its impli-

17 George Murdoch and Caterina Provost, "Factors in the Division of Labor by Sex: A Cross-Cultural Analysis," *Ethnology* 12 (1973): 203–225.
18 For example, Jean-Jacques Rousseau, *Emile*, tr. William Boyd (New York: Teachers College, 1962).

cations for gender issues in contemporary society. In what follows, I shall show briefly how the distinction may apply in several different areas of modern life.

1) POLITICS

Does the *yin-yang* distinction imply that women should be excluded from political leadership and/or political participation as they were in traditional China? Before we answer this question, we should note that in the Confucian past, while the official doctrine reserved political power to males, females were not entirely powerless. They lacked official legalized and institutionalized power, but they were sometimes able to accrue what Pierre Bourdieu calls "dominated power," that is, circumscribed power by proxy.[19] Through their exercise of the right to remonstrate, and through their roles as confidants and advisors to their husbands and sons, sometimes women did manage to place checks on the power of men and influence the direction of power's exercise.[20]

So does the *yin-yang* distinction allow women to be political leaders? From a theoretical point of view, as shown earlier, since *yin* and *yang* take turns in prevailing, there is no reason to restrict political leadership only to males. This then allows us to set aside the *yin-yang* distinction and consider the question from a purely practical point of view. So considered, leadership positions should be awarded to the most capable people regardless of their gender.

In regard to political participation, I cannot comment here on the question whether Confucianism is compatible with democracy, though I believe that it is. What is important is whether or not there should be any disparity in the assignment of political prerogatives among men and women according to the *yin-yang* distinction. In the West, women were debarred from voting in the past because they were thought to lack the required rational capacity and because their interests were seen as fully represented by men as their husbands and fathers. Such a rationale for exclusion is inapplicable to Confucianism where the dichotomy between emotions and reason does not exist. Hence in Confucianism, it cannot be said that women are emotional and men rational.[21] Indeed, as observed by David Hall and Roger Ames, the

---

19 Dorothy Ko discusses these two kinds of power and gives an intriguing account of how women in traditional China negotiated power within the hierarchical gender structure in her book, *Teachers of the Inner Chambers* (Stanford, Calif.: Stanford University Press, 1994).

20 I thank Professor de Bary for reminding me of the dynamic nature of women's power in traditional China.

21 I therefore disagree with Alison Black, who describes the Chinese male as rational and seeking order and females as intuitive and seeking harmony. Black, "Gender and

Confucian ideal of personhood consists of a combination of both male and female qualities.[22] In the same vein, the sage-ruler is supposed to act like the parents and assume the roles of both the father and the mother to the people. Consequently, in Confucianism, women cannot be excluded from politics on the ground that they lack the full human potential as they were in the West.

Nor can women be excluded from politics on the ground that they lack the required capacity to participate in politics. For in Confucianism, the political sphere is not characterized as displaying or requiring only male/*yang* qualities. In the Confucian ideology the political sphere is just the social sphere writ large; it does not carry special characteristics of its own. It therefore should be like the social sphere – in particular the family – and require the cooperation and participation of both *yin* and *yang* forces.

2) THE WORKPLACE

The same rationale for granting equal opportunity for leadership in the political sphere also applies to the workplace: Both the theoretical consideration of the succeeding prevalence of *yin* and *yang*, and the practical consideration of incentives, point to the need to remove the glass ceiling for female workers. A more pertinent question is whether the distinction supports the division of labor along the gender line. For example, should jobs that require more initiative and assertiveness be assigned to males? In answering this question, we have to note that for modern industries it is often difficult to decide which job is of the *yin* nature and which of *yang*. Usually jobs require a combination of various kinds of skills. For example, is computer engineering a *yang* or a *yin* job? It requires patience and attention to details (*yin*) as well as analytical skills and following strict rules of logic (*yang*).

Even for traditional jobs, segregation by gender does not seem justified by the *yin-yang* distinction. Note that I am not claiming that, theoretically speaking, the *yin-yang* distinction can never support a division of labor along the gender line. My point is that we need to be very cautious in scrutinizing each individual case of segregation. Even the seemingly paradigmatic male and female jobs such as the military, on the one hand, and child-care services, on the other, still require more refined distinctions.

Cosmology," pp. 179ff. The dichotomy between rationality and intuitiveness is found in the Western, not the Confucian, tradition, where harmony is sought by the male sage-rulers.

22 Roger Ames and David Hall, *Thinking from the Han* (Albany: State of New York University Press, 1998), p. 90.

Take, for example, the military. A careful look will show that in the military there are many functions to be filled, including, for example, strategy and training, which require specialists in areas such as psychology, economics, and engineering. It is not obvious that any of these areas fall under the *yin* or the *yang* rubric. Even for combat units, it is unclear whether women should be excluded. Not only do they require experts from gender neutral areas such as medicine and communication, but arguably the job of combat in modern warfare does not require aggressiveness and readiness to take initiative as much as it requires perseverance, calmness, and prudence (the *yin* traits). Perhaps there may still be jobs in the military that should be reserved exclusively for men, yet such jobs probably would not come down to a significant number.[23]

Above all, in thinking about the implications of the *yin-yang* distinction in the workplace, we should make good use of the point that the distinction is a fluid concept: One can choose to emphasize either the complementary dimension or the hierarchical dimension. Things can become more interesting if we approach the distinction from the complementary dimension. One implication is that *yin* and *yang*, or female and male, may have very different ways of doing things. Their different approaches to handling cases and solving problems might complement each other. So instead of assigning males and females to different levels in the work hierarchy, or to different kinds of jobs, it might be better to promote diversity and pluralism, practicing different kinds of management, different styles of planning, organization, and problem solving. For example, recent research has shown that in the United States women are more likely to adopt the so-called consultative style of leadership than men. This style stresses consultation and persuasion, rather than exertion of power in leadership.[24] It is also important to fine-tune diversity in response to different industries, companies of different sizes, et cetera. For example, service institutions like hospitals and welfare organizations may require a management style that can encourage and integrate substantial input from frontline workers who have direct contact with clients and women would be better at this. This will be very different from, say, work in a military force where strict discipline and a top-down style of management may be more appropriate. In this way, society will benefit from the complementarity of the different approaches of the two genders.

---

23 My discussion of the domestic sphere in the next section will throw some light on how the *yin-yang* distinction may bear on professions like child-care services.
24 Alice Eagly and Blair Johnson, "Gender and Leadership Style: A Meta-Analysis," *Psychological Bulletin* 108 (1990): 233–256.

3) DOMESTIC SPHERE

Traditionally the domestic sphere is seen as the sphere where *yin* activities dominate. This view makes sense when a large part of family life revolves around reproduction and the nurturing of infants, as nurturing and reproduction are the quintessential *yin* characteristics. However, in saying so, we still need to be careful about what the claim means. To say that nurturing is a *yin* activity does not mean that nurturing must be the duty of the *mother.* Anthropological studies often find that in traditional societies, the responsibility of nurturing a child does not rest solely on the shoulders of its mother. Instead the job is often shared among the females in the extended family, especially among the elderly women. The adult mother, on the other hand, participates directly in economically productive activities, for example, farming and animal rearing.

Furthermore, nurturing and reproduction no longer define modern family life. Reproduction, which used to be the main occupation of women for a long period of their lives, is no longer their "career." While children still need to be nurtured, with the advent of technology, nurturing, in the sense of supplying nutrition and taking care of physical health, is not *the* issue in modern family life. The most important issue is how to raise the children. Reproduction and nurturing are *yin* activities, but is raising children a *yin* activity as well? Raising children involves giving care, affection, guidance, and education; serving as role models; and disciplining children. Some of these activities are *yin* and some are *yang*. Perhaps the idea of shared parenting does not conflict with the *yin-yang* distinction after all. The domestic sphere is the responsibility of both genders.

4) EDUCATION

As we have seen, the distinction implies that *yin* and *yang* be allowed to run their own courses of natural development. Since education helps people develop their potential and fulfill their nature, contrary to the traditional practice, women are entitled to education just as men are. Indeed some people, including women, in traditional China did appreciate the importance of women's education. Pan Chao, the authoress of the famous *Nü Chieh*, explicitly aligns *yin* and *yang* with females and males and makes the following comment about women's education:

> 9 Yet only to teach men and not to teach women – is this not ignoring the reciprocal relation between them? According to the Rites, book learning begins at the age of eight, and at fifteen one goes off to school.

Why, however, should this principle not apply to girls as well as to boys?[25]

Assuming equal opportunity for education, a more pertinent question is whether males and females should share one common curriculum. We have seen that the *yin-yang* distinction suggests essentialism. If so, does it mean that female education should be different from male education? Should male students engage in physical education more than female students? Perhaps. The important thing though is not to ask whether the curriculum is exactly identical for both genders. It is to ask whether the different curricula overlap in significant areas. Traditionally, girls were taught about cooking and domestic management, and boys were educated to prepare them for public life. Diverse curricula are meant to cultivate different skill sets. But if the division of labor along gender lines is not justified, then neither is the traditional curriculum. As the main concern of the Confucian education should be to help people to develop their moral capacity and become *junzi* (君子), it is hard to see how the curricula for boys and girls should diverge in the core areas.

YIN-YANG AND LIBERAL FEMINISM: A COMPARISON

Our analysis shows that when examined more closely, many of the traditional gender practices are not justified by the *yin-yang* distinction. While the distinction implies gender inequality, the difference is of a minor kind and need not affect the distribution of important opportunities and resources. In this way, the distinction can be seen as highly, if not perfectly, consistent with the demands for gender equality. To see the distinguishing characteristics of the Confucian approach to the gender issue in terms of the *yin-yang* distinction, we can make a brief comparison between it and liberal feminism.

By liberal feminism, I mean feminism based on the ideas of liberalism. That is, liberal feminists subscribe to individualism, and value individuals' rights, freedom to choose, autonomy, and responsibility. This theoretical stance is different from that of other feminist theories such as radical feminism – which proposes ideas like the complete eradication of reproductive difference – or Marxist feminism – which calls for an overhaul of the social-economic-political structure of society.[26]

---

25 *Hou Hanshu*, 84 (Peking: Chung-hua Press), p. 2789. I adopt the translation of Professor de Bary. See his *Asian Values and Human Rights* (Cambridge, Mass.: Harvard University Press, 1988).

26 It is important to note that liberal feminism does not agree with the entire liberal doctrine. For example, Carol Pateman points out that liberal feminism sees traditional liberalism as patriarchal and challenges one of its key ideas – the distinction between the private and the public. See Carol Pateman, "Feminist Critiques of the Public/Private Dichotomy,"

The overlapping of so many implications of the *yin-yang* distinction with the position of liberal feminism is quite striking. For example, both support the idea of shared parenting, the elimination of many kinds of traditional sexual segregation in the workplace, and equal opportunity for political leadership and political participation. However we should not jump to the conclusion that Confucianism shares important reasoning and values with liberal feminism. For largely the convergence revolves around the critique of traditional patriarchal practice. It therefore only underscores the lack of theoretical justification and arbitrariness of traditional gender roles and duties.

Instead we can easily see that the two positions might give very different justifications for their critique of traditional gender practices. Take the example of sexual segregation in the workplace. Liberal feminism would criticize the practice on the grounds that it places illegitimate restrictions on individuals' free choices and violates the principle of equal opportunity among individuals. The Confucian approach might challenge the segregation on the ground that it does not appropriately recognize the distinct traits of *yin* and *yang*. By excluding females (*yin*) from the place where they should belong, the segregation interferes with the proper interplay between *yin* and *yang*. At a basic level, liberal feminism aims at the full development and fulfillment of autonomous individuals, the Confucian approach at cosmic unity and harmony.

Besides giving different justifications, liberal feminism and the Confucian approach would also have some very different implications in other areas. Liberal feminism would object to the hierarchy implied by the *yin-yang* distinction, due to its commitment to gender equality. Moreover, its position also differs from Confucianism on gender essentialism. As noted earlier, the *yin-yang* distinction suggests gender essentialism. Liberal feminism, on the other hand, has no theoretical commitment to a particular stance on the issue. Despite this, it can still be said that most liberal feminists reject gender essentialism. Even those feminists who maintain that females have a "distinctive voice" – a different psychological profile and/or moral outlook than men[27] – often attribute the differences to nurture, rather than nature. That is, the gender differences are often seen as, for better or for worse, a result of the interplay of factors such as social conditioning and the social positions in which women are placed.[28]

in *Feminism*, Vol. 1, ed. Susan Okin and Jane Mansbridge (Brookfield: Edward Elgar Publishing Company, 1994).

27 I have in mind people like Carol Gilligan, Nancy Chodorow, and Sara Ruddick.

28 For discussion of these views, see Jane Mansbridge, "Feminism and Democratic Community," in *Feminism*, Vol. 1, pp. 347–352, and Elizabeth Spelman, *Inessential Woman* (Boston: Beacon Press, 1988).

More importantly, liberal feminists, including those who believe in gender essentialism, have different responses than Confucians concerning the normativity of the gender norms. As Nancy Fraser has pointed out, the question of whether there should be gender differences is an unsolved issue which has plagued feminism for the past three decades.[29] According to Fraser, there are two camps: Equality Feminists and Difference Feminists.[30] Equality Feminists believe that the main agenda should be about equal access to opportunities and resources. Difference Feminists, on the other hand, think that the equality approach is self-defeating as it is androcentric and assimilationist. According to them, since the standard for measuring merit, needs, and relevance is a male one, it disadvantages women, who must either try to be like men in order to attain "equality" or become marginalized and denigrated. They therefore advocate another standard that can better reflect the female perspective and reality. "Separate but equal" is their slogan. The bone of contention is whether the "separate" standard is a valid one. The Difference approach is looked upon with suspicion by many feminists, first, because it is unclear whether such difference exists, and second, perhaps more importantly, because the so-called female values/approaches might themselves be undesirable products of sexism. If so, they deserve no celebration as they only handicap women and reinforce the existing sexist hierarchy. In that case, they should be cast away.

Furthermore, even Difference Feminists differ from Confucians on the issue of enforcement of gender norms. Liberalism values individuality. To Mill, the individuals' "experiments in living" should be promoted because of their intrinsic and extrinsic values. The natural consequence of such experiments is a diversity of values and approaches. Consequently, to liberal feminists, people who choose to deviate from gender norms should not be discouraged and a fortiori should not be punished. For femininity and masculinity, like other desirable personal traits such as curiosity and prudence, are optional. Their normative force is conditioned on their noninterference with individual freedom and choices.

Confucians, on the other hand, may be more strict about the normativity of gender traits. A contemporary Confucian might perhaps switch the emphasis placed on the particular *yin* elements: She might stress adaptability and persistence instead of more traditional characteristics such as passivity and obedience. Whatever the favored traits are, she will nevertheless uphold the

---

29 Nancy Fraser, "Equality, Difference, and Democracy: Recent Feminist Debates," in *Feminism and the New Democracy*, ed. Jodi Dean (Thousand Oaks, Calif.: Sage, 1997).
30 Fraser thinks that the recent debate between the "anti-essentialist" and the "multiculturalist" feminists is only a variation of the same question that divides the Equality Feminists and the Difference Feminists (ibid., pp. 103–107).

gender distinction *in accordance with* the traits embodied in the *yin-yang* distinction. Guided by essentialism, she would believe that the traits are "natural" and immutable. Moreover, on her view, following the gender norm is the way to achieve cosmic harmony.

This does not mean, however, that Confucians must advocate a strict and thorough enforcement of the gender norm by the state. As Joseph Chan has pointed out,[31] a paternalistic Confucian government that aims at promoting Confucian values can be a moderate one. That is, it can abstain from using legal coercion to require people to conform to certain values. Instead it can achieve this end by noncoercive means, such as education and subsidies. In brief, Confucians can advocate a conscious effort to promote the gender norms and not hesitate to pass out negative appraisals to people who deviate from the gender norms.

Finally, liberal feminism and the *yin-yang* distinction differ on the issue of the relationship between the two genders. The former is concerned about equality between the two genders, the latter about their complementarity. As long as fairness is maintained between the two genders, liberal feminists as such do not care what their relationship is, or whether there is any relationship at all. Imagine a society where the majority is of one gender which, as a result of fair and freely chosen arrangements, occupies most of the privileged positions. Even if in that society the two genders develop very different styles of living and have little interaction with each other except when mating, liberal feminists would have no grounds to complain. Such separatism, however, would be disturbing to Confucians who believe in the complementarity and dynamic relationship between the two genders.

When we look at the issue in the context of the family, the core social institution in Confucianism, we can see clearly the divergent views of liberal feminists and Confucians. The absence of one gender in the family would not trouble liberal feminists as it would Confucians. Consequently, single-parent families, homosexual marriage, and a single lifestyle would face no objection from liberal feminists.[32] All these arrangements, however, fail to allow for the interaction and *complementarity* between the two genders in the family setting. Hence they would not receive endorsement from Confucians.[33]

---

31 Joseph Chan, "Legitimacy, Unanimity, and Perfectionism," *Philosophy and Public Affairs* 29, No. 1 (2000).

32 Another reason for their endorsement is their support for diversity of lifestyles, regardless of whether the lifestyles conflict with gender norms or not.

33 This rationale, however, need not imply the rejection of homosexuality by Confucianism. For the requirement of the complementarity of *yin* and *yang* should apply to all *important* areas, rather than to every single area. Otherwise, there cannot be events like all male, or all female, sports competitions. In Confucianism, family is an important area; sex, however, is not.

LEGAL IMPLICATIONS

So what would the *yin-yang* distinction imply about laws related to gender? As always, complex considerations are involved when one tries to translate values into laws. For example, we have to consider the practicability as well as the cost of the legal enforcement of values. Can we really go around to check whether anyone has a gender bias that is not justified by the *yin-yang* distinction? We also have to see whether the legal enforcement of these values conflicts with other important values. Confucians would favor minimal legal enforcement of values, for they are concerned that legal sanctioning would induce a wrong motivation for people to behave in a morally virtuous way. Hence, I shall just make some tentative claims about what kinds of gender laws might be supported by the Confucian adherents of the *yin-yang* distinction:

1. Laws ensuring equal opportunity in politics, the workplace, and education:

   Given the entrenchment and the pervasive nature of traditional sexist practices in these realms, and the importance of political participation, work, and education to the well-being of a person, a Confucian can side with the liberal feminists in endorsing the legal enforcement of equal opportunity in these areas. Some qualifications certainly need to be made. Equal opportunity in the workplace, for example, does not imply that all positions must be allotted equally to both sexes. It may even allow that some occupations are reserved exclusively for one sex if it can be proved that the exclusion is justified in accordance with the *yin-yang* distinction.

2. Domestic laws:

   Since families are of the utmost importance to Confucianism, legal measures to ensure that families have parents of different genders would not be ruled out by Confucian adherents to the *yin-yang* distinction. Various means could be adopted to prevent or discourage the choice to become a single parent, to remain single, or to form a couple with another person of the same sex. Divorce laws might be designed in such a way as to prevent and/or discourage people from divorcing (e.g., by requiring family counseling before granting a divorce). There could also be adoption laws forbidding single persons or same sex couples to adopt children, tax laws rewarding (heterosexual) married couples, and even laws outlawing same sex marriages.

3. Laws about deviations from the gender norms:

   As we have said, the Confucian adherents of the *yin-yang* distinction take gender normativity seriously. This however need not imply their endorsement of the legal sanctioning of the norms. Since the gender norms are more closely related to a person's private behaviors and, more importantly, to his or her convictions and values, a Confucian would probably judge that gender norms should fall under the realm of education rather than law. One may educate, persuade, criticize, and morally inspire people who deviate from the gender norms, but one may not force them to conform. Otherwise these people might once again behave correctly but for the wrong reason.

CONCLUSION

In this chapter, I have examined the *yin-yang* distinction as a basis for the Confucian conception of gender. I have traced out the early development of the distinction and noted that it did not have an important place in early Confucianism. I have also examined its implications for issues like essentialism, complementarity and the dynamic character of the two genders, and the nature of male superiority according to the distinction. Next I have turned to the applications of the distinction in the different areas of politics, the workplace, the domestic sphere, and education. I have argued that the distinction implies results that converge to a large extent with the position of liberal feminism with regard to the critique of many traditional sexist practices. The convergence, however, disappears with regard to matters of justification and gender essentialism. Finally, I have offered some speculation about the Confucian position on laws related to gender.

Before I draw this chapter to a close, I would like to advance my personal views on the issue. What I shall say is very sketchy, but I hope it can still shed some light on the future exploration of the issue of Confucianism and gender. From the comparison between the Confucian *yin-yang* distinction and liberal feminism, it can be clearly seen that Confucianism is less tolerant of deviations from gender norms. Such intolerance may be disturbing to a Confucian feminist. There are, I believe, ways to address the issue.

The more radical way is to discard the *yin-yang* distinction and its associated metaphysics and "modernize" Confucianism as a purely humanistic and ethical or political philosophy. The cost of this approach is that Confucianism would then be devoid of all metaphysical and religious content. On the other hand, this need not be a high price, since most contemporary discussions of Confucianism already focus only on its ethical and political aspects.

The second way to address the problem of Confucian intolerance is to detach genders from the *yin-yang* distinction. The advantage of this approach is that the *yin-yang* distinction, with its dynamism and generality, can still serve as a useful explanatory category in Confucianism. This is a feasible solution. Recall that in early Confucianism, *yin-yang* as an explanatory polarity was originally independent from genders. It was only when Dong Zhongshu tried to seek cosmic justification for the social-political hierarchy that genders became codified as the exemplification of *yin-yang* forces. Above all, as Alison Black has argued, gender is not a predominant element in the Confucian *yin-yang* cosmology.[34] If that is true, we can conclude that the *yin-yang* based conception of gender is not an essential element of Confucianism and, hence, it can be detached from Confucianism without tampering with the core Confucian ideas.

If either of the above suggestions is right, the *yin-yang* distinction as a basis for the traditional Confucian conception of gender can be debunked. Elsewhere I have also drawn a similar conclusion about the inner-outer distinction (another basis for the traditional Confucian conception of gender).[35] If my conclusions are right, we would need to seek a new basis for a contemporary Confucian conception of gender. But before we engage in that project, perhaps we need to think seriously and carefully about the following questions: Does Confucianism really require a gender system? Can't and isn't it better that the Confucian role-system combine instead with the ideal of androgyny,[36] which believes that gender should become an irrelevant consideration in how we treat one another, and that all people should have equal opportunity in developing all desirable character traits, regardless of gender?[37]

---

34 Alison Black, "Gender and Cosmology." One reason she gives is that the inner-outer distinction, which also characterizes the Confucian conception of gender, does not cohere with how things are categorized as *yin* or *yang*.

35 See note 2.

36 For discussion of the ideal of androgyny, see James Sterba, "Feminist Justice and the Family," in *Feminist Philosophies*, ed. Janet Kourany, James Sterba, and Rosemarie Tong (New Jersey: Prentice Hall, 1992).

37 I am indebted to the participants of the conference, the two anonymous referees, and my colleagues David Christensen and Don Loeb for their constructive comments on this essay.

CHAPTER 14

FAMILY VERSUS THE INDIVIDUAL

THE POLITICS OF MARRIAGE LAWS IN KOREA

HAHM CHAIBONG

I INTRODUCTION

On July 16, 1997, the Constitutional Court of Korea ruled article 809 of the Civil Code unconstitutional.[1] The article contained the centuries old prohibition of marriages between men and women who have the same surnames and "ancestral seats" (*dongsung-dongbon* 同姓同本). Conservatives and "fundamentalists" were immediately in an uproar. Progressives and liberals rejoiced in the decision. For defenders of Confucian tradition, the marriage prohibition is the backbone of their conception of a well-ordered society. They claim that the court's decision violated the cardinal human principles, that it threatened to destroy the moral and ethical foundation of society. For its detractors, the marriage prohibition was an outdated, anachronistic practice that enforced patriarchalism and male-domination in society, while causing unnecessary pain and suffering for those who dared to flout it. The National Assembly, which has to amend the Civil Code in accordance with the court's decision, has yet to act, suspecting and fearing that public opinion is still deeply divided over the issue. Why did this decision over a seemingly obscure marriage law cause such a furor? What exactly was the prohibition all about?

The issues and debates surrounding this case offer a fascinating example of the ways in which traditional Confucian institutions are being challenged by modern liberal ones. It shows a traditional society in the process of adopting new institutions and adapting to more recently introduced norms and values. To be sure, Korea is a modern nation-state in almost all respects. Its political institutions mirror those of other liberal democracies while its economy, already fully industrialized, is rapidly becoming globalized. However, as this court case indicates, there are still aspects of Korean society

1 The research for this chapter was conducted with the support of a grant from the Institute of Korean Studies, Graduate School of International Studies, Yonsei University.

that are quite "traditional." This will come as no surprise to those students of Korea who have always been struck by the extent to which the society remains deeply Confucian despite all the modern institutional trappings. However, it is much more difficult to pinpoint concrete institutional manifestations of that influence. The marriage law was one of the few remaining ones. Thus, the case provides us with a glimpse into the workings and limitations of a traditional institution within a modernized society. It provides us with a rare opportunity to witness not only a clash of values but also a clash of institutions and to see how such clashes are articulated and what discursive and legal mechanisms are employed to deal with them.

From a normative point of view, the landmark decision was the culmination of a protracted and intense debate that touched upon such fundamental issues as "traditional versus liberal social order" and "family versus individual happiness." The debate has forced Koreans to reflect upon the fundamental way in which to organize their society. This case is particularly relevant as it shows the family, arguably the most important institution for Confucianism, under siege. How much of the institutional features of the traditional Confucian family, which still contains in it a vision of the "good society" that most Koreans still seem to share, should be maintained? How far should society insist on it when, at least for some members of society, it is obvious that "individual rights" and the "pursuit of happiness" are seriously hindered by it? What exactly is the Confucian family?

In this essay, I will use this landmark case as the occasion to rethink the institutional and normative basis of the Confucian family system. I do so first by comparing it with the conception of family that I argue is deeply rooted in "Western" tradition and second by tracing its historical evolution. In the concluding section, I argue that the Confucian conception of the family is still relevant for the modern age although the maintenance of particular features of it, such as the marriage prohibition, is not essential. But first, the case.

2 THE CASE

All Koreans have not only surnames but also ancestral seats (*bon* 本). An "ancestral seat," or a "choronym," is the name of the locality where the first ancestor of a particular clan or lineage purportedly first settled. Some ancestral seats supposedly go back more than a thousand years, while those started up by a particularly famous or illustrious ancestor during the intervening centuries are of more recent vintage. Ancestral seat is crucial in that it, and not surname itself, determines one's ancestry. Two people can have the surname Kim (金) but if one's ancestral seat is "Kimhae" (金海) and the other's is

"Andong," (安東) they are not related. All in all there are some 274 surnames in Korea, but there are numerous ancestral seats for each surname. For example, there are 280 different ancestral seats for Kims, the most common surname in Korea, 240 for Lees (李), and 127 for Parks (朴), the second and third most popular last names in Korea, respectively.

The prohibition of marriage between people with the same surname and the same ancestral seat was instituted in order to prohibit consanguineous marriages. As we will have occasion to see later, the family as an institution occupies a central place in the Confucian world view. It is an institution as important as the individual or the state, if not more so. The family is not only the foundation of one's identity but also the repository of all the values and mores deemed essential for human flourishing, a place where one learns how to become a civilized human being. Given the importance of the family as a sociopolitical institution, rules and regulations governing it had to be articulated and enforced. Elaborate rules and regulations for the family were set down by Confucian scholars and philosophers over the centuries. Rules governing ancestor rituals, proper behavior among the constituents, and inheritance of property were only among the more prominent ones. Marriage laws, essential not only for ensuring the continuity of the family but also for defining its identity and boundaries, were important. The prohibition of marriage between people with the same choronym was the most concrete mechanism by which family identities were maintained, thereby ensuring the integrity of the family as a sociopolitical institution.

The marriage prohibition was particularly relevant when the total population of Korea was about five to seven million, as it was throughout most of the Chosŏn dynasty (1392–1910). However, with the population explosion which coincided with rapid modernization, the number of people having the same ancestral seat increased dramatically. Today there are 3,760,000 Kimhae Kims, 2,740,000 Milyang (密陽) Parks, and 2,370,000 Chŏnju (全州) Lees, the three largest clans in Korea. The chance of meeting and falling in love with someone from one's own clan is much greater in modern-day South Korea, highly urbanized and with a population of forty-five million. According to statistics, in 1978 there were 4,577 couples that were married "illegally." In 1988 the number increased to 12,443, and by 1996, it reached 27,807. Some estimate that the actual number is as high as 200,000 couples, nearly 2 percent of all married couples in Korea. The children born of such marriages were, until the ruling of the Constitutional Court, considered "out-of-wedlock" children. They were not eligible for national health insurance and were discriminated against in matters of inheritance and property rights. In extreme cases, young couples who met and fell in love, only to find out that their love could never be consummated, chose suicide as the way out.

On May 20, 1995, the Family Court of Seoul referred to the Constitutional Court the case brought forth by eight couples who asked the court to evaluate the constitutionality of Civil Code 809. They argued that the code violated the "right to the pursuit of happiness" and the "right to family life" guaranteed by articles 10 and 36, respectively, of the Constitution. Two years later, the Constitutional Court ruled 7 to 2 against it. The majority opinion stated that "the law against marriages between members of the same agnatic lineage descendants violates the dignity of human beings and the right to the pursuit of happiness as guaranteed by the Constitution as well as the right to free marriage and equality." The court also added that "this law originated from a clan-oriented, patriarchal extended family system, as well as an agrarian society where self-sufficiency was the rule," but that "rapid industrialization, population explosion, and rapid urbanization make it impossible to recognize the rationality of this law." The court was not, however, thereby "condoning or encouraging marriage between close kin." Rather, "marriage between close relatives should be regulated by civil codes other than Code 809 while the actual extent of the prohibition should be left to social ethics and morality to decide."

However, the story does not end here. Now that Code 809 of the Civil Code has been declared unconstitutional, the National Assembly has to pass an amendment. However, as of the writing of this essay, fully five years since the Constitutional Court's ruling, the National Assembly has yet to amend the code. In the face of fierce opposition from staunch defenders of Confucian values such as the *yulim* (儒林), "fundamentalist" Confucians who continue to exercise a great deal of influence in rural areas, the National Assembly has decided not to act on the amendment. On December 17, 1999, the Subcommittee on Law of the National Assembly said, "in view of the national sentiment which places a great deal of importance on bloodline the abolition of the law prohibiting marriages between people with the same surnames and same ancestral seats is premature."[2] Afterward, the subcommittee passed an amendment maintaining the prohibition. The executive branch and the Constitutional Court insist that the old law has ceased to be effective. The debate still rages.

3 THE FAMILY, WEST

In the Western political tradition, family has always played a minor, secondary role vis-à-vis the *polis* or the state. In the modern era, it has taken a back seat to the individual and the society. The distinction between private

---

2 *Chosŏn Ilbo* (Chosŏn Daily), December 19, 1999.

and public realms, so crucial to Western political theory, rests on the ancient Greek distinction between the *oikos* (household) and the polis.[3] Although the two realms are dependent on each other for both conceptual and practical purposes, the polis is clearly privileged. The realm of the household was the realm of need, where people engaged in labor to secure the basic necessities for survival. It was relevant for the public realm only to the extent that it was through the *oikos* that economic surplus, or leisure, which enabled the household heads to engage in the activities of the polis, was produced. The household was meaningful only insofar as it provided for basic human survival and the leisure that made politics possible: "Historically, it is very likely that the rise of the city-state and the public realm occurred at the expense of the private realm of family and household."[4]

Because the two realms were so distinct, and because they were organized for different ends, they had different principles and rules of organization. Whereas polis was the realm of equality and freedom, household was the realm of hierarchy, power, and violence:

> What all Greek philosophers, no matter how opposed to *polis* life, took for granted is that freedom is exclusively located in the political realm, that necessity is primarily a pre-political phenomenon, characteristic of the private household organization, and that force and violence are justified in this sphere because they are the only means to master necessity – for instance, by ruling over slaves – and to become free.[5]

The public realm was where things were decided through oration, debate, and fair contests between equals who enjoyed leisure by virtue of being household heads: "To be political, to live in a polis, meant that everything was decided through words and persuasion and not through force and violence."[6] The private realm was where despots ruled:

> In Greek self-understanding, to force people by violence, to command rather than persuade, were pre-political ways to deal with people characteristic of life outside the *polis*, of home and family life, where the household head ruled with uncontested, despotic powers, or of life in the barbarian empires of Asia, whose despotism was frequently likened to the organization of the household.[7]

The ancient Greek understanding of the relationship between the public and the private became the mainstay of Western political theory through the ages. The words "feudal" and "medieval" derive their pejorative sense by virtue of the fact that they refer to an era in which the public realm was all

---

3 Hannah Arendt, *The Human Condition* (New York: Doubleday & Company, 1959), p. 27.
4 Ibid., p. 28.   5 Ibid., p. 29.   6 Ibid., p. 26.   7 Ibid.

but extinguished. Under the "feudal" order private, personal, pre-political relationships and ethics permeated all spheres of life, including the formerly "public" realm such as the court. The typical feudal barony was the exact replica of the ancient Greek household in that the power wielded by its head and the relationship that he maintained with his subjects were "despotic": "the secular realm under the rule of feudalism was indeed in its entirety what the private realm had been in antiquity. Its hallmark was the absorption of all activities into the household sphere, where they had only private signifi-cance, and consequently the very absence of a public realm."[8]

Greek prejudice against the family as the breeding ground for the kind of power and authority unfit for the public realm was shared by early modern political philosophers. For the likes of Locke and Rousseau, family became the symbol of "patriarchy" that assumed for itself powers over individual family members that are for the most part unwarranted and tyrannical. Locke's prejudice against the family is clearly expressed in his famous debate with Robert Filmer. For Locke, men in the state of nature are "all equal and independent."[9] As such, "no one ought to harm another in his life, health, liberty, or possessions," including kings.[10] This was in response to Filmers defense of the "patriarchal" power of the monarch which the latter likened to "Adam's private dominion and paternal jurisdiction."[11] Locke vehemently criticized Filmer for committing a category mistake, for confusing the public with the private. Locke then gave a distinctly modern account of the role of the polis:

> political power, then, I take to be a right of making laws with penalties of death and, consequently, all less penalties for the regulating and pre-serving of property, and of employing the force of the community in the execution of such laws and in the defense of the commonwealth from foreign injury; and all this only for the public good.[12]

Locke, however, did not stop at making a clear distinction between private and public realms. He went on to argue that a father could and should not wield despotic powers even within his own household. The power of a father is not as great as was assumed by Filmer: "the power, then, that parents have over their children arises from that duty which is incumbent on them – to take care of their offspring during the imperfect state of childhood."[13] The relationship between the father and the son and by extension between all family members becomes one of mutual need and support, nothing more,

---

8 Ibid., p. 32.
9 John Locke, *The Second Treatise of Government* (Indianapolis: The Bobbs-Merrill Company, Inc., 1952), p. 5.
10 Ibid., p. 5.   11 Ibid., p. 3.   12 Ibid., p. 4.   13 Ibid., p. 33.

nothing less. In his effort to ensure the public good in all spheres of life, Locke denied a place for despotic power even within the confines of a family, its traditional home. In the sense that he was not willing to grant parents despotic powers over their children, Locke may be said to have dissolved the crucial private-public distinction.

However, the role of the family then becomes highly problematic. The family is an institution necessary for the propagation of the species and for the raising of its new members. However, it does not have a telos of its own. It is not an end in itself. It is but a temporary institution that a society cannot do without but which it is hard put to place neatly within the context of the social contract theory. The only solution for this dilemma is then to claim that the family is but a "temporary" organization. This is exactly what Locke did. He stated that the relationship between parents and their children is "temporary and reaches not their life or property."[14]

An unease with family as an institution was also expressed by Rousseau. If the family is no longer regarded as a distinct realm with a logic of its own, what is its raison d'être? Rousseau also views family as but a temporary arrangement. For him the family is "[t]he earliest of all societies, and the only natural one."[15] However, "children remain attached to their father only so long as they have need of him for their own preservation."[16] Once the children grow up, the "natural bond is dissolved" and the father and his children "become equally independent."[17] For Rousseau, like Locke, the family is of limited and temporary use. In a sense, the social contractarians have a vision of the family even more limited than the ancient Greeks: "if [the children and their father] remain united, it is no longer naturally but voluntarily; and the family itself is kept together only by convention."[18] This is because man is a naturally self-interested being: "This common liberty is a consequence of man's nature. His first law is to attend to his own preservation, his first cares are those which he owes to himself; and as soon as he comes to years of discretion, being sole judge of the means adapted for his own preservation, he becomes his own master."[19] There is very little room or scope for the family. Its only reason for being, even temporarily, is because children have to be born and raised. Rousseau could not imagine an alternative institution to carry out such a function.

Modern prejudice against the family was most clearly expressed by Max Weber. According to Weber's famous typology of "authority," the worst kind is "traditional authority" whose prototype is "patriarchal authority" which is

---

14 Ibid., p. 37.
15 Jean-Jacques Rousseau, *The Social Contract*, tr. M. Cranston (New York: Penguin Books, 1968), p. 50.
16 Ibid.   17 Ibid.   18 Ibid.   19 Ibid.

the authority of the father, the husband, the senior of the house, the sib elder over the members of the household and sib; the rule of the master and patron over bondsmen, serfs, freed men; of the lord over the domestic servants and household officials; of the prince over house- and court-officials, nobles of office, clients, vassals; of the patrimonial lord and sovereign prince over the "subjects."[20]

This is in contrast to the modern "legal" or "rational" authority in which "the legitimacy of the power-holder to give commands rests upon rules that are rationally established by enactment, by agreement, or by imposition. The legitimation for establishing these rules rests, in turn, upon a rationally enacted or interpreted 'constitution.'"[21] What makes this a superior form of rationality is that here "[o]rders are given in the name of the impersonal norm, rather than in the name of a personal authority; and even the giving of a command constitutes obedience toward a norm rather than an arbitrary freedom, favor, or privilege."[22]

Ancient Greeks posited the family as the inferior realm of necessity and despotism as opposed to the superior realm of the public or the polis. Early modern thinkers such as Locke and Rousseau gave even lesser room to the family. Weber then clearly distinguished the modern rational authority needed for modern institutions in opposition to the traditional patriarchal authority bred and justified within the context of the family.

4 THE FAMILY, EAST

It is well known that Confucianism, in contrast to Western political theories, placed a great deal of importance on the institution of the family. Confucian classics are replete with pronouncements and aphorisms concerning the importance of family and values particular to it. What is perhaps less well known, or clearly understood, is the extent to which Confucians tried to define and establish the institution of the family as an integral part of the political order. It was not just that they thought the family should be protected as an independent realm but that they viewed it as the bedrock upon which sound political institutions and a well-ordered society could be built. However, it is not the case that Confucianism placed equal importance on the family throughout its long history. As with any system of thought with a long history, Confucianism continuously adapted itself to changing political and socioeconomic circumstances, reinventing itself by articulating new

---

20 H. H. Gerth and C. Wright Mills, eds., *From Max Weber: Essays in Sociology* (New York: Oxford University Press, 1958), p. 296.
21 Ibid., pp. 294–295.   22 Ibid.

institutional and normative configurations to fit particular historical contexts. Indeed, the Confucian family as we know it today and as it is practiced by Koreans, embodied in such laws as the marriage prohibition discussed earlier, is the conscious invention of *xing-li-xue* (性理學), a particular branch of Confucianism which received its fullest theoretical articulation at the hands of Song Neo-Confucian thinkers and its fullest institutional expression during the Chosŏn dynasty of Korea.

1 FEUDAL CONFUCIANISM

The heart of Confucian political theory is the "rule of li" (*lizhi* 禮治), or ritual propriety. If Machiavelli sought to counter *Fortuna* with *virtus* and Hobbes sought to bring order out of the state of nature by the sheer *power* of the Leviathan, Confucius thought that the only way to establish order out of chaos (*luan* 亂) was through the establishment of government based on the principle of benevolence, or *ren* (仁), and ritual propriety, or *li* (禮). Of course rival schools of thought in pre-Qin China proposed different solutions to the decay of political order and the ensuing chaos which characterized the Spring and Autumn and the Warring States periods (春秋戰國時代). The Mohists (墨家) argued that peace and order could be brought about only through "love" (*jianai* 兼愛) while the Daoists (道家) thought that it is only through "non-action" (*wuwei* 無為) that the human order could be made to coincide with the rhythm of the natural order. The Legalists (*fajia* 法家), perhaps the most famous rivals of the Confucians, argued that the rule of law (*fa* 法), accompanied by the threat of punishment, was the only way to bring about peace and order to all under heaven. However, Confucius thought that the rule of law, for example, could never bring about lasting peace and stability to society because it will only make people look for ways to circumvent the law. The rule of *ren* and *li*, on the other hand, will instill in the people an inner sense of propriety and an accompanying sense of shame, making possible an order which would be self-sustaining without outside enforcement or coercion.

The rule of *li*, as envisioned by Confucius, presupposed a particular type of society, namely that of ancient Zhou (周). The sociopolitical order of ancient Zhou was characterized by two major institutional features: feudal political order and the "*zong*" (宗), or "descent-line," family system (*zongfa zhidu* 宗法制度). The "feudal system" (封建 *fengjian*) was one in which royal family members and aristocrats were given their "fiefs" which they ruled in their own right, maintaining their own courts and armies while acknowledging the nominal suzerainty of the royal house of Zhou. Its main feature was a system of aristocratic ranking, called *gong-qing-daifu-shi* (公卿大夫士).

The elaborate codes of proper conduct that Confucius had mastered and which are recorded in great detail in Chapter 10 of the *Analects* were all based upon the Zhou feudal order and its rules of ritual propriety, designed to coincide with each aristocratic rank. For example, only those above the *qing* (卿) rank were permitted to perform rites for three generations of ancestors, while the commoners were only allowed to perform rites for their immediate parents.[23]

The *zong* family system was one based on the strict agnatic principle, that is, the principle of descent through male heirs. The heir of agnatic succession was always the eldest son who was given the responsibility as well as the duty to perform ancestor rites. He was also the inheritor of the wealth and property of the family. The younger sons were given an inheritance, but the far greater part of the descent-line's wealth was kept intact by being given to the eldest sons. The *zong* system was obviously well suited for the feudal system in which great families needed to maintain their power and wealth through successive generations: "The *zong* system was suited to the Zhou aristocratic system in which the family patrimony was an indivisible office or appanage, rather than private property that could be freely bought, sold, or mortgaged. Brothers were differentiated according to age, with the eldest son responsible for preserving the ancestral rites and the patrimony that supported them."[24]

These two institutional mainstays of Zhou, the feudal and *zong* systems, were eminently suited for the practice of the rule of *li*. The combination of the feudal political order with the *zong* system created a community which was ideal for the realization of the rule of *li*. The "extended family" system provided an environment in which family members could be reared in the intricacies of proper behavior in various interpersonal contexts. The feudal system with its own hierarchical order and a family-like structure and ambience provided a semipublic realm in which the rules of propriety acquired in the extended family environment could easily be applied. Thus, Zhou's feudal order and the *zong* system were the political and socioeconomic context in which Confucius elaborated his theories. Indeed, the Master himself made it abundantly clear that it was the *li* particular to Zhou, or *Zhou-li* (周禮), that he wanted to imitate and restore for his own age. Confucius's ideal of the rule of *li* was very context specific. The problem for later

23 The realm governed by aristocrats of the "*gong*" (公) rank was called "*guo*" (國) while the realm ruled by "*qing*" (卿) and "*dafu*" (大夫) ranks was called "*jia*" (家). The modern term for "state" in East Asia today is "*guojia*" (國家), the combination of the names of the realms ruled by Zhou feudal lords.

24 Patricia Buckley Ebrey, *Confucianism and Family Rituals in Imperial China: A Social History of Writing About Rites* (Princeton, N.J.: Princeton University Press, 1991), p. 56.

Confucians was that Zhou's feudal political order and the *zong* family system, which had been in a steady decline during the Spring and Autumn and the Warring States periods, disappeared completely with the unification of China by Qin.

2 IMPERIAL CONFUCIANISM

The unification of China by the first emperor Qin Shi Huang-di in 221 B.C. was a turning point in the history of Confucianism. The world order that the "hundred schools of thought (諸子百家)," including the Confucians, Taoists, and Mohists, were familiar with and had taken for granted all changed overnight. Of course, the Legalists were the important exception as the new world order was brought about by the literal application of their major tenets. Qin adopted an overtly anti-Confucian policy, most infamously illustrated by the burning of Confucian books and the burying alive of Confucian scholars. More importantly, by reorganizing the governing structure of the empire in a fundamentally new way, Qin destroyed the feudal and *zong* systems, the sociopolitical basis upon which Confucius's ideals rested. After the unification of China, the first emperor explicitly rejected the suggestion that he also adopt a feudal system like all the previous dynasties. Instead, he heeded the advice of his Legalist advisors by adopting the first centralized system of government in Chinese history, in which the emperor ruled the vast empire directly through self-appointed intendants and prefects. To this end, instead of the feudal fiefs, the empire was reorganized into units called *jun* (郡) and *xian* (縣) whose governors reported directly to the emperor. For such a system, Confucian rules of ritual propriety based upon feudal ranking and relatively small units of government were clearly ill suited. The only way in which to govern the sprawling empire was through the rule of law backed by the threat of sanctions. The rise of Qin and the introduction of imperial rule thus seemed to spell the end of Confucianism as known to, and idealized by, Confucius.

How then was Confucianism able to survive the transition to an empire? First, luckily for Confucianism, Qin fell just as suddenly and unexpectedly as it had risen. The seemingly invincible empire collapsed within two years after the death of the first emperor. Second, Han, which reunified China after a brief period of civil war, adopted Confucianism as its governing ideology. Of course, it did not return to the feudal system idealized by Confucius, inheriting instead Qin's centralized bureaucratic system of government. However, it was able to effect a compromise with Confucianism which was to benefit the imperial rule enormously and ensure the survival of Confucianism at the same time. The compromise between the empire and Confucianism was effected by Han Wu Di (141–87 B.C.) who instituted the civil service examination, in which candidates were tested for their knowledge of the Confucian classics. A "national university" was set up where Confucian philosophy was taught and exegetical work on Confucian texts carried out. Han eventually came to be known as the quintessentially "Confucian" dynasty.

Why was it that Han opted for Confucianism in stark contrast to Qin, its immediate predecessor? When assessing the reasons for the sudden collapse of mighty Qin, the founders of the new dynasty focused on the harshness of the Legalist rule which, despite its seeming effectiveness, alienated the populace, leading to its sudden collapse. With this in mind, they sought means by which to soften the edges of the rule of law while retaining it as the governing principle of the empire. It was thought that Confucianism, with its emphasis on "human heartedness" (ren 仁) and "justice" (yi 義), would be able to counterbalance Legalist strictures while Confucian rituals added authority and luster to imperial rule. In other words, the empire needed the trappings and façade of Confucianism in order to make its rule of law more palatable to the populace and thus ultimately more effective. Since Han, succeeding Chinese dynasties all maintained the Legalist-Confucian duality as the mainstay of their rule.

Confucianism, for its part, not only weathered the persecution under Qin but was also able to make a strong comeback as the "state religion." However, Han's solution was only partial, at best. Even though Confucianism survived the transition to empire, it was able to do so only by selectively emphasizing and developing those aspects which could serve the interest of the imperial rule. The bureaucracy and the examination system by which new officials of the empire were recruited, as well as the renewed emphasis on ritual, were all put into the service of the empire. For instance, the great revival of interest in Confucian rituals during the Han almost exclusively concerned the imperial family:

> The new imperial form of government required new forms of political rituals. Because the ritual classics contained no liturgies for royal, much less imperial rituals, from early in the Han dynasty emperors turned to Confucian scholars to devise appropriate court rituals, which they generally did by scaling up items found in the canonical texts. . . . The creation, critique and editing of liturgical texts, and the scrutiny of imperial performance, became a major political activity of scholarly officials.[25]

However, with the emphasis on imperial rituals, the rule of *li* became largely irrelevant for the population at large:

25 Ibid., pp. 34–35.

During the long early imperial period, governments rarely showed much concern with the rituals that common people performed. Some local officials tried to eradicate wedding or funeral practices so deviant that they marked the performers as ethnically non-Han, such as marrying a brother's widow (levirate) or failing to wear mourning clothes. Some would work to eliminate offensive local religious practices, but they were generally too busy dealing with demon worship, insubordinate local gods, and cults involving human sacrifice to worry about minor deviations in ancestral rites or other family rituals.[26]

The rule of *li* was maintained in name only as the imperial and aristocratic families usurped the rituals to serve their own political ends while the empire was run on Legalistic foundations. As such, the only people for whom the rule of *li* had any relevance were the imperial family and other great aristocratic families which survived the imperial rule.[27] The *Da Tang Kaiyuan Li* (Ritual of the Kaiyuan period of the Great T'ang) of A.D. 732 only specified rituals to be performed by the "emperor and other members of the imperial family" and "high, middling, and low officials."[28] Confucianism and its rule of ritual then became largely the provenance of the ruling class who had the power and wealth to maintain their patrimony through successive generations.

The collapse of the feudal order and the bureaucratization of the aristocratic clans entailed the collapse of the *zong* system. It was thus during the Han that the *zong* system, another major institutional mainstay of the Confucian world view, collapsed. With the disappearance of the *zong* system, families were no longer able to maintain themselves as economically, socially, and politically independent institutions. As family property was equally distributed among sons, the size of the share also decreased rapidly except for those rare cases in which a family was able to augment its wealth generation after generation. For most families, the size of the unit became smaller and smaller:

> [I]n the imperial period descent was not thought of in terms of a single line. Younger sons were just as much expected to marry and have children as older ones and would share equally in the family estate if and

---

26 Ibid., p. 37.

27 Of course, the nature of the aristocracy under imperial rule changed greatly. During the Tang dynasty, the great aristocratic clans were ranked by the emperor, based upon meritorious service to the empire. As a result, in contrast to the original sense of aristocracy, "the survival of aristocracy" became "a function of bureaucracy." Peter K. Bol, *"This Culture of Ours": Intellectual Transitions in T'ang and Sung China* (Stanford, Calif.: Stanford University Press, 1992), p. 36.

28 Ibid. The *Kaiyuan li* which prescribed the rules for ancestral rites according to official rank, not the *zong* system, clearly reflected the subordination of the aristocratic clans to the emperor.

when it was divided. Division could rarely be delayed much beyond the death of the father as family head so that it was exceptionally rare for all of the descendants of a great-great-grand father to live together.[29]

The development of imperial rule, despite its adoption of the trappings of Confucianism, seemed to leave little room for the realization of Confucian ideals. Even though there were many institutions created by the Han which came to be regarded as quintessentially Confucian, very little resembled the institutions idealized by Confucius and his preimperial era disciples. By the end of Tang, there were very few manifestations of the familistic orientation that later came to be known as an essential characteristic of Confucianism. The family as a realm coequal to the state or the court and the elaborate rites and code of conduct pertaining to it, which were to become the hallmark of Confucianism, were nowhere (yet) to be seen.

3 NEO-CONFUCIANISM

How then was it that the family (*jia* 家) became so important in the later imperial era, so much so that Confucianism became almost synonymous with familism? The rearticulation of Confucianism with the family as its essential and characteristic component can only be understood within the context of the sociopolitical history of the Song dynasty. As with all Chinese imperial dynasties, Song was founded by a military leader. The founder, Zao Guanying (r. 960–976), a superb military leader as well as a consummate politician, was able to consolidate imperial power by eliminating and otherwise pacifying all rival claimants to power such as warlords and great aristocratic clans. The fall of the Tang and the ensuing political turmoil that lasted for half a century had destroyed most of the leading aristocratic families who had retained great power and influence even under the imperial rule of the Sui, Tang, and the Five Dynasties. This facilitated the efforts of the early Song emperors in consolidating their power.

As a result, Song was able to build a powerful and effective centralized political system. Song was able, for the first time, to implement in earnest the practice of recruiting officials through the civil service examination. The use of the examination system became more widespread and frequent, eventually becoming the means by which the majority of officials were recruited for government service. Another factor which facilitated the bureaucratization and civil domination of Song politics was the propagation of learning made possible by economic prosperity and improvements in printing technology. During the Song, an agricultural revolution was begun with the

---

29 Ibid., pp. 56–57.

intensive development and cultivation of the fertile Yangzi River basin. New strains of rice were introduced as were new fertilizing techniques and irrigation methods. The explosion in agricultural productivity brought about by such developments led to a population explosion as well. Cities with populations close to a million began to spring up with the development of commerce, while the population of the empire as a whole reached nearly one hundred million by the end of the tenth century. At the same time, new advances in printing technology made books widely available. Such changes produced a new breed of scholars who provided a new pool of talent from which the government could recruit its bureaucrats. Song thus began to take on a distinctively "civil" as well as bureaucratic character, more so than any previous dynasty. The great feat of centralization through a purely bureaucratic system was finally achieved by a combination of political leadership and favorable historical circumstances.

It is against this backdrop that we see the rise of a new class of scholar-bureaucrats called the *shi-da-fu* (士大夫). The *shi-da-fu* were members of the gentry class who based their identity on Confucian learning. They were of the class of people who were able to take advantage of the opportunity for learning provided by economic prosperity and the availability of books. They were also the ones who came to supply the vast pool of candidates for the civil service examination. However, unlike the great aristocrats of the previous dynasties, they did not enjoy a power base of their own. They had neither fiefs nor the pedigree and record of continuous and illustrious service with the dynasty that made the great clans of previous dynasties powers to contend with. They were clearly willing to advance their status and expand their privileges, not by challenging the imperial house, but by serving it. In that sense, the *shi-da-fu* were exactly what the new dynasty was looking for. They were perfect for the founders of the Song dynasty, who were able to break from the old pattern of relying on other great families to establish a new dynasty:

> When the first Song emperors patronized the *shi* (士) . . . they did so because the *shi* (士) were willing subordinates, without independent power, who depended on a superior authority for their political position, and who brought to their duties a commitment to the civil culture invaluable to the institutionalization of central authority. Using the *shi* (士) to govern was an example . . . of the imperial desire to use men with ability but without a power base.[30]

Here we see the emergence of the structure of an empire ruled with the help of a loyal bureaucracy versed in Confucian classics and armed with a strong sense of duty toward the society and state. However, as time went on,

---

30 Ibid., p. 52.

it became clear that the situation was less than perfect as far as the *shi-da-fu* were concerned. The problem, at least for those wishing to enter government service, was that the competition became ever more fierce. Whereas during the previous dynasties being a member of an illustrious clan assured one's place in the bureaucracy as well as access to wealth and power, now one had to pass the examination. A bureaucracy based upon the examination system only recognized individual merit. One's birth and pedigree were no longer factors in securing one's position in the social hierarchy. However, with the rapid increase in the number of examination candidates, the possibility of failing the examination became a very real prospect. Given that the examination became the only way to wealth and power for most, the consequence of failure was enormous. For families and individuals wishing to maintain their privileged status from generation to generation, they had to produce successful examination candidates every generation. No matter how illustrious a family was in the past, if it failed to produce successful examination candidates, it passed into oblivion. Thus, the *shi-da-fu* began searching for a means to guarantee their social, economic, and political status even in the event of a failure to pass the examination.

The Song Neo-Confucians sought to resolve this dilemma by reconstructing the family system along the ancient *zong* principle with new rules of propriety. Clearly, for the ambitious *shi-da-fu* families, the great clans of Sui and Tang, not to mention the feudal lords of ancient Zhou, demonstrated the importance of a strong clan in maintaining a sociopolitical and economic base independent of the imperial house. Thus, leading Song Neo-Confucians such as Zhang Zai and Cheng Yi advocated the restoration of the ancient *zong* system.[31] The *zong* system could guarantee the economic independence of a family better than the practice of equal distribution of inheritance among all the sons, a practice which had become standard since Han times: "Ancestral rites celebrate ancestry; the *zong* system evoked images of hereditary officials. Both promoted the independence of the elite from the government."[32]

The Neo-Confucian family was then the result of an effort to strike a middle ground between feudalism and empire. Feudalism guaranteed the independence of great families. It was an independence that the *shi-da-fu* longed for. However, they did not wish to see the complete restoration of the feudal order in which pedigree, rather than merit, was the way to power and wealth. The imperial bureaucracy and the examination system guaranteed the meritocracy that the *shi-da-fu* longed for. However, they did not want to become a mere civil "servant" of the emperor. The rearticulation of the family

31 Ebrey, *Confucianism and Family Rituals*, pp. 56–61.
32 Ibid., p. 65.

along the *zong* system within the context of a centralized bureaucratic empire was the balance that the Neo-Confucians tried to strike.

Of course, it was not just class interest that prompted the *shi-da-fu* to advocate the restoration of the *zong* system. For Neo-Confucian intellectuals their abiding concern was the restoration of order. The great Tang dynasty began to disintegrate in the aftermath of An Lushan's rebellion which effectively put an end to centralized rule. When China was plunged into further chaos after the fall of the Tang, the urgency of restoring order became even greater. The loss of the Central Plains (中原), the birthplace and center of Chinese civilization, to the barbarians during the Southern Song further accentuated the need to restore order and civilization. However, for the Neo-Confucians, restoring order was not just a matter of political and military leadership. The deterioration of civilization itself, not just the lack of military prowess, was what prevented the restoration of order. True to the spirit of Confucianism, they rejected "Legalist" means as inadequate for the task at hand. Instead, they searched for more fundamental causes of the loss of civilization and ways to restore it. Again, true to their Confucian heritage, they agreed that the only way to restore civilization was through the restoration of *li*. And the restoration of *li* required the restoration of the *zong* system which, after all, was the Master's institution of choice.

Thus the most concrete means by which Neo-Confucians sought to establish a lasting order and to restore civilization was by resurrecting family rites. Leading Neo-Confucian intellectuals, including Zhang Zai and Cheng Yi, advocated the restoration of the *zong* system. All of them discoursed on the need for rituals in general but also wrote on the proper ways to perform various family rites such as marriage, funerals, and ancestor worship. The following words of Zhu Xi (1130–1200), the greatest of Song Neo-Confucian thinkers, clearly expresses their way of thinking:

> In order to control the minds of the people, unify one's kin, and enrich social customs so that people will not forget their origin, it is necessary to clarify genealogy, group members of the clan together, and institute a system of heads of descent. (This work should be done year by year.) . . . If the system of heads of descent were destroyed, people would not know their origin. The result would be that they would drift and wander in all directions. Very often there would still be relatives but they would not recognize them.[33]

At the core of this clan system is the ancestor worship ritual: "[E]ach family should have an ancestral temple. (The common people should have halls

---

33 Chu Hsi and Lu Tsu-ch'ien, *Reflections on Things at Hand: The Neo-Confucian Anthology*, tr. with notes by Wing-tsit Chan (New York: Columbia University Press, 1967), pp. 227–229.

with ancestral portraits rather than temples.) In the temple there should be tablets."[34] Zhu Xi then goes into a detailed description of to whom, how, and when the ritual should be conducted. He concludes by saying, "If a family can observe these several items, even its children can be made gradually to understand moral principles."[35] The establishment of the system of descent through the practice of ancestor worship will ultimately yield political returns: "If the system of heads of descent is established, people will know how to honor their ancestors and take their origins seriously. As they take their origins seriously, the power of the court will naturally be highly respected."[36]

The elaborate family rites written by the Neo-Confucians were in effect the governing rules or "constitutions" for the new institution of the family (*jia* 家). Clearly, the *shi-da-fu*'s class interest was part of the reason for this renewed interest in the ancient family system. The effort to revive the family was part of an effort to preserve and maintain status through successive generations under a bureaucratic system which became increasingly competitive. At the same time, however, as far as the Neo-Confucians were concerned, the family was the only realm in which the Confucian ideals of *li* could be taught and practiced. The bureaucratized world of imperial China afforded very little room for the education and practice of *li* as idealized by Confucius. Hence, for both political as well as philosophical reasons, the reconstruction of the family was thought to be essential.

4 THEORETICAL UNDERPINNINGS OF THE NEW FAMILY SYSTEM

It is important to note the connection between the articulation of the new family system and Neo-Confucian political theory. The Neo-Confucian family system and the strong sense of identity as well as independence was what gave the *shi-da-fu* the confidence to articulate a new form of Confucian learning which emphasized the independence and even superiority of their class vis-à-vis the imperial dynasty. Neo-Confucianism, as articulated by the likes of Han You of Tang, but more importantly by Zhou Dun-yi, Zhang Zai, Cheng Hao, Zheng Yi, and the great Zhu Xi, developed three components which became the centerpieces of the new version of Confucianism. They were the "*daotong*" theory (*daotonglun* 道統論), "learning of kings" (*diwangxue* 帝王學), and "*Xing-li-xue*" (性理學). Confucian learning was not only a vocation for the newly emergent *shi-da-fu* but also a powerful weapon against the powers of the imperial family. Neo-Confucians began to argue that it was

34 Ibid., pp. 229–230.　35 Ibid., pp. 230–231.　36 Ibid., p. 231.

individual merit based upon the cultivation of the self and knowledge of the
Confucian classics, not birth and pedigree, that should become the sole
criterion for the right to govern. The famous opening passage of the *Great
Learning* is the most succinct and powerful articulation of this idea:

> The Ancients who wished clearly to exemplify illustrious virtue
> throughout the world would first set up good government in their states.
> Wishing to govern well their states, they would first regulate their fam-
> ilies. Wishing to regulate their families, they would first cultivate their
> persons. Wishing to cultivate their persons, they would first rectify their
> minds. Wishing to rectify their minds, they would first seek sincerity
> in their thoughts. Wishing for sincerity in their thoughts, they would
> first extend their knowledge. The extension of knowledge lay in the
> investigation of things. For only when things are investigated is knowl-
> edge extended; only when knowledge is extended are thoughts sincere;
> only when thoughts are sincere are minds rectified; only when minds are
> rectified are our persons cultivated; only when our persons are cultivated
> are our families regulated; only when families are regulated are states
> well governed; and only when states are well governed is there peace in
> the world.[37]

The passage, clearly meant for not only the scholar-bureaucrats themselves
but kings and emperors, gave canonical authority to this idea. By arguing
that one had to earn the right to govern others by ceaseless self-cultivation
and by adhering to lofty standards of morality, all made possible by rigorous
academic learning, the *shi-da-fu* were actually arguing that they were the only
ones truly fit for government. Self-cultivation, moreover, could not be tested
by the civil service examination. Hence, it was not the success in examination or bureaucratic rank that determined the true worth of a person and his
right to govern. Moreover, the true place where self-cultivation can take place
is in the family.

Self-cultivation in itself would have been a difficult exercise for most
aristocrats and imperial family members to engage in, given their privileged
upbringing, but Neo-Confucian scholars placed an even more implacable
hurdle in their way to acquiring the right to rule. The academic learning that
the Neo-Confucians proposed as holding the true meaning of Confucianism
and the True Way was filled with metaphysical speculations and theories
of cosmology, formidable in their complexity and intricacy for most but the
staunchest initiates. Unlike the Confucianism of old, Neo-Confucianism
erected a formidable philosophical system to undergird Confucian theories of

---

37 Wm. Theodore de Bary, Wing-tsit Chan, and Burton Watson, eds., *Sources of Chinese
   Tradition*, Vol. 1 (New York: Columbia University Press, 1960), p. 115.

ethics and politics. True, this was in response to Buddhist and Daoist metaphysics and cosmology which greatly attracted the intellectual minds of the period. However, it clearly had the effect of putting Confucian learning beyond the reach of all except the most conscientious politicians who kept up their academic learning even while engaging in practical affairs.

An even more overt articulation of the idea that the *shi-da-fu* were the only ones fit to rule was the theory of *daotong*. According to this theory, first articulated by Zheng Yi, the "Dao," or the "Way," was first embodied by Yao and Shun, the mythical emperors, who then passed it on to Wu, Tang, Wen, Wu, and the Duke of Zhou. These were the great kings and emperors who first gave shape to Chinese civilization by embodying the true Way. However, after the Duke of Zhou, the Way was transmitted to Confucius, a private intellectual, not a king, an emperor, or even an aristocrat. Indeed, from then on, the way was transmitted to Mencius, Zhou Dun-yi, Zhang Zai, and Cheng Hao, all scholars, not rulers. What they were claiming through the theory of *daotong*, in effect, was that, at least since Confucius, the true knowledge of the Way was transmitted through Confucian intellectuals who, by implication, were the only ones fit to rule. The rulers who had real power were unfit to rule. If they wished to rule according to the true Way, they had to heed the advice of those Confucian intellectuals who were the true inheritors of the knowledge of the Dao. Again, not to belabor the point, the intellectual and theoretical independence of the Neo-Confucians were to be undergirded by the institution of the family.

5 NEO-CONFUCIAN FAMILISM IN KOREA

The development of Neo-Confucianism in Korea is a fascinating example of the way in which religions and political ideologies developed in one place actually find their fullest and most "orthodox" expression in another. The Neo-Confucian theories and institutions articulated by Zhu Xi found their most ardent followers and ideologues in Chosŏn (1392–1910). The small but influential group of scholars, including the likes of Yi Saek (1328–1396), Chŏng Mong-ju (1337–1392), Chŏng To-jŏn (1337–1398), Cho Chun (1346–1405), Ha Yun (1347–1416), and Kwŏn Kun (1352–1409), became the first generation of Neo-Confucian scholar-bureaucrats in Korea who thought that the new philosophy provided the blueprint for fundamental social change and reconstruction. The transitional period between Koryŏ and Chosŏn in Korea coincided with the dynastic change in China from Yuan to Ming. The disintegration of the five-hundred-year-old Koryŏ dynasty as well as the chaos in China provided the backdrop for the importation and development of new ideas which were thought to be capable of restoring order and renewing civilization. Neo-Confucianism, the newest form of learning at the time, became the ideology of choice for those agitating for change in Korea. Despite some internal dissent, the core group of Neo-Confucians was able to found a new dynasty.[38] They were able to convince the most powerful general/warlord of late Koryŏ, Yi Sŏng-gye, to establish a dynasty in his name but along clear Neo-Confucian lines. Once they assumed power, they immediately set about realizing the Neo-Confucian ideal society. They took the recommendations of Zhu Xi regarding the ancestral shrines quite literally. For example, during the first century after the foundation of the dynasty, its Neo-Confucian architects succeeded in forcing most of the prominent clans of the land to build ancestral shrines. Through massive state-led efforts in translating, interpreting, and disseminating Neo-Confucian philosophy and institutions, they were able to transform Korea, a land of Buddhism for the previous millennium, into an exemplary Confucian society in less than a century. The remarkable story of how they succeeded cannot be fully recounted in the short span of this essay. Suffice it to say that they succeeded admirably. As Deuchler puts it, "the scholar-officials succeeded in reshaping the sociopolitical environment to an extent the Sung Neo-Confucians would never have dreamed possible."[39]

The prohibition of marriage between members with the same surname and from the same locality was one of the means for the rigorous enforcement of the Neo-Confucian family system. Some thirteen out of a total of fifty-three kings of the Shilla dynasty (57 B.C.–A.D. 935) are on record as having married within the royal family while thirteen of thirty-four kings of the Koryŏ dynasty (935–1392) had queens who were members of the royal family. The Neo-Confucian founders of Chosŏn thought this was one of the major causes of the ultimate collapse of these earlier dynasties, as well as a symptom of moral decay. As they saw it, the problem lay in the marriage system. Because the pre-Chosŏn marriage custom was uxorilocal and because lineage descent was not clearly established, marriages between close kin were quite frequent. The Neo-Confucians began to enforce patrilocal marriages. They were quite anxious to eradicate such "immoral" and "unethical" practices which often confounded the hierarchy of a family organized along

38 Chŏng Mong-ju, one of the most respected members of the group, opposed the overthrow of the Koryŏ dynasty for very Confucian reasons, that a subject should not be disloyal to, and hence cannot depose, his king. He was assassinated the year the new dynasty was founded. Later, after the Chosŏn dynasty was firmly established, his former friends and colleagues succeeded in restoring his honor. Chŏng, to this day, has come to symbolize the epitome of the principled and loyal Confucian scholar-bureaucrat.

39 Martina Deuchler, *The Confucian Transformation of Korea: A Study of Society and Ideology* (Cambridge, Mass.: Council on East Asian Studies, Harvard University, 1992), p. 128.

patrilineal descent. They vehemently denounced and began prohibiting the practice of marrying second cousins and other close relatives, then quite common. In 1471, an edict prohibiting marriage between second cousins was promulgated. In 1669, Song Si-yŏl (1607–1689), one of the most famous Confucian scholar-bureaucrats of the Chosŏn dynasty, even tried to pass a law prohibiting marriages between descent groups with the same surname but different ancestral seats.[40] The Ming law which prescribed sixty blows and a forceful divorce for violation of the prohibition was often enforced in Chosŏn as well.

Another practice designed to clarify the agnatic lineage and to prevent marriages between close kin was the keeping of detailed genealogical records. The oldest extant family genealogy in Korea is *Andong Gwon-ssi Sunghwabo*, compiled in 1476. Called *"chokbo"* (*zupu* 族譜), the genealogical records kept a detailed account of all the descendants of an agnatic ancestor, often the first person said to have used the surname. With such records, it would be much easier to police possible marriages between close kin. Through these measures, the Neo-Confucians of Korea tried to maintain the integrity of the agnatic lineal descent groups which, as we saw, were considered fundamental to a well-ordered society. Even today, all Koreans keep a *"chokbo"* of their "clan." These genealogical records, now published by independent publishers, still top the best-seller lists in Korea.

Confucian ancestor worship is not simply a form of religious practice designed to address existential questions. It is a "secular" institution designed for explicitly political reasons. This is not to say that it did not have religious connotations or ramifications. It clearly did. However, its creators designed it for its "secular" rather than "religious" uses. As Martina Deuchler puts it, "For establishing a Confucian-style society, a first crucial step was the implantation of the agnatic principle in the social matrix and the activation of an agnatic consciousness within a descent group. No mechanism was better suited to accomplish this than ancestor worship."[41]

Like the ancient Greeks, the Confucians clearly recognized the family as a separate realm. However, they by no means viewed it as an inferior one. Like modern Western political theorists, Confucians recognized that the type of authority practiced in the context of a family was rather different from the one to be found in the political realm. Filial piety (*xiao* 孝) was the representative value of the family while loyalty (*zhong* 忠) was for the political arena. The father-son relationship was to be mediated by the value of "familiarity" (*qin* 親 in Chinese and *chin* in Korean), while the king-subject

---

40 Ibid., p. 238. 41 Ibid., p. 129.

relationship was to be based on "justice" (*ui*, in Korean, *yi*, in Chinese, 義). However, neither realm was thought to be superior to the other. They were two distinct realms and two distinct value orientations of equal value for the ideal Confucian world. Indeed, if anything, the Neo-Confucians privileged the family over the state. Family was the place where proper ritual behavior was learned and practiced. It was through family rites, which included the all-important ancestor rites, that one learned the codes of proper conduct as well as the values thought to inhere in them. Through the rearticulation of family rites and the concomitant reestablishment of the *zong* system, the Neo-Confucian family became a realm independent of the state in terms of its value orientation as well as socioeconomically. Of course, the line between the family and the state never became so distinct as to make the two realms incompatible. If anything, a great deal of emphasis was placed on ensuring perfect compatibility and harmony between them. This was probably a reflection of the fact that despite all their pretensions to independence, the *shi-da-fu were* their beholden to the imperial, bureaucratic state for their existence. Thus, the codes of conduct and the value orientation to be gotten from the proper practice of family rituals in all its facets were thought to engender those very qualities which would make one a loyal and effective subject of the state at the same time.

5 CONCLUSION: THE CONTINUING DEBATE

The institution of the family that was articulated by Song Neo-Confucians and perfected by their counterparts in Chosŏn was of a very specific type. Its main feature was the agnatic principle, or the *zong* system. By defining the family through the "stem" family consisting of successive generations of eldest male heirs, Neo-Confucianism was able to provide two things that other family systems could not; it gave the family a clear sense of identity based on continuity through successive generations and a "community" large enough to function as a semi-independent economic, academic, and sometimes even political unit. The marriage prohibition between same clan members was a law instituted to ensure the integrity of this particular kind of family system. The Confucian family as we know it today, then, was an institution designed to educate and foster those values and interpersonal rules of proper conduct deemed universal by Confucians. It was also an institution designed to meet particular political, social, and economic considerations arising from specific historical circumstances and needs. It was neither a "natural" institution nor a biological and economic necessity, but rather an institution to serve as the bedrock of social order, political balance, economic security, and universal values.

What possible implications for modern society does such an understanding afford us? Seen from the modern point of view, the family is little more than a necessary evil that must ultimately be overcome. Even in Korea it may only be a matter of time before the National Assembly passes an amendment to the old law prohibiting marriage within the same agnatic descendants. The two sides are divided fairly clearly along generational lines. As the older generation brought up within the social and ethical milieu of the traditional Confucian order passes from the scene, the younger generation with less sympathy for the tradition on the whole will enact a more modern law which will better respect the right to the pursuit of individual happiness. On the other hand, as the National Assembly, an institution perhaps the most attuned to public sentiment, realizes, there is still a great deal of opinion in favor of maintaining traditional values and institutions.

The irony is that an increasing number of young people are flouting the old law in order to form the kind of families they themselves grew up in. It is not the case that the young people are turning away from the institutions of marriage or family. Rather, they wish very much to become builders of families. In this sense, the old law is actually acting as a barrier against the formation of families. For the foreseeable future, then, the changing of the law will actually increase the number of people who build happy families. However, it will certainly spell the end of family as Neo-Confucians had envisioned. A family that does not respect agnatic lineage descent by allowing for the intermarriage of clan members will mean the destruction of family as understood by Neo-Confucians. The family that results from the violation of the Neo-Confucian prohibition of marriage among members of the common descent line will be much more akin to the modern nuclear family that we are familiar with. It would still be a family, but precisely the kind that Neo-Confucians thought they needed to overcome in order to return to the "true" family idealized by the Master.

The modern nuclear family is part and parcel of the modern liberal individualist social order. It is perfectly compatible with a robust form of individualism and gender equality. It is not concerned with creating and maintaining an identity of its own, independent of and sometimes even superseding the individuals that constitute it. As envisioned by the likes of Locke and Rousseau, the modern family is a means for nurturing individuals who are fundamentally and ultimately free, even of the family that nurtured them. Hence, the family in modern societies is clearly in a perpetual state of crisis. True, even in the West, the family has functioned as a haven from social and political upheavals for many people well into the twentieth century. However, with the establishment of welfare states, on the one hand, and the rise of liberalism, on the other, the family is rapidly being replaced by either the welfare state or the individual. The family is no longer seen as a realm worthy of devoting one's life to. That is why "relegating" women or anyone to the family is seen as a mode of repression, as taking away that person's right to individual freedom and self-expression. This clearly reflects the Western and modern bias against the family, a bias that regards family as a lesser realm, a realm of menial labor, or a biological construct at best. Modern political theory seems to acknowledge only two realms, the state and the individual. How then can the family be made into a true realm of its own? Given the criticism that traditional Western conceptions of the family have been under attack for centuries, it is hard to imagine how they can become the basis for an affirmation of the family as a distinctly modern institution.

Confucianism, on the other hand, provides one of the most robust, intricate, and well-articulated conceptions of family, which has not only survived to this day in practice but may be able to prosper in the future, provided it is given a rearticulation that is appropriate for the modern world. The Confucian family has a telos of its own, a telos at least coequal to that of the state. Family is an end in itself. It is the place where one learns all that needs to be learned in order to be a responsible member of society, a true citizen. Of late, "civil society" has become fashionable as the mediating realm, a "moral" space, between the state and the individual. The Confucian family was designed to perform a similar role. It has the added advantage of fostering a sense of intimacy and caring that most "civil societies" tend to lack. As we have seen, Neo-Confucian familism was articulated and instituted in an era characterized by rapid social mobility, urbanization, and commercialization, phenomena that modern society is quite familiar with. As such, there is no fundamental reason why the institution of the family cannot be rethought, rearticulated so that it can be privileged above and beyond society or perhaps even the state. Indeed, it may be the only sensible and logical solution to many of the problems that plague modern postindustrial, postmodern, globalizing society. However, from the liberal, modern perspective, the Confucian family is hopelessly anachronistic. It is hierarchical, authoritarian, and gender biased. It is the realm of a prototypical "patriarchal authority," something that modernity and liberalism have fought so hard against over the past two or three centuries.

The choice is a stark one. There seems no easy way out of the dilemma. Koreans are at a major crossroad in their sociocultural history. The outlawing of the prohibition against interclan marriages will signify the end of one civilization and the beginning of another. What we are witnessing, then, is a "clash of civilizations." As of now, the historical momentum seems to be on the side of outlawing the marriage prohibition. It is, after all, the "modern" thing to do. Of course, changes in such laws being what they are, practices will take much longer to change. Indeed, the change will be initially imperceptible to most people not directly affected by the law. However, the direction of change will be irreversible. Koreans will have opened another chapter of modernity, an "ambiguous achievement," at best.[42]

42 William E. Connolly, *Political Theory and Modernity* (London: Basil Blackwell, 1989).

EPILOGUE

WHY CONFUCIUS NOW?

WILLIAM THEODORE DE BARY

The question, simple enough in itself, naturally breaks into two parts: "Why Confucius?" and "Why Now?" In other words "Why Confucius, the person and the man (rather than Confucianism), and why especially now?" The first part focuses on Confucius himself, whether as a person or as a mythic figure. The second part raises as many questions about our present condition, and its needs, as it does about the past.

I shall defer for the moment these latter questions in order to deal first with this one: Can our present problems be dealt with simply by invoking the teachings of the "original" Confucius? Must not their relevance to our contemporary situation take into account, in some way and to some degree, what they have meant to Confucians historically (i.e., as Confucian tradition or what we call Confucianism, which could also include the Japanese and Korean experience as well as the Chinese). Many twentieth-century scholars have tried to identify the "original Confucius" or interpret the "Original Analects," and any number before them in China, Japan, and Korea have tried to do the same. As just one example, Itō Jinsai and other seventeenth- and eighteenth-century Japanese scholars identified with the "Ancient Learning" movement attempted to peel off the layers of historical commentary and philosophical reinterpretation in order to get at the original "meaning" of Confucius. Scholars in Qing China did the same. The search did not end with them and the process goes on; it will never be definitively settled, because the subject itself continues to be endlessly fascinating and challenging, always open to reexamination. There will be no conclusive or definitive edition of the *Analects*, and "Confucius the Man" (rather than the Myth, as Herrlee Creel put it in mid-twentieth century) will forever be a subject inseparable from what the generations of his interpreters, for over two thousand years, have had to say about him. Past scholarly consensus, or indeed disagreement, will continue to be relevant to any modern reading.

"Confucius," however, is only one aspect of the problem and perhaps not the one most pertinent to the modern scene. The larger question has to do with "Confucianism" as an historical tradition and process. It is true that what we call "Confucianism" (whatever the provenance of the term or the other names given to the "ism") has always, from the earliest records, focused on the teachings attributed to Confucius and his school, whether in the textual or the ritual tradition. But if we are talking here about the possible relevance of these teachings to contemporary problems, then the Confucians' historical practice, and the results thereof, become as important to our understanding as are classically stated values.

As I have said elsewhere in relation to Confucianism and human rights,

> It has sometimes been thought sufficient to find in Asian traditions, and mostly in classical Confucian writings, some evidence of values akin to those associated with human rights concepts. For this purpose quotations have been drawn from the *Analects* of Confucius, or in the case of Buddhism from the sutras or the pronouncements of the early Indian ruler Asoka, to illustrate their humanitarian sentiments. . . . Still, such classic statements serve only a limited purpose. They can illustrate traditional ideals or axial values – which are by no means insignificant – but they do not, in themselves, speak to the historical realities of China in later times or to the twentieth century circumstances in which contemporary issues are embedded.[1]

What happened in the course of history to the Confucians' attempts to implement and live by ancient ideals is of crucial importance. How things worked out in practice, and if it is possible to identify them, what were the limiting conditions in which Confucians tried to act upon and work out these ideals, are questions quite relevant to the implementation of human rights or civil society today. Problems of continuity and change in the evolution of major traditions must be considered. Confucianism should not be thought of as either static or monolithic – that is, taking the sayings of Confucius and Mencius just by themselves, to represent an historically developing, often conflicted, and yet gradually maturing Confucian tradition.

As an example let me point to the case of the community compact which Professor Chang Yun-Shik cites as a possible model, drawn from the past experience of the Korean people, for consensual, cooperative organization on the local level (a case which also bears importantly on the matter of center-local relations discussed by Professor Rozman). The community compact (Chinese *xiang yue* [鄉約]; Korean *hyang yak*) was not a Confucian institution

---

1 *Asian Values and Human Rights* (Cambridge, Mass.: Harvard University Press, 1988), pp. 10–11.

for which there is any literal precedent in the corpus of classical Confucian texts. It is rather a Neo-Confucian construct, mostly of Zhu Xi, who consciously cited eleventh-century Song Confucians as his precedent and model. At the same time, however, for Zhu Xi the compact gave concrete embodiment to traditional Confucian values. Like Neo-Confucianism itself, this concretization of traditional values was a neoclassical construct – neoclassical in much the same sense as neoclassical constructs in the eighteenth-century West, like the American and French Senates, which evoked the civic values of classical Greece and Rome, and which architecturally were housed in neoclassical structures in Paris and Washington, D.C. In Zhu Xi's case the community compact was meant to embody values expressed in the *Analects* and *Mencius* – Confucius's reliance on the inculcation of virtue and ritual respect rather than on laws and regulations as a means of maintaining public order, and Mencius's hierarchies based on the "ranks of Heaven," that is, moral distinctions in contrast to the "ranks of man" (power and wealth) as the basis for a social order.

It was not, however, only the great prestige of Zhu Xi in Neo-Confucian East Asia that led major thinkers and reformers like Wang Yangming in sixteenth-century China and Yi I (Yulgok) in Korea to see in this "newer" Song Confucian institution something applicable to their own historical situations and problems. For them the community compact (though not mentioned in the classics, and thus not "fundamentalist" in the literal reading) was both new and Confucian, drawing on a recognizable continuity of Confucian values to address a contemporary need.

I first drew attention to the importance of the community compact in East Asia almost twenty years ago in my Ch'ien Mu Lectures at the Chinese University of Hong Kong, later published in *The Liberal Tradition in China*.[2] This came at a time when the Confucian tradition was widely viewed as simply a conservative and authoritarian doctrine, to be relegated to a museum of ancient and obsolete artifacts, if not consigned to the proverbial dustbin of history. In that same book I tried to show how important elements of that Neo-Confucian past, long overlooked, had inspired reform efforts in late imperial China and, in the twentieth century, had sparked one of the most striking protests against Mao Zedong's repressive rule (Wu Han's "Hai Rui's Dismissal").

One of my purposes in the Ch'ien Mu Lectures was to show how Confucian ideas and ideals had survived, on their own merits, from age to age, not just from ideological inertia but because major thinkers in the past brought them to bear on pivotal issues of both perennial and contemporary

---

2 *The Liberal Tradition in China* (Hong Kong: Chinese University of Hong Kong Press, 1982).

relevance. What I did not attempt to do, in that series of brief public lectures, was to show what became of these ideas for good or ill, in their own time or in subsequent history – a much larger task than time then allowed for.

Later I did attempt to address this matter in *Asian Values and Human Rights*, using community compacts and community schools as authentic examples of a Confucian communitarianism that contrasted with the spurious claims of some recent "Asian values" advocates who identified Confucianism and "community" simply with the upholding of state authority and social discipline.

A main reason for my citing these two cases, and dealing with them in historical detail, was to show how, despite the importance and persistence of these ideas, they could be distorted and perverted by systemic forces more powerful than the intellectual traditions themselves and become misappropriated by the state. If I devoted two heavily documented chapters to this task – chapters some general readers might well have shied away from as too scholarly and historical – it was precisely to show how even good or challenging ideas do not live in a vacuum; what becomes of them in later history is just as significant for us as their original articulation. This is why the "now" of "Why Confucius Now?" can be dealt with only in the perspective of history, and for the community compacts and schools, in view of all those years in which Zhu Xi, Yi I, and many others struggled – more often than not failing – to accomplish the changes they sought. Any values that we might cite from Confucian tradition today, as relevant to our problems "now," would be subject to the same historical qualification and systemic deflection.

Despite such cautions and disclaimers on my own part, a reviewer of *Asian Values and Human Rights* saw it as arguing "that the Confucian tradition supported what we now call a civil society because it championed the spread of [community] schools and the practice of community compacts." This, he says, "is a romantic view of what schools were ever capable of doing" and "idealized the merits of moral force as an effective check on autocratic government."[3]

In fact, most of chapters 4 and 5 in the book (apparently unread by the reviewer) deals with the inability of Confucian scholars to establish or sustain either of these institutions in their authentic form, as well as with the misappropriation of them to serve the purposes of the state – the point being to get a realistic estimate of how well institutions embodying Confucian ideals could survive in either an uncongenial or inimical systemic environment – certainly as applicable today to modern adaptations and improvisations as it was to premodern circumstances.

3 Lucian Pye in *The Journal of Politics*, 61 (August 1999), p. 867.

As regards the possibility that such Confucian institutions could serve "as an effective check on autocratic government," my views as stated in chapter 6 are quite the reverse of what Professor Pye reported. I said:

> The fate of Confucian communitarianism conceived as consensual rituals fell victim to the superior power of the state system. Thus, regardless of the priority given to ritual or the tradition of Confucian communitarianism, historically the strength of central administration dominated the scene at this crucial level, with dynastic institutions and laws prevailing over Confucian social prescriptions. One could not then expect much improvement on the level of the community, or the emergence of something like a civil society, without addressing the problem of the state.

Further I cited the views of Huang Zongxi in the seventeenth century concerning the effectiveness of moral force and Confucian ritual to restrain autocratic power:

> Huang drew from the Neo-Confucians' unhappy Ming experience a new lesson concerning the individual's need for law and the importance of law for the curbing of imperial power. Prior to this, in the Song, Yuan, and Ming, Neo-Confucians had put their hope in persuading rulers to perform as sage-kings by listening to the advice of wise mentors and observing the moral constraints of traditional ritual. From this hope sprang their strenuous efforts to elevate and reinforce the position of the Confucian minister.[4] Yet as Huang reviewed the results of this effort over several centuries, he could no longer believe that the individual heroism and dedication of the Noble Person (*junzi* 君子) as minister was sufficient to cope with the inordinate power of the ruler or the latter's indisposition to accept the self-discipline that goes with sage-kingship or the restraints embodied in the rites. Something more would be needed: a supporting infrastructure such as that later identified by Montesquieu in *L'Ésprit des Lois* (1748) with the "corps intermediaires" between state and society at large.[5]

In the case of China what was to be learned from the earlier experience with community compacts served primarily to provide an alternative view – a genuine Confucian communitarianism – belying the specious claims of those who would let Chinese Communism speak for it. The authentic Confucian example stood in marked contrast to the communes of Mao Zedong, as Liang Shuming attempted to remind the Chinese in Mao's day.[6] It

---

4 *Asian Values*, pp. 91, 101.
5 See W. T. de Bary and Richard Lufrano, eds., *Sources of Chinese Tradition*, Vol. 2 (New York: Columbia University Press, 2000), 2nd ed., pp. 382–385.
6 *Asian Values*, pp. 138–146.

represented a genuinely consensual and cooperative community – no more than an ideal of Liang, it is true, but nevertheless, one that stood in contrast to, and served as an implied critique of, the autocratic and exploitative character of Mao's state-managed communes – a critique generated from within China's tradition that could not be discounted as alien or as subserving cultural imperialism.

Since neither in earlier times nor in most recent ones did these communitarian conceptions achieve practical realization, one might conclude that they were simply not viable. And yet they did survive as ideals, speaking to still unsolved, perennial problems of Chinese society, which reminds us not only of the intractability of the problems themselves but also of the caution – the restrained optimism or idealism – with which we might look for a solution to these problems in the light of the Confucian experience.

Before proceeding to this larger question, we should consider, in the present context, what this tells us about the Korean case in particular. Historical circumstances differ, and our understanding of them in Korea will affect any conclusions one might draw here, but it is a remarkable fact that, although I have cited the community compacts and community schools as major concerns of Chinese Confucians and key test cases of local reform in China, they were of no less importance in Korean Neo-Confucianism and in the historical development of Korea, where conditions often differed from China, especially as regards the power of the central state and its relative weight in the systemic balance. I am in no position here – either for want of time and space, or competence – to discuss these matters in detail, but certain general points seem to me relevant.

In Korea leading Neo-Confucians attached major importance to the adoption of Zhu Xi's recommendations in regard to both the community compacts and the community schools,[7] with the result that both became prominent features of local life in Chosŏn Korea. One cannot say that these were purely autonomous institutions, independent of the large role played by the *yangban* (兩班) elite and clan organization in the social and political life of Korea, but it would seem that they contributed significantly to cooperative organization and activity on the local level, and community schools to a relatively high level of literacy in the population as a whole. Again, I am not competent to judge but it would seem at least worth asking whether there was not a residual influence of these institutions and patterns in twentieth-century Korea. In other words, I am suggesting that the situation in Korea differed enough from China so that, instead of a scholar like Liang Shuming

7 See Ch'oe Yong-ho, Peter Lee, and W. T. de Bary, *Sources of Korean Tradition*, Vol. 2 (New York: Columbia University Press, 2000), pp. 144–149.

having to talk about the revival and re-creation of the community compact in twentieth-century China as the retrieval of a lost ideal, there may have been much more sustained practice and less erosion of it in Korea. Thus one might expect to build on a continuing tradition of local organization and cooperative life.[8] At least this might seem to have been the case down into the nineteenth century. The question now is whether or not such institutions have any relevance in the twenty-first century. Are they still part of the living memory in rural areas, or are they simply anachronisms?

For any help that Confucianism may be able to give us today, we must look at these questions from a Neo-Confucian perspective. Just as the latter found in their classical legacy no exact models to be followed in their own present situation but had to develop new forms in which to deal with changed historical circumstances, what can be learned today from the Confucian and Neo-Confucian past can only suggest new possibilities, not provide precise models.

Nevertheless, even if community compacts and schools are deemed to be only quaint and rather homespun examples from a remote past, they could still speak to the contemporary need for some concept of valid and viable community. The political and economic globalization of the contemporary world (what Professor Helgesen in his paper calls "the runaway world") has not obviated this problem but only intensified it. This is because it is pervaded by a "throwaway culture" that uses and trashes almost everything, without thought of the long-term consequences. In the United States, with the serious loss of a sense of community and the deterioration of family life, have come intense anxieties over social decay in cities, rising crime and drug problems, a decline in the activity of voluntary organizations, and the disappearance of small towns. The resultant problems have proven resistant to legal and penal solutions and do not lend themselves to remediation by large-scale political programs. Whatever the successes of advanced capitalism and the technological capabilities of the West may be, they have not found answers to these social problems but have only worsened them. With this much at least of the critique of contemporary Western society offered by Professors Hall and Ames in their contribution I would agree, even though I could not attribute it, as they do, mainly to the influence of Western liberalism. (They base their critique of liberalism on John Dewey, as if he were not himself a liberal!)

When Confucius encountered similar problems on a smaller scale and in a simpler form in the sixth century B.C., he tried to rescue and preserve a family

8 See my *East Asian Civilizations* (Cambridge, Mass.: Harvard University Press, 1987), p. 116; and James Palais, *Confucian Statecraft and Korean Institutions* (Seattle: University of Washington Press, 1996), pp. 188–189, 699–700, 735–761.

ethic – the moral and social bedrock of the earlier agrarian society – in the midst of a growing, large-scale organization of political life by military and bureaucratic means. For this recognition of the family, Confucianism has become forever identified as a "family system," though "system" may not be the right word for it. Confucius thought of it as a method of self-cultivation working through the most natural of personal ties and informed by spontaneous human sentiments – far from anything as routine and mechanical as a "system."

This, however, is where Confucianism later encountered its problems with modernity – first with the "modern" Chinese state of the Qin and Han (historians today like to call it the most advanced state and society of its time) and then with its further elaboration in the Tang and Song. "Neo-Confucianism" was a response to this new historical situation which no longer resembled the *Great Learning*'s simple paradigm of person-family-ruler relations. The leviathan state of late Imperial China went far beyond anything that could be managed simply by interpersonal ritual relations – which is why later Confucians began to think of the need for an infrastructure roughly corresponding to Montesquieu's *"corps intermediaires"* – an infrastructure that embodied personal and family values on a higher level of local organization than the family but still beneath the prefecture and county level of centralized bureaucratic organization. Zhu Xi's new school curriculum likewise included a substantial infusion of historical material concerning the workings of the imperial dynasties – historiography unknown to Confucius and Mencius, but generating the institutional studies on which a Huang Zongxi could base his constitutional reformism in the seventeenth century.

The twenty-first-century "modernity" referred to in the question "Why Confucius Now?" has to be viewed in this same historical perspective. Global capitalism, multinational corporations, and gigantic world trade systems pose similar problems as to whether the so-called global village will not actually be as impersonal, as routinized, as mechanical and inhuman in its operation as the earlier leviathan state. Will a world of McDonalds and shopping malls express any of the personal intimacy or group participation democracy that we associate with the family, village, or town meeting?

If the answer is very likely no, what could Confucius or the Neo-Confucians have to do with this new situation? My suggestion (and it is not really an answer) runs along three lines.

First of all, in the Korean case, one could ask whether anything survives of the cooperative spirit or group relations that were supposed to have characterized the community compacts (*hyang-yak*) up into modern times? Everyone today is familiar with the Korean oligopolies known as "chaebol" – even if they know little else. Is there a local Korean alternative that offers a better cooperative model, one more congenial to a shared sense of community or a participatory democracy?

Second, a striking feature of the economic success of Korea, no less than of other East Asian nations, has been the determined pursuit of learning and education that is characteristic of all East Asians influenced by Confucian culture – to such an extent that it could well be considered one of the most essential Confucian values. Against this, however, one might adduce the persistent charge that in those people influenced by Confucian culture – more often than not as an authoritarian system – this eagerness to learn manifests itself mainly in the form of assiduous rote learning, which can just as well lend itself to the routinization of education and assimilation of packaged culture in modern forms. Inescapably one has to deal with the fact that in all East Asian societies there was an abrupt and radical termination of traditional education in favor of modern systems. What one sees in twentieth-century education is a mixed bag, in which it is almost impossible to identify anything simply as traditional. Older forms of routinization may be compounded or substituted by newer ones.

As Professor Helgesen notes in his contribution to this book, when political authorities sanction efforts aiming at permanently changing people's cultural attitudes, as was the case recently in Korea, the outcome (as the effort itself) may be anything but democratic. This is because change itself has to work through some established processes in order to get at and affect others. In this light the problem of both means and ends is heavily conditioned by one's understanding and assessment of what is working and workable in a given culture.

For the most obvious part, education in twentieth-century East Asia has been nontraditional in form and content, however much certain traditional values may have persisted at some levels in the midst of change. First in Meiji Japan (late nineteenth century), then in Korea under Japanese influence or domination, and finally in late Manchu and Republican China, East Asian schooling broke out of the traditional Confucian learning mode, adopting wholesale from the West a more specialized and compartmentalized instruction of a departmental nature. The Neo-Confucian core curriculum, based on a conception of self-cultivation through the study and discussion of classic texts, was lost at almost the same time as advocates of liberal education in early twentieth-century America were conducting a largely unsuccessful, rearguard action against the specialization of the new elective system, hoping to recover some of the core civilizational values that had been central to Western classical learning up into the nineteenth century.

The question of what values can sustain a twenty-first-century world civilization is not of course a purely Asian, East Asian, or Korean one. A new multicultural education for a world community will have to combine an understanding of both native cultures and world cultures. Coming to terms with one's own past culture will be, for everyone and all peoples, an essential element in arriving at the self-understanding that is a precondition for understanding others.

In my view the best way to accomplish this is for every curriculum, as part of a shared general education, to have a place for the reading and discussion of classic texts that have stood as landmarks of the developing traditions in each country. In East Asian countries during the second millennium, these classics were those identified in the twelfth century by Zhu Xi, works that had become standard in most schools. In other words they had become the core of the classical curriculum, supplemented by "local" classics of the later traditions. In China Zhu Xi included, along with the "classical" Confucian texts, the reading of Lao Zi, Zhuang Zi, and the Legalists, as well as the Song Neo-Confucian masters. Japanese in the Edo period included native classics like the *Manyoshu*, *Tale of Genji*, and the *Tsure zuregusa*. In Korea something of the same developed with the reading of major figures like Yi Toegye and Yi Yulgok. Thus in East Asia as a whole, the Neo-Confucian development was formative in the second millennium inasmuch as Zhu Xi and his followers were the ones who emphasized general education and took the lead in building schools on all levels (as distinct from religious training for the initiated).

In the modern setting something like this – a core curriculum in the humanities – is clearly needed, in each case based on one's own tradition but reaching out to others, that is, in East Asia beyond the Confucian core to include, on a higher level, comparable classics from other world traditions – moving from a base in one's own culture to a more expansive multicultural education at increasingly higher stages of learning.

In this perspective one could say that a proper remedial education in East Asia – remedying the lack of attention to core human issues – would include the reading and discussion of Confucian classics in all those countries wherein Confucianism had played a substantial formative role in defining the local (national) tradition and the cultural terms in which it was expressed. Here I would place special emphasis on the importance of discussion (contentious, disputatious learning, not just reading and memorizing) because Zhu Xi himself stressed learning as a social, collegial, and shared enterprise. To discuss the meaning of key texts with one's teachers and peers was important to forming one's own opinion about the texts themselves (that is, to "learning for one's self" [*weiji zhi xue* 為己之學]). Thus *jiang xue* (講學), "discursive learning," was a significant activity at most Neo-Confucian academies.

At this point however, having recognized and taken into account Confucianism as an historically evolving, social, and cultural force – to be sure with its own problems and complications – I think we can return to the question originally posed here: "Why Confucius Now?" This takes us back to the person of Confucius himself, a question deferred earlier. Out of the larger body of Confucian classics, it has always been the *Analects* (*Lun yü* 論語) that has been the most compelling reading. The reason is that over the centuries what has attracted generations of readers has been the person of Confucius revealed in its pages.

No one has thought of the *Analects* as the original or authoritative work of one man known to posterity as Master Kung. It is not the distinctive authorial voice that has attracted attention to the book, but a recognizably human figure whose laconic wisdom, gentleness, modesty, and humane concern – rather than any great claim to authority or prophethood – have come to define the quintessential Confucian sage. Among the great world traditions and their founding patriarchs the figure of Confucius is unique for its engaging personality and character more even than for any specific doctrine he taught. This has been recognized and appreciated from the beginning in what we call the Confucian school – which had other names (the school of Lu, the *Ru* [儒] [*Ju*], etc.), but none more indicative of the character of Confucian teaching than the one identified with the man himself. Neo-Confucians called it the Sagely Way, and tried (with some success) to explain philosophically what sageliness consisted in, but in the end it was the person or image of Confucius himself (who disavowed any claim to sagehood) that provided the irreducible core of the Confucian vision in the later tradition.

This is not to say that, in answering affirmatively the question "Why Confucius Now?" one should expect his teaching to be given a uniquely privileged place in a twenty-first-century education, but only to ask that it should have a definite and special place therein. For all the talk of a global village, it is not, as a matter of fact, being brought together in any meaningful sense; it is a world in great moral and social disarray, and nowhere more so than in education, where there is so much talk of "education for success" but so little attention to the human person underlying cultural differences, technological specializations, and momentary social advances or setbacks. Without this "learning for one's self," people do not become either responsible persons or responsible members of a community. They are just there to be used (for the moment, perhaps, "successful") but then to be thrown away.

The appeal of Confucius as a person lay, not in his worldly success, but in how he triumphed over political failure and achieved a measure of self-fulfillment in difficult circumstances. This was summed up in the passage in the *Analects* (2:4) where Confucius characterized the successive stages in his own self-development – not a process of sudden enlightenment or mystical breakthrough, or a moment of political triumph, but just the culmination of what he had worked at for a lifetime.

> At fifteen I set my heart on learning.
> At thirty I had established myself.
> At forty I was no longer perplexed.
> At fifty I knew what Heaven commanded of me.
> At sixty I could heed it.
> At seventy I could follow my heart's desire without transgressing.

In later centuries this was one of the most quoted, paraphrased, or adapted passages from the *Analects*, because it offered some guideposts on the path of life and some assurance that the path would lead to a meaningful conclusion – that having come to terms with one's self, one's society, and one's culture, one could achieve a sense of personal ease, contentment, and fulfillment. Is this not still a good enough reason for answering the question "Why Confucius Now?" in the affirmative?

INDEX

accountability: and Censorate in Chosŏn Korea, 8, 58–68; modern theory of, 56–7. *See also* discipline
affect, and Dewey's theory of education, 146
affective networks, and social investment in Korea, 14–15, 201–17. *See also* social networks
agricultural revolution, in Song China, 347–8. *See also* well-field system
An Lushan, 350
Allen, Charlotte, 220n8
alternative dispute settlement (ADR), and Confucian perspective on mediation, 25, 275–6, 282
Ames, Roger T., 11–12, 49n54, 125n1, 127n2, 130n4, 140n16, 150n37, 237n1, 315n9, 323–4, 367
Analects of Confucius, The: and benevolence, 290–1; and Confucian view of litigation, 259; and contemporary relevance of Confucianism, 23, 361, 371–2; and image of life of Confucius, 148–9; and importance of harmony, 260, 261; influence of on Confucianism, 1, 220; and material welfare, 223, 237; and Neo-Confucianism, 221
ancestor worship, and Neo-Confucian family system, 350–1, 354, 355
"Ancient Learning" movement, in Japan, 361
Andong Gwon-ssi Sunghwabo (genealogical records), 355
anti-Confucianism: and contemporary relevance of Confucianism, 3; and feudal system in China, 344; and influence of Liang Qichao, 79n16; and succession laws, 301, 309
Anti-Rightist Movement, 83
Araro, A., 212
Aristotle, 122, 135

Asian values: Confucianism and regionalism in East Asia, 198; and contemporary relevance of Confucianism, 364; and debate on Confucianism and modernity, 4; and governance, 55–6. *See also* values
Auerbach, Jerold S., 257
Australia, and succession laws, 297
Austria, and succession laws, 294
authority: and Censorate in Chosŏn Korea, 62; and cities in premodern China and Japan, 189; and contemporary relevance of Confucianism, 363
autonomy: Censorate and accountability of government in Chosŏn Korea, 61–2; Dewey's pragmatism and concept of, 142, 143; and equality in Confucian societies, 140

Barber, Benjamin, 53
Bauman, Zygmunt, 164, 166–7
Beer, Lawrence W., 40n28
Beijing, and urbanization in premodern China, 189
Beijing Spring, 87
Bell, Daniel A., 8n9, 16, 230n34, 243n25, 262n14
Bellah, Robert H., 123
benevolence: as basis of moral virtues, 290–1; and government role in social welfare, 246, 247–8; personal relationships and social welfare, 244–5; and succession laws, 310. *See also ren*
Berkowitz, Peter, 35n10
Biggart, N. W., 206n8
Bislev, Sven, 168
Black, Alison, 323n21, 333
Blair, Tony, 166
Boisvert, Raymond, 142
Bok, Derek, 276

president: constraints on power of in Korea, 118; election of and democratization in Korea, 114

Preuss, Ulrich, 33n5, 45n42

property rights: Confucian constraints on in China, 218–35; and Confucian view of family, 16

public opinion, and government accountability in Chosŏn Korea, 63–4

public/private spheres: and affective networks in Korea, 214–15, 216; and Dewey's pragmatism compared to Confucianism, 137; and Western political theory, 337–40. *See also* domestic sphere

Pusan, and affective networks in Korea, 204

Putnam, Robert, 208n8

Pye, Lucian, 365

Qin Shi Huang, 25, 74, 344, 345

radical feminism, and concepts of gender, 327

Raphals, Lisa, 314, 315n9

rational choice theories, and affective networks, 209

rationalization: and Confucian politics compared to Dewey's Pragmatism, 155–60; and Confucian social forms, 148; and depersonalization of social relationships, 144; and disenchantment of modern world, 145

Rawls, John, 8, 219n6, 223–4n19, 238n6

Raz, Joseph, 35n11

Redfield, Robert, 99

Reed, Gay Garland, 175

regionalism: and affective networks in Korea, 204–5, 208; Confucianism as integrating force for East Asian, 14, 196–200. *See also* East Asia

religion: Confucianism as state religion in China, 345; and Dewey's understanding of social practices, 146–7. *See also* Buddhism; Christianity and churches; Shinto

ren: and concept of ritual propriety, 43; and feudal Confucianism, 342. *See also* benevolence

Republican Revolution, in China, 77–81

reverence, and filial piety, 291–2

Revillard, M. L., 294n25, 301n57

ritual, pragmatic philosophy and Confucian democracy, 133–5

ritual propriety: Confucian concept of as public political norm, 7; and Confucian social forms, 148; and constitutionalism, 42–6; contemporary relevance of, 46–53. *See also li*

Roh Tae Woo, 109, 112, 204

Rome, and civil law, 273

Rosemont, Henry, Jr., 237n1, 319–20

Rousseau, Jean-Jacques, 339, 340

Rozman, Gilbert, 13–14, 222n15, 362

rural areas, community compact and mutual help in Korea, 91–7

Russia, and succession laws, 302, 303, 308

saganwŏn (Office of the Censor General), 58

Sagely Way, and Neo-Confucianism, 371

sahŏnbu (Office of the Inspector General), 58

Sandel, Michael, 35–6n13

sarim, and Neo-Confucianism in Chosŏn Korea, 65–6

Schauer, Frederick, 39

Schrecker, John, 229n33

Schwartz, Louis, 233

Scott, James, 159

Sejo, king of Korea, 60, 65

self: and identification of person with roles in Confucianism, 136; Neo-Confucianism and cultivation of, 352–3

Sen, Amartya, 90, 223n17

Seoul, and urbanization in premodern Korea, 189

Seoul National University, 203

Serageldin, Ismaïl, 170n13

sex differences, gender differences as social interpretation of, 313

Shaffer, Thomas L., 278n71

Shao Jingren, 76

Shao Yung, 316

Sherrin, C. H., 299n49

shi-da-fu, and bureaucracy in feudal China, 348–50, 351, 352, 353

Shiga Shuzo, 268n35

Shinto, and Confucianism in Japan, 192

Shun (sage-king of China), 263

siblings, and succession laws, 307–8. *See also* filial piety

Sima Qian, 263n17

Singapore: and care for elderly parents, 231; Confucian tradition and education in, 48n49; and land tenure, 227

Skinner, G. William, 185n15

social capital, and affective networks in Korea, 208

social democratic theory: Confucianism and democratization in China, 83

socialization, and moral education in Korea, 163–4, 171

social life, Confucian values in family and, 289–93

social networks, and ethics of social welfare, 243–5, 248. *See also* affective networks

social reform, and litigation, 274

CPSIA information can be obtained at www.ICGtesting.com
Printed in the USA
BVOW07s0425150914

366712BV00001B/17/P